PARLOR PONDS

PARLOR PONDS

The Cultural Work of the American Home Aquarium, 1850–1970

JUDITH HAMERA

THE UNIVERSITY OF MICHIGAN PRESS
Ann Arbor

Copyright © by the University of Michigan 2012
All rights reserved

This book may not be reproduced, in whole or in part, including illustrations, in any form (beyond that copying permitted by Sections 107 and 108 of the U.S. Copyright Law and except by reviewers for the public press), without written permission from the publisher.

Published in the United States of America by
The University of Michigan Press
Manufactured in the United States of America
♾ Printed on acid-free paper

2015   2014   2013   2012   4   3   2   1

A CIP catalog record for this book is available from the British Library.

Library of Congress Cataloging-in-Publication Data

Hamera, Judith.
 Parlor ponds : the cultural work of the American home aquarium, 1850–1970 / Judith Hamera.
  p.   cm.
 Includes bibliographical references and index.
 ISBN 978-0-472-07166-1 (cloth : alk. paper) — ISBN 978-0-472-05166-3 (paper : alk. paper) — ISBN 978-0-472-02810-8 (e-book)
 1. Aquariums—Social aspects—United States—History. 2. Aquariums—United States—History. 3. Aquariums—United States—Historiography. 4. Aquariums—Great Britain—Historiography. 5. Home—United States—History. 6. United States—Social life and customs—19th century. 7. United States—Social life and customs—20th century.   I. Title.
 SF457.3.H36   2011
 639.34'4—dc23
                          2011028328

For Thaddeus F. and Dolores Hamera

and, as ever,

for Alfred Bendixen,

with love and gratitude

ACKNOWLEDGMENTS

This is both a curious and an ideal project for a scholar of performance studies. Perhaps it is predictable that it began idiosyncratically. Taking a moment of respite from a Modern Language Association conference in Philadelphia, my husband, Alfred Bendixen, and I were enjoying the fossil collections in the Academy of Natural Sciences when we suddenly found ourselves surrounded by dozens and dozens of very energetic young children freely expressing their considerable enthusiasm for the specimens in loud, high-pitched voices amplified by the marble academy walls. Sensing the potential for things to take a suboptimal turn, Alfred quickly steered me to a refuge in the academy's library, whereupon I picked up H. Noel Humphreys's *Ocean Gardens*. The book opened to the page containing Humphreys's comparison of aquarium viewing to encountering the "fairy wonders" of the theater. That seemed important.

It also, frankly, seemed a little wacky. I am happy to have this opportunity to thank the many colleagues and friends who, over the years of this project, had the deep generosity to offer help, feedback, and encouragement, as well as the kindness to refrain from asking gently and worriedly, "You're writing about *what* now . . . ?"

I owe a great debt to wonderful archivists and librarians, especially Danielle Castronovo, Lawrence Currie, Daniel Matsumoto, and Rebecca Morin of the California Academy of Sciences Library; Dana Fisher and Mary Sears of the Ernst Mayr Library of the Museum of Comparative Zoology at Harvard University; Thomas Lannon of the New York Public Library; Richard Greene of the Smithsonian Institution's National Museum of Natural History Library; and Christina Moretta, Asa Peavy, and Susie Taylor of the San Francisco Public Library.

My dear friend and colleague Bryant Alexander helped keep me grounded throughout this project with his deft and precise theorizing of race and gender politics, savvy readings of institutional politics, and boundless good humor.

I suspect there might have been times when Hae Kyung Lee wished I would just finish this up already and go back to writing about dance. As in all things, her grace and true generosity of spirit meant that I benefited throughout this work from her unceasing support and encouragement, which is palpable even across the miles.

Soyini Madison contributed her deep and brilliant understanding of the flows of power that characterize neoliberal globalization, as well as her unerring moral compass in her analyses of its predations.

Sincere thanks go to Susan Mason for sharing Ibsen's insight that humanity began to go wrong as soon as it climbed out of the water and for her engaging readings of the circulation of power in/as theatricality.

I was honored to share data from this project at the 2006 Beverly Whitaker Long Performance Event at the University of North Carolina at Chapel Hill, where I benefited from feedback from colleagues in communication, performance, and cultural studies. Della Pollock provided crucial infrastructure for refining my argument. Carole Blair's insightful response to the aquarium as a component of visual culture and Lawrence Grossberg's thoughts on the politics of male leisure proved very stimulating. Beverly Whitaker Long's complete enthusiasm reassured me that this really was a performance studies project.

Sincere thanks go to colleagues Barbara Biesecker, Colleen Boggs, Jill Dolan, Shannon Jackson, Paul Lauter, and Janelle Reinelt for their clarifying contributions to this project. Thanks also go to the anonymous reviewers from the University of Michigan Press, whose suggestions strengthened the manuscript.

I am very grateful to aquarists across the country for sharing with me their passion for the hobby and their tank tales. Special thanks go to the late Dennis Gallagher, John Brandt of the Marine Aquarium Council, and Lee Finley of Finley Aquatic Books.

My editor, Tom Dwyer, was excited about this project from the first. I am very grateful for his excellent advice, support, and genuine investment in the success of this book. Thanks also go to Alexa Ducsay and Christina L. Milton for their care and attention during the manuscript and production process.

James M. Rosenheim and the Melbern G. Glasscock Center for Humanities Research at Texas A&M University have been generous supporters of this project from the very start. A cross-disciplinary travel grant enabled me to attend my first aquarium hobbyist conference. The opportunity to present my very early thinking about the work at a Glasscock Center faculty colloquium significantly advanced this book. Special thanks go to my TAMU colleagues Steve Balfour, Dennis Berthold, Margaret Ezell, Maura Ives, Jerome Loving, Pam Matthews, Anne Morey, Claudia Nelson, Mary Ann O'Farrell, Eric Rothenbuler, James Smith, and Gary Varner.

I completed the bulk of the research and all of the writing for this book while serving as head of the Department of Performance Studies at Texas A&M University. I owe the TAMU Dean's Office of the College of Liberal Arts a debt of gratitude for the support, camaraderie, and care that made this juggling act possible. They are a joy to work with, even when the work itself is sometimes joyless.

Words are inadequate to express my thanks to Charles A. Johnson, former dean of the College of Liberal Arts and now senior vice president for research at TAMU. Simply put, without his support, this book would not have been finished on time. Barbara Johnson's warm and sincere excitement about the project and her confidence that it will find a wide and appreciative audience have been very sustaining.

I am so fortunate to work with wonderful colleagues, staff, and students in the Department of Performance Studies. Harry Berger, associate head, intellectual interlocutor, and friend, has always been eager to share ideas. Donnalee Dox generously supplied me with dozens of examples of fish humor, which reassured me that I was on to something after all. Kirsten Pullen offered excellent suggestions for advancing the larger argument of the book. Andrea Imhoff cleared out administrative thickets with her great sense of humor, clarity, and good sense.

My parents, Thaddeus F. and Dolores Hamera, were perhaps the only ones not surprised by my choice of the home aquarium as a research site. They were so enthusiastic that they contributed their research skills, working with me as we combed through the stacks of the temporarily displaced California Academy of Sciences Library, scanning countless dusty issues of hobbyist journals for hours. They were the best research support I could hope for. They said they enjoyed it. I also suspect that, though they are too kind to say so, they are a bit relieved that this project, unlike the anatomy models, ballet costumes, chemistry lab, microscope, shell collection, telescope, and unused dissection specimens, will most likely not end up cluttering their basement.

My thank you to Alfred Bendixen is briefest because my debt to him is the most profound. He is the gentlemanly stickleback of our little tank.

CONTENTS

	Introduction	1
CHAPTER 1.	Promiscuous Vision: The Visual Affinities of the Home Aquarium	15
CHAPTER 2.	Rural Rambles and Rustic Adornments: Early British Aquarium Writing	50
CHAPTER 3.	The Toy of the Day: American Aquarium Writing, 1850–1915	84
CHAPTER 4.	Toy Fish	125
CHAPTER 5.	The Domestic Aquarium	159
CHAPTER 6.	"Foreign in the Domestic Sense": Tropical Fish and the Transnational Aquarium	193
	Conclusion: Reefer Madness	219
	Notes	227
	Index	265

drew on the perceptual logics and plots of the shop window, the theater, the panorama, and literal and fictive travels to become an amalgam of all of them. Aquarium texts—for general readers and, later, for dedicated hobbyists—used recurring tropes, humor, and the odd anthropomorphic potential of tank residents to offer more than just information about the pragmatics of maintenance. The home aquarium's uncanny ability to draw on multiple, even competing visual and textual logics is central to its cultural work. It is an emblematic product of modernity, one using elements of exploration, technology, science, and a commitment to rigorous observation to contain anxieties spawned by industrialization, urbanization, changing gender roles, and relations with the global south.

The tank is all the more potent a cultural actor for its innocuousness. Framed as a mere toy, a decorative frill, or an enthusiasm for children or eccentrics, it operates as a practice of everyday life, at the intersection of work and play. It was one of a number of tools used by the middle class, especially middle-class men, to carve out a seemingly neutral and, for this reason, restorative personal and social space, out of the public sphere yet replete with potential for a selective sociality of hobbyists. The tank was a personal water world that allowed aquarists to feel, paradoxically, both larger through their mastery of "lower" beings and smaller through communion with the glories of nature. It was a place of revelation, fascination, and rejuvenation not because it exempted its enthusiasts from the tides of modernity but because it contained them in a glass box.

Aquariums enabled hobbyists to manage and even seemingly resist the challenges of profound historical changes by using the very logics and products of those changes to construct private refuges against public dilemmas. These challenges were immense. The birth and rise of the home aquarium detailed in this book coincided with a series of cultural shocks that irrevocably altered the American landscape: the Civil War; increasing urbanization and demographic diversity; the changing nature of work; shifting class, gender, and moral relations; accelerating globalization and imperial entanglements; even the size of the buildings Americans inhabited and the types of vehicles that carried them there. As Walter Lippmann observed in 1914, near the midpoint of the period covered here, "The modern man is not yet settled in his world. It is strange to him, terrifying, alluring, and incomprehensibly big."[6] Almost seventy years later, Marshall Berman famously posited this enervating unsettledness as constitutive of modernity itself. "To be modern," Berman writes, "is to experience personal and social life as a maelstrom, to find one's world and oneself in perpetual disintegration and renewal, trouble and anguish, ambiguity and contradiction: to be part of a universe in which all that is solid melts into air."[7] Zygmunt Bauman characterizes modernity in terms that are particularly congenial to the aquarium's cultural work: as a process of dissolution from its "solid," "heavy" iteration—territorial, industrial, bureaucratic, rational—to a "liquid" form that is faster, lighter, though not more equitable or just.

> Nothing has changed in this respect with the passage from heavy to light modernity. But the frame has filled with a new content . . . People who move and act faster, who come nearest to the momentariness of movement, are now the people who rule. And it is the people who cannot move as quickly, and more conspicuously yet the category of people who cannot at will leave their place at all, who are ruled. Domination consists in one's own capacity to escape, to disengage, to "be elsewhere," and the right to decide the speed with which all that is done—while simultaneously stripping the people on the dominated side of their ability to arrest or constrain their moves or slow them down.[8]

Life in liquid modernity "is consuming life. It casts the world and all its animate and inanimate fragments as objects of consumption."[9]

The aquarium was one of a number of technologies that inserted nature into solid *and* liquid modernity, while domesticating the underlying logics of both. Like the shop window, the panorama, and other urban entertainments, it linked seeing to owning, a domestic iteration of imperial orientations to landscape going back to sixteenth-century voyages of discovery. But seeing was not simple. Just as nature was shaped by modernity into a consumable remedy for modernity's own excesses, seeing was refashioned by rationality into an imperative to observe and manage attention that increasingly linked leisure to work. By arresting water worlds and using them as personal ornaments, aquariums celebrated modernity's prowess. But they also revealed another unsettling possibility lurking below the surface: aquarists, not just their finny charges, might also be small fish consigned to glass boxes in which they were ever visible and from which they could not escape. The tank suggests that solid modernity and particularly its construction of nature were, if not fully liquid, at least moist all along.

Ornamental fish keeping does not, of course, begin in 1850. It is an ancient practice. But from the nineteenth century to the present, historians view the modern Western aquarium as the offspring of the Ward Case, an airtight glass environment for growing ferns that we would recognize as a terrarium.[10] The Ward Case was responsible for the fern craze, and with the discovery of complementary respiration of plants and animals, the "aquavivarium" followed as a logical next step. Early on, aquariums were transatlantic affairs. In its first formative decades, British aquarium celebrities, particularly Philip Henry Gosse, provided crucial conceptual infrastructure for understanding and maintaining the tank, as well as its multiple intersections with and repairs to the vexations of urban, industrial modernity. The American hobby started later, stoked by the steady flow of British publications; the first American books were published in 1858. The hobby later expanded to become a transnational site of sometimes literal and sometimes vicarious global exchanges as it included fish from the literal and fictive tropics.

The semiotics of the home aquarium were and remain remarkably variable. There is no simple "typical tank," even within the same period, region, or demographic. Indeed, one reason for the aquarium's enduring popularity is its ability to indulge and contain aquarists' idiosyncrasies along with its residents. Early in the hobby's history, tanks were circular and shallow, spherical and deep, octagonal, or rectangular, with glass on all sides or on only one. Rectangular tanks might have had straight or slanted backs. They were framed with wood or zinc or iron and resembled boxes, birdcages, fountains, or greenhouses (see figs. 1–3).[11] Arthur Edwards, author of one of the first American aquarium books, states plainly that "the vessel may be of any shape and size" (see fig. 4).[12] Variability of tank setup continued to be a key feature of the hobby even after Gosse popularized the four-sided glass rectangle with which we are now familiar. Bottoms could be lined with sand, gravel, a few rocks, or nothing at all. Fish were optional; anemones, crabs, or coral could fill one's water world, and British aquarium writers were particularly fond of them, though Edwards dismissed such arrangements as mere "quiet flower gardens."[13] Tank populations depended on access to native freshwater and saltwater species and, much later, to the vicissitudes of local breeders, markets, and retailers. Darters, dace, and sticklebacks were perennial favorites in American aquarium books from the mid-nineteenth into the early twentieth centuries, but this is most likely a function of both the books and the fish originating in the New York area—preference born of proximity. Initially, plants and their complementary respiration were essential to the survival of tank fish. With the advent of electric aeration technologies in the 1920s, they became optional.[14]

Some tanks were housed in parlors, others in children's rooms; and later,

Fig. 1. Parlor aquarium with fountain: *Manufacturer and Builder* 10, no. 7 (July 1878): 163. (Courtesy of Cornell University Library's Making of America Digital Collection.)

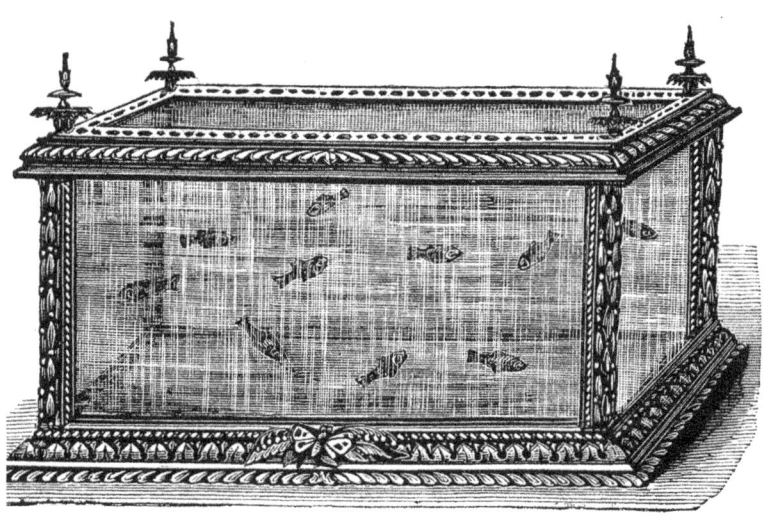

Fig. 2. Design for parlor aquarium, *Manufacturer and Builder* 10, no. 7 (July 1878): 163. (Courtesy of Cornell University Library, Making of America Digital Collection.)

Fig. 3. Aquarium and fernery combined, reminiscent of the tank's origins in the Ward Case. (From Gregory C. Bateman and Reginald A. R. Bennett, *The Book of Aquaria* [New York: Scribner's, 1902], 45.)

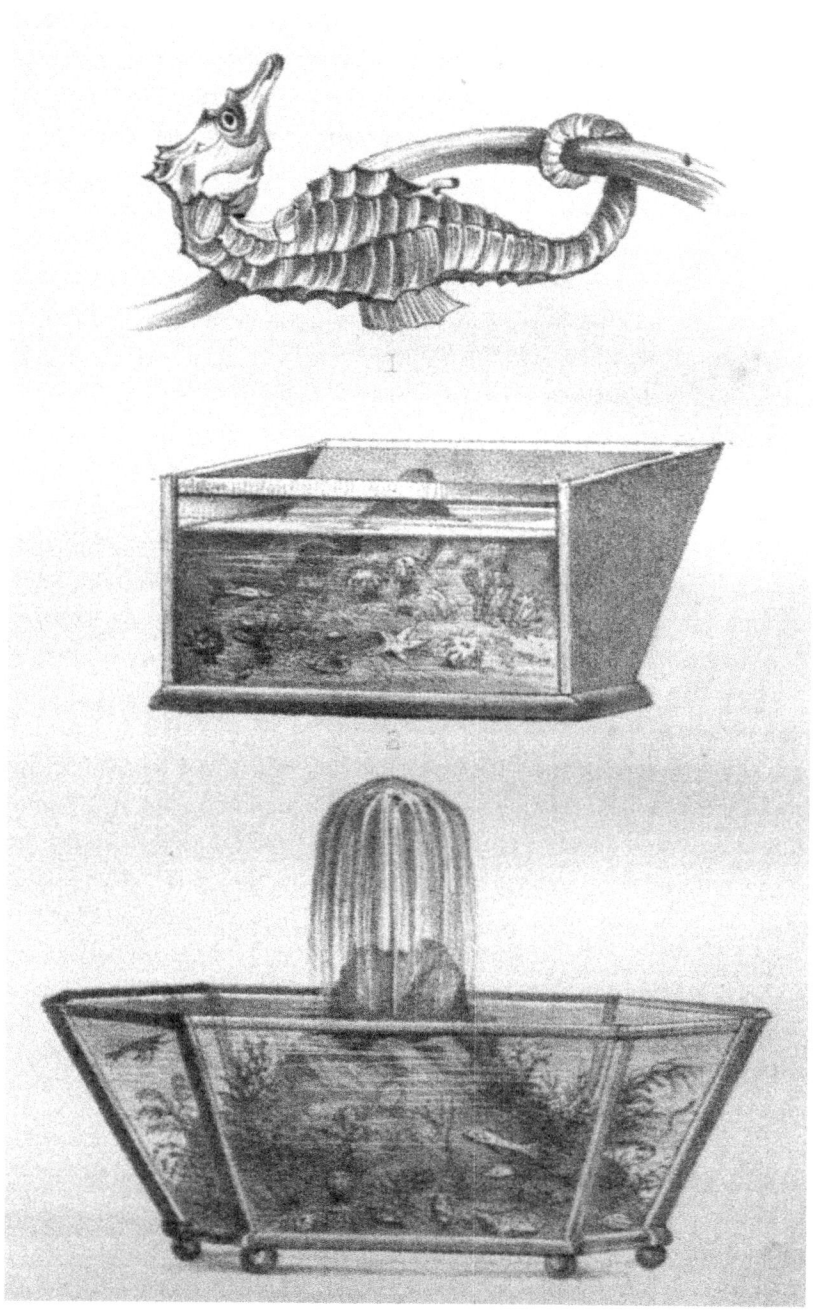

Fig. 4. Cover plate to Arthur M. Edwards, *Life Beneath the Waters; or, The Aquarium in America* (New York: H. Balliere, 1858). Note the different options for aquariums, including a slanted slate back and sides and an internal fountain.

as the hobby increased in popularity and advanced technologically, tanks moved into "fish rooms" dedicated to or reappropriated for the purpose. Typically, these were converted spaces in lesser-used parts of the home, designed both to minimize potential damage done by routine maintenance, especially water changes, and to provide a place apart from the rest of the household for the hobbyist's exclusive respite. In this sense, the tank was an early forerunner of the radio and the television and traced a similar trajectory. Over time, it became progressively less and less like a parlor ornament or piece of family furniture and more an extension of an individual's highly personal habitus—an escape from the interpersonal, if not the literal, confines of both parlor and family. Aquarists' tanks were personal theaters, and while there were certainly general dramaturgical and theatrical principles, as well as scientific ones, to be observed in their construction, authorities from the earliest texts to contemporary ones "leave the student to make his own discoveries, in all mere matters of convenience; as he will necessarily adapt them more aptly to his own peculiar views and wants."[15] For example, despite frequent and recurring appeals from some aquarium authors to maintain the tank as a "natural" landscape, it became, over the time period covered by this book, a site for highly individualized decor, enabled by an emerging industry in tank accessories. No longer parlor ornament, it was itself a potential parlor to be ornamented. When hobbyist Nina Quart wrote about "keeping your aquarium alive" one hundred years after Arthur Edwards offered the basic how-tos, she meant this phrase aesthetically and highly individualistically, not biologically, and "nature" was not necessarily helpful: "Your aquarium setting can and should be as creative an expression as your painting."[16] Because "not all nature is beautiful," an aquarist might add plastic plants, hippos, divers, and treasure chests to the tank; might organize it narratively or visually around a theme or motif; and might even dye living anemones artificial colors "that defy recognition and are quite as dazzling as some of nature's handiwork."[17]

These highly variable semiotics of the tank are not matched by variable demographics of its keepers. This was an urban middle- and upper-middle-class hobby from its earliest beginnings, a way to parlay native aquatic capital into the manageable equivalent of little parlor estates. Enthusiasts on both sides of the Atlantic extolled its ability to alleviate the deleterious effects of increasingly bureaucratic modernity while instilling the very norms central to successfully navigating it: rigorous observation and discipline; a working knowledge of science and technology; access to urban infrastructure and the ability to escape the city, when needed, to collect specimens; specialized books; and recognition of the self as the apogee of progress over against lower beings. This class position has stayed remarkably consistent. Home aquarium keeping is still primarily a middle-class practice and a mark of distinction, signifying the hobbyist's access to resources; mechanical, scientific, and husbandry skills; capital; and good taste. In the United States, the hobby is overwhelmingly white. Further, despite early vigorous marketing to women as a parlor decoration and educational toy for children, it is also overwhelmingly male, dominated by the very population putatively threatened by the feared effeminizing anomie of modern institutions. A close reading of aquarium publications demonstrates that the tank is an unjustly underregarded middlebrow technology for maintaining class, gender, and racial privilege. It manages encounters with difference intrinsic to modern urbanism by unproblematically coupling artisanal rhetorics of personal competence to the promise of exploration enabled by technical and scientific progress. The aquarium unites the mind, the eye, and the hand in productive leisure, honing skills transferable to the workplace even as it repairs the workplace's psychic predations. It is a tool for asserting individual mastery of the home because it is itself a home: the "happy family" inside the tank could reciprocally construct one outside. Yet it can conjure exotic locales through tropical fish, even if those fish come from the United States. These locales and, by extension, global entanglements situated there are made conceptually manageable by demonstrating that colorful foreigners can be consumed unproblematically at home.

The aquarium's visual and rhetorical promiscuity demands an interdisciplinary approach that the field of performance studies is ideally positioned to provide. First, the tank inserts nature into aesthetics and particularly into theatricality. It borrowed the perceptual dynamics and textual conventions of the theater to make its pedagogical and moral contributions to the home and the antics of its residents intelligible to viewers. The aquarium drew back the curtain on heretofore-unseen worlds and presented them through "rhetorics of spectacular display."[18] Stock characters and plots circulate through early aquarium books, lending potential personalities to specimens who were so obviously other that early audiences did not always know what they should be looking at. Finally, as discussed in this book's concluding chapter, the underlying promise of the aquarium is the promise of theater itself: that presentational and representational elements can somehow combine to spawn a brave new world of edification and enjoyment betwixt and between reality and its more domesticated, contained other. In addition to its visual orientation and its plots, the aquarium also inserted the world-making promise of theater into the home.

The first four chapters of this book detail *how* the home aquarium works, through its multiple visual affinities, the narrative and rhetorical strategies of its early British and American proponents, and the queer alterity of fish themselves. These elements trained viewers in how to see the tank—what privileges accrued to spectators, what plots they should look for and what conclusions they should draw, and, most crucially, the difference between observing and merely looking. Thus, the tank exemplified modern attempts to structure spectatorship and attention and inserted these into the home as a comfort and a pleasure, domesticating, aestheticizing, and normalizing operations essential to modernity itself. Chapter 1 examines these visual affinities and what they bequeathed to the aquarium.

Likewise, early aquarium writing provided textual templates that enhanced its potential for cultural work. Slippages between the tank and the sea allowed aquarists a measure of conceptual control over nature and its meanings. The tank expanded to include other landscapes, particularly, in its British antecedents, rural ones. This containment of a premodern, seemingly timeless past served as a palliative for anxieties about industrialization and urbanization while fashioning aquarists into itinerant naturalist-artisans and, at the same time, scientifically literate people of their age. The tank was a tool for self-fashioning, a reflection of elevated taste. In American aquarium writing, it was a home, a business, and a progressive tool for social reform. Chapters 2 and 3 examine British and American aquarium writings, respectively. Chapter 4 analyzes the ways the tank works through a complex surrogacy involving fish, whose own representational fluidity enables them to stand in for a wide range of positions. Their behaviors were read through plots of domestic bliss or strife, martial bravery, busy industry, exotic difference, or equally exotic and sensational violence. Not quite animals and not quite toys, fish were also representationally fungible: they could stand in for people, but, often disconcertingly, people could also stand in for fish—captive, ever on display, and easily disposable.

Chapters 5 and 6 are case studies examining *where* the tank works. Its visual and textual templates endow it with the ability to manage a range of dilemmas, including those dealing with gender relations and foreign others. The first four chapters discuss the aquarium's cultural work as it emerges in publications for those with a general interest in aquariums as well as those specifically for hobbyists. These two chapters focus solely on the latter. Hobbyist magazines and journals offer a neglected but immensely valuable opportunity to explore how and where the aquarium worked for its most dedicated devotees. Issues and dilemmas both large and small were routed through the tank to resurface in editorials, poems, reference articles, and humor, including the seeming caprices of modern commerce; tricky negotiations of balances of power in the nuclear family; science envy and antipathy; and fear of and desire for colorful, exotic others. Hobbyist journals offered opportunities for self-display that matched those of the tank itself. They enabled aquarists to wade into the currents of public life, as in appeals for industry assistance during the Great Depression through Franklin Roosevelt's National Recovery Act. These publications gave earnest amateurs an opportunity to vent their rage or revel in their own "author-ity" through their own cartoons and personal narratives. Above all, these outlets demonstrate the hows and wheres of the aquarium's social work through the words and images of its most ardent enthusiasts.

Finally, the conclusion addresses the *why* of the home aquarium by probing its potential for excess, as well as its participation in and reproduction of the logics of the theater. This is the only part of the book to consider contemporary aquaria and its new rhetoric, born of increasing environmental exigencies that are, in part, the product of those same excesses. The conclusion takes up the tank's overarching mimetic promise and probes some of the less fortunate consequences of its enthusiasts' infatuations.

Though this book is not a history of the hobby, the chapters do proceed roughly chronologically. Chapter 1 examines the mid-nineteenth-century urban entertainment and consumer technologies that made the tank initially intelligible, even familiar. British antecedents described in chapter 2 paved the way for the tank's American popularity. As demonstrated in chapter 3, writings from 1850 to 1915 situated the tank in American private and public life. Chapter 4 offers a survey designed to demonstrate the equivocal construction of fish as pets throughout the period covered by the book. Chapter 5 details various versions of the domestic tank and its attendant gender troubles from, roughly, the 1920s through the 1960s, while chapter 6 analyzes the cultural utility of the so-called tropical tank from the 1930s to 1970.

The hobby changed subtly but significantly after 1970. Technologies for water quality improved, and as a result, saltwater tanks gained in popularity over freshwater versions. Small, highly idiosyncratic hobbyist magazines increasingly gave way to scientific publications or were subsumed into and reshaped by conglomerates in the pet industry. Greater and greater attention was given to ecological concerns. Some of this was defensive. Aquarists had to answer for ecological disruptions and predations, including release of potentially destructive nonnative species and environmentally disastrous collecting practices like the cyanide poisoning of rivers in the global south to more efficiently gather specimens for the trade. In other cases, aquarists recognized the importance of the tank to emerging rhetorics of ecology and sustainability and attempted to both change the footprint of the hobby and use aquaria to communicate larger messages about the fragility of ocean and river ecosystems. Increasing recognition of the potential for global environmental catastrophe was only one of a number of exigencies to be routed through the tank after 1970; these included shifting ideas about the nature and promise of modernity itself. While these recent turns in the partnership between the tank and ideas of the modern are beyond the scope of this book, they paved the way for contemporary reefers, reef tank enthusiasts who, in some respects, bring us full circle back to the madrepores and anemones that so engaged English enthusiasts over a century before. My conclusion considers the reefers as the latest to succumb to the peculiar mix of desire and excess that defines the hobby, a mix, I argue, that can be rendered intelligible by reading the tank as part of the affective and mimetic economies of the theater.

The aquarium makes virtue and ideological utility out of its most basic characteristic. It is a container that holds some things in while keeping others out, a virtue that does not necessarily translate easily into comparable analytical parameters. With the same giddy fear that reefers feel when they contemplate tanks big enough to house every coral they ever wanted, I quickly discovered that the topic had the potential to overflow its artificial limits. It seemed to me that all of American history and culture from 1850 forward could be routed through the intoxicating, world-making power of the tank. Rather than be swamped, I adhered to some artificial boundaries. Though public aquariums are fascinating in their own right, I only discuss them as they intersect with their domestic siblings.[19] Likewise, I focus on aquarium texts and hobbyist culture, rather than mainstream media representations. Though I believe the analyses here can apply to them, I offer no explication of Disney's *Nemo* or discussion of that famous frame in the film *The Graduate* where Benjamin stares blankly through his tank, both master of his water world and a fish out of water. I do not take up detailed discussion of goldfish or aquatic plants. Both freshwater and saltwater tanks are discussed together, demonstrating their technical and ideological similarities.[20] Thus, like even the largest tank, this book is inevitably partial, gesturing to the plenitude left outside.

Aquarists always counsel moderation, even if they don't often heed their own advice. You can't keep everything, so you have to leave something out. But in books as in tanks, the pleasures and surprises come from what you put in. Here, that means the words of aquarists themselves, from the indefatigable Gosse and his citational solidarity with romantic poets; to self-proclaimed fish guy Don Simpson; to Diane Schofield, the Erma Bombeck of the hobby; to others whose prose reveals that the aquarium was not always the progressive force for enlightenment and uplift its early proponents proclaimed.[21] In "Bodies and Their Plots," Hayden White asks us to imagine how the bodies of/in historiography *"sounded, smelled, felt,* and *tasted."*[22] In aquariums, these aren't just human bodies. They include those of soldierly crabs, gentlemanly sticklebacks, and flirtatious bettas, as well as finny celebrities like "Snoz" and "Blanche," introduced in chapter 4, all ventriloquated by hobbyists whose fish were both more and less than pets—toys and alter egos; faithful companions or nemeses; hectoring reminders that predators were not limited to those in the tank or even the sea and that falling prey to them was not a worry only for little fish. I quote extensively from the voices of aquaria, not only for the denotative content of their utterances, which is often remarkable enough, but to capture, if only partially, the textures of their thinking and the grains of their voices. Reduced to the dry two-dimensionality of print, they are as close as I can come to providing readers with a sense of what the hobby has sounded like.

Aquaria flow unseen through so many channels of American modernity, as part of the background, a social force hiding in plain sight in the living room, basement, or fish room. At the same time, fish keeping is a significant industry. The 2009–10 survey of pet owners by the American Pet Products Association found that 14 percent of U.S. households have freshwater or saltwater fish; nearly 183 million aquarium fish are kept as pets.[23] The U.S. Census Bureau estimates that aquarium fish and products comprised over 9 percent of the pet industry's total sales in 2002.[24] In both capacities, the aquarium repays careful attention. And it speaks beyond its boundaries to raise questions about larger interconnections between nature and consumer culture, the consumption of theatricality in everyday life, the construction of hobbyist rhetoric as a tool for managing and wading into public discourse, and ongoing relationships between modernity and the animal. The home aquarium also asks us to take water worlds and their inhabitants seriously, not just as sources of pleasure and respite, not merely as a limitless bounty of found objects that might become our pets. It asks us to regard these worlds as the most praiseworthy hobbyists regard their tanks, as part of a meaningful network of personal and social obligations that demands commitment, concern, and continual investment in the most rigorous and humane stewardship.

※ ※ ※

My acquaintance was outraged. Though an academic herself, she did not hide her disdain for my assertion that the U.S. home aquarium managed and allayed anxieties about industrial, imperial modernity. People keep aquariums, she countered defiantly, because they are beautiful and peaceful and because pretty fish make them happy.

Exactly.

CHAPTER 1

PROMISCUOUS VISION: THE VISUAL AFFINITIES OF THE HOME AQUARIUM

> The wonders of the ocean floor do not reveal themselves to vulgar eyes.
>
> —H. NOEL HUMPHREYS, *Ocean Gardens*

H. Noel Humphreys assured his English and American readers that, to engage the full potential of the aquarium, "it is the *seeing* that is everything."[1] But when it came to the home tank, seeing was not simple. As the preceding epigraph attests, this was not a matter for "vulgar eyes." It was not enough to merely look. The allure of spectacle might sustain the public tank, but to maximize the benefits of this rational amusement in the parlor, one had to pay attention; one had to observe. Thus, seventy-five years after Humphreys's admonition against vulgar eyes, William Innes, one of the pillars of the American hobby, used an editorial in his journal, the *Aquarium*, to reiterate the importance of the perceptual and cognitive synthesis intrinsic to properly observing the home tank.

> This little editorial is a plea for the overlooked possibilities, particularly in very simple and sparsely stocked aquaria, where the field at first sight seems quite limited. Has the owner really seen all that can be seen, learned all there is to know? Hardly.
>
> These are not foolish questions. They have direct scientific bearing, but most of all, they are intended to bring out the fact that observation needs to be systematized, so that it can be increased and made more valuable.
>
> It is pleasant to believe one's self a person with the power of seeing everything at a glance, but in aquarium study (and I suspect elsewhere) "there ain't no such animal."

If this exhortation seems excessively disciplinary for a leisure activity, Innes assures his readers that "perpetual progress" as an aquarium observer "becomes permanent pleasure."[2]

Innes's mid-twentieth-century supplement to Humphreys's mid-nineteenth-century assertion of the visual pleasures of the aquarium and their inaccessibility to vulgar eyes underscores a key feature of the tank as an exemplary rational amusement. Its enthusiasts' emphases on systematic observation as key to intellectual profit and progress link the hobby to the core operation of American modernity: the ability to pay attention. Humphreys's and Innes's assertions reinforce the aquarium's place in the ongoing construction, management, and domestication of modern attention, which, as Jonathan Crary observes, is the operation central to the functioning of a capitalist consumer economy.[3] What, in its British antecedents, begins as an appeal to a cultivated aesthetic and theological vision, one mark of distinction against the merely vulgar, morphs over time into surveillance as leisure. The inculcation of systematic discipline as crucial to the hobby transports the hobbyist from an earlier romantic ethos, one in which the refined soul sees in the tank a solidarity with lyric poets, to an entrepreneurial, managerial one ever on the alert to overlooked possibilities for increasing value.

Yet the aquarium was not only an activity to which attention must be paid. It was also a distraction, a site of seeming respite from the need to pay attention, as J. E. Taylor argued.

> Invalids, or people of sedentary habits, who are much confined within doors, might find comfort and enjoyment from keeping an aquarium. The antics of its little inhabitants, and the little care required to keep this miniature world in a healthy condition, will draw off their attention from many an hour of suffering or care, and unconsciously develop a love for God's creatures.[4]

The aquarium did not just demand the heightened vigilance and cultivated engagement required of the modern subject; it was also the antidote to them. Whether as a task to be effectively managed or a refuge from such tasks, the home tank was part of a Foucauldian "network of permanent observation," one in which concentrated attention, its refinement and recalibration, increasingly colonized leisure time.[5] How did the home aquarium so easily accommodate these two seemingly incommensurable visual operations—focused attention and respite—within a larger construction of attentiveness?

This chapter examines the perceptual dynamics of the home aquarium through its visual affinities. The aquarium's uncanny ability to draw on a wide range of such affinities and their operations is crucial to understanding its social work and its enduring popularity. These affinities inserted the tank, its residents, and its viewers into preexisting logics of perception and consumption, along with their embedded narrative logics, organizing what and how to see, as well as why. These visual and textual logics worked together to establish and enhance the appeal of the hobby. Chapters 2 and 3 focus specifically on the rhetoric of home aquarium texts, which relied heavily, if seemingly unconsciously, on the tropes and templates discussed here. Thus, aquarium texts were much more than "foils" for the tank's visual affinities, more than "rival modes of representation."[6] On the contrary, the garden, the window, panorama and the theater, the sightseeing vacation, and the ideological utility of the domestic landscape itself undergird these texts. Over the course of the hobby, visual and textual elements engaged in an ongoing process of mutual redefinition. This chapter focuses on mid-nineteenth-century landscapes and technologies that coincided with and contributed to the emerging popularity of the hobby, but one obvious example is contemporary. The rise of the nature documentary, especially its easy availability on that other domestic leisure box, the television, coupled with the increasing circulation of ecological rhetoric in the public sphere, contributed enormously to the popularity of the reef tank, discussed in this book's conclusion.

This chapter examines perceptual foundations for the home aquarium. It begins by briefly outlining familiar domestic landscapes that accustomed viewers to the type of world and associated benefits the aquarium offered: the garden and the collection. Like the aquarium, both operate within a larger iconological economy of the domestic(atible) landscape. The aquarium benefits from this economy and troubles it in its continual reminders that the underwater world is both inaccessible and very strange. The chapter then turns to more-extensive discussions of the diverse architectural and entertainment technologies that acclimated consumers to specific forms of modern spectatorship and prepared them for the landscapes in the tank.

DOMESTIC(ATED) LANDSCAPES

The aquarium entered the public and private spheres as versions of the landscape. W. J. T. Mitchell's "theses for landscape" could just as easily serve as a poststructuralist definition of the home tank—a piece of the sea removed to the parlor, both a real ecosystem and a highly artificial ornament, a framed portion of aquascape gesturing toward an unframable whole. Mitchell writes,

Landscape is a natural scene mediated by culture. It is both a represented and presented space, both a signifier and a signified, both a frame and what a frame contains, both a real place and its simulacrum, both a package and the commodity inside the package.[7]

In mid-nineteenth-century America, the liminal both-and aspect of the landscape provided a particularly potent tool for imagining national unity and constructing a seemingly stable, comprehensible, and harmonious nature while minimizing the unpredictability of both. Angela Miller calls this "the formula of the middle landscape" in visual art of the period.[8] The aquarium was both a logical extension of this representational strategy and an exception to it. Collecting and containing specimens from rivers, streams, and the ocean itself was certainly one way of making national patrimony visible. It paralleled American landscape painters' representations of geological forces on canvas. Like these paintings, the aquarium attempted to contain the ultimately uncontainable, making it reassuringly available for display and thereby intelligible. Yet, while a bucolic pond might be easily recognized as a site of restorative repose or a nostalgic marker for rural scenes now lost to urbanization, even here the conventional landscape schema only skims the iconological surface.

At the birth of the aquarium in the United States in the late 1850s, water worlds could not yet be fully enclosed by the conceptual and material frames of capital. They were simultaneously essential for yet resistant to national and later global annexation and exploitation. These were sources of raw materials and modes of transporting them, but their depths, expanses, and flows could not be easily tamed by entrepreneurs, painters, scientists, or tourists. Unlike the geological wonders painted by Thomas Cole, Frederic Church, and other members of the Hudson River school, underwater landscapes were wholly inaccessible, even by the most intrepid adventurer. The seas and mighty rivers so crucial to the nation's self-fashioning were vehicles for progress yet also threatening, impenetrable, seemingly inexhaustible—howling wilderness not yet completely transformed into restful, restorative nature nor fully subsumed into the productive networks of culture. Indeed, water worlds were as much reminders of the limits of human progress as vehicles for it. Melville's *Moby Dick* is only one obvious example, as is the prevalence of imagery of wrecked boats in American luminist painting of the middle to late nineteenth century.[9] The sea and the great rivers of the interior were also cast as sources of primeval national vitality and routes to the elemental sublime. Paintings could easily organize the picturesque aspects of water worlds for viewers, but the materiality of the aquarium's actual water—sloshing, spilling, evaporating, leaking—was a constant reminder that the tank held only "fast-fish," even as it gestured toward incalculable conceptual and material "loose-fish." As Melville observed in *Moby Dick*, "A Fast-Fish belongs to the party fast to it. A Loose-Fish is fair game for anybody who can soonest catch it."[10] Fast-fish were enlightening and reassuring diversions. Loose-fish seemed inexhaustible and eternal.

The home aquarium reassured the viewer of the power of technology and the individual to miniaturize water worlds for private consumption, even as its very artifice served as a reminder of the highly circumscribed nature of that power. Perhaps it was this ambivalence—reassuring through technologically enhanced frames while pointing to the unframable—that kept the "picture frame aquarium" at the margins of the hobby.[11] Despite occasional references to the aquarium as a living picture, water's three-dimensional materiality and symbolic potency strained the conventions of the two-dimensional landscape. Literal and ideological maintenance were problems. Water in picture frame aquariums, like that in actual ponds, rivers, and seas, didn't always do what technicians and consumers wanted it to, and when it stubbornly went its own way, it swamped the entire frame, exposing it as always already inadequate. Perhaps this accounted for a metaphoric slide to other, less ambivalent, more obviously domesticated three-dimensional landscapes to normalize the aquarium.

The title of Humphreys's book *Ocean Gardens* points to the domestic landscape most analogous to the home aquarium. Consumers could view the tank as a garden. Garden imagery was common in early aquarium literature on both sides of the Atlantic. Henry D. Butler asked his readers,

> Would you desire an aquatic flower-show?
> The sea and the lake have their gardens, beside which the garish beauty of man's proudest efforts at floriculture pale into sickly impertinence. Behold them, reproduced in the Aquaria![12]

The prevalence of garden references in early publications was in part a reflection of biology, a recognition of the variety of undersea botanicals and animals, like the anemone, that were frankly flowerlike. Anemones were discussed like plantings, especially in books that emphasized the decorative possibilities of the tank, including Shirley Hibberd's *Rustic Adornments for Homes of Taste*, discussed in chapter 2. It was also a function of genealogy, of the widely held view that the aquarium was an outgrowth of the Ward

Case, a miniature greenhouse for growing ferns. Both the early incarnation of the aquarium and the garden were literal places of cultivation.

More substantively decorative home gardens offered a well-established model of aesthetic and domestic virtues that the aquarium was poised to share. They simultaneously demonstrated mastery of the earth and independence from it.[13] For the emerging urban middle class, a small garden might supplement the larder, but it was far from subsistence agriculture. In this respect, it paralleled hobbyists' relationship to aquarium fish: having the resources to cultivate them without the economic imperative to eat them. Gardens were reassuringly controllable elements of nature incorporated into the home, where they were appreciated as pedagogical and artistic goods. Moreover, as products of individual or family initiative, they reflected the inner cultivation of their owners—imagination, the coupling of leisure and hard work or the ability to employ others to do it, access to materials and perhaps even to Old World landscapes through travel or publications.[14]

In both aquatic and garden scapes, the pleasing appearance of physical space reflected a mastery of facts, especially, in the case of gardens, a "botanical vernacular" that marked the command of the upper-middle and emerging middle classes over genteel natural history as well as their distance from utilitarian peasant understandings.[15] Like the garden, the home aquarium offered the opportunity to subsume the natural within an expanded notion of the domestic self by inserting it into domestic space. In both cases, the process made nature into a consumable. Further, both the garden and the aquarium relied on and reinforced practices of an emerging managerial ethos within the domestic routine as the leisure-time equivalent of "the language of calculation, system, and diligence into which efficiency engineers poured their new and stricter meanings."[16] These practices included sorting desirable elements from undesirable ones using arbitrary classification schemes ("plants" versus "weeds"), a "good eye" (a putatively democratized version of innate "taste"), discipline and vigilance needed for regular maintenance, and/or the ability to delegate and supervise "lower order" tasks. Beyond this, the garden had utopian affinities from the admittedly ambivalent Garden of Eden to the medieval "bower of bliss."[17] This utopian aspect was an especially potent antidote to increasing urbanization and industrialization. The garden offered the middle-class family a private park as the aquarium offered a parlor sea, a way to view and manage nature as a palliative, a pedagogical tool, and a pleasure.

These shared attributes aligned the home aquarium much more closely with the home garden than with the zoo. Though the tank was certainly a way to stage the domestic self as erudite, handy, and tasteful, it did not partake of the same visual rhetoric of gross power as private menageries. Historically, American public aquariums actually preceded zoos. P. T. Barnum installed tanks in his American Museum in 1856, and Henry Butler and James Cutting opened the Boston Aquarial Gardens in 1859. Though the charter establishing the Zoological Society of Philadelphia was signed that same year, the zoo itself—the first in the United States—did not open to the public until 1874. Add to this the fact that the labor of the home tank, like the labor of the garden, was personal, an extension of domestic space and management. The zoo might have presented the world's fauna, but the tank was its owner's personal world.

The quality of relationships between viewers and residents in zoos also marked a crucial difference between these institutions and home or even public aquariums. This difference was another component of the overall strangeness of water worlds. It was not just the water itself that made these landscapes inaccessible, inconvenient, and unintelligible. It was the nature of the residents themselves. Biologist Todd Newberry describes this difference in contemporary terms.

> Aquariums are where we confront scaly swimmers, animals without backbones, animals whose heads don't turn, creatures without faces. Aquariums have animals that never touch the ground and others that settle to the ground and never move again. They have animals that look like plants or stones or the water itself. Strange appearances are signs of strange lives.[18]

It is this alterity, the radical otherness of the residents, that aligned aquarium inhabitants to garden plants. Audiences could identify with the animals behind bars but faced significant limits to empathizing with residents in the tank. How to engage them other than as things or food was not clear or, as yet, scripted. Aquarium residents simply did not call forth the same affective range summoned by zoo residents, from the cuddly to the terrifying to the seemingly human. Aquarium writers generated the templates for relationships with tank fauna by casting them as recognizable character types based on obvious behaviors. Ultimately, as indicated later in this chapter, the theater was a far more useful prototype than the zoo for understanding tank residents and relating to them. In theatrical terms, zoo animals are Stanislavskian. They invite emotional recognition. Aquarium residents are Brechtian. As Newberry suggests, their physiology, their physiognomy, and their very surroundings constitute built-in alienation effects.[19] Early in the hobby, authors overcame this alienation, not by turning aquarium residents into individual personalities, but by casting them as recognizable stock figures to make them seem less alien and more familiar. Yet stock figures were interchangeable and disposable; there is little indication in this early literature of lasting personal attachment to tank residents as a whole or as individuals, as would emerge later in the hobby. Early aquarists frequently express surprise that their fish seem to recognize them, willingly eat from their hands, or allow themselves to be touched. They were characters, not fully "beings." Even their exoticism was opaque. They may have lived strange lives, but early in the hobby, those lives were local and did not conjure mysterious faraway places like the Amazonian jungle or the African savannah. It took years for the hobby to develop the affective vocabulary and narratives in which to set tank residents. This process is explored in chapters 2, 3, and 4. At this early stage, aquarium residents were neither exotic specimens nor fully pets.

The collection provided another way to understand the landscape dimension of the home aquarium. Indeed, the tank is a collection in the most literal sense, "a set of natural or artificial objects, kept temporarily or permanently out of the economic circuit, afforded special protection in enclosed places adapted specifically for that purpose and put on display."[20] It reframed relatively commonplace specimens (at least early in its history) and set them into new contexts (domestic, scientific, decorative, allegorical) and new forms of attention (observation and reprieve from the imperative to observe).[21] Stocking a tank before widespread availability of store-bought specimens meant taking literal collecting trips, which effectively rendered the sites of these trips extensions of both the tank and the home, both the "original" context and a new, domestic one. Further, as noted earlier, the queer alterity of tank residents often positioned them in early literature as something between an animal and an object or curio, generally more of the latter. The aquarium worked as parlor displays of seashells or butterflies did. They were "rustic adornments for homes of taste."[22] They offered manageable nature on display as evidence of travel or adventure. Like private "cabinets of curiosities," they combined exoticism and pedagogy in ways that reflected favorably on the unique tastes of the household. In this sense, the collection might be less a function of the objects displayed and more an affirmation of the cultivated vision, technological savvy, discipline, and abundant resources of the modern collector.

The collection, like the garden, was a world-making endeavor, and in the case of nature collections, the worlds constructed were preurban and preindustrial, antidotes to the dislocations of modern progress, decorative "Noah's arks" for vanishing wilderness.[23] The aquarium demonstrated this world-making aspect of the collection more literally than most. Though the early days of the hobby cannot compare with contemporary tanks in the sheer amount of equipment needed, the glass, cement, buckets, and other accoutrements testified to the hobbyist's ingenuity, leisure time, and disposable income. The labor of world making required capital and was celebrated through the tank as a display of what capital could buy. Then, as now, reproduction in the tank was a testament to excellent husbandry, further underscoring the hobbyist's creative prowess and adept command of both natural and material fecundity.

Above all, the home aquarium, like other natural history collections, reframed nature as a collectible in ways that marked distance from both the "primitive" economy of manual labor and the "equally savage" marketplace. This was neither a gathering of resources to ensure survival nor a matter of vulgar display of wealth. Instead, it demonstrated the gentility of mastery over nature, technology, scientific knowledge, and the transatlantic *au currant*, for, as Arthur M. Edwards, one of the first American aquarium writers, noted in 1858, in England, "a parlor is hardly considered furnished" without an aquarium.[24] Aquariums demonstrated the conflation of knowledge and good taste. Like museum objects in institutions organized during this same period, specimens functioned as both synecdoches and metonyms. A fish and an anemone stood for the pond or the shore and for the know-how that reproduced them in the home. Independent of individual collectors' motives, the tank functioned like trophies of animal heads on the wall. This was a domestic and domesticating iteration of imperialism, even if very partial given the dynamics of aquascape. Natural abundance was tapped, claimed, and contained, rendering it a private good and casting the owner as master, explorer, and authoritative interpreter of his personal water world.

Domestic landscapes, especially the garden and the collection, showed aquarium viewers *what* they could see in the tank. This included nature shaped into and managed as a pedagogical and aesthetic good; a utopia, a respite from the demands of urban life; a fragment of vanishing wilderness reassembled by cultivated hands and eyes into alternative worlds; and a testament to the quality and level of this cultivation. However, to learn *how* to see the unique elements and potential of the tank, consumers could turn to urban visual culture.

VISUAL AFFINITIES

In "Simulated Seas," his discussion of contemporary aquarium exhibits, Dennis Doordan describes contemporary public facilities as places of "promiscuous vision where natural and enhanced forms of seeing are mingled."[25] This visual promiscuity is not unique to contemporary public tanks. On the contrary, from its earliest incarnations, the aquarium benefited from its ability to allude to, absorb, and adapt a wide range of spectatorial technologies, media, and positions, including the window, the theater, panoramas and dioramas, and real and vicarious travel. The aquarium was one of what Jonathan Crary calls "a related group of strategies through which a subject is modernized as a spectator traverses a range of seemingly different objects and locations"; it was part and parcel of the nineteenth century's "'frenzy of the visible.'"[26] Engaging aquarium landscapes seemed far less odd than it otherwise might because such engagements benefited from overlapping and mutually reinforcing technologies that already acclimated viewers to highly mediated visual consumption in commerce and in leisure. If, as Humphreys argued to his nineteenth-century readers, "it is the *seeing* that is everything," viewers came to the tank well versed in its multiple options for spectatorship.[27]

The Aquarium as Window

> Today it is easy to take the aquarium for granted, but one must wonder how awesome it must have been 150 years ago to peer through a window into a truly alien world.
>
> —BERND BRUNNER, *The Ocean at Home*

The sheer number of references to the aquarium as a window on aquatic worlds suggests that the latter functions as perceptual training for the former. This relationship is crucial to the aquarium's ability to both expose and manage a range of modern anxieties. Modernity and transparency are intimately linked, and glass makes this possible.[28] The aquarium is one example. It is impossible to imagine the aquarium without glass, but it is the specific configuration of the window—as aperture and as frame—that defines the modern aquarium. Crucial in this process was the distinction between the rectangular framed aquarium now most familiar to most home hobbyists, the glass globe or jar used early in the history of the hobby, and the goldfish bowl. Jars and globes were used from the earliest interest in fish keeping and continued to serve the mid-nineteenth-century aquarist as a way to isolate specimens and prevent them from being poisoned by toxins leaching from metal-framed tanks. Though globe-shaped tanks continued to be advertised in aquarium magazines into the early twentieth century, goldfish bowls were decried in the United States as early as 1858, denounced as amateurish and cruel, their popularity the unfortunate result of greedy merchants and an ignorant public.[29] Dozens of variants on rectangular designs for framed tanks appeared in early highly influential books by British aquarists, including Hibberd (1856) and Humphreys (1857), and were popularized by Philip Henry Gosse, based on rectangular and octagonal designs for the London Zoo in early 1850s. As U.S. aquarium periodicals amply demonstrate, the steady flow of British books across the Atlantic contributed to the spread and standardization of the rectangular design, with the two earliest American aquarium patents issued for tanks of this shape, both in 1858.[30] Increasingly, the American public and home aquarium came to be an iteration of the picture window and not the specimen jar.

Anne Friedberg argues that windows served as metaphors for the rectangular frame of the picture plane; the "modern function of the window is to frame a view."[31] The aquarium engaged its viewers through their familiarity with both the window and the picture. Like the window, the clear tank front functioned as a "membrane between inside and outside."[32] Isobel Armstrong observes that "glass is an antithetical medium. It holds contrary states within itself as barrier and medium."[33] The glass-fronted rectangular aquarium replicated and called attention to the ambivalence of transparency that "enabled a perceiver to make a seemingly unbroken transit from subject to object." Yet this "felt presence of transparency, interposing between the self and the world" was ambivalent, introducing perceptual complications even as it seemed to solve them, by "creat[-ing] a heightened awareness of mediation and its anxieties."[34] In its affinity with the window, the aquarium reproduced one of the paradoxes of modern spectatorship: greater visual access enabled by a medium that was, itself, a source of anxiety, through two interrelated operations.

First, the illusion of unbroken transit between terrestrial and aquatic words was simultaneously offered and framed as utterly impossible by the unique characteristics of the landscapes on either side of the glass. The aquarium was a window into an alien world that always already reinforces its very alienness and inaccessibility to the viewer and, in so doing, underlined the artifice of the entire apparatus. As Todd Newberry notes, "The more we pretend that we are looking through a porthole in Captain Nemo's submarine, the more we come up against the constructed setting."[35] Second, as noted earlier, this alienation effect is further reinforced in the specific spectatorial relationships enabled by a view through the porthole, relationships with other beings who may or may not be looking back and whose glass-enclosed world gives few sensory clues—no smells, no tactility of vegetation—to their relational potential. This was vexing to early public aquarium viewers, especially those looking at marine invertebrates. Pioneering German aquarist Gustav Jäger "witnessed cases in which educated individuals, after long periods of moving from one tank to the next, walked out and asked the ticket officer angrily: 'What in heaven's name am I actually supposed to see in there?'"[36] Some of this was a question of differential vision; indeed, one objection to goldfish bowls was that they seriously disturbed the fishes' sight and hampered their ability to recognize their keepers. But confusion over different visual mechanics was also a proxy for larger questions about empathy, identification, mutual recognition, and connection.

> [H]ow can I feel affinity with fishes, medusae, and sea stars? I see them well, but they see me only dimly or not at all. And the glass between us keeps me from any possibility of detecting . . . detecting I know not what. Do they even know they are trapped? Do they care? I am sure the porpoise does, as much as the zoo's tiger, and I am beginning to think that great sharks must too. But as far as the rest? . . . These are tentative acquaintances.[37]

Aquariums both enabled and underlined the unsettling tentative acquaintances made possible by spectatorship in the middle to late nineteenth century, as did apartment windows opening onto the increasingly diverse populations on crowded urban streets, department store windows framing manufactured clothing modeled by blank-eyed mannequins, and workers laboring in the cubes of glass-sided skyscrapers.

Yet the aquarium also helped its viewers to manage the uncanny nature of relationships governed by modern spectatorial technologies in several unique ways. First, the "constructed setting" reinforced a very specific form of human domestic agency by being, literally, constructed. Though ready-made tanks were available in major metropolitan shops and by mail in the latter part of the nineteenth century, serious hobbyists were encouraged to build their own.

> Tanks can be obtained at prices from a few cents to many hundred dollars, but without question the one that will be appreciated the most by the owner

will be the one he has made with his own hands. At least that particular tank will be the one he will point out to his guests and say "I made it," illustrating that trait or qualification in his disposition that indicates a well-balanced mind, viz., that of producing something with his own hands.[38]

Here, constructing the tank was itself a palliative, even an antidote to the effects of alienated labor in the modern marketplace, and a testament to core mental, mechanical (and manly) virtues that, as discussed in chapter 3, were increasingly seen as casualties of modern middle-class life, potentially imperiling American men and boys. By building one's own tank, the hobbyist would gain intimate acquaintance with the fruit of his own mental and physical labor and with a unique combination of practical engineering, mechanics, and popular science that continues to characterize the hobby to the present. This same combination of technical and aesthetic skills guided viewers in how to see the aquarium, as well as how to make one. As noted earlier, it was not enough to simply *look*. If the home tank was to be pleasant and profitable, it must be *observed* with the same discipline and precision that characterized its construction. For "the student, the artist, the scientist, and for those who simply love pets," the aquarium offered "a window where that which we see is only limited by our own capacity for observation."[39]

Second, placement of home aquariums near windows in the house, important to ensure adequate lighting, made the nature of one coextensive with the familiar function of the other. The aquatic landscape thus became one more aspect of a domestic one, an extension of a yard or familiar view glimpsed through one of the home's windows. Another option was to explicitly link the frame of the aquarium to that around a painting. Klee notes two early U.S. patents for picture frame aquariums (1892 and 1912), before a new wave emerged in the 1930s.[40] Though, as noted earlier, they remained at the margins of the hobby, picture frame aquariums capitalized on desire for and comfort with paintings as high-status consumables that offered direct and unproblematic relationships between beholder and beheld. But one more iteration of that relationship normalized the tentative acquaintances of aquarium viewing even more productively: the shop window.

Friedberg argues that the display frame of the mid-nineteenth-century shop window, "a consequence of improved glass technology and the commercial exploitation of its visual display, . . . enacted the *entre libre* principle of the department store, where the consumptive mode of 'just looking' had its own price, not in the obligation but in the desire for purchase."[41] Armstrong captures the visual potency of the shop window in terms reminiscent of aquarium viewership: "The sensuous allure of light and transparency created optical overload."[42] The shop window commodified a wide range of tentative acquaintances across glass membranes. If aquarium residents stood in for nature in the parlor, the visual resonance with the shop window also enfolded them into a logic of consumption and display within the home, with "every home a shop."[43] The core operations of the department store—"unconscious surveillance, clear visibility without handling, illuminating engineering, an inoffensive barrier"—paralleled the aesthetic and operational imperatives of the home aquarium.[44] Further, as major stores added departments selling pets and produced their own theatrical entertainments, they reproduced familiar relationships between literal theaters and aquariums in urban visual culture, while anchoring both in larger imperatives to desire in public and to consume in private.

The Aquarium as Theater

The window gave visual normalcy to the aquarium, making it contiguous with and intelligible through familiar domestic and commercial landscapes. But theater, as metaphor, context, and source of vocabulary and design, also provided frames through which the aquarium was viewed and understood. In its visual connections to the theater, the aquarium extended associations that go back to the Renaissance and the idea of the "theater of nature." Ann Blair argues that this view, in contrast to "the book of nature," emphasizes visual consumption, multiple vantage points, and a sense of both immersion and control, precisely the elements actualized in the aquarium. Blair describes this theater of nature as offering "a complete and coherent view of the world in one gaze." The viewer's task "is not to act out a role, but to watch and contemplate," and "the spectator is still part of the scene, ambiguously both observer and participant in nature."[45] The word *ambiguously* is the key to this description, for this spectatorial liminality ("both observer and participant"), shared by the panorama and the diorama, contributed to the characterization of aquarium viewing as a vicarious undersea journey, as discussed later in this chapter.

Scholars have increasingly noted the connections between theater, performance, and the popularization of science in mid-nineteenth-century Britain and the twentieth- and twenty-first-century United States.[46] Theatricality and spectacle are seen as so central to the construction and consumption of science in this period that even scientific literature is viewed in terms of performance. Yet within this performance-saturated environment, the relationship between aquariums and theaters is especially intimate. First and foremost, institutional and public relationships between theater and aquariums helped cast the home versions of the latter as spectacle or domestic drama and encouraged viewers to read the tank as they would read the stage. Viewers examined aquariums for action as well as landscapes. They were to be seen as plays, not simply gardens: "In history, in the drama, in painting, in sculpture, it is action-action-action! . . . It is action that renders the Aquarium the most attractive spot at the Zoological Gardens."[47] Further, theater trained middle-class viewers in the suspension of disbelief so crucial to sustaining the illusion of intimate contact with life beneath the waves, not just behind the glass. Looking head-on at or down on a proscenium stage directly paralleled the experience of viewing aquariums, particularly those with glass fronts and solid backs. It accustomed audiences to holding the putatively natural and the highly artificial in the same productive and pleasurable tension that also encouraged views of the aquarium as vicarious travel. Finally, visual training in consuming worlds onstage encouraged audiences to see aquarium residents as actors—as allegorical, moral agents or stock characters. Such personifications supported the rhetorical positioning of the aquarium as a vessel of uplift and laid groundwork for attachment to and relationships with individual fish and invertebrates.

Relationships between theaters and public aquariums were mutually beneficial. In return for offering a model for productive viewing, the aquarium lent a quasi-scientific, pedagogical ethos to entertainments in a wide range of venues. Particularly in the United States, aquariums were one means to "purify" the mid-nineteenth-century theater, to recast it as pedagogical space and thus safe and appropriate for middle-class audiences. As Neil Harris observes, the museum provided the prototypical venue in which performance per se was inoculated by pedagogy.

> Museum lecture rooms . . . were not theaters but could do what theaters did: mount dramatic entertainments or present variety acts under the guise of education and public enlightenment. However transparent, the fiction was effective and museum owners lost no time exploiting their advantage . . . The devil lurked only in playhouses; museums were out of his territory, and so safe for ordinary folk.[48]

No American museum owner exploited his advantages more than P. T. Barnum; aquariums figured prominently in his strategy for his American Museum in New York and its popular lecture room. "Performances of a chaste, interesting, and wholly moral nature will take place on stage every afternoon and evening," he advertised for the American Museum, and similar events were also featured attractions at Barnum's Aquarial Gardens in Boston.[49]

British aquarists appeared unimpressed with Barnum's contributions to the form, which were dismissed as ancillary to simple, vulgar entertainment rather than as a pedagogical good to which public aquarists should aspire. Consider, for example, J. E. Taylor, who relegated Barnum to a footnote in a section on "aeration of aquaria," specifically excluding him from discussions of milestones in aquarium history while unintentionally highlighting the spectacular nature of every facet of Barnum's aquatic enterprise.

> In 1861 Barnum had two white whales captured for him at the mouth of the St. Lawrence, and conveyed alive to his museum at New York, where they were exhibited in large tanks constructed for the purpose. Other tanks were shortly afterwards constructed by him, in which sharks, porpoises, "angel" fish & c., were shown. These animals were kept alive by a stream of salt water from high tide. This was the first rude attempt at aquaria in America.[50]

Alas for the whales—at least one became a spectacle in a way Barnum didn't intend. One of a depressingly large number of fires consumed his museum in July 1865 and "left a dead whale in the street for two days."[51]

Barnum's Boston predecessors, James Cutting and Henry Butler, proprietors of the Boston Aquarial and Zoological Gardens, also explicitly linked aquariums and theatrical performance, featuring "Ned" the "Marbled Seal" and "The South African Aborigines" as "an exhibition from 9, A.M., to 10, P.M." The latter included "an exhibition of their NATIVE SONGS and DANCES, every Evening, commencing at 8 o'clock" (see fig. 5).[52] A subsequent program announced the three-act drama "Latakoo! Or A Yankee Among the Kaffirs!" followed by the Arabian horse "Abdallah," the Central African SPHYNX, and the Educated Bear, as well as the Performances of The Seals Ned and Fanny (see fig. 6). As these aquarium programs suggest, the exoticism of viewing life beneath the waves, even if that life was relatively local, was enhanced by and contributed to a wide range of other "exotic" displays in the overall theatricality of these venues. The role of the home aquarium in domesticating "foreign others" is discussed in chapter 6.

But the theatricality of the aquarium went beyond public venues and their associated performances. Home aquariums were themselves theaters of nature. In his 1858 book on the home aquarium, Henry Butler asked his readers,

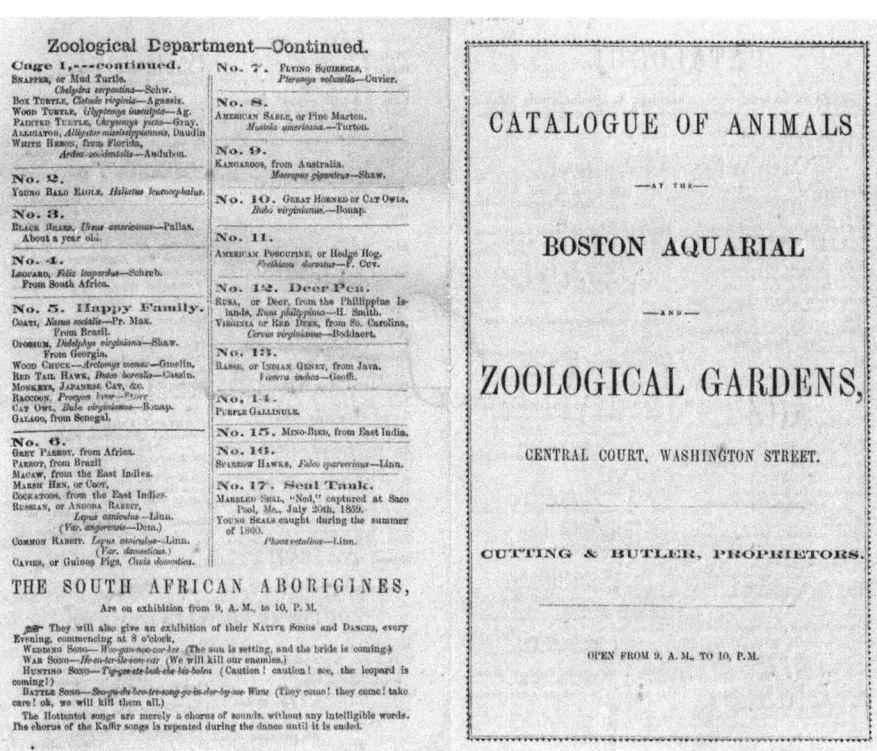

Fig. 5. "Catalogue of Animals" with "The South African Aborigines," Boston Aquarial and Zoological Gardens program, 1860(?). (From the collections of the Ernst Mayr Library of the Museum of Comparative Zoology, Harvard University.)

> Would you witness the grand spectacle of Life, as performed in that other theatre of being, to which nature has so long refused even to sell us a ticket of admission?
>
> Turn to the Aquaria! Ring up the curtain of your thoughts. *There*, indeed, is comedy and tragedy, broad farce and exciting melodrama.[53]

The physical appearances of both public and home aquariums reinforced connections to the stage; they drew on conventions of then-contemporary theater design, with its self-conscious and often-excessive acknowledgment that the scene depicted was representation, not reality. Sides of tanks were sometimes ornate, with embellishments recalling the architectural details that framed actual stages, including base and column ornaments. In some cases, the tank offered ornate framing and the additional theatrical artifice

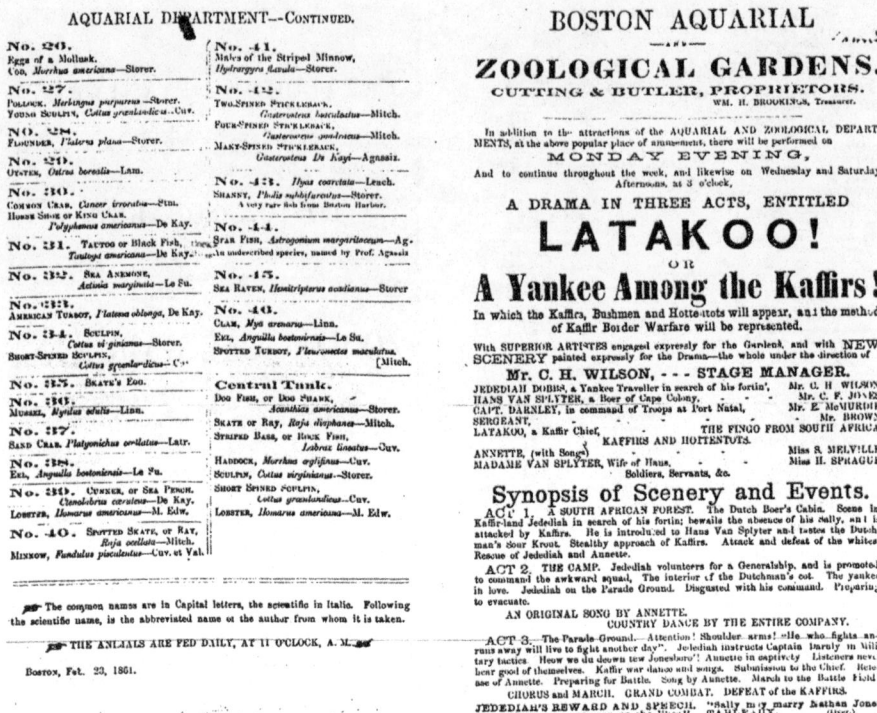

Fig. 6. "Latakoo! Or A Yankee Among the Kaffirs," Boston Aquarial and Zoological Gardens program, February 23, 1861. (From the collections of the Ernst Mayr Library of the Museum of Comparative Zoology, Harvard University.)

of its own fountain. Fish and invertebrates were cast as dramatis personae in their own glass theaters. These visual elements, textual references to theater, and uses of stock characters to refer to specimens gave viewers designs for seeing and plots for understanding the tank. If, as noted earlier, spectators had difficulty determining exactly what they should be looking at, theater offered perceptual templates that imparted action to aquatic gardens and motives to their inscrutable inhabitants. A scientific approach to these residents demanded at least some specialized knowledge, and empathic engagement required the status of companion or pet, but to appreciate the grand spectacle of life in the home, one only needed a basic familiarity with common theatrical types. Butler, who was Barnum's aquarist and author of one of the first American aquarium books, pitches the goings-on in the domestic "theatre of being" like a barker hawking attractions at the American Museum. For "warriors," there was the goby. For the lovers of Arthurian romance, the stickleback offered "all the gentle complaisance of the knight-errand of old" when dealing with "his mistress" and "adores the tournament." The starfish and sea cucumber, invertebrates characterized more by their inertia than their theatrical potential, were cast as "sentimental performers" who deliberately commit suicide" by "exploding" themselves "when irritated." There were "comic actors too multitudinous to detail," "gymnasts," "rakes," "beauties," and "Jeremy Diddlers."[54]

Butler was not unique in his view of the aquarium as a playhouse. An exact contemporary of his, the anonymous author of "My Aquarium," also saw the tank as an underwater stage filled with colorful characters. One illustrative excerpt is worth quoting at length.

> The Bernard Crab in the front, so leisurely pushing away the sand before him with his broad, flat claws, quietly enjoys the meal he finds, undisturbed by fears of a failing supply. There is less of enterprise than complacency in his character, and I call him Micawber, for he is always expecting "something to turn up." Twice since March has he changed his coat and thrown off his tight boots and gloves for new ones. The disrobing seemed to give him little trouble, though he sat dozing at the door of his cell some hours after, as though fatigued by the unusual effort. Very becoming is the new costume; and the red coat is prettily relieved by the gray tint of his Diogenese-like dwelling.
>
> There goes a military cousin of his, striding along, with his heavy armor clattering against the glass as he walks. A pugnacious fellow is that same soldier; and if he meets an opponent, you may see the tug of war.
>
> Speaking of spiders,—here are two Spider-Crabs, the very monkeys of this menagerie. The small one climbing the post is Topsy . . . Now look at her sister sprite, Crazy Kate. Her head is adorned with a long plume of Coralline, she is tearing ribbon-like shreds from the silky lettuce and hanging them upon her already fantastic person. Anon she dances in mad glee, and next her arms are solemnly stretched upward in grotesque similitude to one in prayer.[55]

Of course, theater was not always such a generative frame. In some cases, specimens were subject to the classic Platonic suspicion of actors as, at best, other than they appear and, at worst, thoroughly disreputable. Consider J. E. Taylor's description of "the nontubed worm."

[T]he *Neries*, for example, although not so brilliantly colored, are very graceful and pretty marine creatures. The habits of some of the prettiest, however, belie their lovely appearance; for they are not infrequently those of the well-clad stage ruffian who struts about in garments which have been obtained by means of murder and robbery. Not a few of the "errant," or wandering worms, live by stealthily preying upon objects actually more highly organised than they.[56]

Unlike "stage ruffians" of the human variety, however, these characters imparted moral uplift and affirmed virtue, even if sometimes by negation.

Come and sit by this indoor sea, day by day, and learn to love its people. Many a lesson for good have they taught me. When weary and disheartened, the patient perseverance of these undoubting beings has given me new impulses upward and onward . . . Seeing the blind persistence with which some straying zoöphyte has refused to follow other counsel than its own, I have learned that self-reliance and strength of will are not, in higher natures, virtues for gratulation, but, if unsanctified, faults to blush for.[57]

Like the private natural history collection or the public museum, the aquarium was a rational and moral amusement; it purported to teach as well as entertain. Its many connections to the theater ensured that the amusement didn't take a back seat to the rationality. In the period before tank residents were fully pets, the theater "emplotted" tank residents, giving them roles through which their behaviors could be understood. But the theater also emplotted aquarium viewers, telling them how to consume the new technology. It had the pedagogical potential of allegory, the spiritual potential of natural theology, the disciplinary potential of a science tutorial, and, perhaps most important for the enervated modern consumer, the potential entertainment value of the music hall and the playhouse. This last was all the more enjoyable because its "merry twists and laughable eccentricities" were available "unsolicited" in the comfort of home.[58]

Aquatic Panoramas

The aquarium also drew on the logic of and familiarity with the panorama, a genre of painting as popular culture that provided both exceptional verisimilitude and the illusion of immersion in the landscape or historical event depicted. Aquarium writer Shirley Hibberd, whose work is examined in the following chapter, explicitly describes the freshwater aquarium as a panorama because it offers "delightful" and amusing entertainment.[59] Though developments in theater scenography contributed to its evolution, the panorama did away with the actors and the disreputable reputations of theaters themselves, to emerge as a preeminent form of rational amusement for the middle class in England as early as the late eighteenth century and in the United States in the early to middle nineteenth.[60] In its American iterations, the visual potential of the panorama was linked to larger cultural values of progress, mobility, and optimism; to discourses offering "visual etiquette" for viewing and interpreting landscape attractions; and to long-standing connections between seeing and owning, as exemplified by Ralph Waldo Emerson's famous formulation "property in the horizon."[61] Like the theater and the department store window, the panorama was primarily, though by no means exclusively, an urban phenomenon.

Panoramas were large, protocinematic paintings wound around rollers such that they could be unfurled at a steady pace to convey the sense of traveling through a scene or landscape or, more accurately, of the scene itself traveling for the benefit of the viewer. Consumers could be passively enveloped in the scene as a kind of respite, they could observe and learn as a pedagogical opportunity, they could vicariously command that it unfurl before them, or they could have a combination of these experiences. This reconciliation of multiple modes of attention was bequeathed to the tank. The panorama's images, often accompanied by narration, could be revealed on a cylindrical surface—a rotunda or gallery—to give the sense of a 360-degree view. The twin illusions of control through visual command and immersion were central to the pleasures of panorama viewership. Audiences could be simultaneously subsumed in and masters of the scene; they were "installed in the picture."[62] Crary writes,

> Like the name itself, the setup of the panorama presumes to present a total view, characterized by a seemingly self-evident wholeness. And one important definition of the adjective *panoramic* as it was used in the nineteenth century is the notion of a full 360-degree view that has no obstructions, nothing blocking an optical appropriation of it. In this sense the panorama provided an imaginary unity and coherence to an external world that, in the context of urbanization, was increasingly incoherent.[63]

If urbanization was incoherent, underwater worlds, because they were heretofore unknown, were even more so. The aquarium remedied this as the panorama did. Its glass construction imposed "flux into form" and "infinity into frame"—imposing literal coherence onto the inchoate liquid environment while maximizing its visual consumability.[64] In addition, as discussed in chapters 2 and 3, the rhetorical construction of the aquarium as a self-sustaining whole based on biological interrelationships between plants and animals, as well as metonymic slides between the tank and the actual sea, reinforced the view that the aquarium offered more than *a* highly artificial reconstruction of a world. It offered access to *the* hitherto unseen and unseeable depths.

The panorama's ability to make scenes both visually accessible and coherent was especially appropriate for sharing details of distant landscapes and the passage of time. In this capacity, it reinforced viewers' engagement with the tank as a mode of vicarious travel to the geographical and chronological depths, as discussed later in this chapter. One distinctly American example is found in Nathaniel Hawthorne's short story "Main-street," which uses the device of the panorama to narrate the visual history of a New England town.[65] Like Hawthorne's panorama, the tank provided visual access to history, both natural and social, with tank residents cast as specimens in the former and as allegorical agents with pedagogical potential in the latter. Sensitivity to design and a measure of technological savvy were key to the power of both media, as they were to the theater. As Grau observes, the construction and particularly the lighting of the well-executed panorama ideally made it "difficult to distinguish between an *imitatio naturae* and real nature," in ways that parallel the aquarium's status as both "natural" and highly artificial.[66] Like the aquarium, the "authority of the panorama was founded in limitations of subjective vision, on the inadequacy of a human observer."[67] The panorama compensated for the viewer's inability to take in the entirety of the scene, either because the viewer lacked an adequate spatial vantage point to take it all in or because she or he lacked the perceptual and interpretive resources needed to assemble a coherent picture from disparate sights. Likewise, the aquarium could access, arrest, and frame inaccessible landscapes for the viewer, making them potentially comprehensible even as and indeed because they were made visible.

The visual and interpretive power of the panorama proved invaluable to the popularization of science as one form of nineteenth-century rational amusement, particularly in presentations of optical illusions and geological deep time.[68] Unlike the telescope or the microscope, which also opened up previously inaccessible vistas to middle-class audiences for visual consumption, the panorama and the aquarium functioned as windows and theaters did: as both social and individual viewing experiences simultaneously. Indeed, the tank was posited as superior to both the telescope and the microscope precisely because of the element linking it most closely to the panorama: its self-evident artifice that, at the same time, made its visual pleasures seem all the more natural. Henry Butler addresses these relationships directly.

> The telescope is our substitute in the "blue empyrean" . . . The microscope reveals much to us that is sublime, beautiful, and profoundly interesting. It has remained for the wondrous AQUARIUM to do more. That extraordinary combination of science and art may be called the crowning glory of the spirit of discovery characteristic of the nineteenth century. It opens to our inquisitive gaze the hidden chambers of the deep . . . It presents us with a miniature fac-simile of the fascinating reality in its exquisite colors, and replete with its inexplicable revelations. It exhibits, in other words, LIFE BENEATH THE BILLOWS in all its surprising shapes and amid all its amazing phenomena.[69]

Like the telescope and the microscope, the tank "reveals" by acting as a "substitute"—or, more accurately, a supplement—to human vision, compensating for biologically imposed limits. But the tank does more. It is science and art; it reveals and constructs an accessible "fac-simile." The plenitude of the copy is reinforced: it shows *all* of the original's surprising shapes and phenomena as it textually slips in this passage from a reproduction of life below the billows to the actual scene. This same rhetorical slippage characterizes aquarium writing of the period, as discussed in chapters 2 and 3.

Like the window and the theater, the panorama and aquarium did not require contorting normal vision by staring through an eyepiece. It enabled the viewer's play of the vicarious in the scenes represented and their appreciation for the technology producing the representations by holding both in pleasurable, productive tension—in Richard Schechner's formulation, not the scene itself but not not-the-scene either. This same liminality is key to the pleasures of aquarium viewing as a kind of subjunctive immersion wherein the ability to *see* underwater slides into the ability to *be* underwater.[70] Further, Butler's coupling of science, art, and the contemporary "spirit of discovery" underscores connections between the panorama, the aquarium, and the visual operations of empire, specifically the relation between seeing, aestheticizing, and owning that defined both internal and overseas expansion.

These visual elements also characterized the diorama, which emerged as a fixture in U.S. museums in the late nineteenth century. Combining the perceptual dynamics of the window (the sense of transparent, unmediated access) and the theater (a proscenium orientation and identifiable characters) with the two-dimensional landscape painting of the panorama, the diorama provided a three-dimensional "'shock of the real': visual immediacy, usually combined with a strong claim to the truth."[71] Three-dimensionality and "dramatic taxidermy" enabled more direct "relationships" between viewer and characters.[72] American museums explicitly foregrounded the expeditions that provided specimens and data for the installations, adding to both the narrative potential and the truth claims of the form. Viewers could participate in both the scene and in the scientific and imperial adventures that produced it.[73] Dioramas were part of spectacularizing science: drawing on explicitly theatrical stagings of nature while, at the same time, using institutional sobriety and an increasingly professionalized presentation of science to disavow theatricality in favor of "the real." In addition, after the turn of the century, dioramas in U.S. museums referenced the ambivalence of modern progress by adding a salvage narrative to the mix. Quinn argues for the diorama as part of a "wilderness ethic," a response to destruction of habitat and loss of the American frontier.[74] The romance of scientific adventure, technological and artistic virtuosity, and an increasingly remote and imperiled wilderness all contributed to the "drama in the diorama," just as they did to the home aquarium.[75]

The aquarium fit easily within the visual logics of the panorama and diorama. It allowed access to an inaccessible landscape by showing the actual medium rendering it inaccessible, the water, along with the live inhabitants. Further, it continually reminded viewers of their own privileged positions as viewers: seeing without being contained, apart from yet a part of and even vicariously immersed in the scene. Indeed, the aquarium's resemblance to the diorama presages its relationship to another, later box with a proscenium orientation—the television—such that the former could make a living diorama out of the latter.[76]

Voyages of Discovery

Ralph O'Conner observes that "representatives of distant times and places at the theaters and panoramas[/dioramas] provided a crucial template for the concept of the 'imaginary voyage.'"[77] The aquarium was just such a representative; like the theater and the panorama to which it was also indebted, the conflation of the tank and travel served the hobby by providing visual and narrative templates to its viewers. They could be underwater tourists. Moreover, casting aquarium landscapes and residents in terms of travel enables complex ideological work. Nostalgia-infused rural landscapes and tropical locales were first subsumed and then normalized as part of a domestic "consumer imperium" through the trope of the tank as travel.[78] Aquarium viewing benefited from this template and, in so doing, both reflected and contributed to an American middle-class "culture of international travel" that took root in the latter half of the nineteenth century. Kristin L. Hoganson characterizes this culture as

> permeated with reports and images of foreign travel, a culture rife with ersatz travel experiences . . . a culture in which the sum was greater than the constituent parts . . . [and] resulted in a sense of living in a time and place marked by mobility and touristic encounters. And finally, by a culture of international travel I mean a development that drew even those who did not have the means—or the inclination—to truly go abroad into its net.[79]

Aquarium fish themselves were eventually drawn into this net, too, as evidence of and impetus to travel. First and foremost, though, they served as synecdoches for the destination, which was as much supranational in its excess of state boundaries as it was either intranational or international.

The increasing availability and popularity of travel books provided a vocabulary through which the aquarium could be imagined as a real or vicarious journey under the sea; it served as a manageable surrogate for largely unmanageable travels. From the late 1850s to the present, the pleasures of the aquarium are often described in terms of travel and tourism in a radically foreign place, the better to consume and appreciate it at home as a kind of living souvenir or to examine its inhabitants for details of their lives as one would the natives of exotic cultures. Introducing the aquarium to its American readers, *Godey's Lady's Book* doubled the travel trope by using a tourist trip to the Regents Park Gardens aquarium as an opportunity to proclaim, "It was not only novel, but wonderful to behold the creatures of the deep sea face to face without the aid of diving-bell, diving dress, glass-eyes, or the pains of submersion."[80] Moreover, aquarium viewing was actually superior—because more technologically advanced, more domestic, literally more alive and thus repeatable—to tokens of the sea brought home by actual travelers: "The sailor, who brings home to his friends a bunch of dry seaweeds to hang over the chimney as a weather-guide, may now be astonished to find forests of sea-weeds flourishing under the parlor window."[81]

The image of the aquarium as vessel for vicarious undersea travel was enhanced by two popular developments, one literary and one technological. Jules Verne's *Twenty Thousand Leagues under the Sea* was published in 1869 and quickly translated into English. The novel itself is a travel diary, a "submarine tour of the world."[82] Its panoramic visions of undersea sightseeing were quickly appropriated by aquarium discourses of the day, and connections to the book persist to the present, most recently by lending the name of its central character to that of the Disney company's animated fish odyssey *Finding Nemo*. Struggling to convey the wonders of his tour beneath the waves, Verne's narrator, Professor Aronnax, is as vexed as a terrestrial travel writer wrestling with representing the magnitude and novelty of a foreign scene: "And now, how can I convey the impression left upon me by that walk under the waters? Words are impotent to relate such wonders."[83] The spread and popularity of the book so whetted the appetite for vicarious undersea travel that even professional aquarists drew on it, specifically its imagery of submarine tourism, to extol the virtues of the home aquarium that "has made it possible to practically walk dry-shod along the river-bed or ocean-floor, and see life as it is below the surface at first hand."[84]

The advent of underwater photography did indeed make it literally possible to see life beneath the waves. Simon Lake, the first American to master the feat, used his submarine the *Argonaut* to bring underwater landscapes to the readers of *McClure's Magazine* in 1899; one episode from his adventures reverses aquarium viewership by positioning the humans as contained curiosities for an aquatic audience: "[First mate] Jim said that he would often see fishes come swimming up wonderingly into the port[hole]. They would remain quite motionless until he stirred his head, and then they vanished instantly."[85] The novel and the photographs worked as contemporary travel narratives and panoramas did. They provided vicarious experiences that stimulated appetite for the "real thing"—here, real access to the visual wonders of the deep—and offered a kind of visual etiquette for consuming the objects of such travel: what, where, how, and why to see and, by extension, to learn, enjoy, and acquire.

Aquariums inspired actual as well as vicarious travel. As the example from *Godey's Lady's Book* indicates, public venues were major tourist destinations, particularly in Europe, where they were considered less as museums of past glories than as technological wonders, equivalent to the Crystal Palace and the Eiffel Tower. Throughout the history of the hobby, collecting specimens for the home aquarium required some measure of travel, and soon the relationship worked both ways, with a trip raising opportunities for collecting as well as the latter obligating the former. The pleasure of such a trip included contact with both literal and moral landscapes: "It is greater than that of the sportsman who goes out to kill, and creates kindlier feelings towards man and beast and brings nearer home the great fact of the community of all life. It takes you out into the sunshine and the air, to forest and meadow, to rippling streams and quiet ponds."[86] Consistent with its status as a pedagogical entertainment, the aquarium offered a productive use for two other modern commodities, leisure time and the family vacation, as routine components of middle-class and upper-middle-class life.

> Now that a large portion of the American people are taking their annual hegira, forsaking comfortable city houses and suburban residences for the purpose of breathing the sea-air through the medium of fashionable first-class hotels, or the less aristocratic quarters of little coves and fishing towns, we would say to one and all, Commence an aquarium . . . [It] will occupy all your leisure moments, which are usually so many and hang with such leaden weight upon scores of summer idlers, who, their daily bath and bowling over, look with dismay upon the weary hours which must intervene before they can again go through the same diurnal process.[87]

Collecting provided exercise, both mental and physical, each in pleasing, if undemanding, proportions depending on the specimens involved. Thus, *Harper's Bazaar* assured its readers that "the gathering of sea-anemones is certainly a very pleasant addition to the seaside holiday, first, because it supplies an object for the morning ramble; second because they are just such company as is most desirable on a drowsy, hot afternoon, amusing enough to awaken speculation, without requiring any great exercise of either the intellect or the attention."[88]

Children, in particular, would benefit from engagement with marine fauna enabled by the aquarium while on summer holidays. Such engagements were cast as both adventurous and idyllic, as in "Our Babies among the Butter-Cups and on the Sea-shore," which imagines these idylls as if springing from a rustic landscape painting in Romantic and, at times, even literally Wordsworthian terms. "Gertrude" and "Blanche," the vacationing youngsters, are not aimless summer idlers, however. Their mother's home aquarium has imbued them with a sense of mission that will, in turn, enlarge their sentimental, if not their "scientific," education, even as "we children of larger growth" incorporate the pleasures of watching their "expedition" into those of adult respite from rigors of upper-middle-class urban life. Here, the journey to the seashore, children, the fauna, and the sea itself are domesticated, enchanted, and consumed through romantic visual and textual tropes.

"I wish we could find a sea-anemone," says Gertrude to Blanche; "it would be so nice to take it home for momma's aquarium." Then they go off on a pleasant voyage of discovery, looking for treasures in all sorts of likely and unlikely spots, and through the clear, translucent sea-green waters peering down upon such faery-like sights as were seen in Southey's verse:

> "And here were coral bowers,
> And grots of madrepores,
> And banks of sponge as soft and fair to eye
> As e'er was mossy bed
> Whereupon the wood-nymph lie
> With languid limbs in summer's sultry hours."[89]

Invocations of two English poet laureates frame this new world of putatively more democratic leisure consumption in the literary and visual terms of a Romantic ramble through Old World or even timeless landscapes that are both rustic and aesthetically elevated.

This same imagery circulates through English aquarium texts, P. H. Gosse's in particular, and contributes to the idea of the specimen as an artifact of a vanishing rural past, hence a rustic adornment for the modern home, as discussed in the next chapter. Here, "Gertrude" and "Blanche" approach the scene to "search for treasures," but specimens like those collected for "mamma's aquarium" became living souvenirs who were also the functional equivalent of summer friends, even decades after romantic appeals to Southey were abandoned: "There is no reason why boys and girls should not continue their acquaintance with certain of the small creatures met on a vacation at the seashore. Some of them can be transported home and maintained in a marine or sea-water aquarium."[90] These "small creatures" often served as synecdoches for nature itself and as evidence for travels through open and wild spaces that were seen as in increasingly short supply: "Walks through open fields and the excitement that comes with finding something new and strange are part of the pleasures of collecting wild fishes. These enjoyable expeditions to ponds and brooks will more than repay the boys and girls who keep aquariums containing fishes they captured."[91]

As these references to the excitement of "expeditions" resulting in the capture of "something new and strange" suggest, fantasies of children's collecting trips were imbued with nostalgia for wilderness and visions of juvenile ontogeny recapitulating colonial phylogeny: American youngsters reproduced earlier "voyages of discovery" that birthed the nation and tamed the frontier, stabilizing and internalizing that enterprise in the process of repeating it. These pleasures were not limited to youngsters. A wide range of general interest and hobbyist publications framed the collecting trip and aquarium viewing as observational exercises aligning the aquarist as much with the adventurer-naturalist and the scientist as with the tourist on holiday.

In the mid- to late 1800s, connections between travel and natural history as modern visual operations supporting imperial, entrepreneurial ones crystallized in three iconic images. These three persisted into the next century as stock figures, each a popular caricature of an approach to nature and science and to American modernity itself. Further, each suggested a specific visual stance vis-à-vis the objects of travel to be adopted by readers and audiences who vicariously participated in their work. The aquarium hobby drew, to varying degrees, on all of them. The first was the rugged frontiersman, whose scientific objectives were a function of his manly perseverance and sheer physical toughness. His visual orientation emphasized mastery of self, environment, and specimen as the experiential matrix into which scientific minutiae were set. John James Audubon cast himself in this role; John Wesley Powell and Theodore Roosevelt, among many others, also occupied this naturalist/explorer/hero position in the popular imaginary. The Great Man of Science inserted the natural world into global, especially western European, systems of canonical knowledge. If the naturalist hero could master and define American natural patrimony in aesthetic, spiritual, and utilitarian as well as scientific terms, the Great Man translated it into international intellectual capital. Louis Agassiz embodied this position and the point of view that combined a panoramic command of the larger scientific conversation with microscopic focus on the data that fed it. Intellectual prowess, rather than physical stamina, made the Great Man a mirror opposite of his adventurous counterpart. Finally, there was the specialist-bureaucrat working within institutional constraints and using the pragmatic focus defined by them. The bureaucrat scientist, regardless of the actual physical and intellectual challenges of the job, lacked, by definition, the rugged individualism and/or the personal charisma that neutralized concerns about the collectivizing, putatively effeminizing effects of modern institutions. The first two naturalist travelers observed to domesticate. The career naturalist observed from within institutional domestication. This was the figure lampooned by Mark Twain in *The Innocents Abroad* as "a common mortal . . . [whose] mission had nothing more overpowering about it than the collecting of seeds, and uncommon yams and extraordinary cabbages and peculiar bullfrogs for that poor, useless, innocent, mildewed old fossil, the Smithsonian Institute."[92] Twain saw the specialist-naturalist as a diminished thing. Sometimes amateur aquarists did as well, particularly when this position enabled favorable distinctions between the passionless professional and the daring and dedicated hobbyist. More commonly, though, aquarists recombined and then drew on all three figurations of the traveling natural scientist to legitimate aquarium viewing.

Early on, the aquarium was described as a parlor pleasure that solved a larger scientific travel problem, as in the 1854 article "Customs and Manners under the Water."[93] That problem was how to "invade the depths of the sea" and examine "with calm, observant eye, the forms and manners of its inhabitants."[94] As the image of invasion suggests, the overall mission of this operation was a domestic extension of what Mary Louise Pratt calls "the imperial eye" underwater.[95] Obviously, the standard repertoire of the frontier hero did not suffice: "This has not been accomplished by means of perilous adventure—and indeed no perilous adventure could have achieved the feat."[96] Further, even great European men of science, with all the technological resources at their disposal, were not adequate to the task.

> The French zoologist who proposed, some time ago, to pay a domestic visit to the fishes of the Mediterranean, provided with a water-tight dress and a breathing-tube, would have come back doubtless well able to furnish a pleasing superficial sketch, but quite ignorant of those minute details of individual life which form the materials of natural history.

The home aquarist provides the answer: "[I]t was necessary, in short, for the purposes of science, to have *a piece of the sea* laid upon our table."[97] The home aquarist, then, focuses on the "strictly biographical," "those minute details of individual life," like the systematic, professional naturalist observer. However, she or he can succeed where the heroic adventurer and the scientist cannot, because the domestic lives observed in the tank are natural extensions of its placement in the home, allowing the hobbyist to witness underwater intimacies, "goings on" and "family secrets," that reinforce the extrascientific implications of "those minute details of individual life."

A larger "fictive travel movement," including travel writing, panoramas and dioramas, and public lectures by scientist-adventurers, contributed significantly to the intelligibility and desirability of the aquarium.[98] It provided readily adaptable narrative frameworks, including those of undersea travel and holiday respite; visual training in how to *observe* rather than simply *see;* vocabulary for describing natural wonders and cultural curiosities (e.g., "Customs and Manners") and their sensory pleasures; and a roster of identities, from the frolicking child to the adventurer-scientist, that positioned and trained the aquarist as a purposeful traveler. Fictive travel also provided a rationale for the activity: as exploration, adventure, parlor science, or productive leisure. But the visual pleasures and potential of the home aquarium as real or vicarious travel exceeded those of the naturalist hero and the systematic observations—or domestic spying—of the amateur scientist-biographer. In addition to exposing unseen, inaccessible worlds of deep water, these pleasures included the possibility of traveling back to deep time.[99]

As suggested earlier, one key component of the relationship between the aquarium and time travel was nostalgia, the harkening back to fantasies of childhood collecting, exploration, and play in an Edenic "nature" over against an alienating and alienated urban commercial landscape. But two other intertwined and equally important connections between time and the aquarium contributed to its popularity. Increasing scientific interest in the deep sea, coupled with the spread of evolutionary thinking, fed recognition that—in addition to serving as vehicles for commerce and conquest—seas, lakes, rivers, and warm little ponds might also be sources of kinship. From this perspective, the "goings on and family secrets" observed in the tank could be those of one's distant relatives. Specific relationships between the aquarium and various evolutionary discourses are briefly discussed in the following chapter. Suffice it to say here that the aquarium accommodated a wide range of evolutionary thinking, from an embrace of natural selection to the more general view of continuing progress central to modernity itself. The aquarium became the capacious vessel for containing this range of positions by making the "evidence" of both the remote past and contemporary progress visually available in the form of the primitive at home.

Henry D. Butler seems to address the full range of relationships between the aquarium and time travel in the first few pages of his book *The Family Aquarium*. He begins by speculating about a vestigial "monster," a survivor of the biblical flood and, as such, "a prisoner on parole" roaming the depths, "a messenger of God's infinite wonders in that universe of mysterious romance."[100] Butler maintains that though "[i]t is not for us to unveil the awful secrets interred by his hand," the aquarium, "the crowning glory of the spirit of discovery characteristic of the nineteenth century," opens access to, at the least, a "miniature fac-simile" of life beneath the depths. Butler's aquarium accommodates multiple temporalities simultaneously, linking nineteenth-century progress to biblical chronology and, finally, to a landscape that seems out of time, albeit one cast in terms of Old World grandeur observed on the Grand Tour. If the tank "does not actually place us where our foot-prints may be seen among the jeweled corridors, the many-pillared halls, the shining temples, the pebbled grottoes, the incomparable gardens where time's ravages are unknown and eternity seems stamped on all this is matchless in its grandeur, it gives us, at least, a faithful copy."[101] Butler demonstrates that the aquarium has temporal, as well as visual and rhetorical, elasticity. It attests to modern technological progress, exposes the putatively timeless, and hints at ineffable mystery. The promiscuous temporality of Butler's aquarium reinforces Carlene Stephens's point that relationships between time and modernity can be viewed as "a kind of web, spun from ideas about nature, religion, civil authority," and technology.[102]

Emerging ideas about a far vaster temporality than is suggested in the Bible also contributed to this web. As Thomas Allen has argued, increasing acceptance of geologic time—the idea that the earth was millions, not thousands, of years old—"prompted many thinkers in the nineteenth century to contemplate a nature whose immensity was beyond human comprehension."[103] Geologic time, coupled with popular coverage of the "bone wars" between Othniel Marsh and Edward Drinker Cope and the introduction of the dinosaur to the larger culture of display, generated a potent combination of fascination, anxiety, and outright resistance, not only because it challenged biblical narratives, but also because, in raising visible evidence of an expanded timescape that included extinction, it exposed larger ambivalences about the distance between "progress" and "the primitive," a distance central to the very idea of the modern.[104]

As W. J. T. Mitchell points out, the dinosaur, that poster monster for this new expanded temporality, "is the animal emblem of the process of modernization, with its intertwined cycles of destruction and resurrection, innovation and obsolescence, expansive 'gigantism' and progressive 'downsizing.' [It] also stands for the fate of the human species within the world system of modern capitalism, especially the 'species anxieties' that are endemic to modernity."[105] In the United States in the middle to late nineteenth century, these "species anxieties" included, among other things, fears of degeneration and even extinction at the hands of putative "primitives"—racial and ethnic "others"—within. As a form of travel back in time, the aquarium offered an antidote: a managed atavism that reminded and reassured its white, urban, middle-class viewers of their place on an ascending staircase to progress and prosperity—to the apogee of what it meant to be modern—while ameliorating anxieties about the dislocations of that upward momentum. In this, the aquarium functioned as panoramas and tours of Old World ruins did: to reinforce one's own local present and future prospects over against the "'mouldering stones,' 'ruined castles,' and 'falling towers'" of others' pasts.[106]

In her study of atavism at the American fin de siècle, Dana Seitler notes that the word *atavism* itself came into widespread circulation alongside ideas of the modern at the end of the nineteenth century; atavism is "a 'reproduction' and a 'recurrence' of the past in the present, a recurrence that is specifically one of ancestral prehistory" and is intrinsic to modernity.[107] Atavism is inherently ambivalent, operating alongside narratives of evolutionary progress while raising specters of potential regression back to animality and alterity. The aquarium shares and attempts to master this ambivalence by literally containing and domesticating it. In Butler's terms, it frames and exhibits a "fac-simile" of the past in the home. Here, inaccessible aquatic and evolutionary recesses are made reassuringly available for visual consumption through modern scientific and technical contrivances, even while pointing to uncontainable origins in deep water and deep time.

Even as dinosaurs muscled their way onto the popular evolutionary stage, fish retained a genealogical pride of place. W. P. Pycraft's *The Story of Fish Life* is illustrative.

> Fish hold, says Dr [sic] Bashford Dean, an important place in the history of vertebrates or backboned animals; their group is the largest and most widely distributed; its fossil members are by far the earliest of known vertebrates; and amongst its living representatives are forms which are believed to closely resemble the ancestral vertebrate.[108]

Butler invoked the biblical flood and Old World vistas to describe the aquarium's ability to forge a visual connection to the past. Pycraft anatomizes the connection in his focus on the backbone and vertebrate lineage. Ida Mellen, the first American female professional aquarist, used elements of both.

> Dividing the world of Nature into two parts, we may call them the Old and New Testament of Nature. In the Old Testament are all the spineless forms;

in the New Testament, all the animals that possess a backbone. We know little of the way in which groups of creatures of this Old Testament are related to one another, but, beginning with the fish, the first animal with a spinal cord, we can trace the higher developments almost step by step . . . [O]ne fact is certain, and that is that without the fish there never could have been any human beings.[109]

Mellen's answer to "the why of fish" captures both the aquarium's ability to manage multiple dimensions of highly racialized atavism and its utility for containing and dispensing with difference through a complex surrogacy using fish.[110] As demonstrated in chapters 4, 5, and 6, this operation is especially effective because it is both obvious in its effects and opaque in its mechanics, albeit not in this particular case. As noted earlier, fish do not lend themselves to simple anthropomorphism as easily as other animals; their alterity is more perceptually and behaviorally complex. They have a representational liquidity as well as a logistical one, standing in for "exotic others" (primitive, colorful, promiscuous, or just strange) at one point, in solidarity with "higher beings" against the undifferentiated spineless reminders of a vanished past at another, and sometimes both at once. Though Mellen does not employ a specifically Darwinian framework, she clearly uses tank residents to naturalize racial-theological hierarchies as evolutionary ones.[111]

In the passage just quoted, the underwater world demonstrates an undisguised and possibly unexamined Christian triumphalism to which Mellen sees her readers as unquestionably indebted by virtue of their being human. Christian supremacy gets coded as textual succession and further neutralized and naturalized as biological advance. This is "Nature's" Old and New Testaments. "Old Testament" beings are "spineless." Who knows how they are all related. They are inscrutable, unintelligible. They offer "higher development" nothing, or at least nothing intelligible. They are not truly creatures of the scientific book. Fish, in contrast, bequeath the necessary saving condition of humanity in the form of a backbone. If the New Testament offers a word made flesh, fish offer flesh capable of generating words and readability itself, specifically a linear step-by-step account of human development from lower animals. The aquarium rendered this entire operation reassuringly visible, while disguising it at the same time. "New Testament" fish show the viewer how to be(come) human through their simultaneous relationship to and distance from "Old Testament" "spineless forms," who might be their tank mates.

Fish endured. Unlike the dinosaurs, they had the good grace to resist extinction. In the aquarium, they made visually available both the collective vertebrate past and our individual pasts as well, as demonstrated in accounts spanning almost one hundred years: Millicent Washburn Shinn's (1899) observation that the prototype for human infant movement "may be seen in any aquarium; they are survivors of the period long before the ape-like stage, long before any mammalian stage, when our ancestors had not yet abandoned life in the waters"; and Neil Shubin's contemporary assertion that "the earliest creature to have the bones of our upper arm, our forearm, even our wrist and palm, also had scales and fin webbing. That creature was a fish . . . There isn't just a single fish inside of our limbs; there is a whole aquarium."[112] Aquarium residents were primitives who knew their place; they were instructive and decorative, like native peoples on the Midway Plaisance of the Chicago World's Columbian Exposition. If modernity exposed the deep past in order to dramatize a break with it, the aquarium reassured its viewers that the upward momentum of progress was not reversible. The remote past was available for daily inspection and edification in the parlor, where it was contained as unproblematically as "a few Indian arrow-heads . . . treasured up as memorials of a vanished race" conjured by Hawthorne's panoramist.[113]

Consumers embraced the aquarium as a domestic version of middle-class popular entertainments, as well as a new iteration of familiar landscapes. The garden and the collection domesticated the home tank. Mid-nineteenth-century visual and travel cultures rendered familiar its intermingling of natural and enhanced ways of seeing. As a place of promiscuous vision, the aquarium demonstrated a remarkable ability to subsume, recode, and even harmonize a wide range of sites and practices. From the reassurance of a well-tended flower bed to the enervating prospect of a submarine tour, from a "theatre of fairy wonders"[114] to panoramic command of a primeval landscape and acquaintance with distant relatives, all come together unproblematically in the water world in the parlor.

CHAPTER 2

RURAL RAMBLES AND RUSTIC ADORNMENTS: EARLY BRITISH AQUARIUM WRITING

> Each culture generates its rhetoric, finding it consistent, convincing, and, of course, useful. This rhetorical screen is particularly durable in those cultures with an imperial bent since it justifies practices that without it would reveal their self-interest. Such rhetoric has a synthetic and unifying role in cultural life. It removes the need to examine disturbing issues, giving each subscriber a sense of comforting identity and firm destiny. It defines the common good and will not tolerate its redefinition. It maintains itself through both its own energy and the rewards it offers.
>
> —BARBARA NOVAK, *Nature and Culture,*
> preface to the previous edition

The home aquarium functions rhetorically as landscape painting does in Barbara Novak's landmark study *Nature and Culture*, the source of the preceding epigraph. The aquarium contains and harmonizes a wide range of issues and anxieties associated with imperial modernity. But whereas Novak describes a genre of painting with rhetorical strategies that did not tolerate redefinitions, the aquarium accommodates them, proving that its visual elasticity—its ability to draw on multiple media to normalize its pleasures—is second only to its discursive elasticity.

The aquarium is a useful and unifying vessel for cultural work precisely because of this capacity to adapt a wide range of sometimes-contradictory discourses to characterize its appeal. In *The Cultural Politics of Emotion*, Sarah Ahmed describes a metonymic slide in which, through a series of substitutions, terms slip from one to another to form an implicit argument with emotional force, if not cognitive coherence.[1] Discourses surrounding the aquarium operated to the same effect using this strategy and its mirror opposite: both sliding/substitution and accretion. In addition to rhetorically productive slippages as, for example, between the tank and the sea, diverse tropes, imagery, and textual tactics stick together like polyps, one to another, accumulating over time, resulting in a deceptively simple, putatively organic discursive construction of seemingly obvious social and personal virtue. Thus, the aquarium was an element of decor, a teaching tool, and a testament to the manly virtues of handiness in its construction and hardiness in collecting residents. It was scientific, an invitation to observe and chronicle specimens of national patrimony; and it was spiritual, a chance to behold and marvel at the genius of the Creator. It was therapeutic in its invitation to repose, morally demanding in its inculcation of responsibilities for lower beings, and intellectually bracing in establishing norms of rigorous, systematic study. Most of all, it offered a comforting reminder, reassuring its viewers that modernity could generate its own technologies of respite and renewal by bringing them aesthetically close to nature even as it kept them conveniently apart from it.

This chapter is the first of two to examine the remarkable rhetorical inclusivity of the home aquarium. As chapter 3 indicates, American popularizers certainly included uniquely nationalist elements in their advocacy of the hobby, but from its earliest inception, rhetoric surrounding the home tank was a transatlantic affair. It was inconceivable without the profoundly romantic prose of its English enthusiasts. This chapter discusses the British textual templates that guided the hobby through its formative stages; in some cases, these are easily discernible in American aquarium publications over one hundred years later. Key narrative and rhetorical precursors were established by British natural historians in the mid-nineteenth century. Some of these figures were also foundational to the aquarium hobby. The most important of these was Philip Henry Gosse, whose volume *The Aquarium: An Unveiling of the Wonders of the Deep Sea* is examined in detail. This book's genre conventions, narrative strategies, and rhetorical tropes set a framework for the hobby and were enriched by other naturalist aquarists, including H. Noel Humphreys, Shirley Hibberd, and J. E. Taylor. Domestic landscapes and urban visual culture provided perceptual templates for viewing the aquarium. These media also offered general narrative contours within which the tank and its residents could be understood: as allegorical actors, souvenirs from a vanishing wilderness or vanished childhood, distant relatives, or distant peoples with exotic manners and customs. If these landscapes set the stage for the hobby's cultural work, its remarkable persistence, and seemingly endless capacity to harmonize a wide range of modern discourses and anxieties, then British aquarium writers provided the scripts.

NATURAL HISTORY AS TEXTUAL TEMPLATE

British aquarium writing emerged directly from larger discourses and practices of natural history, which was itself central to imperial modernity. Natural history as an imperial enterprise emphasized the move from seeing to describing to owning. So foundational were these observational and taxonomic operations that Mary Louise Pratt and Susan Scott Parrish convincingly argue for the frenzied cataloging and exploiting of New World resources as "crucially formative of modern European ways of knowing."[2] By the mid-nineteenth century, British natural history writing advanced complimentary aims on the domestic front: a kind of reciprocal nation building in response to the ongoing management of empire. Exotic flora and fauna "over there" were matched by indigenous wonders "over here." This domestic wilderness awaited only trained eyes, rich vocabularies, vivid powers of description, and the appropriate scientific and spiritual matrices into which specimens could be set.[3] In the mid-nineteenth century, at a time of increasing industrialization and urbanization, domestic nature study could extend its imperial mission abroad into the empire's own parlor, with the evidence of "conquest" and appreciation displayed in cabinets of local curiosities; lavishly illustrated volumes; fern, feather, bug, and butterfly collections; and, later, the aquarium. The naturalist collector could create an "empire of things."[4]

Local nature study was also of an ideological piece with the imperatives of emerging industrial capitalism that it often purported to mitigate. It scientized everyday fauna while providing a new way to comply with increasingly familiar mandates for discipline, order, and rigor. From this perspective, parlor collections of specimens were the domestic middle-class and upper-middle-class iterations of enclosure acts—once uncultivated "commons" now spatially segregated as private goods for cultivated consumers.[5] Local nature study created new practices and discourses of citizenship rooted in exploring and explaining a "local wilderness," one that could only emerge as such in contrast to the rigors of bourgeois civilization, its commercial metropolitan landscapes, and the longing for what those landscapes destroyed or displaced.[6] This did not require a multiyear stint on the *Beagle*. Nature study could be done at home, so, to paraphrase Elizabeth Bishop's "Crusoe in England," the more the populace engaged in it, the more they could feel—and create a polycentric understanding of—home. This polycentric understanding included the aesthetic and the scientific, work and leisure, romance and realism, the mundane and the divine, all harmonized in natural historians' prose. These textual templates would contribute directly to writings extolling the virtues of the home aquarium, including those that crossed the Atlantic and defined the hobby.

Romantic piety permeated natural history discourse in mid-nineteenth-century England and crossed the ocean in a variety of forms: publications, lectures, and research collaborations. This discourse was birthed from the larger discipline of natural theology. It fused art, science, and religious devotion to techniques of systematic observation, recording, and classification in ways that were soon used to characterize the pleasures and utility of the home aquarium. Consider, as one representative example, the writings of English zoologist and illustrator William Swainson (1789–1855), a collaborator of John James Audubon. Swainson, who opposed the possibility of the mutability of species, cast natural history firmly as a science and argued for a rigorous, holistic approach to collection and classification.[7] He supported his position by seemingly teasing a rhetoric of science apart from that of art and aesthetics using the ur-concept central to his larger view of the natural world: immutability. He argues, "Mutability in science only belongs to *error*: for truth, no less than nature, is unchanging; whereas mutability, on the contrary, is a necessary accompaniment of art, and is interwoven with its excellence."[8] Yet, not a full page later, Swainson turns to art, as well as technology, to argue for the spiritual benefits of natural history study. Its ultimate significance exceeds a focus on classifying facts. Swainson makes the case using an intricate coupling of aesthetics and spiritual piety, remarkable both for its rhetorical typicality and its resonances with later writings extolling the virtues of aquariums. It is worth quoting at length.

> Another advantage, almost exclusively belonging to the natural sciences, is this, that they carry the mind from the thing made, to Him who made it. If we contemplate a beautiful painting or an intricate piece of mechanism, we naturally are led to admire the artist who produced them, to regard his superiority with respect, and to enquire who and what he is. We mention his name with honour, and take every fitting opportunity of extolling his talents. If such are the effects of contemplating human excellency, how much stronger will be the same train of thought and of feeling in the breast of every good man, when he looks into the wonders of the natural world, and thinks upon the surprising phenomena which it exhibits! When he sees that this globe is inhabited by incalculable millions of living beings, all different from himself, his pride will be humbled by this conviction, that the earth was not made for him alone. And when he finds that all these beings, however minute, or, to the

vulgar eye, contemptible, have their allotted station and hold their distant cause in the great operations of the universe, he is led to enquire into his own nature, and to look towards that Great First Cause, whose bounty created, and whose providence sustains, such hosts of creatures.[9]

Swainson exemplifies the rich rhetorical template offered by natural history writers who preceded the popularity of the home aquarium in England and the United States. Contributions to later aquarium literature are easy to identify. Here is the admonition against "vulgar eyes" that would appear in Humphrey's *Ocean Gardens* over twenty years later, as well as the call for systematically observing as the antidote to vulgar seeing. References to species' immutable "allotted station" offered cosmic and social order and predictability to English modernity in ways that presaged the aquarium's useful management and display of atavism in the United States, whether or not individual aquarists believed in evolution. The superior "allotted station" of the aquarist was reaffirmed by the ability to reproduce that of "minute," "contemptible," and primitive beings within the home. Rigorous contemplation of nature to more accurately and humbly assess one's own spiritual progress and cosmic place was also a virtue of aquarium study, as in the observation of lessons learned from the "straying zoöphyte" described in chapter 1. Natural history provided the taxonomic insights to sustain aquarists' very modern balance of technologically mediated mastery and spiritual submission, a theologically secure middle place in a changing world. Swainson firmly aligns science with unchanging truth and art with mutability.[10] Yet in the passage just quoted, the creator and, indeed, the ultimate significance of the entire enterprise are linked rhetorically not with the unerring scientist but with the artist, whose name "we mention . . . with honour" and "take every fitting opportunity of extolling his talents," thus ensuring the persistence of aesthetic and technological creativity in the discourse. The naturalist brings observational and analytical skill to bear on the seamless excellence of the creative act, like a good art critic. By no means a simple flaw in his argument, Swainson's (and others') use of the artist as metaphor for a divine creator was rhetorically productive for early aquarists, aligning their construction of parlor ponds with both foundational and aesthetic acts of creation, world making and/as art making. Even as these writers sought to establish the rigor of the hobby, repeated references to the literary and visual arts both assumed and ensured a broad and deep appeal beyond that of a strictly observational science.

In early to mid-nineteenth-century England, natural history was both empirical and spiritual, aspirationally a science and inextricably textually linked to the arts. It conferred all of this on the home aquarium on both sides of the Atlantic, along with one other crucial element: a kind of putative observational democracy that cast the practice as local, accessible, and, above all, individual. Swainson explains,

> The successful prosecution of natural history, like that of all demonstrative sciences, depends upon facts; and when we consider the number of data necessary to complete the history of an individual species, and then reflect on the hundreds of thousands of species which exist upon the earth, we shall immediately perceive that every attentive observer has the power of contributing something towards his favorite science.[11]

This prospect of making an individual contribution to science animated aquarists for generations. It appears in descriptions of aquarium practices and pleasures, including its characterization as "a piece of the sea laid upon our table," the better to detail the "goings on and family secrets" of its residents, and in William Innes's plea to scrutinize simple tanks for "overlooked possibilities," both quoted in chapter 1. Further, these contributions were not airily cerebral. Natural history was "a very hands-on kind of endeavor," and the marine science that fed contemporary aquariums was particularly so.[12] Thus, in addition to its potent mixture of art and science, natural history bequeathed the ability to straddle one more binary. It required both thinking and doing, both sustained repose necessary for successful observation and analysis and physical vigor to ensure that one had something to examine.

Finally, Swainson, like P. H. Gosse, Reverend J. G. Wood, and other natural historians and aquarists, was not a professional man of science. He was an amateur, one of the "spider stuffers, country parsons and the like" who contributed to natural history literature, fads, and crazes of the mid-nineteenth century outside of formal institutions of higher learning.[13] But this amateur status of its proponents was part of its overall palliative effect. Natural history offered an alternative to the increasing atomization of knowledge in a world of emerging bureaucracies and highly credentialed specialists. It promised a renewal of civic virtue and national identity in the acts of reproducing colonial exploration and discovery at home, energetically identifying and describing domestic patrimony and sanctifying "nature" as an alternative to industrial modernity, conducted by anyone who could hop on a train to the shore with a bucket and a dredge. This seemingly egalitarian aspect of natural history's amateurism obscured the larger reality that it was typically only the relatively well-off who could marshal the leisure time and resources to fully participate. Nevertheless, the enabling fiction of natural history as an arena open to all enterprising amateurs was both durable and particularly attractive to American aquarists.

The descriptions and textual templates provided by natural history blurred elements of romanticism and realism into a hybrid in which meticulous recounting of specifics supports a theological sublime using the elevated language of or references to aesthetics. The arts provided a vocabulary for reckoning with the abundance, beauty, and complexity of creation. Science contributed an appeal to systematic rigor and a commitment to descriptive precision. The enterprising individual was the key contributor, with bountiful nature being the source of inspiration that links data to the divine. Intellectual and physical prowess were essential to manage the entire operation but it did not require highly specialized training by or the imprimatur of the emerging scientific elite. Contemporary scholars have mixed reviews on this blurring of genres. Amy M. King argues that natural historians' devotion to detail is echoed in realist novels of the period.[14] D. E. Allen asserts that natural history writers overlaid an orthodox theism onto the Romantics, "emotionally relabeling" them for the pious middle class, a "pose" that ultimately devolved into shallow sentimentality.[15] For their part, mid-nineteenth-century British aquarists and readers found this "half-breed" genre and the textual strategies comprising it eminently generative and useful.[16]

"The indefatigable Gosse"

No one seized the potential of this half-breed genre more vigorously than Philip Henry Gosse.[17] His zealous advocacy of public and private aquariums grew directly out of his love for natural history, and his unique combination of precision, piety, and a "poet's heart" engaged British and American readers. The introduction to his aptly titled *The Romance of Natural History* (1860) serves as a rhetorical précis to both the larger genre and his approach to aquariums.

> There are more ways than one of studying natural history. There is Dr. Dryasdust's way; which consists of mere accuracy of definition and differentiation; statistics as harsh and dry as the skins and bones in the museum where it is studied. There is the field-observer's way; the careful and conscientious accumulation and record of facts bearing on the life-history of the creatures; statistics as fresh and bright as the forest or meadow where they

are gathered in the dewy morning. And there is the poet's way; who looks at nature through a glass peculiarly his own; the aesthetic aspect, which deals, not with statistics, but with the emotions of the human mind—surprise, wonder, terror, revulsion, admiration, love, desire, and so forth—which are made energetic by the contemplation of the creatures around him.[18]

Here, as in most of his aquarium writings, Gosse firmly aligns himself and his readers with the field observer and the poet against the Gradgrindian scientist in terms that anticipate American aquarist Don Simpson's characterization of the "fish guy" versus the ichthyologist over one hundred years later (discussed in chapter 3).[19] In his highly influential book *The Aquarium: An Unveiling of the Wonders of the Deep Sea* (1854), Gosse deployed his observational, lyrical, and ministerial sensibilities in support of a literal look at nature through the glass.

The Aquarium is a rich and fascinating work, enormously influential and profitable in its day. Biographer Anne Thwaite reckons the book's final profit at around sixty thousand dollars.[20] Reviews were extremely favorable on both sides of the Atlantic.[21] The work is enhanced by six color plates, Gosse's own delightful illustrations. It also includes eight atmospheric prints. Half of these work like cinematic establishing shots; they depict the rural context of Gosse's collecting adventures. The remainder present aquarium designs and a specimen detail. To reach readers who could not afford the more expensive volume, Gosse published an updated stand-alone chapter, minus the plates, as *A Handbook to the Marine Aquarium* (hereafter, *Handbook*) in 1855. A full accounting of *The Aquarium*'s rhetorical style and its place among Gosse's writings exceeds the scope of this volume. Instead, in the following pages, I examine five key tropes that structure the work as a whole, align it with writings by other English aquarists, and discuss how Gosse's tropes and narrative strategies surface in aquarium discourse for decades. These tropes and strategies are essential to understanding the aquarium's larger rhetorical work.

The first set of narrative strategies depended on the rhetorical utility and discursive fungibility of landscapes. In Gosse's writings and those of many of his contemporaries, the most foundational of these strategies centered on slippage between the aquarium and the sea itself. This is not just a simple matter of the former substituting for the latter, though Gosse certainly does this. In addition, the overall flow of the book, structured around collecting trips and descriptions of specimens, often makes it difficult to discern precisely where Gosse's observations of creatures actually take place, whether in his tank or in "the wild." This is a rhetorically productive ambiguity. It serves both the hobbyist and the modern national imaginary by turning the sea into a domestic landscape—a source of rational entertainment, not only transportation and natural resources. The idea of "unveiling," as in the title to Gosse's book, is crucial here. It positions the aquarium as a tool enabling two kinds of exposure: one involving heretofore unseen and inaccessible wilderness and the other a gentle, restorative nature hiding in plain sight.

Other landscapes—celestial and terrestrial—are also central to the rhetorical work of the volume; it links detailed, highly visual descriptions of (especially) rural landscapes to the social life of and in the aquarium. The aquarium is itself a kind of landscape, a classic illustration of W. J. T. Mitchell's argument that the genre "naturalizes a cultural and social construction, representing an artificial world as if it were simply given and inevitable, and it also makes that representation operational by interpellating its beholder in some more or less determined relation to its givenness as sight and site."[22] In Gosse's case, the use of landscape as a textual device involves more than describing the scenery, the incidental backdrop of specimen collecting. Rather, as with slippage between the aquarium and the sea, it is rhetorically productive. The aquarium comes to encompass the sites with which it is associated both visually and textually, each with its own established conventions of "givenness," "inevitability," and rhetorical potency. These conventions were bequeathed to the aquarium as permanent discursive features. Thus, the tank becomes a tool to imagine utopian urbanity and to encounter a fragment of the picturesque preindustrial past, coded as bucolic periphery, through its real and imagined links both to the landscapes themselves and to norms of viewing them.

Gosse not only links the aquarium to the apparent "givenness" of national and natural landscapes. He interpellates "the made" as well in his inclusion of poetry from Homer to Keats. This "citational solidarity" aligns the aquarium and nature itself with both divine and human artifice, art and/as world making. Further, as Gosse states in *The Romance of Natural History*, the "poet's heart" infuses human emotion into the observational enterprise, inoculating it against the "mere accuracy" of "Dr. Dryasdust." Poetry inserted affect and sensuality into analyses of aquarium residents and, by extension, into the hobby and its enthusiasts as well, enabling it to function as a pursuit inflected both artistically and scientifically. Citational solidarity organizes Gosse's readers and potential aquarium hobbyists into communities of shared taste and shared sentiment by enfolding the hobby itself into a literary, particularly a romantic, sensibility.

Gosse calls *The Aquarium* a "personal narrative," and it is both highly individual in its stylistic idiosyncrasies and individualizing in its effects.[23] The book manages to bestow character on aquarium specimens without anthropomorphizing them, and it inserts them into literary—not simply scientific—discourses like those of Shakespeare and Scott, with whom the author aligns himself. Though he treats some residents as a species, many others are discussed as individuals, and none are simply resources ripe for exploitation. Nor are they pets in the conventional sense of the term. Through his use of induction and allusion, he establishes a template for one-on-one relationships between the aquarist and his charges that persists to the present. These relationships are the subject of chapter 4.

Finally, Gosse establishes and then navigates one more binary that characterizes the hobby: easy and effortless versus difficult and demanding. Advocates of the hobby, particularly in its early years, manage this same binary to both enhance its spread and praise the prowess of its practitioners. Gosse's discussions of aquarium pragmatics are prescient. They reveal the hobby's dependence on an urban context, even as that context is disavowed or distanced by the predominance of rural landscapes in the work. Further, Gosse demonstrates, more clearly than his contemporaries, the rhetorical connections between managing the tank and managing the emerging modern organization, connections dependent on discipline, paternal care, and systematic observation. But he also firmly establishes the tank as spiritual respite from these same rigors, in prose that positions "facts and figures subservient to Faith," poetry, and the sheer joy of communing with little water worlds.[24]

Id(yl)ling: Gosse's Landscapes

The Aquarium firmly establishes one important pattern shared by aquarium writers for over fifty years, one that persists, with adjustments, to the present: slippage between the aquarium and the sea itself. This pattern was central to the hobby's promise of unveiling: taking viewers on a walk beneath the waves and making the wonders found there visually accessible, as noted in chapter 1. Gosse makes this slippage definitive in the overall flow of his narrative. The aquarium becomes raison d'être for complex, sustained engagement with the sea and shore as extensions of domestic space. The tank brings the sea to the parlor but also "parlorizes" the sea, making it a logical extension of the individual's and nation's living space, not simply its commercial or military one. In a paradox that stands at the center of the hobby, the sea does not fully exist as an intimate, domestic location until the aquarium allows consumers to make its acquaintance, to learn the local "comings and goings" that make this world intelligible and consumable beyond a mode of transport and a source of food. As promised in the title, the tank and the book unveil the unseen world of the sea by inserting its wonders not just into glass boxes but into discourses that shape "flux into form, infinity into frame."[25] The aquarium transforms the sea from untamed and inaccessible wilderness into manageable and restorative—because consumable—nature. It domesticates the sea; in so doing, it enables the substitution of the latter for the former in the parlor, as narrative focus in Gosse's book, and, frequently, in the hobby itself.

From this perspective, the most striking aspect of the book as a whole makes sense: for a work entitled *The Aquarium*, very little of it actually deals with the mechanics of the practice. Specific how-tos are confined largely to chapter XI, the final one of the book, which was published separately as the *Handbook* the following year. Gosse describes this chapter as a "postscript of a lady's letter; though placed last it contains the most important part of the volume."[26] At 53 out of 302 pages (less than 20 percent of the text), however, this is debatable. Further, slippage between the aquarium and the sea explains the curious placement of Gosse's descriptive section titled "My Own Tank," which occurs not with the how-tos of chapter XI but about a third of the way through chapter V, as an extension of his collecting idylls in Weymouth. This chapter is an especially obvious demonstration of the ambiguous sites of his observations—in the tank or in situ?—to the conclusion that it doesn't matter because the one is interchangeable with the other.

Gosse writes largely about the seaside and its environs, in both chapter V and the work as a whole. The bulk of the book reads as a richly textured travel narrative to the extent that the author himself anticipates and responds to his readers' imagined impatience: "But what connexion [*sic*] is there between all this and the Marine Aquarium? Well, I have said, be indulgent! I have been idling, I confess; but still I am on duty."[27] What seems like a set of odd digressions and "proliferating descriptions" of picturesque locales if read as a practical primer makes sense from a broader view of Gosse "on duty."[28] The cultural work of this volume is not so much the outlining of pragmatics (though it does this) but the establishment of the hobby's conceptual matrix: the "mimic sea" makes the real sea and its residents even more real by literally and metaphorically containing it.[29] It sets new terms for a relationship between the sea and middle-class audiences by offering a new vocabulary, practices, rituals—a new habitus—to engage it.[30]

The operation works rhetorically through layered sets of parallels. The liminality of the shore—site of most of Gosse's idling in this book and the de facto boundary of the nation—is matched by the liminality of the tank, which is not the sea but not not-it either. This blurring of boundaries, in turn, reflects the hybrid genre of the book: the tank as an artifact of science, art, and technology parallels the narrative fusion of travel writing, thick description, theological tract, and "personal narrative" broadly construed.[31]

This layered hybridity establishes the discursive groundwork for the tank as a container for a wide range of uniquely modern practices, landscapes, and longings. For Gosse, these longings were spiritual. He was deeply religious, a biblical literalist and staunch opponent of evolution. The book is rich with Bible quotes and includes a lengthy chapter, seemingly dropped into the volume at random, entitled "The Right Use of Natural History." Much of this reflects a more vehement and developed approach to the conventional romantic piety of his naturalist contemporaries.[32] One discussion, however, stands out as an example of how slippage between the aquarium, the divine, and the sea enabled utopian yearnings about, and the rhetorical incorporation of, seemingly unrelated modern landscapes: Gosse's characterization of the work of "coral worms" housed in his own tank as "earthly shadows of heavenly substance."[33] This occurs in chapter V, as an extension of his description of his own tank. He writes,

> When I look on the multitudes of Polypes inhabiting such a structure as I have alluded to, each bearing his starry crown, and all engaged in harmony, building up, wall by wall and cell by cell, an edifice whose walls are of crystalline clearness, often studded with what look like gems, and whose cells are closed with pearly doors; when I watch the building growing up into a City, a commonwealth, of myriad individuals; when I know that, besides the separate life of each, there is a common life, a bond of identity, that constitutes the vast assemblage but one Being—One though Many—I cannot help thinking of the heavenly city, the Jerusalem which is above.[34]

The celestial city may have been uppermost in Gosse's mind in this passage, but terrestrial ones were nearby. Because coral are so compact, productive, and such proficient builders, a mass like the one in his own tank "may bear rank, for multitude, with Vienna, Paris, or perhaps London."[35]

Gosse was in fact living in London from 1853 to 1857. Contrast the bejeweled assemblage of crystalline clarity in his tank with the opening lines of Dickens's *Bleak House* from this same period.[36]

London . . . Smoke lowering down from chimney pots, making a soft black drizzle, with flakes of soot in it as big as full-grown snow-flakes—gone into mourning, one might imagine, for the death of the sun. Dogs indistinguishable in the mire. Horses scarcely better; splashed to their very blinkers. Foot passengers, jostling one another's umbrellas, in a general infection of ill-temper, and losing their foothold at street-corners, where tens of thousands of other foot passengers have been slipping and sliding since the day broke (if this day every broke), adding new deposits to the crust upon crust of mud, sticking at those points tenaciously to the pavement, and accumulating at compound interest.

Fog everywhere.[37]

In the material city, there is no crystalline commonwealth, only filthy deposits randomly trampled into layers of sooty mud "at compound interest," the effluence of commerce. Further, the mud and fog of Dickens's London are outer manifestations of a deep inner estrangement, as in book VII of Wordsworth's "Prelude."

> O Friend! One feeling was there which belonged
> To this great city, by exclusive right;
> How often, in the overflowing streets
> Have I gone forwards with the crowd, and said
> Unto myself, "The faces of everyone
> That passes by me is a mystery."[38]

Raymond Williams, referring specifically to Wordsworth but in an analysis easily encompassing Dickens's "indistinguishable" dogs, horses, and pedestrians, argues that such descriptions contain "a failure of identity in the crowd of others which worked back to a loss of identity in the self, and then, in time, a loss of society itself, its over-writing and replacement by a procession of images."[39] Against such contemporary dystopic views of the terrestrial city, Gosse's aquatic "vast assemblage but one Being" stands as counterexample and antidote.

In an increasingly urban nation with wealth and difference concentrating in cities, London in particular, Gosse's polyps present an organic model of beauty, individuality, and common purpose. Urbanization was incoherent. Coral, the aquarium reveals, was not. Where London landscapes delivered ugliness and alienation, the commonwealth of polyps offered harmony and inspiration. The tank that housed them made them more coherent still by framing them precisely as Gosse does: as occasion for respite and reverie, nature contained at a comprehensible scale to answer back to the overpowering size and intrapsychic and interpersonal dislocation of the metropolis. Gosse's meditation on the coral worms includes an excerpt of James Montgomery's poem "The Pelican Island," inspired by a voyage to Australia and the coral reefs found there. It is also replete with characterizations of corals as cooperative laborers, architects, and masons constructing an alternative, organic, and enduring city. Throughout this discussion, Gosse's rhetorical slippage between the aquarium, the divine, the sea, and the city enables the tank to mediate between the metropolis and the wilderness and to find the one in the other. The invertebrates offer not only an allegorical Jerusalem but also a template for civic industry, individuality, and solidarity, all from the comfort of home. The imagined city in the tank both represents and restores the harmonious, generative connection between humanity and the natural world, suturing, at least for a moment, the seeming breach between the two that characterized mid-nineteenth-century urban industrial England.

Gosse's reference to Vienna, Paris, and London is something of an aberration. There are few overt mentions of a specifically urban context in the book. Implicit acknowledgments of that context appear in the pragmatic chapter XI/*Handbook*, however, in the form of arrangements and an individual dealer that support the hobbyist. These references point to the birth of the market for aquariums and to the "machine in the garden" moments that mark the hobby itself as an increasingly urban diversion, dependent on metropolitan infrastructure to produce underwater wilderness at home.[40] With these few exceptions, the book makes the aquarium seem, overall, like the product of prolonged immersion in rural England, a world away from the railways, steamer ships, and commercial networks that became essential to sustaining it. This was more than just an acknowledgment of the obvious sites for collecting specimens. Gosse honed his craft as a naturalist and writer through field observation in Newfoundland, Alabama, and Jamaica. Relationships between the imperial center and periphery are implicit in this work. His highly visual descriptions of travel and local specifics contributed significantly to the conflation of the aquarium with real and vicarious travel. However, unlike his books set abroad, *The Aquarium* seems concerned less with exploration than with the recuperation of rural towns, with their picturesque scenery and colorful locals. Authors credit Gosse with stoking the seaside collecting craze, but one can easily see the enervated urban reader perusing the book for hints to a refreshing holiday destination in the country—a bucolic escape—with collecting as just an alibi.[41]

Page after page of the book is filled with thick descriptions of oxen in fields, verdant dells, moody ruins, and seemingly timeless seaside villages.[42] Even aquarium fauna are cast in a pastoral idiom, as in Gosse's description of (peri)winkles as "unowned cattle on the American pampas."[43] Gosse's quasi-pastoral imagery is complex and a particularly interesting illustration of the rhetorical operations of substitution and aggregation in aquarium discourse. Just as the society of coral worms in the tank becomes a manageable version of the celestial and material city, the aquarium subsumes the rustic village. It can accommodate an urban utopia, a rural idyll, or both. The connections between rural landscapes and the aquarium are reinforced visually by the text's prints. As noted earlier, half—four of the eight—are establishing shots of the countryside. Three represent types of tanks, and the remaining one depicts specimen details (leg cilia). The landscapes are placed in the first half of the book; the tanks appear only in the last half, in close proximity to the pragmatic chapter XI. Taken as a whole, the relationship between the two sets of places appears metonymic, a progression from container to contained. The tank becomes one more rural village in the English landscape. It both contains and becomes a village, not only by housing specimens collected nearby, but also, in Gosse's prose, through the alignment of the sea and its inhabitants with the look and residents of these bucolic hamlets.

Gosse's aquarium invertebrates are immersed in the largely pastoral scenes he describes, but that pastoralism is not simple and repays careful attention. It is certainly a celebration of rural life, especially obvious given the amount of space allotted to such descriptions and the virtual absence of urban ones. These scenes reinforce links between the sea, the tank, and fictions of "the land," always already rustic and preindustrial, in ways that emerge with remarkable directness in writings by other aquarists, especially Shirley Hibberd. But Gosse's celebration of the rustic and its rhetorical utility for aquaria has a very specific cast, as illustrated in an account of a trip to collect medusae.

> I continued my walk over the Ferry Bridge, and along the ridge of pebbles, to the fishing village of Chesil. It has an aspect of venerable antiquity, arising chiefly from its being built, even to the poorest fishermen's huts, of massive stone; the door-posts, the window sills, the lintels, all of the grey freestone which constitutes the staple of the island. The vast over-hanging cliffs of the west side add to the grandeur and impact an awfulness to the scene, which reminded me of an exhumed town. The people visible were few, and those were still, grave, and seemingly only half awake, quite unlike the "fast living" people that one is accustomed to see in these days.[44]

This is, first and foremost, a "natural" scene, both picturesque and "awful." The stones comprising even the poorest houses are the staple of—indeed, the very core constituents of—the nation, making the village one with the "vast over-hanging cliffs" and Britain itself. It is a timeless, "venerable" landscape, but not simply a sentimental one. The town seems visually "exhumed" by the viewer, and the description of its people as "grave" suggests that it is both deadly serious and simply dead. Yet, like the tide pools Gosse investigates, there are "indications of habits and doings" that merit observation, even admiration. The labors of the locals are not erased or sentimentalized. They are not dispensable, nor are they necessary nuisances as in some later aquarists' accounts of collecting trips to the global south.[45] A fisherman's hands are "palsied"; girls collect fresh water. All are engaged in the hard work of making a living, just as Gosse's invertebrates compete and kill, devour and get devoured. Also important, given Gosse's staunch antievolutionism, is the complex sense of temporality that characterizes this passage.[46] The medusae, the work of God, might persist unchanged over eons, but here was a human scene returned from the grave to remind the reader of the "stalwart" authenticity of the preindustrial past, a rhythm very different from the "fast living" of modernity and so natural that it is rooted in the very geology. Gosse's aquarium is not only a tool to expose the essential dynamics of sea and shore; it is also an archeologist's trowel that exhumes the essential rural past and incorporates it, replicating the relationship of the book's first set of prints to the second. The tank and the village organize orderly and enduring landscapes and essential rituals, with the mechanics of survival clearly visible in both. Just as the aquarium "parlorizes" the sea and models the city, it subsumes the rugged village that, in its stark and timeless aspects, reflects the rigors of "nature" without the anarchy of either the metropolis or the wilderness.

In *The Victorian Parlor*, Thad Logan identifies a parallel between "Victorians collecting specimens at the shore and Victorians gathering various cultural resources to the imperial bosom."[47] This identification is both true and somewhat imprecise. Certainly, imperial exotics are discursively housed in the family tank during this period, particularly in the writings of Shirley Hibberd. With the advent of air travel, the tank becomes a literal repository of the exotic at home. But Gosse's writings, as well as those of his contemporaries, operate on a somewhat different logic, albeit one directly enabled by imperial diffusion of people and resources. This logic centers on domestic recuperation of the rural, made rhetorically urgent by the coupling of urbanization and empire. Gosse's repeated invocations of the "slighted and enduring" countryside are of a piece with his descriptions of the heretofore invisible yet persistent residents of the tank.[48] The hobby offered enervated modern viewers access to both.

In literary terms, Gosse's descriptions of these rural villages are more aligned with the georgic than the simple pastoral. They emphasize "the value of intensive and persistent labor against hardships and difficulties," while reinforcing putatively essential connections with the land that were central to the conflation of the rural and the natural.[49] This georgic mode was particularly useful rhetorically in an empire with comparable designs for its colonies, designs that would ideally replicate the relationship between center and periphery that characterized the bucolic countryside—source of raw materials, site of restorative reverie—vis-à-vis the enervating city of commerce and capital. As the aquarium hobby and its associated markets developed, "the tropics" would replace the rural village in the rural-nature conflation, and an expanded notion of "wilderness" would replace nature. Ultimately, in the reef tanks discussed in the conclusion to the present book, the wilderness would stand alone as the rhetorical utility of specific landscapes in the hobby shifted with the tides of modernity.

Citational Solidarity

Throughout *The Aquarium*, Gosse relies on more than his own "poet's heart." He enlists a wide range of other poets as well: Homer, Ovid, Cowper, Bryant, Charlotte Smith, James Montgomery, Spenser, and Keats, among others. This practice was certainly not unique to Gosse. It was increasingly common in midcentury natural history texts, to the extent that David Allen observes, somewhat sardonically, "For a time it became all but obligatory to work into every book or article on natural history a quota of lines from Wordsworth. Even sober works of science were not immune from this."[50] Allen dismisses this citation practice as "pandering" to the market for sentimentality, but "spangling" *The Aquarium* with "snippets of assorted verse" was actually rhetorically useful. As Ralph O'Connor observes in his nuanced discussion of the practice in British geology texts of the period, quotations from a shared literary history signaled a community with educated readers and rendered unfamiliar objects intelligible within an aesthetic tradition.[51] Marine fauna, like geological deep time, certainly benefited from being placed in such a context.

Gosse's liberal use of quotations, like that of his contemporaries, is a rhetorically productive exercise in citational solidarity, a way of forging precisely the kind of conversation between the field observer's "fresh" facts and the poet's "aesthetic aspect" that he describes in *The Romance of Natural History*. In her essay "Performing Writing," Della Pollock observes, "Citational writing underscores the double movement of quotation. It stages its own citationality, re-sighting citation, deploying it in an accumulation of quotations or self-quotation or quotation from beyond the borders of academic prose . . . with the primary effect of reclaiming citation for affiliation."[52] Gosse's citational writing actively claims multiple affiliations: a solidarity of learned middle-class readers, as noted earlier; a solidarity of sentiment; and, most of all, a solidarity of artifice built on the recognition that nature, the tank, and the poem are all artfully created things.

O'Connor notes that "[b]eginnings and endings were natural locations for locating a science in a larger moral framework," with "the epigraph a favorite slot for gnomic quotation in poetry or prose."[53] So it is in *The Aquarium*, with Gosse establishing his citational solidarity of artifice early in an explicit reference to the divine artificer. The book's epigraph is from the Psalms: "The sea is His, and He made it." It both establishes the slippage between the aquarium and the sea that undergirds the entire volume and locates the source in the foundational condition of each: both are created things. This is reinforced and expanded on by the next epigraph in the volume, that of chapter II from William Cowper's "Love of Nature."

> The love of Nature's works
> Is an ingredient in the compound, man,
> Infused at the creation of the kind.
> And, though th' Almighty Maker has throughout
> Discriminated each from each, by strokes
> And touches of his hand, with so much art
> Diversified, that two were never found
> Twins at all points—yet this obtains in all,
> That all discern a beauty in his works,
> And all can taste them.[54]

The aquarist and the poet can approach and recognize God through a solidarity of artifice because all are makers. But as the Cowper epigraph suggests, this begets yet another solidarity. The Almighty Maker, here both an artist and a chemist, infuses a deep appreciation of the beauty of his creation—Nature—so innate it is almost physiological: "all can taste" it.

The connection to creation linking the naturalist aquarist and the poet to the divine is extended to the reader as a solidarity of perception: all love beautiful things. Beauty, according to Elaine Scarry, incites "an impulse toward begetting."[55] It is generative, an invitation to participate or an acknowledgment of shared presumptions and thus relational infrastructure.[56] It is not only that Gosse's poetic citations tell readers how to feel about nature and the residents of the tank, though this interpretation is certainly important. Recall that early tank viewers of invertebrates in particular didn't know what they should be seeing. Gosse showed them they were actually reading poetry—or at least engaging the raw materials. He inserted fish and invertebrates into literature. Further, Gosse's use of poetry reinforced a solidarity of sentiment in his community of readers by acknowledging and reinforcing what they probably already felt, extending an ongoing textual conversation rooted in a shared appreciation of nature seemingly hardwired into humanity or at least into the readers of natural history. The author's task, in this view, is that of the art critic: to uplift and refine sentiments readers already share by using an established and refined rhetorical tool to explicate them. Sometimes that tool works by casting aquatic landscapes in pastoral terms, another way to link the tank, the sea, and the countryside, as in Gosse's use of Milton.

> Forthwith the sounds and seas, each creek and bay,
> with fry innumerable swarm: . . . .
> . . . . . part single or with mate
> Graze the sea-weed their pasture, and through groves
> Of coral stray; or sporting with quick glance,
> Show to the sun their waved coats dropp'd with gold.[57]

At other times, poetry, like a good dredging tool or the tank itself, exposes the aesthetic potential of a formerly inaccessible scene, as in Gosse's use of an excerpt from James Gates Percival's "The Coral Grove."

> The floor is of sand like the mountain drift
>   And the pearl-shells spangle the flinty snow;
> From coral rocks the sea-plants lift
>   Their boughs, where tides and billows flow.[58]

Forging citational solidarity through poetry is rhetorically useful for aquarists well into the twentieth century. By this time, though, that poetry is often humorous doggerel, and its function is to capitalize on shared frustrations or anxieties and not shared aesthetic traditions.

The Aquarium uses citation to cement affiliations in other ways, most notably to establish connections between natural history, the aquarium, and the classical world. Here, quotations function like references to contemporaries in professional science (e.g., Louis Agassiz) or fellow aquarists (e.g., Anna Thynne, wife of the subdean of Westminster Abbey). Gosse is staging textual conversations between artists, amateurs, and scientists that establish the hobby as a rich interchange of multifaceted knowledge and pleasures, one that goes back to the ancients. In so doing, he effectively creates both an expanded discursive palette and an expanded history of the hobby before Robert Warrington and the Ward Case. In this august history, both Homer and Ovid are contributors. The former offers pertinent descriptions of the cuttlefish, the latter both specimen description and instructions for effective dredging.[59] Of course, Gosse also stages himself in these conversations. His interests include both descriptions of the natural world and "the feelings they excite in my own mind"—completely consistent with his characterization of the book as "a form of personal narrative."[60] His use of quotation here functions as ventriloquism. Poets often finish his own sentences, supplying charming biographical detail (as with the "lucky stone" rhyme) or amplifying his already vivid description of a beautiful day with a bit of Keats.[61] This very intimate use of citational solidarity to extend the author's own voice with even more highly affective language than his typical prose persists in aquarium literature, especially amateur publications, and underscores the links between the personal idiosyncrasies and idioms of aquarists and those they see and create in their tanks. Gosse clearly establishes the very individual and affective elements of the hobby through his various textual affiliations. Individuality and emotional appeal are central to the aquarium's longevity and its cultural work. Like Gosse's personal narrative, the tank becomes a tool of self-assertion and an extension of the aquarist's and modernity's sensory and emotional lives. Interestingly, there are no quotations from poetry or the Bible in the *Handbook*, suggesting that if one is ready for the pragmatics of actively establishing an aquarium, affiliations detailing its pleasures are unnecessary.[62]

Personal(ities) Narrative

The Aquarium is a travel book and a personal narrative, but it is also, explicitly, a "biography."[63] Gosse's decision to use "biography" to describe this work is, at its simplest, a ratification of the inductive methods of field study, with its focus on the individual specimen. It also includes an explicitly religious aspect, as the munificence and pervasiveness of divine order are, for Gosse, best revealed in nature's "minute but graphic particulars."[64] Gosse's definition of biography is expansive, again including both the naturalist observer and the poet, and he is adamant about the rigor inherent in the combination: "Shakespeare and Scott, who treat of man as an individual, are not inferior in this walk of science to Reid and Stewart, who describe him as a species."[65] As his reference to Shakespeare and Scott suggests, Gosse literally characterizes specimens, imbuing them with—if not personality—at least intelligible motivations and discernible qualities. Further, he develops his characterizations by setting specimens in dialogue with the aquarist, to the extent that to conduct rigorous inquiries into lives of crustaceans in the tank, one must "ask the Crab," who, "as soon as it is dropped into the Aquarium," responds, "Though I am a Crab, you see I have learned to behave myself in some things like my courtly cousins the Lobster family."[66] Yet Gosse is never a crude or sentimental anthropomorphizer of his specimens. They are not little marine people. Nor are they "pets," at least by one relevant criterion: they were not given personal names.[67] With considerable regularity throughout the book, they dispatch one another or just die, as, presumably, in the wild. As Thad Logan suggests, there is an unmistakable sensationalism in all this killing, predation, and cannibalism.[68] On one level, the tank offers a way to glimpse the putative brutality of "primitive" life, serving as a surrogate for domestic and imperial "primitives," even as it provides the antidote in its association with bucolic landscapes.[69] Gosse does not mourn the casualties and doesn't hesitate to dissect them, recounting these incidents with relative dispassion, in stark contrast to his deep sense of loss at the death of his beloved cat.[70] The textual treatment of his specimens proved important and even foundational for the hobby. The aquarium's considerable affective rewards and pedagogical value lie in the peculiarities of its residents as individuals and in the ongoing relationships between them and the aquarist. *The Aquarium* provides the narrative template for describing and understanding these relationships.

Gosse typically characterizes his specimens by using fairly generic roles—biblical and mythic characters and even other animals—rather than attributing complex personalities or desires. This is another characteristic textual mingling of the poet's "aesthetic aspect" with the naturalist's focus on behavior. The strawberry crab, "a climber," recalls "The Orangatan" [*sic*].[71] His sepiole "can be a real Cain at times," gratuitously slaughtering his fellow cephalopods.[72] The velvet fiddler crab, "gloomy and grim, strong, ferocious, crafty and cruel," recalls the giants "infesting Cambria and Cornwall in 'good King Arthur's days.'"[73] In other cases, his descriptions suggest, if not personalities, at least dispositions. Thus, the tansy is a worthy choice for aquarists because, although "some specimens are ugly enough," it is amusing, "displaying a mixture of impudence and timidity, coming out fiercely to snatch a morsel of food from before a fellow fish's mouth, and then darting charily under the shadow of a rock to eat its treacherously gotten booty."[74] Gosse walks a fine line in these descriptions, keeping emphasis on actions rather than the seeming inner lives of his charges. Typically his characterizations are embedded in detailed and denotative accounts. Like his use of citational solidarity, these idiosyncratic elements, especially allusions to biblical and literary figures, provide narrative matrices in which specimens otherwise unintelligible could be understood and enjoyed without compromising a real sense of their marvelous otherness.

Gosse appears to have a particular fondness for crabs. They inspire some of his most delightful characterizations. The doings of fish appear dull by comparison. In contrast, he seems to have relationships with the little crustaceans, and in delineating their behavior, he offers insights into how those relationships could be constructed and sustained: through recognition of small commonalities alongside the animal's overall oddness; through a font of creative, domestic analogies; and, most of all, through good humor. His discussion of Pennant's *Ebalia* begins prosaically enough, with a systematic survey of its body in sometimes minute detail. Though these particulars recall both a "toad" and a "tiny cabinet," "[t]he face, when examined with a lens through the glass walls of the Aquarium, has a most funny expression, being singularly like that of an ancient man."[75] Gosse is similarly charmed by the housing habits of the hermit crab. Here, as if to emphasize that his own relationship to these creatures is not mere personal idiosyncrasy, he incorporates the observations of a colleague, who demonstrates that Gosse is not the only one to whom crustaceans seem to speak. Set shell-less into the tank, the crab investigates a shell placed there "for the purpose of seeing if the house were to let."[76] On finding it suitable,

> he looks so funny—such *at homeishness* there was in it; he was so different from the poor, houseless vagabond with a driveling tail, that one seen miserably crawling about a moment before: he looked right up in your face, and said as plainly as looks can speak, "How d'ye do? here I am quite at home already."

Interestingly, these observations are much closer to simple anthropomorphism than Gosse's own and highlight his care to focus on analogies for unfamiliar actions and appearances rather than attribution of motive. Perhaps quoting his colleague gave Gosse permission to indulge in such a vivid characterization.

As noted earlier, certainly part of Gosse's delight in such relationships with specimens was of a piece with his faith. As Lynn Merrill observes, Gosse's "investigation of nature was a form of religious experience," and details of marine life reaffirmed for him the wondrous intricacy of divine order.[77] So pervasive is this sentiment that Gosse even celebrates the anal evacuations of the sea mouse by using psalms that describe the riches of God.[78] Yet there is also a very secular pleasure evident in these relationships, one that hinges on the queer alterity of marine life—so clearly related through physiognomy and literary resemblance, yet so alien. The pleasures of contacts enabled by the tank happen not despite this alterity but because of it. It is precisely the thrill of discovering and attributing quasi-human characteristics to these little extraterrestrials' behavior that sustains aquarists to the present. Chapter 4 of the present book focuses on specific dynamics linking aquarium residents to aquarists and demonstrates the long afterlife of Gosse's narrative strategy in the hobby.

Tank Management

With the exception of a few opening paragraphs, the narrative voice of chapter XI and of the *Handbook* adapted from it is very different from the rest of *The Aquarium*. Aside from an epigraph for the chapter, which, as noted earlier, does not appear in the *Handbook*, there are no snippets of poetry, no biblical passages or conversations with crabs. Beginning with the section entitled "The Tank," the two works are virtually identical.[79] Both offer an unadorned testament to the rather remarkable amount of work required of the early aquarist. Nothing in the volume prepares the reader for this. On the contrary, Gosse's discussion of his own tank in chapter V of *The Aquarium* focuses primarily on the specimens themselves. The only other significant reference prior to chapter XI suggests that "nothing is easier" than housing sea flora in a tank—an enterprise so undemanding that the aquarial gardener can simply use a "soup plate."[80] To be sure, the first chapter of the book includes a prosaic discussion of early experiments, Gosse's and others'. But these are folded into his more typical accounts of his travels. The effect is to reduce these early experiments to a necessary but now obsolete formative stage in the hobby, supplanted by greater understanding, better technology, and improved circumstances.

After two hundred pages of charming idylls, the rigors of tank construction and maintenance seem especially bracing. There is the actual assembly: metal frame, glass, putty, all in appropriate dimensions and scrutinized for potential toxicity to future residents. Buying a vessel is a bit easier but still requires considerations of shape and, if pottery, glaze. There is access to light to negotiate, and construction of an appropriate and congenial tank bottom. Then comes the seawater. Gosse gives a recipe for making it, along with a list of chemicals and proportions that, to contemporary eyes, would certainly seem to give an armchair chemist of the day at least some pause. Securing actual seawater requires its own miracle of logistics: from selecting an appropriate container (tannins from some wood barrels can leach into the water to the detriment of the stock) to obtaining the real thing, which, Gosse assures the reader, "may be easily obtained, by giving a trifling fee to the master or steward of any of the steamers that ply beyond the mouth of the Thames, charging him to dip it in the clear, open sea, beyond the reach of rivers."[81] All of this is preliminary to the ongoing work of collecting and maintaining the residents. For all of his frequently florid prose, Gosse is a steady, sober guide throughout the chapter/*Handbook*, his sobriety mirrored in the specifics of his advice. He cautions aquarists, giving advice as applicable to hobbyists as to colonial administrators: "[B]e moderate in your desire of dominion. Do not overcrowd your Tank."[82] And he reassures them while reminding them of their duties: "Death, which spares them not at the bottom of the sea, will visit them in the Aquarium; and hence the vessel should be occasionally looked over, *searched*, as it were, to see if there be any of the specimens dead."[83] He is equally restrained when extolling the tank's pleasures in these sections.

For all of his romanticism, Gosse is resolutely pragmatic in discussing the demands of aquariums, and he exemplifies one side of the curiously binary response to the labors required of the hobby. He does not in any way conceal or diminish the work involved, even as he celebrates the virtues of marine study generally. His contemporaries, including American aquarists, are more likely to operate on either extreme, casting the practice as effortless, as easy as decoration, on the one hand, and, on the other, as difficult enough to serve as a tool of bracing and virtuous pedagogy. In contrast to the rural imagery that comprises the bulk of the volume, Gosse's actual advice reads as a set of managerial imperatives transferable from a little glass box to an office or a household: systematically evaluate available resources, buying rather than making if time is more dear than money; be prudent, a good steward of those resources; be disciplined, observant, and systematic. As this advice indicates, the aquarium offers more than the artist's ability to make a work and the naturalist's ability to understand it. At the most basic level, it required the administrator's ability to manage it. In so doing, it contributed to the ongoing normalization of technobureaucratic rhetorics of efficiency by inserting them into the home and recoding them as leisure.

GOSSE'S CONTEMPORARIES

Gosse's aquarium book was not the only one to cross the Atlantic, though it was among the most popular, judging by the number of American reviews it received. Other British naturalist aquarists employed and expanded Gosse's rhetorical and narrative strategies, keeping them familiar and even commonsensical in widely read accounts of the hobby circulating in the United States. There were many such accounts published as books, pamphlets, and essays in compilations. Especially noteworthy were the works of influential writers James Shirley Hibberd, Henry Noel Humphreys, and John Ellor Taylor.[84] Gosse used the aquarium to domesticate the sea. These British writers who published after him domesticated the aquarium, shifting from a focus on travel and field study to rhetorically situating the tank within the home. This is not to say that the rhetorical conflation of the tank and the "outside"—the sea and the rural/"the land"—was diminished in these accounts. If anything, ties to national landscapes large and small were further reinforced, increasing the popularity of the tank as an element of decor and a source of personal and social virtues. The shift from a tool for observation and a kind of living poem to a "rustic adornment for homes of taste" was accelerated by the development and popularity of freshwater tanks. The pastoral pond and the local river were obvious, accessible, and familiar components of nature, in many ways less demanding than the sea, both logistically and conceptually.

Also central to this shift was a new, more explicit articulation of the aquarium's core operating principle, which had its own rhetorical potency. It was cast as a "philosophy," one that was extremely productive for domesticating the tank. In his description of this principle, Gosse offers a relatively prosaic account of relationships between plants and animals, harkening back to Priestley's discovery of oxygen.[85] Hibberd, in comparison, states the principle boldly and succinctly: the tank "is a self-supporting, self-renovating collection, in which the various influences of animal and vegetable life balance each other, and maintain within the vessel a correspondence of action that preserves the whole." Key words here are *self-supporting, balance, cor-*

responding action, and *whole.* These words render the tank an organic unit, like the sea, the ideal nation, and the family. First, this makes slippage between the tank and the river, pond, or ocean definitive: with these principles clearly part of the tank's operation, it is explicitly "an imitation of Nature on a small scale. The tank is a lake containing aquatic plants and animals." Note that between one sentence and the next, the tank morphs from "an imitation" to the actual "lake." Second, because "these [plants and animals] maintain each other in the water in the same way as terrestrial" communities do, this organic philosophy of the aquarium was fungible, a model for analogizing and naturalizing life outside as well as inside it.[86] This fungibility of "natural" operations would prove especially useful in cases where gender trouble in the tank served as a proxy for gender relations in the family, as discussed in chapter 5 of the present book. Other writers went further. The tank was not just a lake. It was a whole world in miniature: "The marvelous principles of adjustment of animal to vegetable life, and contrariwise, is as much in active operation in a portable aquarium as on a planet."[87] This characterization of the aquarium as a world is central to its ability to do cultural work, especially that involving national and transnational concerns like relations with the global south, as discussed in chapter 6 of the present book. With this organic principle clearly articulated, relations between the tank and the world were even reversible. The tank was a world in miniature, and its self-sustaining mechanics made the world one giant aquarium.[88]

In mid-nineteenth-century Britain at the birth of the hobby, conflations of the tank and a wide range of landscapes proliferated even beyond Gosse's georgic descriptions. In some titles, that slippage was complete; the aquarium *was* an ocean or river garden, seemingly harmonizing incommensurabilities between wild places (oceans, rivers) and domestic ones (gardens).[89] Personal landscapes were also interpellated into the tank, as in Humphrey's argument for the aquarium as the logical extension of his pond, site of boyhood reverie and naive collecting adventures, a move underlining the hobby as a vehicle for nostalgic time travel, as noted in chapter 1 of the present book. The aquarium's ability to conjure the "rustic" was a feature across all of these books; indeed, rusticity was even an explicit feature of aquarium design (see fig. 7). No one did more to extend Gosse's pastoral rhetoric linking nature, the rural countryside, and the aquarium than Shirley Hibberd in his *Rustic Adornments for Homes of Taste.* The opening to the book is so remarkable and so useful in its summary of the multiple elements coming together in the tank at this formative moment that it is worth quoting at length.

Among the emblems of our nationality, not one is more strongly cherished by us than OUR HOME. We pride ourselves on the strength and healthiness of our domestic life, and we challenge the world to produce an example of a people more fondly attached to their native soil, or in whom the fireside affections have a broader development or a higher aim . . . It is because we are truly a domestic people, dearly attached to our land of green pastures, and shrubby hedgerows, and grey old woods, that we remain calm amid the strife that besets the states around us, proud of our ancient liberties, our progressing intelligence, and our ever-expanding material resources. Those resources daily multiply the means of exalting our social life, and invention keeps pace with the demands of an improving civilization; so that while

> "The thoughts of men are widened by
> The progress of the suns,"

the facilities for calm and healthful enjoyment increase with the growth of more elevated desires. The "Home of Taste" is one of the latest fruits of the high tone to which social life has attained in this country of late years, and its complete development may not be so far off, but that the present generation may witness the union of Nature and Art in happy ministration to human sympathies within doors.[90]

Hibberd began the 1856 and 1857 editions of *Rustic Adornments* with chapters on the aquarium. It was given first place as the preeminent rustic adornment. The 1895 edition relegates the tank to the end of the book, a reflection of the waning British aquarium craze. Yet even then it encompasses five full chapters, including its own introduction. The introduction to the volume quoted previously and the work as a whole read as a veritable summary of aquarium rhetoric. As a rustic adornment, the tank emphasizes rural nature as national patrimony and domestic diversion. It is inextricably tied to "Art" by Hibberd's citational solidarity and its own artifice, as well as to the intellect and the sentiments to which it ministers. It is the product of invention, part and parcel of the advances of modernity, while enabling viewers to recall the ancient liberties made possible by the surrounding seas. The aquarium is a testament to "higher aims": simultaneously spiritual, political, and personal. More than anything else, this passage demonstrates the remarkable rhetorical sleight of hand that shifts the great expanse of national landscape into the home to soothe away the "demands of an improv-

Fig. 7. "A Design for the Aquarium Mounted in Handsome Rustic-Work." The rusticity of the presentation complemented the aquarium's evocation of the English countryside in multiple tank-management books. (From H. Noel Humphreys, *Ocean Gardens: The History of the Marine Aquarium and the Best Methods Now Adopted for Its Establishment and Preservation* [London: Sampson Low, 1857], pl. xii, 34.)

ing civilization." The rustic adornment, particularly the aquarium, is the ideal conduit linking one to the other. The organic nature of the tank reinforces an intrinsic connection to "the land" and the holistic, self-sustaining "HOME," an especially important illusion given the textual and conceptual sprawl of empire. Urban contexts are barely mentioned except as forms of dis-ease remedied by the aquarium, which repairs "estrangement from ruralities" through collecting trips and living souvenirs.[91] The relation between rural countryside, home, and tank enables imperial amnesia of precisely where many of the "expanding material resources" Hibberd mentions actually came from. The country is one with its ponds and hedgerows; the effluence of commerce is abstracted into "resources," "social life," and "an improving civilization." This, in turn, negates culpability in overseas adventures and exploitation: "a domestic people's" cosmopolitanism is purely self-contained, owing nothing to and asking nothing from the periphery but, instead, offering a model of "calm" to other states. This is precisely the role landscape plays as the rhetorically useful blend of nature and culture in imperial societies described in Novak's epigraph to the present chapter. Nature outside the home becomes decor and palliative inside it. It erases local and global inequities, substituting an organic, self-sustaining fantasy of "OUR HOME," including our tank. The term *domestic* is here polyvalent, a reflection of nation in/as home. The aquarium was quickly emerging as a rhetorically powerful tool for negotiating the complexities and anxieties in both.

The aquarium's full potential to contain international elements and issues required the expansion of markets in specimens and, especially, air travel. Yet even this early in its history, there are hints to its ability to register transnational fascinations and imperial anxieties. The tank contained foreign, even exotic landscapes as well as indigenous ones. These included scenes from German legends and bullfights.[92] Most interesting are those characterizations tinged with orientalism, broadly construed, including discussion of the golden carp as a private pleasure of the imperial Chinese court.[93] Anemones are especially susceptible, linked to the Peri flower from Thomas Moore's *Lalla Roohk* or to "the Indian blossom that the Brahmin believes to be endowed with life."[94] Ignorance of the basic principles of marine study is cast as "Egyptian darkness."[95] Observation itself is described in imperial terms: "physiological Alexanders, weeping for new regions to subdue, may hail the Aquarium as a fertile source of other conquests."[96] Lurking around the edges of these descriptions are the structures of fascination and desire central to the everyday life of empire, but there are attendant anxieties as well, found most obviously in recurring references to the "black hole of Calcutta" that reappears like a fetish in multiple books on aquariums.[97] The references emerge in cautions against overstocking and the resulting oxygen depletion, but their recurrence suggests an underlying unease about relationships between empire and captivity. Potentially suffocating confinement through foreign entanglements was a risk of imperial expansion, an ambient anxiety that could be rerouted into and contained in the tank.

As the example from *Lalla Rookh* indicates, citational solidarity with poets is a continuing feature of aquarium writing after Gosse. Hibberd is, by far, the most generous in his use of quotation as affiliation. For him, romantic poetry is itself a rustic adornment, a testament to the shared taste of author and reader. Further, the proliferation of citations in his books seems to position the aquarium as part of the same canon, as one more turn in a venerable tradition of celebrating the natural and domestic spheres through artifice and then using both to elevate public and private life. As a group, these works contain far less Gossean ventriloquism of poets finishing authors' sentences and a much broader network of affiliations, a testament to the spread of the hobby evidenced in references to scientists, professional aquarists, and public institutions.

Despite frequent allusions to Socrates, Dumas, Pope, and others, Humphreys actually ruptures Gosse's rhetorical equivalence of "Nature and Art." Art, in Humphreys's view, is aesthetically inferior. "[I]n the most fanciful pictures," he argues, poets "do not surpass in strangeness the wonders of the world beneath the sea."[98] Further, whereas Gosse, "the biographer," aligns himself with Shakespeare and is quick to defend the rigor of the association, Humphreys, opting for a less inductive approach to observation, finds the Bard of Avon wanting.

> Even the intellectual giant, Shakespeare, could not see clearly many of the minuter things of Nature. In his line upon the slow-work, for instance, vulgarly called the blind-worm, which he describes as
>
> "The eyeless, venomed worm,"
>
> are concentrated two mistakes . . . But it is useless to multiply examples of the physiological errors of great men who had not learned to *see* Nature.[99]

To correct such errors, one needs not a poet's heart but more rigorous observation, the focused attention demanded by industrial modernity. Hibberd does Humphreys one better. Whereas Gosse used poetry to set marine life into existing matrices of aesthetic appreciation, Hibberd offers the possibility of reversing the relation. The aquarium may spawn new types of poetry: "How will future poetry be affected by the revelations of the aquarium, and how far will the sober facts of scientific research influence the pictures and incidents of romance?"[100] Thanks to the aquarium, the "sober facts" of Dr. Dryasdust can now touch the poet's heart. In J. E. Taylor's book, published in 1876, there is no poetry at all. But aesthetics are not divorced from the aquarium even here. They are only shifted from a shared solidarity of artifice with the divine to shared solidarities of taste with homeowners and of denotative observational practices with amateur scientists.

The sobriety of focused attention to denotative fact was not the only virtue inculcated by the aquarium. All three writers continue to attest to its spiritual benefits. Evolution did not diminish this discourse. Seventeen years after the publication of *On the Origin of Species*, Taylor argued,

> The enormous strides which natural science has made since the publication of the "Origin of Species" have necessitated large aquaria, where the new study of embryology could be more easily followed . . . The fact that evolutionists and non-evolutionists have taken sides over zoological questions, renders it imperative that both shall observe more and theorise less. It has been found, also, that large aquaria may be rendered places of the highest amusement, as well as of the easiest and pleasantest instruction. Hence their numbers are increasing, and we doubt not the time is not far distant when all our large towns will be provided with them, so that all classes may know more of the marvelous works of God.[101]

As David Allen notes, in Britain, "[n]ot all naturalists found the facts of evolution spiritually dismaying, and those who did reacted in different ways. There was no recognized 'line' on the matter in natural history circles. If anything, because of the closeness of naturalists to the controversy's raw material, the spectrum of attitudes among them was even wider than in general."[102] Yet the aquarium was able to contain both positions, as Taylor suggests, and thus could advance science, faith, and pragmatic domestic concerns simultaneously.

Though the aquarium attested to the elevated sensibilities of its owners, it was more than a mere ornament. It could also regulate the emotional climate of the home, ensuring not just good taste but also good cheer.

> Fresh-water aquaria especially, may be arranged so as to add to the usual cheerful aspect of our English homes. The sight of the moving objects, and of the green water-plants covering and shooting above the surface of the water is undoubtedly cheering. Invalids, or people of sedentary habits, who are much confined within doors, might find comfort and enjoyment from keeping an aquarium. The antics of its little inhabitants, and the little care required to keep this miniature world in a healthy condition, will draw off their attention from many an hour of suffering or care, and unconsciously develop a love for God's creatures.[103]

The "happy family" in the tank reflected the equilibrium of sentiments in the one outside it.[104] Its effects were almost medicinal. Further, the benefits were not limited to invalids. The home aquarium could "eradicate" the temperamental dislocations endemic to urban industrial modernity by diverting the mind from "the mill-like repetition of worldly affairs [that] brings on a torpor of mind, in regard to all without the narrow circle of selfish interests and easily purchased pleasures."[105]

For Taylor and other aquarists, though, the ultimate value of the aquarium was as a form of moral pedagogy, not simply in instilling the generic glories of the creator, though this was certainly important. The aquarium was also a crucial component of training in compassionate living.

> To children, aquarium keeping may be the means of imperceptibly teaching those feelings of humanity towards the lower animals which have hitherto been too much neglected. The "hunting instinct" is strong in most boys, and a love of natural history might direct this so that it would benefit man and beast alike: not infrequently it assumes the character of unconscious cruelty, and the possession of *might* soon passes into the belief that its exertion is *right* . . . There is only too much truth in the sarcastic remark that when an Englishman is on a visit to the country and writes home to say he is enjoying himself, you may be sure he is killing something! Anything which can neutralise this tendency to cruelty, or develop a more tender regard for the lower organised of our fellow creatures, becomes a means of moral education. This, we contend, might easily be brought about by keeping an aquarium, and interesting children in the funny ways of its inhabitants.[106]

As Taylor indicates in this remarkable and rhetorically typical passage, "lower animals" in the tank can teach children how to be human/humane. The aquarium rewrites the emotional terrain of relationships to the countryside, substituting compassion for killing. Interestingly, many twentieth-century aquarium writers would abandon Taylor's concern for boys' "hunting instinct" and substitute instead worries about their effeminacy.

Taylor and his fellow naturalist aquarists saw the potential for moral education and healing cheer in the "funny ways" of aquarium residents, but there is actually far less characterization of those ways in their writings than in Gosse's book, where the various crabs sometimes seem like odd relatives. Taylor does offer his own colorful asides on the hermit crab, but this is a rare and very brief departure from his typically denotative description of species rather than individuals.[107] Hibberd casts tank residents generally and collectively as "weird residents of lonesome pools" or "fairy fishes from the mountain tarn." They are not characters so much as surrogates for native landscapes. Though he writes that "in their recognition of our attention the basis of an intimacy resembling friendship" may develop, it is clear from his next sentence that the real object of intimacy he refers to is an idealized English countryside: "Here are the finny favourites of our rills and lakes, the mosses of our own moors, the ferns that we have wandered miles to see waving under their native waterfalls; the traditional glories of our own English water scenes."[108] Fish, like mosses and ferns, remind his readers of what is "ours." They are a form of national patrimony, a way of reassuring residents of a far-flung empire that their identity is the product of organic and timeless ties to "our" land. This is accomplished through two moves: first, the metonymic slide from fish to countryside to the nation and, second, the presentation of fish as a category, not as individuals.

Perhaps the dearth of characterization in these books is due to a shift from inductive prose capturing an individual to deductive reckonings with groups. Perhaps it is due to all three writers' considerable fondness for and attention to anemones over other invertebrates or fish. Anemones' flower-like appearance and their liminality—seemingly betwixt and between plant and animal—stimulates highly visual descriptions, but their immobility and lack of faces make them far less amenable to individual depictions. The lack of characterization in these later aquarium books may also be a function of writers treating specimens as objects, whether of decor or of a dispassionate gaze well schooled in how to "*see*" Nature." In any case, Gosse's narrative strategy of inserting specimens into characters and relationships would emerge again in works by American aquarists, largely, though not exclusively, in the twentieth century.

The antics of the tank's little inhabitants contributed to the positive emotional climate of the household, but its success depended on one more element: the "little care" required to maintain it. All three writers more actively assert the ease of the hobby than Gosse does, though their descriptions of setup and maintenance duties are also august. Certainly, this was one consequence of the developing market for aquaria and the authors' own interest in serving it. All three demonstrate awareness of potential objections to the hobby based on the work involved, and all are eager to dispel them. Taylor argues that there are "few 'hobbies' which require less trouble"; whatever difficulties owners encounter reflects their ignorance of its basic principles or laziness in applying them.[109] Hibberd adds affective duties to the pragmatic and intellectual ones to be mastered. In uncharacteristically blunt terms (given his usual ornate romantic prose), he frames his instructions using an image that recurs in reckonings with fish as pets. "[W]hether filled with fresh or salt water, and no matter large or small," the tank "is a prison"; "as birds in cages require special care to compensate for their confinement," so, too, do the tank's residents.[110] He goes on to affirm that the requisite special care is "love." The conflation of fish and prison marks an ambivalent detour from the image of fish living in a world in miniature and comes perilously close to reminding readers of the fetish of the "black hole of Calcutta," albeit one redeemed by love. As discussed in chapter 4 in the present book, the conflation of the aquarium and the prison is one register of a larger modern anxiety about confinement and captivity, an anxiety that the slide from the tank to the sea is supposed to counteract. Further, the image of the tank as a domestic prison to be administered with love figures prominently in its ability to contain gender trouble in the home and beyond, as discussed in chapter 5.

The spread of aquariums, both public and private, greatly expanded models and sources of help available to the hobbyist. Large public institutions are discussed in the works of Hibberd, Humphreys, and Taylor. Public aquariums further linked home tanks to urban amusements, professionals, and the emerging market in specimens and supplies, as well as to rural "English water scenes." Perhaps the very ubiquity of public tanks in England's major cities contributed to the waning interest in the hobby later in the nineteenth century. Why should one take on the considerable work and expense of a home tank if ocean and river gardens were accessible on a grand scale and accompanied by other amusements, not always rational? Perhaps, as David Allen indicates, "enthusiasms" simply faded.[111] The naturalist Rev. J. G. Wood asserted that "the aquarium fever had run its course, never again to recur, like hundreds of similar epidemics."[112] Wood was needlessly pessimistic. The hobby had already crossed the ocean, where it persisted, not as a fever or epidemic, but as one current in the quickening flow toward a more urban, increasingly industrial economy and an emerging sense of national modernity.

CHAPTER 3

THE TOY OF THE DAY: AMERICAN AQUARIUM WRITING, 1850–1915

> It could not be expected that such a novelty would long escape the vigilant gaze of American enterprise.
>
> —HENRY BUTLER, *The Family Aquarium; or, Aqua Vivarium*

The American home aquarium predates the Civil War. News of the Ward Case and its watery relative appeared in an eclectic range of American periodicals in the early to middle 1850s, nurturing a "domestic" aquarium practice in multiple senses of the term. These writings, along with the first commercial public aquariums in Boston and New York, increased awareness sufficiently to support the publication of two books devoted to the hobby in 1858. From this point forward, aquarium writing developed along two parallel tracks to appeal to two interrelated constituencies: one internal, for dedicated hobbyists; the other external, aimed at reaching new audiences. The hope was to turn the latter into the former. Like their British counterparts, American aquarium texts proved that the hobby was remarkably adept at containing seemingly contradictory aspects of emerging modernity and remarkably useful for illuminating relationships between nature, domesticity, and mid-nineteenth-century consumer culture.

This chapter examines American aquarium writing in its first formative seventy-five years. It begins with a brief discussion of articles introducing the tank to American readers. Next, it turns to Henry Butler's *The Family Aquarium* and Arthur M. Edwards's *Life Beneath the Waters*. These two books are especially important, not because of their longevity—many later writers either did not refer to them at all or represented them inaccurately—but because they offer a rhetorical template for the hobby that persisted unexamined like a collective unconscious almost to the present. In contrast to the disparate articles that came before, Butler and Edwards both pay requisite obeisance to British forebearers but make specifically American claims for the hobby. They operate within larger currents of American art and public discourse and set the tank into a complex relationship in which the city and nature mutually construct one another. They establish the tank as (and for) the family and constitute its residents as pets. And they present the hobby as an explicitly commercial practice, at the intersection of urban entertainment, retail infrastructure, and a managerial ethos, expanding its promiscuous and seemingly irreconcilable affiliations. Thus, the tank held the howling sea, the theater, happy families, virtuoso acrobats, tenants of good repute, and prisoners, as well as the unassailable good taste of its cultivated manager/owners. This crucial period in the tank's development established the larger discursive patterns that enabled its cultural work. After the Civil War, the aquarium operated alongside increasingly professionalized American science and, still later, discourses of progressivism extolling nature study as a personal and social antidote to a range of modern ills, from effeminization to the tenement house. The aquarium accommodated each of these discourses and, in so doing, reached new consumers and consolidated communities of dedicated hobbyists. As in its British incarnation, the tank continued to demonstrate an uncanny rhetorical capaciousness during this period, one that functioned not to resolve the contradictory attributes imputed to it but to demonstrate that industrial modernity itself required these contradictions to persist unresolved.

A NEW DELIGHT

American aquarium writing in the early 1850s was literally Gossean. Many of the articles in popular magazines and journals of this period were reviews of Philip Henry Gosse's books, particularly *Rambles of a Naturalist on the Devonshire Coast* (1852) and *The Aquarium* (1854). Others quoted from these books so extensively that they might as well have been reprints. This was as true of articles written by and for Americans as of those reprinted from British sources and appearing in publications like the *Albion* and the *Eclectic Magazine of Foreign Literature* Gosse's books were so influential that they became interchangeable with actual aquariums, offering the same pleasures and decorative potential: one periodical reported, "[M]any of our readers will doubtless get the volume [*The Aquarium*] for themselves, and, independently of its other merits, they will find it a fitting ornament for the drawing-room table."[1] Reprints of British articles emphasized the glories and rigors of natural history, often as part of a larger natural theology: "What a change from the temper of two generations since, when the naturalist was looked on as a harmless enthusiast, who went 'bug hunting,' simply because he had not the spirit to follow a fox."[2] Further, aquariums, like natural history generally, inoculated intellectually and observationally inclined upper-class men against charges of weak spirits and profligate wastes of time on nonsense. They also redeemed women from frivolity, imaginative and economic irresponsibility, and just plain artlessness.

> [I]f Mr. Gosse's presages be correct, a few years more will see every clever young lady with her "aquarium"; and live sea-anemones will supplant "crochet" and Berlin wool! Happy consummation!—when women's imagination shall be content with admiring Nature's real beauties, instead of concealing their own idleness, to the injury of poor starving needle-women by creating ghastly and unartistic caricatures of them.[3]

The tank worked here presumably as these publications themselves did for their American readers: as indicators of the overall global cosmopolitanism of a cultivated subscriber who, from a position on the relative periphery, could participate in the day-to-day workings of empire, if only vicariously, by adopting its most current accessories.[4] Certainly, this was part of the hobby's appeal, even in articles written by Americans. In these texts, it was described as highly fashionable "in England and on the Continent"; the cultural authority of the Old World legitimated the spread of the tank in the New World.[5] But in ways that anticipated claims in Butler's book, the aquarium was also presented as so inevitably proto-American as to be almost an entitlement, one not to be restricted by provenance to English parlors. It was "destined" to become an American favorite as well.[6]

Despite their own heavy dependence on Gosse's prose, articles by American authors were decidedly un-Gossean in one respect. Perhaps American middle-class and upper-middle-class women were less idle, and its own poor starving seamstresses were less visible or compelling; perhaps harmless bug hunters had not yet taken on the respected scientific mantle of professional naturalists. Despite the use of Gossean tropes and literal invocations of Gosse himself, appeals to the glories of observational natural history as a productive intellectual endeavor do not generally appear in articles by American authors. Even an 1857 article in *Scientific American* with, presumably, a readership especially interested in such matters does not belabor or extensively extol the tank's scientific virtues.[7] Indeed, one article complains, "It is a lamentable fact [natural history] is in little esteem in the education of the young."[8] As discussed later in this chapter, a very different domestic construction of naturalists and natural history required early American enthusiasts, including both Butler and Edwards, to distance themselves from these discourses in their books.[9]

American writers presented the tank as entertainment more than a scientific tool and appealed explicitly to consumer values of novelty, pleasure, and ease. Thus, the tank was a "toy," an "ornament," a fashionable amusement. And it was a retail phenomenon. Gosse's seaside rambles might have made for charming reading, but busy urbanites had no need to replicate them. In Gosse's books and others like them, retailers are almost invisible afterthoughts; rigorous observation, divine providence, the rustic countryside conveying seemingly essential "Englishness," and romantic poetry worked together to position a practice birthed from science, art, artisans, and God. Early American aquaria are, in contrast, positioned between the sea and the store. The editors of the aforementioned *Scientific American* article actually commissioned it from a well-known New York dealer, Charles E. Hammett, Jr., whose "modesty forbids his intimating . . . that he is prepared to furnish tanks of superior construction."[10] One article even suggests that it was better to buy one of Hammett's already stocked aquariums than to bother buying and reading the book it was reviewing, Humphreys's *Ocean Gardens*.[11]

As the terms *toy* and *ornament* would suggest, there was some underlying confusion and even ambivalence about the relationship between the self-evident artifice of the tank and the close contact with nature it purported to enable. Though both Butler and Edwards, like their British counterparts, adopted the strategy of unproblematically slipping between the tank and the sea, many of these early articles are more restrained. They assure readers that the tank "is not unnatural," and they turn to landscapes more amenable to its then unfamiliar representational liminality: not quite the sea but not not-it either.[12] The garden was especially useful, combining natural raw materials and the agency of design in ways that were transferable to the tank. The aquarium became a flower bed, and specimens, especially the anemones, were easily intelligible as underwater "chrysanthemums," "dahlias," "daisies," and "marigolds."[13] Maintenance was thus not a set of unfamiliar practices required to domesticate an alien wilderness. It was a matter of keeping one's "subaqueous lawn close mowed."[14] In fact, some saw the tank as a literal garden, a place for potentially commercial propagation. The editor of *Horticulturalist* posited that just as the Ward Case's chief value was not its appeal to "scientific persons and to invalids" but as a transport vessel for new and rare plants, so, too, the aquarium was potentially important for "the possible discovery of new coloring matters, modes of propagation of fish, & c."[15] In other cases, instead of slipping between the tank and the sea to make the former an iteration of the latter, nature itself was redefined in terms of manufactured materials; one was not inherently more natural than the other. For example, in his account of the aquarium at the American Museum, "Uncle Hiram," the kindly sage of *Merry's Museum and Parley's Magazine* for children, defines the tank as an "artificial pond, for raising aquatic plants or animals."[16] When further pressed by his inquisitive charges as to how something as amazing as an artificial pond could be accommodated in a building, Uncle Hiram reassuringly replies with the magic of redefinition: "Why not? a pond is not necessarily very large. This fish-globe may be called a pond." This was, admittedly, not a definition widely shared. Indeed, another way to affirm the naturalism of the tank was through negation, specifically of goldfish bowls and globes, which were denounced as "ridiculous" and cruel.[17] Yet other authors wholeheartedly embraced the conceit that the tank was the sea. Some even went beyond this to suggest that the aquarium afforded the opportunity to replicate a choice of actual, specific underwater environments—the very unseen and inaccessible sites the tank was meant to introduce—as an element of decor: "[T]aste may dictate designs and scenery of the bottom of the Atlantic or those of the bed of the Hudson."[18] This was literally a way to bring the world into the parlor by casting its particulars as a set of decorating options. In addition, the complementarity of respiration between plants and animals established the tank as natural in its most basic operations, ones shared with the sea itself.

These early articles also present ambivalences about tank residents, who do not yet emerge as fully pets as in Butler's and particularly Edwards's books. In some cases, they are allowed the possibility of individuality, which was itself seen as "somewhat amusing."[19] In others, their animality seems both excessive and highly sensational. The black goby is a "ferocious little cannibal," a "robber," and a "murderer."[20] Others are "pranksters" or "unruly offenders."[21] The reality of predation in the tank is so disturbing that Uncle Hiram has to reassure little "Elsie," using the opportunity to forge a reciprocal relation routed through Benjamin Franklin: fish kill each other as men do, and men eat other animals as fish do.

> Well, dear Elsie, it is so the world over. Man is not the only destroyer. Dr. Franklin, you know, once thought it wrong to eat any kind of animal food. But when he found, as a fish was opened in his presence, that he had been

feeding on another fish, he concluded that that was according to nature, and so gave up both his theory and his practice.[22]

The aquarium afforded viewers the opportunity to put these finny criminals "up in a witness box and make them give account of themselves."[23] But it was also a home and therefore an opportunity to spy on residents' "private lives" while they were "making love, and rearing their young families."[24] Their interdependence and close quarters made them ideal surrogates for imagining all sorts of domestic arrangements, as discussed in chapters 4 and 5 of the present book and as evidenced by one author's observation that "they agree better than the heroes and heroines of Mr. Hawthorne's *Blithedale Romance.*"[25] As these publications suggest, the queer equivocality of fish was present from the very beginning of the American hobby. They were both very exotic and very familiar.

The aquarium introduced in these publications also offered early enthusiasts a world-making agency positioned betwixt and between "life, art, and mechanics."[26] American authors extended this option to "ladies," not to replace their ugly and destructive alibis for idleness, but because an aquarium provided an outlet for displaying "skill, delicacy," and good taste at a reasonable price; a suitable vessel could be purchased at any glass shop. Aquarium keeping was not demanding, but it was not mindless either. It demonstrated effort, but no special talents were required. One did not have to be a Gosse; the aquarium was equally manageable for those with flair and an aqueous green thumb as for those who were simply consistent and dogged: "if there is natural aptitude in the individual, he will soon make a progress; even if there is no taste, he will have filled up some vacant hours in a healthful occupation at a trifling cost."[27] The requisite skills were the same ones needed to maintain a well-run home: "patient perseverance, regular attention, and, above all, perfect cleanliness."[28] Finally, the aquarium was both a mark of aspirational consumption, like fine art or a professionally managed garden, and democratic, like a potted plant. As such, it had the potential to enlighten and amuse across a wide range of demographic boundaries.

> The wealthy are availing themselves of the aquarium to add to the graces of their homes. Why should not the poor man have the enjoyment too! We look forward to the day when every village school shall be furnished with it for the instruction of youth in natural history, and when it will be a common ornament in the parlor window of the mechanic in town, and the farmer in the

country. The family geraniums may have to clear away to make room for it. It may even compete with the flower-stand and the bird-cage; but it will compete honorably, and pay for the little space it occupies in an exhibition at once novel, pleasing, and wonderful.[29]

These early articles offered Americans a basic vocabulary and a set of visual tropes through which the aquarium could be understood. It was a toy, an ornament, a garden, a self-sustaining replica of the sea or an actual iteration of it. It had some scientific potential but offered even more as entertainment. Above all, its characterization in consumerist terms as a novelty and a pleasure, rather than the Gossean fusion of field observation and a poet's heart, established it as something desirable to buy and use, whether to learn about one's "finny neighbors," while away leisure time in a "healthful" pursuit, or demonstrate one's good taste. It was a retailer's baby, and science's only maybe, and that was a plus. Aquariums entered American parlors in part out of a desire to affiliate with transatlantic elites. They endured as opportunities to create water worlds for self-gratification. In their book-length treatments, Butler and Edwards consolidated all of these elements, giving them a kind of narrative coherence that took readers through the processes of setting up and stocking home tanks, then giving them more detailed scripts for what and how to see inside. These scripts did little to resolve the already contradictory aspects of the tank as both a toy and the sea, a home and a predator-filled wilderness. In fact, they added even more.

BENEATH THE WATERS, IN THE PARLOR: THE FIRST AMERICAN AQUARIUM BOOKS

Early American aquarium writers owed much to their British predecessors, including textual strategies like the rhetorical slippage between the tank and the sea and the image of the tank as container of national landscapes, with all their attendant anxieties and longings. The most important debt, though, was genealogical. British aquarists established the aquarium's Western pedigree and created its cultural capital; its popularity "over there" was evidence of its intrinsic worthiness as a pursuit "over here." This transatlantic affirmation surfaces, albeit in different ways, in the two earliest U.S. aquarium books, Henry Butler's *The Family Aquarium; or, Aqua Vivarium: A "New Pleasure" for the Domestic Circle* and Arthur M. Edwards's *Life Beneath the Waters; or, The Aquarium in America*, both published in 1858. Edwards states that the aquarium was "so popular in England [that] a parlor is hardly considered furnished without one"; he issues a special appeal to American women readers, "whom I hope soon to see taking as much delight in the fitting up and management of these beautiful parlor ornaments as their sisters on the other side of the Atlantic."[30] It's hard not to sense an undercurrent of provincial inferiority in Edwards's appeal to England's well-appointed parlors and the resourceful women who furnish and manage them. Likewise, these same parlors and leisured women underscore the upper-class and upper-middle-class constituency of the hobby, one presumably transferable to Americans seeking to project their own status as well-off and *au courant*. Butler handles this differently. First, he explicitly links the hobby's Old World and class bona fides to American homes as well: the tank was "almost a necessary luxury in every well-appointed household, both of Europe and America."[31] Then he acknowledges the hobby's debt to the British craze, one repaid with interest by American ingenuity.

> An Aquarium-mania seized upon the public mind. The Aquarium was on everybody's lip. Morning, noon, and night, it was nothing but the Aquarium . . . It could not be expected that such a novelty would long escape the vigilant gaze of American enterprise.[32]

In Butler's view, American vigilance disciplines an unruly and seemingly unproductive British mania; the enterprising American spirit quickly recognizes the aquarium's larger aesthetic, spiritual, and, above all, commercial potential.

In Butler's narrative, it is P. T. Barnum who embodies the "vigilant gaze of American enterprise." His Grand Aquaria at the American Museum "has no competitor whatever in the western hemisphere, and is, beyond dispute, the largest, most costly, most complete, and most elegant production of the kind on the face of the globe."[33] There was no need to envy or even replicate the tank in the well-appointed European parlor, when American know-how perfected the form, far exceeded what was heretofore possible over there, and was ready to share its expertise for a price. There was no need to replicate Gossean construction and collecting labors, when the American Museum itself manufactured and sold fully fitted and stocked tanks: "[W]hat is there to prevent the Aquaria from becoming the universal embellishment of the private parlor or the sittingroom, the conservatory or the garden, as well as the place of public entertainment."[34] Butler was not a disinterested reporter/naturalist. He was an aquarist, manager, and nominal co-owner of Barnum's American Museum and, with James A. Cutting, proprietor of the

Boston Aquarial and Zoological Gardens, which was itself purchased by Barnum in 1862.[35] His affiliation with the American Museum is stated explicitly as a source of his credibility; the museum itself is advertised in the back matter of the book.

Butler's (and Barnum's) entrepreneurial bent marks an even more decisive departure from British strategies of aquarium writing than in earlier American articles. In British texts, P. H. Gosse's pervasive influence meant that the tank entered the well-appointed parlor initially as a form of rational and moral pedagogy. It certainly required means and leisure, but these were obscured by larger appeals to a highly aestheticized natural theology. Further, Gosse's peripatetic collecting and his conflation of the aquarium with rustic landscapes and their weathered inhabitants linked the tank explicitly to fantasies of unalienated labor as intrinsic to its production. The naturalist aquarist was both a modern field scientist/technician and a premodern artisan. Gosse wrote the spiritual script for the hobby, parts of which were borrowed by both Butler and Edwards, but it was not primarily a commercial one. Shirley Hibberd transformed the tank into a consumer good by framing it as an object of decor, a rustic adornment, but even here crass commercialism was masked by appeals to an essential, preindustrial English countryside always already part of the individual and national home. In contrast, from one of its first publications, the American aquarium was an explicitly urban commercial affair, linked to spectacle and the acquisition and display of status.

In this respect, the tank was perfectly positioned to benefit from as well as minister to the emerging industrial economy. As business historian Stanley Buder observes, between 1840 and 1860, when the aforementioned articles and Butler's and Edwards's books were published, "the percentage of the workforce engaged in agriculture declined from 63 to 53 percent, and Americans employed in manufacturing rose from 14 to 19."[36] Though the percentage increase in manufacturing-related employment was only 5 percent, it nevertheless represented "the cutting edge of occupational change." By 1860, urbanization had also accelerated to the extent that "nearly one out of every ten Americans resided in cities and almost one out of 10 lived in the 'great' cities of 100,000 . . . or more."[37] The urban middle class experienced both the dislocations accompanying these changes and a "domestic revolution" that brought greater access to cheaper consumer goods and the retail opportunities that provided them.[38] If Butler constructed the American Museum as the ideal retailer to satisfy future aquarists' desires, Edwards constructed the ideal consumer, one who was likely to avail himself of just such a source: "'a citizen of credit and renown' in New York."[39] The aquarium may have been a beautiful and enlightening form of moral pedagogy, at one with the quintessentially American vision of landscape, but as Butler and Barnum in particular demonstrate, it was also a business.

Nature in/and the City

Natural history offered valuable textual templates to British aquarium writers. This was not so in America. Despite occasional nods to established naturalists, Edwards and Butler did not have a comparable genre to draw on. This was due in large measure to the very different objects and politics of natural history in the United States in the mid-nineteenth century. American naturalists shared two core convictions of their British counterparts: the commitment to progress through documentation and display of the natural world and the belief that nature was a moral teacher, illuminating the munificence of a divine creator.[40] Yet their operations were circumscribed by regionalism, which was itself exacerbated by poor transportation and communication infrastructure; hampered by lack of institutional support; constrained by bias toward knowledge that was obviously useful, particularly botany; and caricatured as the pedantic, slightly ridiculous devolution from the adventures of earlier explorer heroes.[41]

James Fenimore Cooper's Obediah Bat, "Battius," the doctor/naturalist character in *The Prairie*, exemplified this view.

> Is the power to give life to inanimate matter the gift of man? I would it were! You should see a Historia Naturalis Americana, that would put the sneering imitators of the French-man De Buffon, to shame! A great improvement might be made in the formation of all quadrupeds; especially those in which velocity is a virtue. Two of the inferior limbs should be on the principle of the lever; wheels perhaps as they are now formed; though I have not yet determined whether the improvement might be better applied to anterior or posterior members, inasmuch as I am yet to learn whether dragging or shoving requires the greatest muscular exertion.[42]

As his plan to surpass Buffon by redesigning mules with levers or wheels demonstrates, Battius was a cautionary figure whose catalog of faults included delusions of personal glory on an international stage, a potentially blasphemous hubris, and a basic ignorance of the pragmatics of manual labor born, presumably, of never having done any. But these were not the naturalist's only potential character flaws. Soullessness was another, as Emerson observes in "Blight."

> But these young scholars, who invade our hills,
> Bold as the engineer who fells the wood,
> And traveling often in the cut he makes,
> Love not the flower they pluck, and know it not,
> And all their botany is Latin names.[43]

In this view, the naturalist is just as ignorant and hubristic as Battius. He prefers "names" to "things," arcane formulations to essence. Like his partner, the engineer who reduces things even further to their instrumentality, the naturalist neither knows nor loves nature and is therefore thoroughly alienated from its "truths." Further, the engineer and the naturalist are both destroyers, eradicators of nature, if not literally by the ax then discursively, even spiritually, reducing its potential restorative powers to "Latin names."

With these antimodels haunting the popular imagination, American aquarium writers, heirs to their British antecedents' views of the tank as an enlightening, ennobling union of art and science, had to make their case while navigating between the Scylla of impotent pomposity and the Charybdis of spiritual aridity. They did so by explicitly distancing themselves from the strategies of citational solidarity deployed by their British counterparts. As discussed in chapter 2 in the present book, Gosse, Hibberd, and Humphreys used citational solidarity with both scientists and poets to frame the aquarium as the logical outcome of a conversation between art, pedagogy, and observational rigor. Butler, however, quickly disavows this rhetorical move in the very first sentence of his preface: "I conceive it but just to say that, in the following little work, I have indulged in no attempt at scholarly display or literary effect."[44] This disavowal was more tactical than truthful. As the excerpts cited later in the present chapter amply demonstrate, Butler's book deploys both scholarly and literary effects and sometimes extraordinary uses of the latter. Butler's false modesty is symptomatic of his fear, realistic or not, that elevated prose in either register would alienate his audience. Edwards, who includes even less poetry in his book than Butler, acknowledges up front the ambivalent popular image of naturalists, stating that the wonders of the aquarium "attract and rivet the attention not only of scientific men, but of those who, until lately, have looked upon the votaries of science as forming a useless class."[45]

In both books, readers are explicitly inoculated against potential aversions to science. Butler reassures his readers that they were not expected to undertake "expensive or erudite experiments."[46] They could enjoy the tank as relatively passive spectators and not impinge on their well-earned leisure by turning it into a demand for intellectual productivity. Edwards, who suggests that collecting can be outsourced to "any of the country urchins for a few cents," encourages rigorous observation of specimens while offering reassurance through a rhetorical question: "Now tell me, reader, is the Aquarium such a deeply scientific affair . . . ?"[47] Early British tanks were *in* the marketplace but, rhetorically in the works of Gosse, Hibberd, and Humphreys, not *of* it. The American tank is presented explicitly as an artifact of the marketplace, including the ability to delegate any associated manual labor. The British aquarium became modern through its distance from the marketplace, a distance established in its romantic celebration of highly personal interactions with nature. The American aquarium became modern through its early embrace of market pragmatics that could offer owners both nature and respite from much of the intellectual and physical work required to reproduce it.

Natural history was a problematic rhetorical partner for early aquarists, but "nature" was not. Butler, Edwards, and the aquarium itself were ideally positioned to enter two felicitous rhetorical currents in American nature discourse. The first of these can be labeled "transcendental" broadly construed. I am not suggesting that either author was a transcendentalist. As Philip F. Gura indicates, the movement itself was fluid; its various flows entered popular discourse and imagery to become, later in the century, "part of the nation's popular mythology."[48] Two transcendental elements were especially supportive of the aquarium and contributed to characterizations that, in their broad contours, paralleled those in British books: the views that nature was a worthy source of spiritual and aesthetic guidance and that increasing pressures of urbanization and a market economy cut citizens off— geographically and psychically—from nature's healing potential. The aquarium offered a way to convert the by-products of that economy (disposable income, leisure time, high-status consumables) to access that very spiritual-medicinal potential; urban residents could buy nature to heal themselves. In addition to these transcendentalist elements, the American aquarium would also benefit from the larger use of nature to forge national solidarity. As Miller, Novak, Stowe, and others indicate, landscape had a profoundly affirming and consolidating function in the emerging national imaginary: "to ground national unity in the ministry of nature" and forge "a bond that transcends politics."[49] This was particularly important in the 1850s, as battles over slavery increased sectional rhetorics on all sides. The actual meaning of "nature" was itself in flux during this period. It was both the howling wilderness and a domesticated, pastoral ideal. The aquarium was able to capitalize on both definitions. It could offer an "aquatic flower show" and reject connections to the "quiet flower garden."[50] It did so using the discursive mutability and the conceptual cohesiveness of water.

Water was an especially powerful image in larger rhetorics of landscape, as a vehicle for personal healing and an image of national solidarity; it stood in for nature in its most sublime, useful, and restorative capacities. Its force was centripetal, channeling diverse flows of national life and visions of nature into a conceptual union rooted in shared geography. Water—from the Atlantic to the Pacific—defined the seemingly natural limits of the nation's manifest destiny. Water—first the great rivers, then the Erie Canal—made it navigable, increasing its commercial potential. And water, particularly the bucolic pond, soothed psyches enervated or consumed in the process of harnessing that potential. Thoreau, most famously, captures this harmonizing force in *Walden;* the pond is "blue at one time and green at another, even from the same point of view. Lying between the earth and the heavens, it partakes of the color of both."[51] In partaking of the colors of both heaven and earth, water symbolically unites them, suturing them together through color, and it offers this same possibility to the nation. In Oliver Wendell Holmes's poem "Brother Jonathan's Lament for Sister Caroline," written shortly after South Carolina's secession, water both defines and heals the Union.

> Our union is river, lake, ocean, and sky,
> Man breaks not the medal, when God cuts the die!
> Though darkened with sulphur, though cloven with steel,
> The blue arch will brighten, the waters will heal![52]

Water reflects the Union's intrinsic wholeness: the Union *is* river, lake, ocean, and sky. The visual connection between sea and sky further ensures that the healing flow includes the celestial as well as the material and so will repair both rhetorical and spiritual ruptures; as it is above, so it will be below, and vice versa. Water's constitutive force and harmonizing flow were stronger than the steel of division.

Butler and Edwards benefited from these transcendental and nationalist currents in American art and public discourse. These two currents further enabled the same slippage between the tank and the sea that characterized

British aquarium writing of the period, allowing both authors to capitalize on the symbolic potency of water as a restorative unifier on national and interpersonal scales. This productive slippage, paradoxically, became even more powerful when it was acknowledged as incomplete, as in a remarkable passage by Butler.

> Who loves not the billowy ocean, with its wild, weird-like, melancholy wail, and its light, dancing foam-tops, shaking, as they go, their "loosening silver in the sun"? Who loves not the glistening river, and the wide, solemn lake, in whose glorious face, all day, but heaven itself seems mirrored, and at night, whose bosom "throbs with stars like pulses"? Yet here, in the Aquarium, we have their "counterfeit presentment," faithfully drawn by nature herself, in her most artistic moments, and finished up to life with all her tintings of romance. Here we may sit face to face with reality, in
>
> > "Silent speech—a converse that affords
> > Surer communion"
>
> than the babbling of the schools, or the dim picturing even of eloquent books. Here we may still learn something in the simplest act to expand our narrow circle of useful knowledge. Here we may, indeed, find "sermons in the brooks," for every pebble in the Aquarium is a text, and every leaflet on it a living accordance for study and consultation. A new world of wisdom will be opened for our private instruction.[53]

The home aquarium can contain the wailing ocean, the glistening river, the solemn lake, and, as in Thoreau and Holmes, the heavens it reflects. It is both counterfeit and faithful, artifice and reality, because it is finished up to life by nature itself. The aquarist is not the maker; nature is. The tank educates without the pedantry of books and schools; these are reduced to tedious babble, in contrast to the potentially restorative babble of a running brook.[54] Every pebble in the tank trumps arid Latin names in its ability to edify. Finally, the aquarium offers not merely a manageable observational tool but a whole world of wisdom, because it contains the whole world of water: ocean, river, and lake. In the same relation that characterizes British texts, water worlds and the wisdom gleaned from them are made more whole—because observable and accessible—by their aquarium counterfeits. So expansive is Butler's view that even the rain is illuminated by gazing into the tank, which discursively swells to contain all of aqueous nature. Just as important, the aquarium offers "private" tutorials and "silent . . . converse," benefits especially welcome in the context of an urban marketplace filled with its own babble. This reference to privacy points to a crucial component of the tank's appeal as a commodity as well as to an additional indicator of its urban context (which I discuss later in this section). Butler's framing of the tank as interpersonal and "face to face" reflects an emerging urban view of nature as a private good in a double sense: aesthetically, morally, and pedagogically felicitous and an individual/family consumable within the confines of home.

Edwards, more restrained than Butler, establishes this same slippage through his repeated references to the tank as a "miniature ocean" or "miniature pond," affirming its constructedness while asserting its claim to the real. It is not a counterfeit of these natural forms; it is the same, only smaller. This relation is further reinforced by a shared core principle. The dynamic, organic unity of plant and animal life in the tank is governed by the "fixed and unchangeable" laws that regulate all underwater life. Thus, the tank does not just house specimens as isolated objects, like butterflies pinned to a board or a shell lost in a cabinet of random curiosities. That would be a soulless naturalist's mistake and a violation of the fundamental unity of nature, as Emerson indicates in "Each and All."

> The delicate shells lay on the shore;
> The bubbles of the latest wave
> Fresh pearls to their enamel gave,
> And the bellowing of the savage sea
> Greeted their safe escape to me.
> I wiped away the weeds and foam,
> I fetched my sea-born treasures home;
> But the poor, unsightly, noisome things
> Had left their beauty on the shore
> With the sun and the sand and the wild uproar.[55]

On the contrary, the aquarium was "each and all," specimen and context, the actual living mollusks and weeds and, according to aquarium books, the wild uproar as well. Its organic governing principle points to a conceptual wholeness: a miniature ocean at one with the larger sea, inextricably linked by their shared and immutable submission to natural law. According to Edwards, because of this shared foundation, even the "miniature" would one day drop away, and the tank would even more fully become the sea. It would house its own tides and tempests, as well as sharks, whales, "and, perhaps, the veritable sea-serpent itself."[56]

The tank offered "surer communion" in multiple senses. Much more than just clearer communication about nature, it provided a visual relationship with both the dynamic harmony of mutually sustaining respiration inside its walls and larger natural forces of aquatic interconnection—river, lake, ocean—outside them. At a time of economic change and dislocation, patchwork loyalties (to city, state, or region), and particularly escalating sectarian tensions, this domestic technology of unification was especially resonant. Nature's larger harmonies were respite from and antidote to personal and collective anxieties; the waters might heal the home on many levels.

Yet the strategy was not without profound ambivalences. Angela Miller argues that "America's vaunted love of nature proved to be a contradictory amalgam of desire and memory better served by images than by the thing itself, a dream of possession and a sense of loss made more poignant by the recognition of something itself never fully experienced."[57] Appeals to a majestic and unifying nature during this period were themselves often rhetorical sleights of hand that became increasingly difficult to execute smoothly. For example, slips between nature and artifice could be disconcertingly reversible; nature might "authorize" an image, but that image might reciprocally conjure its wild object, which could then offer more wilderness than bargained for. Aquarium discourse shared this same rhetorical situation. For all of the lyrical invocations of the wailing ocean, actual and symbolic seas and rivers were forces of primal anarchy as well as images of national cohesion and personal restoration. They could potentially swamp interpretation, flood aesthetics (and one's parlor floor), even capsize the ship of state. Fortunately, slippage between the tank and the sea was reassuringly, not threateningly, reversible. The sea made the tank larger, but the tank also made the sea smaller, containable, and consumable. In this context, Edwards's repeated use of the adjective *miniature* to modify "ocean" or "pond" established both verisimilitude and manageability, an ideal modern approach to engage nature prophylactically from an unassailable position of strength as creator and consumer.

A second internal contradiction in the rhetoric of the unifying landscape operated synecdochally. One part of the putatively harmonizing landscape came to stand in for the whole region, section, or country, erasing its partiality in the process.[58] The aquarium has a particularly rich relationship to synecdoche; as noted earlier, its own partiality comes to stand in for the aqueous whole through textual slippage between the tank and the sea. Yet these same texts show that the tank's conceptual promiscuity (and visual promiscuity, which I discussed in chapter 1) operates alongside and sometimes even swamps synecdoche. Ocean, lake, river, and pond—the aquarium may contain just a part of each, but it can also, as Butler indicates in the preceding quote, contain all of them. This textual promiscuity with aquascapes became quite chaste when it came to terrestrial ones, and synecdoche became more obvious and potent. For example, the British texts discussed in chapter 2 offered a variant of this strategy by framing the aquarium's "Englishness" as a function of its connection to the rustic countryside. The urban context of the practice, including those "homes of taste" adorned with tanks, were virtually erased. The "American aquariums" of Butler and Edwards also operated synecdochally in the sense that neither book was the expansive attempt to capture and describe the national oceans, lakes, rivers, and ponds it claimed to be. Their partiality, though, worked differently from that of their British counterparts, especially in the treatment of urban and rural contexts.

It is important to note that both authors claim to introduce readers to the "American" aquarium; Edwards has this in his subtitle. "American," though, is here more of a consolidating fiction of an "us" constituted against the European "them" who bequeathed the practice to U.S. readers. Butler claims multiple levels of comprehensiveness for his volume: "It is a complete adaptation to American peculiarities of every species of useful information upon the subject to be met with in the elaborate volumes of European authority."[59] His book does indeed cast the wider geographic net of the two; it includes many references to New England and passing mentions of western states. These are rarer in *Life Beneath the Waters*, which features lengthy descriptions of New York City and its environs. Certainly, some of this bias was a simple adaptation to logistical realities. The Northeast offered easiest proximity to the hobby's requisite amalgam of freshwater and saltwater environments, transportation infrastructure, intellectual and financial capital, and retailers, as well as the spectacular urban entertainments that trained the public in how and what to see in the tank. But this partiality also reflected larger biases in both the natural history and the landscape painting of the period. As Philip J. Pauly observed of botanist Asa Gray's similar synecdochal strategies, "Gray, like the nationalistic landscape painters Asher Durand and Frederick Church, imagined a continental empire that was essentially an extension of their native Empire State. From Gray's biogeographic perspective, the South in particular was an afterthought."[60]

The domestic aquarium was an urban phenomenon from its earliest inception. Though valuable contributions would come from Cincinnati and San Francisco, the cities of the Northeast first provided the formative conditions: the psychic and physical breaches with nature it was supposed to repair and the resources and technology to do so. British aquarium writers of the time sought to repair "estrangement from ruralities" by erasing the city or imaging it as a celestial democracy of coral. Butler and Edwards, the latter in particular, embraced it. Perhaps this hearty embrace was a function of a commercial imperative, recognition of a market that could profitably view aquascapes as leisure because it didn't have to wrest a living from them. Whatever the cause, rustic fishing villages and weathered fishermen do not appear in these pages as in Gosse's. In Butler's book, references to rural collecting rambles are limited and generic; there is one mention for freshwater specimens and two for the marine.[61] The latter are more august enterprises, and Butler advises, "In the first place, provide yourself with an attendant," who can carry the tools and execute much of the manual labor.[62] Or, if readers prefer, "it may be frankly confessed" that they can dispense with the collecting trip altogether and simply buy the entire setup: "Your personal sacrifice of time and attention is wholly superfluous except as a matter of entertainment."[63] Actual Gossean immersion in nature may be edifying, but it is unnecessary when that edification could be construed and consumed as entertainments, purchased like other contemporary diversions. Time and attention were precious commodities in the urban marketplace; buying the tank and its residents was simple, efficient, and eliminated the need to sacrifice either one.[64] Butler's emphasis on retail solutions marks the further consolidation of the intimate relationship between the hobby and its supporting businesses.

Gosse and his British contemporaries portrayed the tank as an extension of the countryside, its pleasures, and its quintessential Englishness. Retailers are afterthoughts. For Butler, Edwards, and later aquarium writers, urban retailers are more viable partners in the practice than the rustic sites in which specimens actually lived. Butler's appeal to the efficiency of retail acquisition and his suggestion for hiring an "attendant," if needed, to do the dirty work of collecting reflect a managerial ethos echoed in Edwards's suggestion to hire a few "urchins" of the human variety for collecting labors. Coupled with slippage between the tank and the sea, it underscores the view of the aquarist as an able administrator of his own private world. As such, he is in sole control of its resources. This position must have been doubly reassuring to urban middle-class men in an emerging industrial economy, poised between the enormous wealth of owners above them and the seeming swarms of laborers below them. The aquarium offered the heartening possibility of active agency, safely outside the circle of the sometimes predatory interdependence contained in the tank, rather than part of it. The aquarist was not just one more fish in the metropolitan sea.

Edwards offers much lengthier accounts of collecting, but these also reveal a very different relationship between the aquarium and the local landscape than in Gosse's rural rambles. Gosse's rustic reveries were punctuated by rare "machine in the garden" moments: intrusions of industrial modernity that seemingly disrupt but actually ultimately construct "nature" as a site of respite from its rigors. In *Life Beneath the Waters*, relationships between technology and nature are not only direct and unproblematic; they are positively enabling.[65] As in Butler, this is a much more textually and operationally efficient vision of collecting than recorded in Gosse and his contemporaries; there are no digressions extolling the venerable beauty of the countryside, no conflation of aquatic and rural landscapes. On the contrary, the collector is so indigenous to city environs that instructions on appropriate dress are required, because "we are not going to promenade on Broadway."[66] The urban landscape is the primary frame of reference, and immersion in nature is not assumed to be more natural than walking in the city.

In Edwards's account of collecting from the shore of the East River, written in the second person, so the reader is enfolded into the scene as in a textual panorama, the six-cent "city car" delivers the aquarist to his specimens, who are themselves virtuoso theater performers; the antics of the pipefish, for example, exceed the acrobatics of M. Seigrist at Drury Lane.[67] Edwards celebrates neither preindustrial vistas or labor nor an essential "Americanness" of rural landscapes. Rising sectional tensions made the former a fraught subject, and larger monuments of wilderness supplanted the rural pastoral in public discourse. Instead, he argues that the tank and its now optional collecting operations repair not the alienation of living in the city but the "ennui" caused by leaving it, as "when you are staying in the country, and missing the flag-stones of the city, confessing yourself 'bored' with nothing to do, and feeling the want of balls, parties, theatres, and operas."[68] British aquarium advocates used the home aquarium to bring nature to the city and imagine a coralline utopia. American aquarists brought the city to nature in order to view it, in part, as a theater that rendered it intelligible and desirable. Transcendent landscapes might civilize the industrial metropolis, even the nation, but these aquarium texts reveal that the underlying pragmatics of managing "nature" (as opposed to conquering the "frontier") as a private good required the city to set the wild into its own idiom of theaters, operas, and acrobats.[69] The aquarium profited from this seemingly contradictory blend of transcendental appeals and urban social infrastructure.

Happy Families, Tasteful Homes

Another set of civilizing matrices organized the tank and contributed to later characterizations of the hobby as good pedagogy and useful container of gender anxieties: the family. Here, the tank is domestic in multiple senses of the term. It is not just American, not just an accessory for the home. It is itself a home, a way of creating and managing family life on multiple scales. Butler's book is particularly and explicitly concerned with family, as indicated in both his title and subtitle. The pleasures of a tank in the home are, for Butler, a way of privatizing and replicating those shared in public venues, particularly, of course, the American Museum. Just as middle-class attendees were assured of that institution's propriety and unlimited potential for moral uplift, so Butler's readers were continually reminded that the tank was an "innocent," "chaste," and "pure" pleasure, "neat and elegant."[70] Butler, even more than Edwards, relied on the theater and other potentially dubious public entertainments to render the tank intelligible. If he was going to situate the equivalent of a *bal masqué* or "the brilliant tumult of a carnival" in the home as a domestic entertainment, it was imperative that the aquatic participants have "good character, suitable habits, and prepossessing wardrobe."[71] In short, the residents inside the tank and the little water world as a whole must conform to and even model modern middle-class norms of comportment.

Butler adopted a two-pronged strategy for marketing the tank as a family amusement. Residents were, after all, "tenants" requiring "honest testimony" to vouch for them, and what could be more persuasive than a reference from the Almighty?[72] In Butler's view, the aquarium offers a carnival with the spiritual force of a religious service: "And if we hymn the Creator's praise in admiring the perfection of His works, is not the study of the Aquarium an honest, an ennobling devotion?"[73] In this, Butler uses the same pious pedagogical potential identified by Gosse, leavening it with Barnum's rhetoric of spectacle. Yet the second element of his strategy departs from Gosse's approach to his specimens, who remained just that: interesting protocharacters. For Butler, in addition to its spiritual utility as an ennobling devotion, the tank's moral potential was established through the "natural happy family" inside it, a mirror, presumably, of the happy family outside that would be made even happier by tank ownership.[74]

Both Butler and Barnum drew on the "happy family" motif, a domestic(ated) variant of the visual trope of the "peaceable kingdom." Best known through Edward Hicks's series of paintings with the same title, executed between 1820 and his death in 1849, the peaceable kingdom works illustrated scenes of (un)natural harmony, especially the biblical prophesy of Isaiah 11:6.[75] Wildly incompatible predators and prey share the frame. These works were highly allegorical, imagining "nature's" peaceable kingdom shoring up political harmony between multiple constituencies in the new nation—another example of forging national solidarity through spiritually infused and representationally contained wilderness. Like the landscape paintings discussed earlier, these images held a troubling potential for reversibility. In its 1829–30 iteration, the predators seem uncannily wide-eyed, either profoundly surprised at finding themselves in such an odd situation or, to modern eyes, hypnotized or drugged so as to stay put. In the 1846–48 painting, the wolf could have its front paws crossed in repose, or it could be poised to leap onto the calf it has fixed in its gaze. By midcentury, increasing tensions over slavery meant that a "happy family" was more conceptually manageable than a peaceable kingdom.[76] The American Museum housed a number of "Happy Families."[77] Butler, too, exhibited a "Happy Family" at the Boston Aquarial and Zoological Gardens.[78] On one level, the entire attraction was a kind of happy family, a giddy yet harmonious amalgam of species united under one roof—regional, national, and global diversity bound together, sometimes in the same tank.[79] The fiction of an inherently benign domesticity was crucial here, and it, too, was rhetorically reversible, though reassuringly so in this case. The family, presumed to be an essential and "natural" unit of harmony, regulated the more primitive drives of the marketplace and bestowed its disciplinarity onto curious collections of natural enemies. Displaying such collections, in turn, demonstrated that civility, routed through the trope of the family, was, if not "natural," at least manageable in public as well as private life.

Butler's construction of the tank as a "natural 'Happy Family'" informed pragmatics of construction and maintenance and generated a new way of characterizing residents, not only as wildlife or pleasant and instructive diversions, but as iterations of modern urbanites with the same middle-class needs and desires as their owners. They were, after all, "at home."[80] "Home," for tank residents as for their owners, was simultaneously public and private, an opportunity for display and a place of respite. Thus, even in this "new theatre of life,"

> the fish, like other creatures more human, like to retire at times to the privacy of their own apartments. There, amid the rockwork, weeds and flowers, whether engaged in their toilette with a view to coquetry and a conquest, or whether seeking to enjoy a siesta in the sultry noon, too much light makes them restless and unhappy.[81]

The challenge for the aquarist was to manage these little tenants so that desirable elements of their natural potential were maximized and the undesirable ones eliminated.

> It is our wish to render them plump and hearty; to bestow on them all the beauty of shape and brilliancy of coloring of which they are susceptible. To effect this, they must be made happy and contented; they must be so well fed as to make life an enjoyment to them; their wants and necessities must be so anticipated as to rob them of all disposition to forage upon each other, or thin themselves in their endeavors to hunt up a banquet.[82]

In their well-regulated wildness, fish resembled children or the urban marketplace. In both cases, a dearth of "nature" depleted vitality, like "biscuit or bread" dampened fishes' colors. Yet too much nature of the "foraging" and "hunting up" variety threatened to rupture the social bond, exposing it as always already fragile. This threat was a particularly undesirable one to install in the parlor; indeed, in the emerging conventional wisdom of separate spheres in an industrial economy, this was a problem both the aquarium and the parlor were supposed to solve.

Butler adopts a "Goldilocks" approach to specimens, offering just the right amount of wildness and narrativizing it through recognizable types. Gosse's specimens dispatched one another with regularity; his narrative dispassion offered a quasi-scientific and objectively sensational look at how the other (aquatic) half lives, a look that could easily encompass urban toughs and imperial subjects that were also framed as wild and uncivilized. Butler, instead, offers reassurance that nature can be ordered through kindly interpersonal relations and understood through familiar figures: the gallant gentleman, the warrior, the clown, and the bully. Thus, residents can be hand-fed and offer "grateful recognition" to their owners while others deploy their "weapons" in martial competitions.[83] Not that this minimizes specimens' potential for conjuring the exotic or the sensational. Consider, for example, the pugnacious stickleback, "his own landlord," who is "somewhat of a Mormon in the polygamous principle of his domestic economy, it must be confessed; but this failing aside, he is a model husband."[84] Butler's aquarium offers the paired potentials for communion with pets and titillation at their strange domestic arrangements, rhetorically fungible to include human others. His discussion of plant propagation offers another potentially titillating glimpse into the intimacies of nature, one, like the stickleback's polygamy, that further marks the presumed tank owner as urban middle to upper class and therefore removed from the routine husbandry essential to agricultural productivity. Propagation was here a matter of leisured voyeurism, not one of livelihood.

While Butler clearly frames the aquarium as a family pursuit, Edwards's implied reader, appeals to women aside, appears to be a well-heeled boulevardier, at home with the theater, the opera, and strolls down Broadway. Taken together, the two books point to the evolving market for the hobby, one that characterizes it to the present day: families using it as pet or pedagogical tool and men within or outside of the circle of family who were interested in a new technology for mastering nature and the relationships that can result. Edwards characterizes specimens more specifically as "pets" who are, literally, pettable.[85] He also has more reservations about families inside and outside the tank. "Happy families" inside must be constructed with care lest their animality break out. Those outside must be watched as rigorously as the tank itself to guard against other eruptions of instinctive behavior: "youngsters [who] are rather too fond of finding out 'what's inside the drum that makes the noise'" jeopardize the residents' well-being.[86] Like Butler, Edwards is managerial in his orientation to the tank, advising readers to keep naturalists' diaries to hone their observational skills and develop quasi-professional expertise, both skills that enhance opportunities for productive modern work as well as leisure. Yet he remains especially interested in fish as pets and in the equally explicit world-making dimensions of the hobby. If the tank is "a world in miniature, . . . nature on a small scale removed to our parlor," it is not fully satisfying to simply manage from a distance.[87] Instead, one hopes for a certain mutuality and shared feeling or, at least, shared recognition. The ennui of the countryside was not the only one reparable through intimacies forged by the aquarium; interpersonal isolation could also be remedied.

> One of my tame minnows is quite a pet, and has received the appellation of "Minny;" he has a peculiar way of staring me in the face through the side of

his glass-prison, especially when he considers feeding time has come. He will, also, allow me to stroke him gently, but sometimes he resents such familiarity, by turning suddenly around and giving me an astonished look, as if wondering at my impudence.[88]

There is a certain ambivalence in this passage alongside Edwards's clear delight in his relationship with Minny. This suggests that in addition to the restorative world of ocean, river, lake, and pond brought home to the parlor, the tank offers another, very modern one: a glass prison where power relations can affect veneers or even genuine moments of tenderness, recognition, and resistance. The tank could conjure both the office and its antidote.

Both Butler and Edwards offered retail solutions to problems of tank construction yet also proposed these labors as edifying, even therapeutic ways of uniting one's head with one's hands. Gossean work was optional; taking it on was a virtue, building an artisanal self-satisfaction and intellectual and technical capital. But putting together the box and procuring the water were only the basics. If, as Butler and Edwards established, the tank was a kind of theater, the aquarist was a set decorator. In this respect, the tank functioned less like the sea and more like the parlor—as a stage for the domestic self, an opportunity to assert one's taste and, by extension, the means to express it. Thomas Schlereth and Katherine Grier describe the quasi-public parlors of the midcentury urban middle class as "exhibit spaces," "family museums," and "stage[s] for special domestic events," "comfortable theatres" where, perhaps, compositions like Jacob Becker's "Aquarium Waltz" could serve as or accompany the entertainment.[89] As a stage itself onstage, aquarium decor could not be left to chance.

Butler is particularly concerned with establishing the proper aesthetics in the tank. Verisimilitude is his guiding principle, and failure to adhere to it is a mark of ignorance, if not vulgarity, whatever the class position of the owner.

> To render the "fitting up" picturesque is one thing—to give it *vraisemblance* is another. Branches of coral might look pretty enough in a freshwater tank, but they would be as ludicrously out of place as warming-pans in the tropics, or grapes growing in Nova Zembla. And yet we have been shocked with just such *niaiseries* in the Aquaria of gentlemen who profess no small share of *goût* and refinement. Eschew it, good reader, we advise you, altogether! Arrange your rockwork in its details, artificially as you please, but let its *tout ensemble* be quiet and natural.

In this passage, Butler's and, by extension, the aquarium's cultivated bona fides are performatively stabilized through the use of French, allusions to faraway places with which the learned reader is presumably familiar, and others of unimpeachably—if, in this case, mistakenly—refined taste. The task of the aquarist, like that of the urban nouveau riche, is to affect abstemious elegance and, above all, not to overdo: "Do not overload with filagree embellishment or exaggeration." Here, verisimilitude is not an aesthetics of accuracy. The aquarist can pile on as much artifice as possible, but that artifice must look, at the same time, restrained and plausible, so as to "display . . . much ingenuity and correct taste."[90] The unruly promiscuity of the tank—its potential to contain ocean, river, lake, and pond, to say nothing of theaters, operas, and carnivals—had to be managed with Protestant aesthetic prudence. The rigors of scientific observation might be one way to accomplish this, but as noted earlier, it was a suspect strategy. Instead, a domestic discipline of "correct taste" ensured that nature in the parlor reinforced the natural cultivation of its owner.

Of course, none of this was natural at all, as Edwards's description of the tank as a "glass-prison" attests, and this went far beyond the obvious artifice of a parlor pond. "Correct" taste was an acquired taste in multiple senses: learned through class aspiration and reinforcement, bought and paid for. Further, displays in/of natural correct taste marked distance from those urban others who were framed as entirely too natural and therefore putatively threatening: working-class, black, and immigrant others. Nature in the home and in the tank was not to be primitive, voracious, and scary; the metropolis held enough of that. Yet restraint, in fact, enabled indulgence. Butler cautioned against excessive ornament because it limited the "valuable space" available for fish. In this, Butler recalls Gosse's counsel of moderation as opposed to his own wildly overstocked tanks, as well as the pleasures shared by contemporary reefers discussed in the conclusion to the present book. Abstemious decoration also spoke to the aquarist's intellectual cultivation, made more refined through an understanding of the principles of respiration supporting the tank. This combination ensured correct taste while avoiding cruelty. In Edwards's book, the French offered a cautionary, not an aspirational, tale, in this case involving the very personification of *La volupté du goût:* "It is said that Madame Pompadour, to her other sins and weaknesses, added that of setting this fashion of studying the, really, tortures of poor fish." Using aquarists' favorite imperial fetish, he goes on to compare these "tortures" to "the dreadful tale of the sufferings of hundreds of persons, shut up at night in a prison called 'the black hole,' at Calcutta, to which there were but two openings."⁹¹ Proper aquarium management not only demonstrates the owner's aesthetic and intellectual refinement; it demonstrates his kindness.

Taken together, Butler's and Edwards's books provide the first overall narrative arc for the American hobby, one that progresses from a new wonder of august Old World provenance, through the pragmatics—retail and otherwise—of acquiring and managing it, to the details of the little lives within that make it even more wonderful. It set the tank in relation to the outdoors and urban amusements like the American Museum, which, in turn, lent their own narrative strategies to tank viewers. On a larger scale, this arc fit smoothly into contemporary art and public discourse that positioned nature as personal and social balm, a way to mend even the split between heaven and earth. Yet if narrative generally offers imaginary resolution of real contradictions, these books do the reverse. In a pattern that repeats over decades of aquaria, they reveal still more contradictions even as they try to contain them. The tank was the sea, but the sea was also a tank—not too wild, just wild enough. It was a theater, a family, and a prison; intellectually respectable but not scientific; entertaining and a riot of reproduction but innocent and chaste. It repaired isolation from nature by using nature to ease separation from the city. And it framed that nature as an explicitly commercial and retail phenomenon: a private good. As such, it was both a thing and a virtue, a way of bringing a happy family to a well-appointed parlor that reciprocally constructed its owner as an efficient manager and a cultivated soul.

American aquarium publications did not fuel a craze like the one in Britain, but the tank did enjoy a steady popularity, even during the Civil War. One example demonstrates how the hobby functioned within the intimate routines of the middle-class household during this transitional period: the diary of Horatio Nelson Taft (1806–88), an examiner for the U.S. Patent Office, who diligently recorded his efforts to maintain his aquarium alongside his observations of events in Washington, D.C., during the Civil War.

> Rain again most of the day. Many of the troops are in an exposed condition and suffering for shelter. The NJ troops came in early this morning, over 3000 in the rain and could find no shelter for sometime. Drilling of RI soldiers in the Halls of the Pat office all day. Everything outside looks wet and gloomy. Did not go to the Ave this evening, but got a plate of glass and put in the Aquarium, one was broken. (May 6, 1861)

> After church and after dinner went out with the three boys to the "Monument" pond after aquatic plants and fish for the Aquarium. On our return met four Regts. of N.Y. troops on their way over the River. (November 28, 1861)

> The news looks favorable for further Victories to be heard of before long. The whole country is jubilant over the post. I have not been out tonight. After dinner I cleaned out the Aquarium and put in fresh water. The Eel has been burrowed in the sand all winter, have not seen him before in three months, he is very active. (February 19, 1862)[92]

Taft's entries reveal that his aquarium is a noteworthy feature of his private life, one folded into the fabric of the household, but his juxtapositions of the logistics of military mobilization and the banal details of tank management are especially striking. They speak to the tank as both a soothing diversion and a technology reinforcing personal control, if only of a little glass box of life, over against the enormity of unfolding events.

The image of over three thousand soldiers, shelterless in the rain, "wet and gloomy," is answered by Taft's repair of a personal water world, one aspect of private home maintenance. Both Taft and the Union soldiers are restoring shattered homes, but individual agency, enabled by middle-class professional privilege, (re)assures the former of easier and quicker success. Likewise, victories over which the whole country is jubilant find their domestic parallel in the return of the active eel, once seemingly vanished—a reassurance that losses and setbacks, both large and small, might be temporary. The rituals of war—drilling indoors—are echoed in the domestic ones that include the tank: church, dinner, collecting. Both are affairs between men—the trip to the pond with the three boys as much as the troops on the move. In this, Taft's diary is prescient; increasingly from this point on, though general interest and women's publications continued to position the tank as a desirable feminine pursuit, the American hobby is constructed as a province primarily for men and boys. In these brief, prosaic entries, the tank and the war mutually construct one another in a kind of palimpsest. We look through nature as an uncontrollable and dismal impediment ("Rain again most of the day") to see it also as a manageable little room requiring modest repairs, and we look through the artifice of indoor drills to that of the glass parlor pond with the result that both the tank and the war are simultaneously natural and not. Further undergirding this relation is the interpenetration of the nation and the home: both are domestic; putatively natural yet also, to some extent, constructed; repairable and demanding maintenance. Taft's entries offer early bracing insights into the tank's unfolding ability to contain domestic anxieties and, later, foreign others and to serve as a surrogate for nature, nation, and home, often all at the same time.

After the war, the aquarium's fortunes rose along with those of its northern enthusiasts in the professional/managerial class. The next fifty years saw the hobby incorporate two additional and interrelated cultural currents: a progressive ethos and an increasing focus on science as an obvious public good. This was something of a move back to the future, a return to tropes of much earlier British aquarium writing, particularly when it came to the tank's potential as a moral and/because observational tool. Butler's and Edwards's books hovered at the margins of these emerging discourses like textual ghosts. The narrative arc and tropes they offered the hobby—the tank's relationship to nature, the sea, the city, and the store; its ability to signal inner and outer cultivation; its establishment of fish as pets both very wild and very tame(able)—were absorbed into the general discourse, even if their specifics were often forgotten or misconstrued. Many of these new books asserted their own status as the primary and foundational American accounts; an emerging national confidence and commitment to science is reflected in this need to repeatedly reclaim the tank from its European antecedents and, perhaps, from the humbug of Barnum's museum as well.[93]

Discourses of domestic progressivism and scientific advance operated both separately and together as the hobby expanded in two directions. The first was toward a broader market that was especially amenable to arguments that more knowledge, more nature, and more imagination would ensure personal and social uplift. The aquarium was ideally positioned to build on genteel, liberal Protestant values of progress, education, and the link between mastery of self and of world; it did so in part by framing nature as a technology enabling modern viewers to engage the primitive past through the discipline and rigorous observational skills that secured their prosperous futures. The second direction was not broad but deep: an appeal to aquarium aficionados as specialists. The end of the nineteenth century and the beginning of the twentieth saw the birth of the first aquarium journals and societies and the increasing presentation of the hobby as a space apart—from the workplace, even if it required many of the same skills, and from the feminized private sphere, even if it demanded its own form of housekeeping. Hobbyists established new boundaries for aquaria, boundaries predicated on the pairing of science as an ideal end and amateurism as the ideal means, a do-it-yourself entrée into the increasingly respectable and professionalized study of nature. The modern aquarium that emerged during this period was both an example of "the promise of American life" and a way to showcase that promise in miniature at home—a reminder and a reinforcement. Both the tank and the promise required intelligence, discipline, education (even/especially if self-taught), and planning. Aquarium publications showed the way.

THE PROGRESSIVE AQUARIUM

Almost immediately after the Civil War and increasingly around the turn of the century, the aquarium was presented as more than a toy, an entertainment, or an element of decor. It was also described as an important observational and pedagogical tool, a way for amateurs to advance the previously neglected "study of Aquatic Natural History" because it made it visible and accessible.[94] In short, the American home aquarium became much more consistently "scientific." In this, it benefited from an increased federal commitment to natural science, marine science in particular. "Culturing fish," understanding their habitats and behavior, became an aspect of national development and spawned institutions including the U.S. Commission of Fish and Fisheries (1871), research facilities like the one at Wood's Hole in Massachusetts (1882), and public aquariums in major cities. Fish entered public discourse in new ways, very different from the "happy families" inside Barnum's museum or Butler's book or even from preindustrial approaches to aquatic production. These new institutions recalibrated the overall relationship between nature and consumers. It was still, of course, consumable, but scientific bureaucracies, with their new vocabularies and protocols of viewing, made it both more familiar and less so—more familiar because it could, at least theoretically, be viewed comprehensively; less familiar because, in this new regime, specimens fostered learning first, enjoyment second (if at all). Spectators had to be reeducated in how to see them through this new conceptual lens. In this new paradigm, science was a tool of progress, and nature was an economic resource, reflecting what Philip J. Pauly has called a "biotechnological view" wherein organisms were explicitly cast as raw materials, manipulatable for pragmatic commercial ends, to be mastered intellectually as well as logistically.[95]

The biotechnological view operated alongside the romantic, transcendental one of nature as soul-sustaining antidote to increasing industrialization. As in its British incarnations decades earlier, the aquarium benefited from both, readily adopting a rhetoric of science while never fully abandoning its earlier scripts that included allegorical agents ("happy families"), performers ("acrobats"), and primitives ("cannibals" and "criminals"). This uniquely potent combination enhanced its appeal to the general public. The preface to Collier and Hoop's 1866 book *The American Parlor Aquarium* offers an early example of this curious rhetorical amalgam. Its heady mix of multiple idioms merits quoting at length.

> Our Ichthyology, or history of fishes, is as yet in its infancy, no popular work has yet appeared, descriptive of them, so that we have groped our way as it were in the dark. Few species only are generally known, the few familiar ones being confined to those varieties whose capture is a sport, or a remunerative employment.
>
> But the Aquarium opened a path to a field of science hitherto trod by few of "Nature's votaries"; it enkindled within the minds of many a desire to become better acquainted with the "life that moves beneath the waters." The gems of Nature's handiwork enshrined beneath the sparkling wave, and hidden deep in its cavernous depths were almost wholly unexplored, their beauties, habits and peculiar formation were to us a sealed book. Little did we dream that at the depth of hundreds of fathoms, the waters teemed with life, that *Anemones* or Animal Flowers existed there rivaling in brilliancy of coloring, or delicacy of marking any of Nature's terrestrial gems. It had always been considered a fact that below a certain depth, animal life ceased to exist; to contravene this we have the testimony of the scientific officers who conclusively established the fact of animal and vegetable life existing at even the greatest depths. Our friend Capt. J. H. Mortimer of Savannah, an enthusiast in marine mollusca, has dredged many curiosities to science, some of which were from the greatest depths he was enabled to fathom.[96]

In this excerpt, the aquarium accommodates all comers, old and new: transcendental "Nature's votaries," "scientific officers," and the amateur "enthusiast." It is an indispensable aid to ichthyology and a window on nature's treasure room. It opens a previously closed book and, as such, is a modern technology of the mind, not work of the hands like a sport or a job. It adds facts, but just as important, it reveals hidden beauties and peculiarities. It was intellectual and sensational. The sensational gradually receded into the background as contributions to science took pride of place, but it never disappeared.

As discussed shortly, committed hobbyists were especially eager to exploit the new "scientific potential" of the tank, but this addition to its rhetorical repertoire also appealed to educators and middle-class to upper-middle-class parents, whose increasing concern about the damaging effects of industrial modernity paralleled the increasing rise of early childhood education as an academic specialty. "Nature study" generally and the aquarium in particular were ideally positioned to benefit, particularly now that the tank was an element of science and not just a miniature version of the theater. Clifton Hodge's *Nature Study and Life* (1903) is especially useful for understanding the tank's cultural work as a children's pedagogical tool and the elite's ideological one in the new century. For Hodge, "[n]ature study is the sheet anchor of elementary education, all the more necessary as modern life tends to drift away from nature into artificialities of every sort," and "[n]o piece of nature-study apparatus is capable of serving so many and so various uses as an aquarium."[97] In a new iteration of the productive slippage between the tank and the pond, the obvious artifice of the tank did not concern him; other "artificialities" of modern life were more pressing.

The potential ravages of early twentieth-century modernity were clearly set forth in the book's introduction by Hodge's Clark University colleague G. Stanley Hall, by then the country's leading authority on child and adolescent education and the emerging discipline of psychology. Hall's introduction details the modern ills that nature study is meant to cure, and he sees this as part of an explicitly national program of development. This is as complex and contradictory a set of imperatives as any for the aquarium and is particularly helpful for explaining why such internal contradictions in aquaria persist over decades. Nature and particularly the aquarium were potent and useful because they normalized and domesticated precisely these contradictions, as well as the race, class, and gender privilege that required them, as examined in the following chapters of the present book. All of these contradictions were rendered seamlessly "natural" because, in Hodge's book and others like it, they were legitimated first by God and then by biology. Thus, for Hall, nature study offered both "an increasing unity between the school and the home" and an antidote to "institutionalizing influences." Nature appeals to the "poetic, sentimental, and religious" impulses, but the child's own nature can be turned to its study by other appeals, this time to "the practical, unsentimental, and utilitarian side." Further, nature countered "overconfinement" and the related danger of "effeminization."[98] The implied ideal child/product of this curriculum was well schooled in the "essential and salient points" yet never fully institutionalized, in touch with a "deep instinctive love" of nature and able to transmute it into a utilitarian and unsentimental mastery, and, finally, able to harness nature as a way of resisting the effeminizing effects of modern bureaucracies.[99] In short, he was a little proto–Teddy Roosevelt.

For Hodges as for Hall, the larger aim was to shore up an imperiled Anglo-Saxon masculinity, increasingly estranged from inner and outer wildness, by using a nature that was more scientific than science itself. This iteration of nature reactivated the individual hero's "ownership" of a personal discovery so characteristic of early naturalist explorers. Nature, particularly its savagery, was both good pedagogy for the boy and good medicine for the man. Even in a little glass box, it could counteract the debilitating effects of a changed workplace that now emphasized "labor of the brain over that of the muscles."[100] Those most in danger of succumbing to a seemingly all-pervasive neurasthenia were precisely the core constituency of the aquarium hobby: middle- and upper-class Anglo-European men whose putatively "highly evolved bodies" had been physically and psychically weakened by the increased speed of production enabled by steam power and the telegraph.[101] Consistent with Hall's suspicion of overconfinement in the sedentary and potentially emasculating classroom, the emphasis on nature "study" was less conventionally "studious" than one might expect. There was no requirement to amass a "bewildering array of facts and technicalities."[102] Instead, the student found an individual voice by doing "original research" on his own in nature's laboratory. This relationship mirrored another putatively natural one included in Hodge's book: man's "dominion" over the earth as biblical and historical fact. The child's and the hobbyist's utilitarian views of nature as a personal lab outside of bureaucratized discourse were modern examples of primitive man first domesticating beasts, ontogeny recapitulating phylogeny.

Of course, some class positions were more naturally predisposed to benefit from this new version of dominion through nature study than others. In another deeply class-inflected version of outer cultivation literally underlining an inner one, Hodge includes two plates, one of "A Home" (his figure 4) and, immediately after, one of "A Tenement House" (his figure 5). The former is lushly landscaped with trees and decorative shrubs. The latter is stark by comparison, offering only a weedy lawn. Hodge quickly explicates the allegorical potential and the social stakes of these two images for the future of the nation.

> Sociological studies suggest that city life wears itself out or goes to decay after three or four generations, unless rejuvenated by fresh blood from the country. Thus these deeper relations to nature are not only ancient and fun-

damental but are also immanent and persistent. While I should not advocate teaching trades in the public school, although we are wont to say that every boy should learn one, this study is so much deeper down in the warp and woof of life, so immediately supports the whole structure of civilized social organization, and is so closely associated in the creation and maintenance of the home, as distinguished from the camp on the one side and the tenement-house barracks on the other, that it stands on quite a different footing.[103]

Here, the full scope of this project of nature study, including the aquarium as its prime technology, is revealed by the full scope of modern specialized wisdom. Both the natural and the social sciences, sociology and biology, together reinforce the timeless wisdom of renewal by the "country," presumably one free of Native Americans, struggling farmers, and rural poverty. The city was a literal source of civic decay. This was innate and inevitable; an attentive reader might note that for most American metropolitan areas, the requisite "three or four generations" had already passed. Proximate causes for decay went unmentioned but were easy to identify at the turn of the century, in the unruly and demographically undesirable concentrations of working-class and immigrant labor, including blacks moving north to escape the Jim Crow South. With the presence of such "undesirables" as one symptom of degeneracy, it was important to emphasize that nature study was not itself a trade, not a form of labor; Hodge's readers would not be expected to dirty their hands to make a living from it. On the contrary, it was "deeper," innate and fundamental, though presumably it still needed to be taught. Nature creates civilization; both are epitomized in the well-appointed, seemingly suburban home. The tenement house is another iteration of the primitive camp discussed earlier in Hodge's book as a relic of earlier relations to plants and animals; it is separated only by time, making its own primitiveness all the more reprehensible and unnatural for being modern. Throughout the book, nature circulates in an endless tautology: creating civilization, then curing it because it was its opposite; innate but not to all; part of science but without the technicalities; effort but not labor. In his elevation of the tank as the premier technology for nature study, Hodge seemed largely unaware of the irony that the tank itself could be and sometimes was viewed as both a home and a tenement house.[104]

Hodge's book and others like it were pitched toward policy makers, teachers, and middle-class and upper-middle-class parents eager to secure or preserve their class privilege. These works were part of a much larger current advancing education, particularly in the sciences, as crucial to national and individual development. This view received particularly forceful and concise articulation in Herbert Croly's *The Promise of American Life* (1909). Croly argued, "It is by education that the American is trained for such democracy as he possesses, and it is by better education that he proposes to better his democracy."[105] Further, science held pride of place because it was self-evidently true and, as such, offered an unimpeachable and authoritative standard exempt from the vagaries of other social processes.

> In the Hall of Science, exhibitors do not get their work hung upon the line because it tickles the public taste, or because it is "uplifting," or because the jury is kindly and wishes to give the exhibitors a chance to earn a little second-rate reputation. The same standard is applied to everybody and the jury is incorruptible. The exhibit is nothing if not true, or by way of becoming or being recognized as true.[106]

The aquarium and larger discourses of "nature" as respite from institutions and technicalities, as in Hodge's book, always had a slippery relationship to "science," but appeals to self-evident truth made that relationship seem unproblematic; the tank was, after all, precisely the window through which some of these "truths" could be viewed.

By the time of Croly's book, the aquarium was so fully assimilated into the vocabulary of science and so completely fit the vision of an obviously true exhibit that slippage between the sea and the tank was no longer a purely literary matter. It was both a scientific tool and the environment that the tool revealed, something parents could provide to their children to better themselves as they bettered their democracy. In this new progressive incarnation, there was little need to establish the value the aquarium added to the upwardly mobile household. It was more urgent for aquarium writers to establish what it wouldn't take away: specifically, time from the lady of the house, who would, presumably, have to manage it as part of her domestic routine. Thus, Eugene Smith, editor of one of the first hobbyists' journals, begins his book for general readers by asserting that the tank actually demanded less than other popular and conventional home accoutrements and, on the purely pragmatic level, offered more benefits.

> An aquarium in a living-room or parlor is more easily maintained than houseplants or birds.
> It requires less attention, bears changes of temperature more readily, and if neglected for a time does not suffer. A bird must have constant care,

houseplants need regular watering, security from cold drafts in winter from without, and from the dry heat within doors, and must be guarded against destructive insects . . .

There is no danger to health, no damp soil to produce exhalations; on the contrary, it is well known that all clean water absorbs gases and acts as a purifier of the air. The evaporation of the water, especially during the winter season, will also give much needed moisture to the air of our usually overheated rooms. In these ways, the aquarium becomes of sanitary value in our homes.[107]

Rev. Gregory Bateman makes a similar case on his first page: "Few things are more interesting and less troublesome than a well cared-for aquarium. It makes no litter to annoy the tidy housewife, and no noise to distract the student. Besides, if properly arranged, it is very ornamental."[108] So fully scientized was the home aquarium that less than sixty years after early writers described it as an ornament and a toy, a new generation could affirm those characterizations to refute them.

Another prevailing notion is, that the small aquarium is simply a plaything serving to amuse the children or to afford an outlet for the energies of an occasional crank and that its only other excuse for existence is found in the fact that the green plants and goldfishes make a bright spot in the room. Even if this were all, who will deny that its existence is justified? But excuses are not necessary. Let it serve for one as a plaything or a bright spot in the room, but for the person who cares to study life in the aquarium—and there is a constantly increasing number—the aquarium becomes a piece of scientific apparatus from which can be learned many of Nature's laws that regulate the outside world.[109]

In earlier books, the aquarium was framed as a home theater, but its newfound scientific utility meant that mothers should "put less money into theater tickets" and more into the home tank, the better to produce young men who could become disciplined and diligent "experts" and no less manly for it: "no sportsman following his quarry was ever more eager" than the fifteen-year-old boy pursuing his ambitions in the hobby.[110] Indeed, the manliness of the enterprise was repeatedly established by comparing it with sports; the pleasures of collecting, for example, were "greater than that of the sportsman who goes out to kill."[111] The aquarium offered the right balance of manly endeavor to produce the right kind of modern middle-class man: it resisted effeminization, on the one hand, and brutality, on the other, and so was an ideal technology for shaping boys who were not yet in the middle class, especially in groups. Louisa May Alcott's Plumfield School in *Little Men* had an aquarium; so did New York City's "vacation schools," designed to transform "street Arabs" who, in one account, were barely recognizable as human into "law abiding citizens."[112] In this capacity, observing and maintaining the tank was a form of what Shannon Jackson has called "civic housekeeping," a strategy of social reform routed through the image of the orderly home.[113] In an updated version of the old "happy family," the tank could showcase both nature's wisdom and/as the well-run household; the little beasts inside could help civilize the young savages outside.

Progressive science gave middle-class parents new motivation to buy an aquarium, but it also gave confirmed hobbyists new permission to enjoy one. In an Americanization of its earlier appeal as a British rational amusement, the tank was a tool for learning and, therefore, self-improvement. Hobbyists vigorously defended the tank as a tool of science, even jettisoning one of the domestic fixtures that initially normalized tank viewing: the collection.

> A true aquarist is a scientist; an investigator delving in the veiled mysteries of a many-sided Nature. The mere possession of a collection of fish means no more than a collection of postage stamps, not as much, unless the owner can demonstrate that they mean more to him than a mere piece of bric-a-brac in his parlor.

For truly serious practitioners, it was time to put away childish things—including, by the 1910s, the muscular nature regime of Hodge and Hall—in favor of facts: "Tramping about the country netting fish is, no doubt, a very healthy occupation, but it does not rise to the dignity of science, or merit regard as an intellectual pursuit."[114] Presumably, the objects of this intellectual pursuit could be efficiently purchased at a local retailer, but this was unproblematic because science, not nature rambles, separated the men from the boys and, of course, from the women and their own parlor bric-a-brac.

Certainly, there were other reasons to buy an aquarium and devote time and funds to it: status, pleasure in creative production, refuge in personal time apart from the demands of work and family, beauty, and reverie. But learning, especially if scientific, was an unimpeachable and manly alibi for all of them. Consider, as one example, the personal narrative that opens J. H. Wagner's pamphlet *The Home Aquarium or "House Pond"* (1915), part of publisher August Roth's Hobby Series; it is emblematic of justifications for investing in aquariums, past and present.

I have often been asked why I make a hobby of the aquarium and its occupants, how I can content myself puddling in my aquaria and spending hours, days and months in studying the effects of certain elements on fishes . . . My invariable answer is: "Simply an innate desire to learn something new."

Smithson said: "Every man is a valuable member of society, who, by his observations, researches and experiments procures knowledge for men."

It is not only a pleasure, but is an education, to create an aquarium or terrarium in the miniature, with its grottoes, rookery effects; its beautifully colored and tinted aquatic plants, its freakish-shaped and colored fish, . . . batrachia and mollusks, and to observe their mode of living, their curious antics, and, when properly treated, their instinctive appreciation of the attention accorded them by their more fortunately created superiors.[115]

This excerpt is remarkable for its blend of rhetorical appeals. The tank itself is an education, not just a tool. In another example of citational solidarity, the potential of the tank and of the aquarist is attested to by none other than James Smithson, whose bequest funded the Smithsonian Institution. Smithson's quote establishes both the individual and social significance of the hobby, which was especially useful if one was to spend "hours, days and months" on it. It is important to add here that, in contrast to Butler, this view of the hobby was not necessarily a family affair: "DON'T allow more than one person to take care of the aquarium."[116] It was a highly individual practice. Yet shades of Butler are still visible; his "shining temples and pebbled grottoes" find their echo in new grottoes and rookery effects, though the latter could now be as easily purchased as imagined.[117] After Smithson's august endorsement of learning through observation comes the potentially voyeuristic pleasure: the sensual description of the tank's beauty and the titillating prospect of watching its freakish inhabitants, a combination of the garden and the carnival midway. Education was an undeniable virtue, but the inhabitants' curious doings were as much of a draw as the pugnacious black goby's "cannibalism" sixty years before. The tank could still be a theater, one, moreover, where the actors were both grateful and a continual affirmation of the superiority of the spectator. It was a vessel for learning but also an island of agency, a way for aquarists, still typically men, to become benevolent and beloved dictators over their water worlds and their time, with Smithson assuring nagging wives and incredulous uninitiates that this was both personally and collectively worthwhile.

This new rhetorical affiliation with science could be shared by dedicated hobbyists through an increasing number of specialty journals and societies.

The sociality within the tank birthed one outside it, as aquarists joined together to share information and specimens and carve out even more free time for the making of self and world. The short-lived *New York Aquarium Journal* was the first of its kind; its inaugural issue appeared in October 1876. Hugo Mulertt's journal, the *Aquarium,* was initially published in Cincinnati in 1878, suspended publication, then revived in 1892 when relocated to Brooklyn, where it operated through 1897. Eugene Smith served as the first editor of yet another journal entitled the *Aquarium,* this one published in Philadelphia beginning in 1912, under the joint auspices of the New York, Brooklyn, Chicago, and Philadelphia aquarium societies.[118] It folded in 1914. *Aquatic Life* was also published in Philadelphia, beginning in 1915 and somewhat erratically thereafter until 1942. On the west coast, the *Aquarium Journal* was founded in 1928 and published by the San Francisco Aquarium Society for thirty-six years.[119] Societies were organized in many major U.S. cities, often in cooperation with the local public aquarium. A review of rosters of officers for five such societies in 1912 showed that all were men; meetings were once or twice a month (generally exempting summers) and in the evenings.[120] Initiation fees were typically one dollar, and annual dues were from one to two dollars. J. H. Wagner, author of *The Home Aquarium or "House Pond"* (quoted earlier), was the secretary of the aquarium society of Washington, D.C. Journals and societies continually advocated for each other, again under the rubric of continuing education rather than simple fellowship. The obligation to "keep . . . in touch with advancement in the study of aquaria and aquarium organisms" required a certain intellectual cosmopolitanism, with particular attention to Germany and Japan; hobbyists were encouraged to subscribe to foreign journals as a part of their commitment to greater learning.[121] They were also boosters for the national hobby, noting with evident satisfaction, for example, that England, home of the aquarium craze, did not yet have a single aquarium society—another triumph of Butler's "American enterprise" over an unruly Old World mania.[122]

Journals did more than present the comparatively advanced state of the American hobby; they were particularly boosterish, even a bit defensive, on the subject of native fish, in an early example of a "Buy American" appeal. Increasingly in the mid-1910s, hobbyists were attracted to "tropicals" from Asia and South America, with many species coming from Germany after earlier domestication there. Perhaps the very developments in domestic aquatic biology that buoyed the hobby contributed to a sense that native species were simply banal, too close to conventional sport and commercial fish to be of interest now that more exotic specimens were available. "Our neglect of the native species is much to be deplored," argued one editorial.[123] To choose exotic species at the expense of native ones was a waste of time and money, smacked of the derided "stamp collector" mentality, and, most of all, failed science, which would benefit from close work *by* rigorous amateurs *for* rigorous amateurs.

> A deal of information [*sic*] is still to be learned regarding the life histories of many species. Much that is known is hidden away in abstruse scientific works not accessible to the average man, even were he able to comprehend the obscure terms used in the usual technical descriptions. Good work can be done placing this information in popular language in the hands of aquarists.[124]

World War I required aquarists to make virtue out of necessity, as imported specimens were meeting the same sad fate as other transatlantic passengers; perhaps, in a reversal of normal aquarium relations, fish were "gliding gracefully over the remains—silent guardians of those who devoted so much thought and attention to them in life."[125] The war thus offered an opportunity for aquarists to become an "Agassiz, Audubon, [Barton] Evermann, [David Starr] Jordan," or other famous naturalist aquarist by systematically investigating native specimens.[126]

Yet there was an unmistakable tension underlying hobbyists' appeals to science. While aquarists might aspire to be an Agassiz in their local society (if not nationally), they were also often as suspicious of Latin names as Emerson and as disdainful of technicalities as Hall and Hodge. Societies and journals offered a secure middle place to assert their own expertise. In some cases, this meant challenging aquarium professionals on their own terms. Mulertt, for example, declared in the pages of his journal that the proposed plan for the New York Aquarium "will not work!" Noting further that it "had been constructed on the wrong principles from the very start," despite praises from New York newspapers, he praised a proposed redesign.[127] Given his own august history as an aquarium pioneer, he would almost certainly carry more credibility with fellow aquarists than either the New York professionals or the general press.[128] Journals were just as likely to ridicule the ignorance of the uninitiated as to call out the shortcomings of the professionals. In "How I Became a Fish Fan," "Frank Humor" describes his seduction by the hobby after beholding his friend "Mr. X's" tank. "Frank" is clearly, deeply, and naively infatuated with this "piece of fairyland"; heretofore his only contact with fish had been at the market, where "their peculiar odor made me sick." "Frank" has already established himself as thoroughly ignorant of the most basic elements of nature, having tried unsuccessfully to "collect" a skunk that was both "pretty" and "seemed so tame," to predictable results. His stupidity thus documented, he is clearly meant to be the butt of a joke about fish value when he figures that if he can buy a dead one for fifteen cents, the little fish he so admires in Mr. X's tank must be worth the same. It is not: "That fish is worth $100!"[129] Within the secure confines of the journal, the apparent idiocy of spending an exorbitant sum on a little—and inedible—fish is productively reversed. The true idiot is the uncomprehending everyman who is incapable of recognizing real value, one so unschooled in science that he thinks "spawn" is a disease of plants. In aquarium society meetings and in the pages of aquarium journals, an expansive definition and rhetorical utility of science offered even more than leisure time, good company, and the mastery of self and world. It offered a way for middle-class and upper-middle-class men to talk back to professionals and peons alike from the security of hard-won personal expertise and the backing of a cohesive community with shared passion.

What science giveth, science taketh away. J. H. Collier viewed the home aquarium as a boon to ichthyology, but a hundred years later, ichthyologists had other ideas. In an indication of the increasingly widening gulf between amateur aquarists and professional scientists, the San Francisco–based *Aquarium Journal* was renamed *Ichthyologica, the Aquarium Journal* in January 1966. With this change came the accompanying requisite shift in cultures from a "general aquarium magazine" of considerable idiosyncrasy and charm to that of "a rigorously scientific publication." This new culture differed so markedly from its predecessor that even the persistence of the word *aquarium* in the new title was presumed to require justification. It was offered, first and foremost, by an appeal to economics ("the aquarium fish trade is beginning to rival that of the food-fish industries") and, second, as a nod to individual biographies (many ichthyologists apparently first learned about exotic fish from their home tanks), not by invoking the intrinsic scientific worthiness of the hobby itself.[130] Science made the tank important by casting it as more than a toy. Perhaps it was not surprising that, as professional science increasingly saw the hobby as its "other," aquarium devotees responded in a tone that recalled P. H. Gosse's dismissal of "Dr. Dryasdust," as in Donald A. Simpson's essay "How Do They Get That Way?"

> Fish people, I'm talking about . . . I do not mean the ichthyologist, he studied for it, worked hard too, but he gets his kicks out of a dead anemic look-

ing specimen in a jar of formalin. The biologist? No. He studied, too, but his joy is in experimentation and the number of scientific papers he can churn out in a lifetime. The hobbyist? Closer, but he is not necessarily a fish person, though he *might* be . . .

The guy (or gal) that I am talking about is the 100 percent dyed-in-the-wool fish guy that would rather work with live fish than anything else in the world; that would rather catch them, keep them happy, study them and above all enjoy them. The guy that is willing to walk miles to put a fish he no longer wants back where he caught it.[131]

As with Edwards's "Minny" and Butler's "happy family," enjoyment "above all" is key to the aquarium for true "fish people." Study is important—the tank is not, once again, a toy—but it is not paramount. Fish people have an emotional investment in keeping fish happy and are willing to walk miles to prove that their charges are not disposable. Professional scientists' pleasures, by comparison, are almost perverse, a necrophiliac attachment to the anemic dead or a mechanistic churning out of product using them as mere raw materials. Simpson's paean to fish people, with their wacky inefficient many-mile walks and goofy openheartedness for their finny friends, points out one enduring aspect of aquaria across the many decades of the hobby: the tank may contain the sea or the city and may function as a toy or a scientific tool, but a key component of both its enduring popularity and its cultural work is the queer and compelling alterity of aquarium fish.

CHAPTER 4

TOY FISH

> Small fishes have taken so definite a place in the home that a living-room without an aquarium is almost as desolate as a fireside without a cat . . . Unlike most animals in captivity, fishes do not return their owner's affection, and it is therefore possible to enjoy them while they live and refrain from mourning when they die.
> —IDA M. MELLEN, *Fishes in the Home*

> I amputated that yellow angel[fish]'s fin and I gave it mouth-to-mouth. Don't tell me that fish doesn't know I saved its life.
> —PAULA, attendee at the 2006 International Marine Aquarium Conference

The gulf between Ida's and Paula's views of home aquarium fish is, in one sense, historical. Mellen, one of the few female public figures in the early American hobby and professional aquarist at the New York Aquarium from 1916 to 1929, is, in many ways, heir to a Gossean strategy of representing one's personal specimens through behavioral sketches, as protocharacters, in contrast to Henry Butler's "happy family" and Arthur Edwards's affectionate pet "Minny." Paula, a very self-aware and articulate critic of the incipient sexism in the still male-dominated hobby almost eighty years after Mellen's book, adheres to an increasingly refined and expansive view of pet keeping; from this perspective, boa constrictors, tarantulas, rats, and, of course, fish are every bit as much "companion species" as the family cat lounging by the fireplace and are every bit as worthy of mourning.[1] This gulf is also conceptual, centering less on evolving standards of pet keeping and more on the nature of fish as beings. On the one hand, fish are both animals and the equivalent of plants or objects in terms of their relational potential. On the other, the yellow angel is not only as fully animal as the family cat but also worthy of lifesaving intervention and potentially aware of and grateful for it. The formulation used as the title of this chapter was coined by Mellen herself. It spans these historical and conceptual gulfs and points to the larger, equivocal nature of fish as pets, sites of deep attraction and attachment yet still "it" toys, other in their animality in ways more explicit than dogs or cats or even their aquatic neighbors dolphins and whales. This queer alterity is key to understanding the theatricality, relationality, and rhetorical elasticity so central to the aquarium's popularity. Specifically, fishes' ambiguous animality enables them to serve as surrogates for negotiating otherness, including gender, race, and geography, in unique ways, as discussed in chapters 5 and 6.

This chapter examines the conceptual and representational potency of aquarium fish as another core component of the tank's rhetorical utility. It begins with a theoretically informed discussion of fishes' animality. Simply put, are fish "animals" in the same ways dogs, cats, and cows are? This is not just a rhetorical question. It vexed early aquarium viewers who didn't always know what they should be looking at or how to interpret what they saw. As discussed in previous chapters, Henry Butler and others needed to supply the plots and landscapes, from melodrama to the garden, to render them intelligible as objects of spectatorship different from their dead kin in the market. Further, fish push up against the limits of critical animal studies, which is generally more concerned with mammals.[2] Not only are mammals biologically closer to us, but in aesthetic and behavioral terms, they are all veritable charismatic megafauna in comparison to aquarium fish. Early aquarists were also keenly interested in the limits of and possibilities in fish animality, particularly in their relational potential. What could they know or feel? What affective benefits could they offer to their caretakers? Next, this chapter turns to three key tropes that recur in aquarium hobbyist texts and particularly in aquarium advertising and humor: fish as people, the fish as captive, and the fish as food. All three tropes offer insights into fish as surrogates used to negotiate and sometimes expose modern anxieties. Finally, the chapter concludes with a discussion of the processes that individualize fish, using as examples two relative celebrities, "Snoz" and "Blanche," who help answer the question, "How can one love a fish?"

ZOOESIS AND FEELING WITH FISH

Animals are good to think with, as Aesop's fables and the Muppets attest. They are even better to feel with: consider the film *Marley and Me;* Knut, the Berlin zoo's star polar bear; and the late, lamented Alex the grey parrot, whose last words to his human companion were "You be good. I love you."[3]

The emotive potency of animals, especially pets, illuminates relationships between affect, alterity, and modernity with special clarity, even though (or perhaps because) it is so deeply embedded in the materiality of everyday life and circulates so widely in popular discourse that it hides in plain sight. Una Chaudhuri has coined the term *zooesis* to describe a critical project at the intersection of the "rhetoric of the animal" and its theatricality.[4] Zooesis takes as its object "the vast field of cultural animal practices" and examines the ways human and animal actors mutually construct one another.[5] With its emphasis on mimesis and the productive overlap of cultural and performance spaces and places, zooesis is an especially generative frame within critical animal studies for understanding animal acts as socially and politically consequential. On one level, the aquarium fits easily within zooesis; its reliance on the visual norms and textual tropes of the theater offer a very clear example of how culture makes meaning and eases anxieties using animal bodies and/as mimesis. Yet the equivocality of fish—their "toyness"— also challenges and expands zooesis. It demands conceptual precision to account for different types of animality, differences produced as much by history as biology.

Ambivalent Animality, Reciprocal Relationality

Aquarium fish enter modernity differently from other animals. Akira Mizuta Lippit, amplifying an observation by John Berger, argues, "Modernity sustains . . . the disappearance of animals as a constant state . . . [T]hey exist in a state of *perpetual vanishing.*"[6] Environmental destruction certainly accounts for this, as does urbanization and specialized industrial agriculture that supplanted the connections between small producers and their livestock—the "disappeared animal of the modern meat industry."[7] Yet the relationship between aquarium fish and the emergence of modernity is one of appearance and persistent visibility as much as disappearance and vanishing. From the discovery of oxygen, through the manufacture of plate glass, to revolutions in transportation, the aquarium used modern technology to make fish visible through the illusion of undersea travel, as discussed in chapter 1.[8] This habitat is now also imperiled, with coral reefs in particular facing extinction; the contemporary reef tanks discussed in this book's conclusion certainly operate in the spectral economy of vanishing beings Lippit describes. But from the mid-nineteenth century until relatively late in the twentieth, aquarium residents were modernity's found objects. They demonstrated human ability to make what was hidden appear. They were novelties, like microbes seen through a microscope or automated toys, as much created through science-infused artifice as creatures. Thus, they could stand in both for the loss of nature (or rurality or wilderness) intrinsic to industrial urbanization and for modernity's ability to manage or even improve it. Again like microbes, they were not fully contemplatible outside the technology that kept them visible. Aquarium residents may not have been machines in Descartes's sense of the term, but they were visibly, obviously closer to animal-technology hybrids than either livestock or the family dog. They were always already mediated, as much a part of a "hallucinatory space" as Eadweard Muybridge's cinematic horse. Yet if the latter seemed to be "racing against the imminent disappearance of animals from the new urban environment," the former celebrated that same environment's ability to make the previously inaccessible easily domestic and ever present.[9] As Steve Baker notes, all animals can be and have been reduced to objects vis-à-vis the human subject.[10] Most obviously, they were merchandise, whether as part of a rural livestock market or produced for the urban pet trade. But the self-evident thingness of the aquarium extended to and enveloped its residents and turned them into objects by extension.[11] They were conceptually part and parcel of the new toy or parlor ornament because they were literally inseparable from it.

It is not only their technologically enhanced objectness that makes fish exceptional within a zooetic economy. It is also their questionable capacities as sensory and sentient beings. If, as Derrida suggests, inscrutability marks the animal as humanity's other, pet fish are more "other" than most. In a now well-known passage, Jacques Derrida theorizes animal alterity through an encounter with his cat.

> [The animal] has its point of view regarding me. The point of view of the absolute other. And nothing will ever have done more to make me think through this absolute alterity of the neighbor than those moments when I see myself naked under the gaze of my cat.[12]

What about the gaze of one's angelfish? Seventy years after Butler used the theatrical fourth wall to construct a one-way visual dynamic for the tank, this was still a pressing question, both for the hobbyist and for the emerging aquarium industry rapidly expanding beyond the urban northeast. In *1001 Questions Answered about Your Aquarium,* Mellen addressed the issue of whether or not fish recognized their owners.

Some [fish] can see farther under water than others. They can see people through the glass of the aquarium. It has been observed that fishes long kept in home aquariums swim away when strangers approach, but swim forwards when those who care for them walk near the aquarium.

The late Mr. E. K. Bruce of the Bruce Goldfish Fisheries, Iowa, wagered $50 that his fishes knew him, the decision being based on whether they came to him and not to the stranger. He always won the bet, for invariably the fish came to him but swam away from the stranger. These fishes had been in his possession for many years. Doubtless they learn the gestures peculiar to individuals. It is not to be supposed that they recognize the features of a person's face or shape of his hands.[13]

In visual relationships with fish, the issue was not just what, if anything, they thought. It was as basic as what they actually saw. Did they recognize individuals? Did they do so using idiosyncratic behaviors, or could they engage "face-to-face"? Mellen's passive-voiced, qualified, and anecdotal answer suggests that, even at a booming moment for the hobby, the jury was out on fishes' capacity for visual reciprocity, even at the level of physiology.

Here, Chaudhuri's performance-based zooesis is especially useful for describing the layers of estrangement in viewing aquarium fish. As I noted in chapter 1, this is a Brechtian experience. The entire scene and the peculiarities of the inhabitants are always already as alienating as they are inviting. In addition to the glass barrier, the water, and their questionable perceptual capacities, there is the denotative queerness of how the fish look when they look back. Fish don't return the gaze as mammals do, because they don't have faces with the same orientation of features. Many have eyes on the sides of their heads,[14] and they lack eyelids. They regard viewers from one side or another as well as straight on, making "face-to-face" encounters with fish very different iconographically from Derrida's exchange with his cat. In "Animal Body, Inhuman Face," Alphonso Lingus argues, "A face is where consciousness and passion exist in the world."[15] The very literally inhuman faces of fish were continual indicators of an equivalent gulf in consciousness, one that resisted the easiest type of anthropomorphism through shared physiognomy. As Desmond observes, "Take eyestalks . . . Now *there* is a real impediment to identification."[16] Moreover, fish lack other signal features that render mammals comparatively "Stanislavskian," that is, inviting empathy rather than alienation: they have no limbs, no hands or feet, no easy way to determine sex.[17] There was also the curious matter of their aging process. Differences between fry and adults were readily discernible, but after that they seemed to age like objects, indeterminately. This was not just a matter of individuals, who did not gray like the family cat or dog. There was confusion about how long aquarium fish could actually live, in part because of lack of research, as well as a sense of their easy disposability, like Mellen's characterization of fish as not mournable. Later aquarium journals stepped into the vacuum with tables giving average life spans, but these are only really useful if breeders spawned the fish themselves.[18] In the absence of specific information about particular species and very careful observation, it is almost impossible for the average viewer to determine fishes' ages. Aquarium viewing is so alienating in its particulars that John Berger uses it to underline the estrangement of animal photography wherein *"all animals appear like fish seen through the plate glass of an aquarium."*[19]

If Derrida's cat and animal photography both represent alterity, then aquarium fish are a limit case. Yet as the earliest known animals with backbones, fish are also relatives, whether "Old Testament" in Mellen's terms or "embryonic" in Millicent Washburn Shinn's (see chapter 1 in the present book). Donald Simpson, hobbyist turned professional aquarist and self-professed "fish guy," defended his passion for aquariums to his readers using literal kinship.

> [W]e are all familiar with paths of evolution leading us back to the time where the fishes were getting ready to venture upon the land, eventually producing the likes of you and me. And so perhaps I am merely paying homage to my ancestors, many of them, I must admit, being pretty zany characters. Meet some of them . . . and see for yourself. It might even give you a lead on what made Uncle Harry such a bum![20]

Fishes' evolutionary antiquity was ambivalent, a record of protohuman potential floating up from deep time and so very "proto" that they could be justifiably regarded as primitive by comparison to other animals.[21] Fish were impressive survivors and dismissible relics at once. Aquarium fishes' technology dependence, physiognomic differences, and evolutionary connections made for ambiguous animality that was rhetorically useful precisely because it was so shifty and noncommittal. Owners could love them without mourning them, relate to them through rituals of care and commerce that reinforced the shared confinements and creativity of modernity, embrace them as family with comparable idiosyncrasies, and ignore then as nonsentient, sometimes all in the same day.

Grier observes that ambiguity about relationships with animals and overlapping categories ("pet" versus "food") characterized pet keeping generally in the late nineteenth century.[22] Aquarium fishes' ambiguous animality entered this already-complex conceptual terrain as a practical challenge to aquarists and their audiences. It was just not clear what, if anything, they were behaviorally and affectively capable of. Popular periodicals offered intriguing hints suggesting that fish might have more in the way of consciousness than met the eye, "shrieking in terror" or demonstrating an uncanny and admirable "tenacity of life."[23] Some offered hypothetical potential to counter real affective limits because "it is easier to like any thing better than a fish."[24] They were unpleasant to touch and so couldn't be petted or hugged. Yet some suggested that this view was shortsighted, the result of simple ignorance. Absence of evidence for a fish's emotional life might not be evidence of its absence.

> Nor must we suppose that, if it were possible for us to take a journey through the watery regions of the fish-world, that we should meet with no instances of constructive skills, or intimations of that maternal affection which reaches its full development among the mammalian tribe.[25]

The hypotheticals and double negatives in the preceding sentence seem to almost wrest emotional potential from the reproductive habits of, in this case, the stickleback. Further, in a reversal of the way fish usually stood in for raced, gendered, and geographic others, putatively "primitive" physiology might not always signal limited capacity. Fishes' biological hearts might have been very simple, but their metaphoric ones might be quite refined.

> [T]he fish family may have oral discussions and concerts of their own, the performers being able to execute passages which an opera *prima donna* would be astonished to hear. This certainly opens a new view of submarine society. It may, after all, be diversified by other incidents, besides devouring and being devoured; fishes may exchange such thoughts and sentiments as their feeble brains may form, and their existence may be rather more than
>
> > "A cold, sweet, silver life, wrapped in round waves,
> > Quickened with touches of transporting fear."[26]

Fish might be companions, even artists of a sort, as well as ornaments, and not just brilliantly colored bundles of instincts.

The general public needed more convincing, as Hugo Mulertt learned the hard way. A pioneer in aquarium display, he reports in the pages of his journal, the *Aquarium,* that "we mourned the loss of choice specimens that had been stolen" when showing tanks "unprotected."[27] People extracted them with baited hooks, in a literal example of slippage between the aquarium and the pond. Even the policeman in charge of protecting the tanks was taken in, not by the beauty of fish society, but by the "small boy with the proverbial 'pin hook'" and his apparently uniquely effective bait. But fishing in the new glass ponds was not the only problem. Even when the tanks were screened at the tops, people attempted physical contact with the fish.

> The spectators would now poke their parasols or fan handles through the screens, and when the mesh of the screens proved too small for these, some did not find it too much trouble to use their hat-pins for the purpose. It gave them so much pleasure when they hit them "right close to the eye."[28]

Mulertt attributes this behavior to a seemingly uncontrollable impulse to "poke" animals in captivity, but the example of the hat pin suggests an alternative explanation: a desire for evidence of animality and conventional "liveness," which was so questionable that spectators were unburdened by thoughts of empathy or cruelty or fear of harm. The fish they poked might have seemed precisely like what early publications said they were: ornaments and toys.

The "feeding-fiend" demonstrated equally problematic but opposite misrecognition. Here, the fish were animal enough; actually, they were more like lunch companions than menu items.

> Of course, no one but "city folks" could think of preventing these dear little fishes from partaking of their luncheon—consisting principally of homemade pie. They would go to the trouble of breaking it into sufficiently small pieces and force it through the meshes. Two young ladies we will never forget, as we caught them in the act, busily engaged both on the same tank, feeding the fish with sponge cake, using the protective (?) screen for a grater. Good-natured and polite, we stopped their proceedings, and were informed by them that we need not fear any bad effects, because they had baked the cake themselves, it being no "bought stuff."[29]

Jane Desmond notes that "[p]eople's zoo behavior, feeding or taunting, often aims at getting the animals to move, to *do* something."[30] Fishes' ambivalent animality exacerbated such behavior further. In addition, Mulertt's challenges also point to underlying class dynamics of viewing aquarium fish: fish were food to the boy with the hook and the cop on the beat and were friend and fellow diner to lunching ladies of relative leisure. He solved the perception problem using scenography, borrowing from the "show window" and theatrical lighting to frame fish as, simultaneously, merchandise and actors. This display strategy suggested a relational, rhetorical stance. Specifically, in this new visual context, one reinforced by other urban entertainments and aquarium texts, what fish could experience in a relational exchange became less important than what they could give. Department store displays and actors onstage didn't talk or love their viewers back, but they did offer real pleasures, and popular audiences understood this without themselves jumping into the mise-en-scène. The affective dimensions of fish keeping were framed in similar terms. Defined as an object or in role, whether or what fish themselves actually felt was immaterial. Their companion qualities were defined reciprocally through the effects they produced in their owners. This was not merely a function of the tank's relative novelty, quickly relegated to rhetorical obsolescence once it and the "pet potential" of aquarium fish became more familiar to the general public. Dedicated hobbyists continually relied on the same formulation in in-group accounts of fish as healers, both of individual aquarists and of actual patients.[31] Fish were companions, not necessarily because they could respond per se, but because they could stimulate response.

The remarkable and often contradictory discourses about the pleasures of fish keeping are discussed in chapters 2 and 3. Fish were exciting and soothing, edifying and cautionary, a mark of intellectual and aesthetic sophistication and a devotional tool. They had the potential to teach viewers to be more human and more humane. This last turn is particularly important. Fish always occupied the outer edges of the "domestic ethic of kindness" that ultimately birthed state and national anticruelty groups in the late 1860s. As noted in previous chapters, goldfish bowls were repeatedly denounced. But aquarium fishes' conceptual position in anticruelty logics was complicated by two contradictory factors, both hinging on their "thingness." On one hand were the wielders of hooks and hat pins in Mulertt's audiences. While some may have regarded the suffering of the abjectly powerless as a joke, as Grier suggests in her discussion of American anticruelty discourse, their actions are more likely indicative of viewing fish as objects and/or food, with a purely utilitarian functionalism enabled by the sense that the animals lacked a capacity to suffer.[32] On the other hand, fishes' complete and obvious dependence on their human caretakers for environmental basics rendered them objects of pathos. Rev. Gregory Bateman observed:

> To see a miserable bird in a cage is bad enough; but it is far worse, I think, to see dying fish in foul water. There are so few pets which require such little care as fish, but it is absolutely necessary that they should have some attention; and he who keeps fish and neglects them is just as much guilty of cruelty as he who is summoned for working a horse with sore shoulders.[33]

Grier notes that modern views of animal cruelty arose out of the elevation of the virtue of self-control: "[C]ruelty to animals was fundamentally a social malady that grew out of individual failing, especially on the part of men of any class who were victims of their own passions."[34] From this perspective, cruelty to pet fish arose from two vices that were even more fundamentally modern: laziness and ignorance.

In any case, aquarium fishes' ambivalent animality kept them largely outside the purview of mainstream anticruelty movements during their formative period. It was not until 1915, almost fifty years after its founding, that the American Society for the Prevention of Cruelty to Animals agreed to support those bringing specific cases charging neglect of aquarium fish. The crusade for ASPCA backing was the project of S. Chichester Lloyd, president of the American Federation of Goldfish Fanciers. Efforts were focused, as might be expected, on goldfish and dealers, but "Mr. Lloyd also stated that all persons who kept fish in aquariums would be held responsible for their care."[35] In a repeat of the reciprocal construction of their relational potential, wherein they could be cast as able companions because of feelings they inspired rather than possessed, fish were deemed worthy of kind and diligent care because they could be objects of cruel treatment. In both of these constructions, "animalizing" and "companionizing" happened simultaneously. Fish were made into companion animals through their owners' responses, and the process was even more thoroughly inferential than for other pets, as it was unaided by purrs or snuggles, the fetching of slippers, or the warbling of songs. In the absence of a range of responses to read and interpret, owners substituted their own wholesale.

Yet dedicated hobbyists wanted more from their pets than the limited emotional range reflected in Mellen's dispassionate prose or Mulertt's errant audiences' pokes. In their own publications, they continued to debate fishes' actual affective potential, even while relying on its effects to extol the tank's virtues in accounts for the general public. They shared among themselves anecdotal evidence of fish cognition and affection and tales of how "reason," not "instinct," accounted for behavior. These included a *polyacanthus* who "has intelligence enough to die" of grief after the death of its mate and a goldfish troubled by the bottom-feeding ways of its catfish tank mate "teaching" it to rise to the surface for flake food.[36] These were not "biographical" accounts of exceptionally charismatic individuals, like "Snoz" and "Blanche" discussed later in this chapter. Rather, they represent a more general grappling with the relational potential of cross-species encounters and drew on available authorities to support a view of specimens as more than toys, decor, or organized reflexes: "Darwin aptly says, 'since animals possess the same senses, it follows they must possess the same fundamental intuitions as man.'"[37] Shared fundamentals, however, did not make equals across the glass or across town.

The weighing of species' comparative relational potentials was ideologically potent beyond the tank walls, part and parcel of larger efforts to generate scientized racial, class, and gender hierarchies that, in turn, stabilized established structures of privilege on the shifting terrain of modernity itself. As indicated in chapter 1, the rising popularity of the hobby coincided with atavistic, evolutionary, and eugenic preoccupations of the American fin de siècle. When weighing his place over against the sensory and intellectual capacities of his pets, the white, upper-middle-class aquarist of the early to middle twentieth century could also solidify his or her own place on a socio-evolutionary taxonomy that included fish, fowl, African Americans, and the growing immigrant working class. The tank was one of a number of epistemo-visual technologies providing observational "evidence" for the conflation of social position and evolutionary hierarchy, operating alongside Cesare Lombroso's photographs of male and female offenders (1911, 1895) and Havelock Ellis's schematics of "criminal noses" (1890).[38] Within these popular, putatively scientific taxonomies, quick observational assessment of intelligence was key to determining one's proper sociocultural place. Thus, the issue of fish intelligence was not a trivial one, because, according to Rev. Paul Wagner Roth, owner of the aforementioned grief-stricken *polyacanthus*, "The livingness of any form of life is measured by its intelligence. It is this that places the animal higher in the scale of being than the plant; the man higher than the animal; the intellectual man higher than the savage."[39] Fishes' very liveness could be read into them through an assessment of their intelligence; intelligence could redeem them from mute "thingness." Further, grappling with their cognitive capacities led both to a "truer possession of our pets" and, in yet one more iteration of the reciprocal fashioning of fish-aquarist relationality, to one's own self-production as an "intellectual man" and thus to a "truer possession" of one's own social place.[40]

Surrogation

Fish became things through their literal immersion in the technology that kept them alive in the home. They become companion animals because they could be constructed as objects of owner's responses to them (e.g., becoming peacefully or attentively engaged) or actions against them (cruelty, neglect). They become social actors because, in the zooetic great chain of being, both their thingness and their liveness give them a unique rhetorical fluidity. Lorraine Daston and Gregg Mitman point out that animals generally are useful figures for cultural work because they resist simple symbolic fixity.

> Animals are not just one symbol system out of many, one of the innumerable possibilities to externalize and dramatize what humans think. They are privileged and they are performative. They do not just stand for something, as a word stands for a thing or a rhetorical trope figures something else; they do something.[41]

But even in this expansive context, fish offer a larger repertoire for figuration and substitution: from the evolutionary "primitive" to a technological advance, from a resident of unseen depths to a constantly visible domestic amusement or pet, actively real and thoroughly artificial, sharing affinities with human caretakers and yet absolutely other.

In *Cities of the Dead*, Joseph Roach describes surrogation as a process of substitution that fills vacancies in the social fabric.[42] Certainly, the aquarium as a whole operates as a surrogate, suturing the various ruptures of modernity together and making the process and result reassuringly available for repeat viewing in the home. Thus, as the early aquarium writings discussed in chapters 2 and 3 demonstrate, the tank repairs estrangement from both nature and the rural countryside. But surrogation is not only a process of plugging the holes to fill these putative vacancies. It is also a managerial strategy in which a model-substitute offers laboratory opportunities for imagining ongoing social complexities, tweaking aspects of the model along the way to accommodate and negotiate new variables. The aquarium generally and fish in particular are exemplary and productive surrogates in this regard because they offer a representational golden mean to use as a model: not a blank slate where projection gets free rein, but just blank enough. Fish offer palpable liveness and recognizable behaviors without even the limited capacity for back talk of the family dog or cat; most don't bark, bite, cuddle, or flee. Their liveness, combined with their mute "thingness," makes them representationally fungible; they can serve as surrogates for a wide range of subjects and objects, relatively unencumbered by the typical historical baggage that frames thinking and feeling with animals—timeworn formulas like the loyal dog, independent cat, and treacherous serpent. They can stand for bodies of water, even entire continents, and through the partnership of condescension and dominion that characterizes pet keeping, they make these places and peoples conceptually docile and manageable as well.[43] Yet, as Roach indicates, the process of surrogation is always imperfect; the hole is never perfectly plugged. Like national landscapes in the mid-nineteenth century, there is always the potential for disconcerting ambivalences and slips that reveal new anxieties while containing others. The representational fungibility of fish meant not only that they could stand in for places and people but also that people could just as easily stand in for fish—captive, mute, consumable, disposable.

ANTHROPOMORPHISM AND ITS DISCONTENTS

The utility and ambivalence of fish as surrogates for shoring up gaps in modernity emerges with special clarity in hobbyist discourses. For dedicated aquarists, tanks were tools of self-expression and self-fashioning not only because they represented mastery of water worlds but also because they were communal currency, ways to talk about and around a wide range of seemingly unrelated topics. Chapters 5 and 6 discuss the aquarium as a surrogate site for managing gender and geographic difference, but this section examines even more basic, foundational tropes: fish as people, fish as captive, and fish as food. All three involve anthropomorphism as a core device. It manages ambivalent animality by both humanizing fish and, in some cases, animalizing aquarists. Anthropomorphism is by no means the only tactic used to insert fish into a domestic zooetic economy. There are also plays on fishes' "thingness," often hinging on the confluence of species' common names and any associated objects. Examples include cartoons by Edward C. Symmes, Jr., of a pointy pencil fish sporting an eraser and a "rummynose," with a proboscis shaped like a flask, as well as poetry like that about "a man who managed one fine aquarium," who keeps

> my shad in shadow, and my sunfish in the sun
> My Triggerfish most carefully I fix upon a gun.[44]

Yet anthropomorphism, which arose as a term alongside industrial modernity itself, remains the most important element in the aquarium's ideological repertoire.[45] Desmond argues that fish are poor candidates for anthropomorphism. On the contrary, their very distance from humans, coupled with their ambivalent animality, makes them especially playful and potent in these types of figuration.[46] The aquarium's ability to operate as a surrogate, filling in modernity's gaps however imperfectly, hinged on both the representational links and estrangements between fish and humans.

"Are fish people?"

The happy couple in the ad for Tropicala fish food is dressed for a night on the town. He sports a jacket, cane, bow tie, and fedora. She is stylishly attired in a flirty skirt and a flowered hat, worn coquettishly to one side, and carries a parasol; she is also tastefully made-up, with meticulously arched brows, long lashes, and luscious lips. They are fin in fin, apparently walking, after a fashion, on their unclothed tails. Random bubbles reinforce the fact that these urbane consumers are underwater. Faced with a pair of savvy dressers like these, it seems perfectly reasonable to ask, "Are fish people?" and, given the tails and bubbles, to conclude, "NO . . . But like People, the Fish in your Aquarium love Good Food."[47]

Anthropomorphism is a consistent feature of aquarium hobbyist texts, especially advertising and humor. Like their animality, fish anthropomorphism is complex. Daston and Mitman rightly observe,

> Before either animal individuality or subjectivity can be imagined, an animal must be singled out as a promising prospect for anthropomorphism. We do not choose to think with any and all animals. There seems to be no simple explanation as to why some species are singled out as good to think with and others not. Phylogeny may be part of the answer, and domestication, another: chimps and dogs are prime candidates, amoebas and eels are not.[48]

Fish, much closer kin to eels than to chimps and seemingly unblessed by familiar physiognomy and evolutionary proximity, are nevertheless excellent to both think and feel with, as a post on the blog *Sea Creatures & Me*

(*SC&M*) vigorously asserts. Acknowledging that there are good scientific reasons to frown on anthropomorphizing tank residents, *SC&M* uses clear reflexivity to establish better reasons for embracing it.

> I want you to know that I know that I'm anthropomorphizing. I'm doing it deliberately. It's fun and it conveys some of the joy I experience in watching my sea creatures. I'm fond of these creatures . . . Anthropomorphism conveys this fondness, this attachment . . . I'll keep my attachment, my affection, my joy—and my anthropomorphic expression of these emotions—thank-you-very-much. Anthropomorphism is, more often than not, a sign that the human cares about the animal they are anthropomorphizing. In short: I write the way I do because I care. This is who I am.[49]

So much for eels' dearth of anthropomorphic capital. *SC&M* finds this even in "tiny amphipods" and, in so doing, highlights core features of fish-aquarist relationality that undergird the pleasures of the anthropomorphic aquarium.

This spirited defense of anthropomorphism has three components, all representing similar arguments implicit or explicit across the history of the hobby. One, presented in *SC&M* as almost an afterthought, answers back to science's dismissal of the practice by recasting it as a scientific tool. The anthropomorphic observer is a careful observer whose very precision may produce new knowledge. The second component concerns the defense's self-reflexivity. Like the urbane couple featured in the Tropicala ad, this anthropomorphism is not sentimental sloppiness or conceptual confusion. It is almost parodic and thus much closer to the art works Steve Baker discusses in his essay "Sloughing the Human."[50] Consistent with *SC&M*'s view of anthropomorphism as knowledge making, Baker sees works by William Wegman, Man Ray, and others as "art's exploration of the animal." These works are iconographically similar to Tropicala's fish in fedoras in that they are explicitly both "outlandish and preposterously transparent"; they make no denotative claims to the "nature" of the animal per se. Instead, they "suggest playful exchanges between the human and the animal, or between one animal or another, which may allude to borders and distinctions but are not impeded by them."[51] For example, Donald Simpson's disclaimer to his unpublished manuscript "Something Fishy" offers another playful turn, reminiscent of earlier discussions of fish as opera divas with elevated souls. He gently suggests that a comparative assessment of fish-human relational potential does not always find the fish wanting. In Simpson's view, anthropomorphism may not be the sincerest form of flattery.

> If any of the characters in this book resemble persons living or dead, it could be a pleasant surprise to the author. The fish, however, are on their own and, whereas I have seen fish that resembled people, I doubt if this would be an occasion for rejoicing on the part of the fish.[52]

In the third component, consistent with my earlier discussion of aquarium fishes' affective potential, the relational vacuum created by their ambiguous abilities is filled by human feeling and self-assertion ("my joy," "the way I am"). Fish are happy because they make the aquarist happy. This is hardly simple narcissism. These sea creatures are also happy because they are healthy; they are not just objects of representation and affection but objects of genuine care. In an almost Levinasian loop, the writer's anthropomorphic response to the sea creatures begets an ethical response—better care—which, in turn, sustains the creatures' own albeit limited response: staying alive.[53]

Anthropomorphism alludes to the relational vacuum in fish-aquarist contact and fills it. Further, this relational vacuum generates a commercial one: "What can fish feel?" becomes "What do fish want?" As the Tropicala ad demonstrates, anthropomorphism fills this vacuum, too. These appeals work through a rhetorical sleight of hand dependent on the permeable boundary between pet and owner, the liminality of which recalls the mimetic link between the tank and the sea: you love "Good Food"; your pets are not you but not not-you either; therefore, they love it, too. Fish become surrogates for exercising consumer agency, not to make them more human (like buying a sweater for one's Shih Tzu), but because they both can and can't be rendered as such depending on the particular appeal or need. This very ambivalence is itself an invitation to play with the diverse possibilities of fish animality and companionship through the mediation of specific products. Aquarium residents are rendered more alive and more petlike because they can consume as such.

Anthropomorphism in aquarium ads can be organized into three overlapping categories based on type of appeal. The first, empathy, relies on relational reversibility and asks the consumer to think like a fish, while playfully suggesting that fish think like people. The second uses the power differential, Yi Fu Tuan's "dominance," in the pet-owner relationship, along with the image of the tank as a "happy family" or personal water world, to cast the fish as a child or subordinate.[54] The third works by emphasizing the pathos in a particular exigency. The Tropicala ad works through empathy and the limits and possibilities of fish-human interchangeability. Similarly, the Aquarium Stock Company argues that fish require their own medicine chest because "Fish Are Like Humans": "When we feel a cold or a mild illness coming on, the first thing we do is head for the family medicine chest."[55] A bundled-up and clearly unwell human of indeterminate gender, thermometer protruding from the mouth, peers into an open medicine cabinet, matched by an equally under-the-weather fish wearily eyeing a box of Aqua-Stock remedies, a pamphlet, *Tropical Fish Diseases*, clasped in its fin.

Appeals to power differentials use anthropomorphism to do more than establish playful equivalences. They emphasize asymmetrical obligations, using the quasi-Levinasian loop of care and response noted earlier, by casting fish as human subordinates. Grier discusses the evolving characterization of the pet as a child; though she does not include fish, their abject dependence on their caretakers makes them ideal and highly mutable objects for this form of anthropomorphism.[56] One early example is the ad for Mulertt's Condensed Fish Food on the back cover of his 1909 pamphlet *The Aquarium: Information for the Care of the Parlor Aquarium.* Three fish with bibs "sit" at the table, each with a full bowl and spoon before it. The smallest (youngest?) seems to have upset its bowl. The three are smiling broadly to illustrate the caption, "They feel well, because 'fed' well!" (see fig. 8).[57] Here, fish are and are not hungry children at mealtime, admittedly an awkward fit given the tails, which seem to blend into the folds of the tablecloth. Yet fishes' relational potential is indeed childlike, given their total dependence on their caretakers, which is actualized in the circle of care ("fed well") and reward ("feel well").

Power differentials are crucial to anthropomorphic aquarium ads, but the appeals were not limited to casting fish as children. The Nicholas Wapler Company, wholesalers, constructed fish as citizen-workers at the height of the Great Depression (see fig. 9).

<blockquote>
President Roosevelt's NRA
Gives us a SQUARE DEAL

How about our aquatic pets? Don't *they* deserve a "square deal" too? . . . May we suggest, for the sake of your little "animal kingdom," that you use our highly specialized foods?[58]
</blockquote>

The aquarist could manage his or her water world through benevolent codes of fair competition and "wage support," just like those implemented by the National Recovery Administration. This was presented as a matter of simple

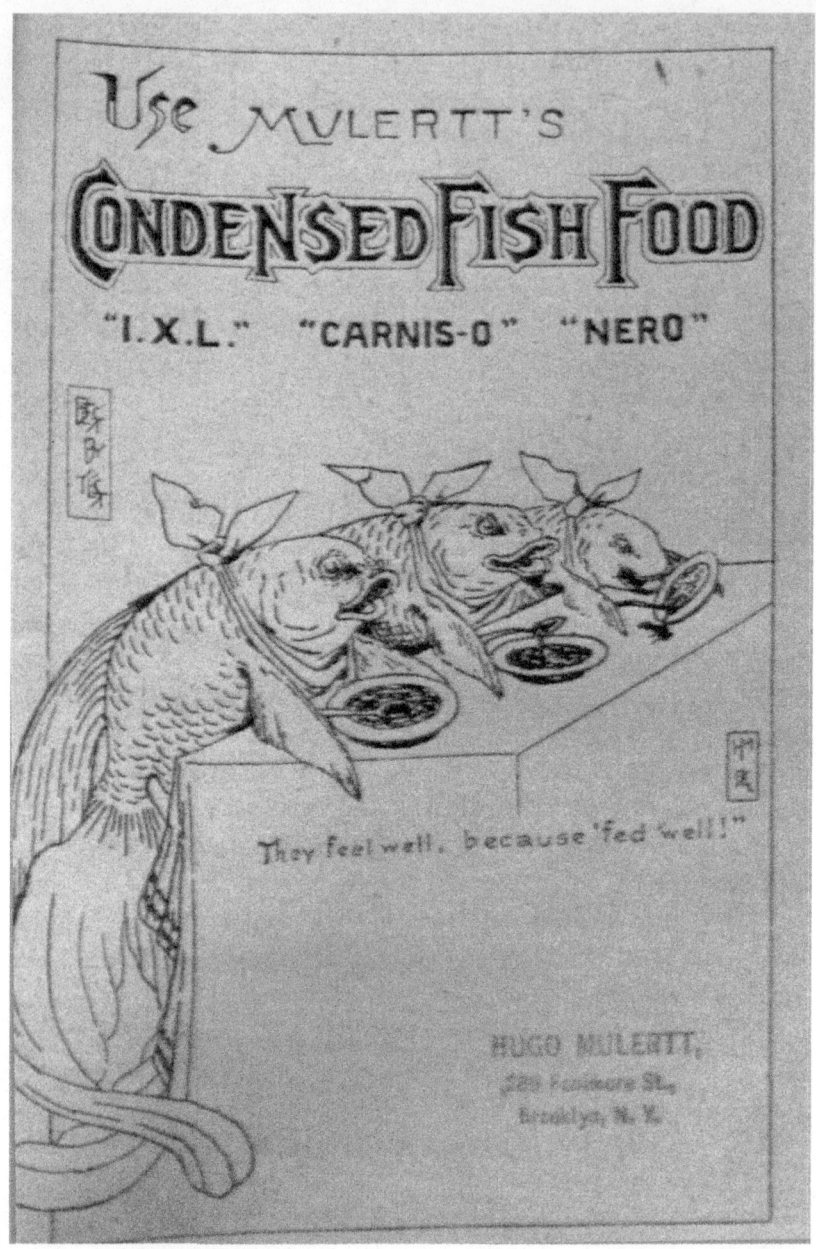

Fig. 8. "Use Mulertt's Condensed Fish Food," advertisement, on the back cover of Hugo Mulertt, *The Aquarium: Information for the Care of the Parlor Aquarium* (Brooklyn: Hugo Mulertt, 1909).

President Roosevelt's NRA

Gives us a SQUARE DEAL

How about our aquatic pets? Don't *they* deserve a "square deal" too? Simply feed them well and keep them healthy with foods recommended by expert aquarists; foods that are tested and approved and not boosted in price because of their superior quality. We *preach* the *best* — we *practice* what we preach. May we suggest, for the sake of your little "animal kingdom," that you use our highly specialized foods?

GEHA-PISCIDIN-UNISONO
These foods keep indefinitely.

ANTIDISCRASSICUM
A cure for sick fish — A tonic for aquatic plants
SOLD BY LEADING DEALERS
A card will bring you our new catalogue of Aquariums and Accessories

WAWIL-WELKE-RELPAW
Do not become moldy or rancid.

NICHOLAS WAPLER COMPANY
43 WEST 23rd STREET   Wholesale Only   NEW YORK

Fig. 9. "President Roosevelt's NRA Gives us a Square Deal," advertisement, *Aquarium*, December 1933, xx.

fairness and just deserts, hinging on both the shared vulnerability of workers and fish and the shared wisdom, authority, and good stewardship of FDR and the aquarist. The hobbyist could be the agent of his or her own remedy through the surrogacy of his or her pets. The fish as worker also surfaces in an ad for the San Francisco Aquarium Society's Brine Shrimp Sales Company. It features an exuberant fish seated on a stool by the dinner table, waving a knife and fork and proclaiming, "Boss, I *Love* that frozen brine shrimp!"[59] One can't help but admire his pluck and enthusiasm and give him a gastronomic raise, performatively reinforcing one's own authority by enacting the role of boss and, once in role, executing it benevolently for the good of the pet-self.

Appeals to pathos also turned on cross-species identification and powerlessness. A staggering fish on crutches, tearful, its tongue hanging out, begs, "Please Tropi-Cure Me."[60] An Aquarium Stock Company ad for decorative aerators combines exigency with attitude in its anthropomorphism. A large fish, done up in a boater hat, shirt, tie, and suspenders, fan in fin and sweating profusely, proclaims, "Boy . . . Am I HOT! Don't you know I need lots of aeration during Summer hot spells."[61] As a plus, the smiling hippo aerator to remedy the problem would "redecorate the joint." The juxtaposition of this "big fish's" colloquialisms and his dress suggests that he is too feisty to endure such poor conditions passively and too refined to have to. Printed in 1956, before the widespread availability of home air-conditioning, the aquarist probably understood the discomfort of poor air circulation in the summer heat very well.

Anthropomorphism was certainly not limited to aquarium commerce. As is indicated by the repeated invocations of the "black hole of Calcutta" noted in earlier chapters, it was also a tool for instilling norms of aquarium care and banishing anxieties about colonial confinements, using the tank as a surrogate. It operated using a rhetorical construction of empathy through shared discomfort. In a twentieth-century iteration of the caution against overcrowding the tank, the new "black hole" was public transportation.

> Did you ever sit on a crowded bus or subway . . . you know the kind I mean . . . the one where you're squeezed in between some large lady in a polka dot dress who has on her lap an immense grocery bag with stalks of celery hanging out . . . and on the other side of you sits this gentleman who insists on reading his newspaper while he rests his elbow in your gut and turns pages like there is no tomorrow. Does this agonizing commuter situation ring a bell? . . . What I'm trying to say is that a crowded subway scene is similar to the conditions of a crowded community aquarium . . . those poor fish in close quarters are experiencing the same tortures.[62]

The "tortures" of modern sociality could be remedied, if only vicariously, through good stewardship of the water world one could control.

In addition to forging empathy with their pets and using them as surrogates for managing collective anxieties, hobbyists used anthropomorphism to comment on their own eccentricities, as in a cartoon from the *Aquarium* where the humor and pathos come not from fish being human but from their not being human enough. Slumped in his chair, holding a plastic bag full of his pets, a grimacing man is confronted by an unsmiling bureaucrat, his position signaled by the "Internal Revenue" sign above him: "I know how you feel, Mr. Wilson. But, totally dependent on you for their support or not, they're simply not deductible."[63] Hobbyists also used jokes about anthropomorphism per se to enforce not just norms of good care but moderation and sobriety over against the intoxication threatening the aquarist who became too immersed in his or her water world. Here, the humor comes from anthropomorphizing not wisely but too well, as in a Rube Goldberg cartoon from the *Saturday Evening Post*, reprinted with commentary (Goldberg drew a *scalare* upside down) in the *Aquarium*.[64] The strip has three vignettes. In the first, a man queries a companion who is sobbing operatically into a handkerchief, "What's the matter—lose a relative?" His tearful interlocutor replies, "Worse—my pet guppy died." In the second, a young man gazes wistfully into his tank, observing, "It looks like a romance between Julia and Charlie." His sweetheart stands behind him, hands on hips, clearly impatient: "How about throwing a little romance my way?" In the final panel, a worker bursts into an office proclaiming, "It's a fish!" The caption below explains, "They used to come dashing into the office yelling, 'It's a boy!' . . ." For *Post* readers, the cartoon was funny because it captured the eccentricities of harmless oddballs. For readers of the *Aquarium*, however, it and others like it raised the uneasy possibility that a productive use of leisure in service to nature, beauty, or science could become a dangerous obsession that threatened to animalize the aquarist through misdirected passion, a kind of aqueous "going native."

Captives and Cannibals

Going native and confusing fish with family was one mistake of aquarium anthropomorphism, but humanizing one's pets held other dangers. There was also the possibility that the very conditions that defined their pethood—captivity, confinement, perpetual surveillance—might be disconcertingly reversible, revealing not just the aquarists' mastery of personal "little animal kingdoms" but also their own immersion in and dependence on modernity's managed spaces. The ambivalence of captivity is a recurring trope in aquarium humor. It operates differently from discourses of unease with captivity in zoos. As biologist Todd Newberry observes, "At the zoo, I feel an affinity with the captives, as though we spoke the same warm-blooded language."[65] Fish's evolutionary distance, physiognomy, and ambivalent animality made for a more distant and ambiguous kinship. In addition, fishes' abject dependence on the conditions of their confinement makes them both more pathetic and less fraught. They could not "rage against the machine" or even comprehend its contours. An escaped gorilla could rip your arm off, and a runaway lion could maul you, but a fish jumping from a tank to the floor would just shrivel up and die. Further, most home aquarium fish are small, and water was water; could they really know the difference between freedom and confinement by assessing the relative amount in which they were immersed?

Aquarists, like zoo personnel, were certainly sensitive to charges that captivity was in and of itself an abomination. William Vorderwinkler, a giant in the hobby and editor of *Tropical Fish Hobbyist*, responded to such charges with a paternalism reminiscent of "The White Man's Burden."

> Something these people [aquarium critics] do not realize is that a fish which is kept in average good conditions never had it so good when he was swimming in the Amazon, the Congo, or wherever he came from.
>
> A fish in his native waters is always in danger of becoming a meal . . . In an aquarium it is a different story . . . [The aquarist] gives them the attention which he knows is best for them.[66]

Anthropomorphism enabled fish themselves to answer back to charges that aquarium keeping was cruel and to outline the specifics of "average good conditions" from "their" point of view. One example is the "Twelve Commandments," delivered unto aquarists by a nameless überfish. Yet even here, in what amounts to a simple, if grandiosely framed, outline of basic aquarium protocol, there is an uneasy recognition of the tenuousness of the social bond underlying both pet keeping and human relationships, especially when cast as purely private and individual matters, absent institutional protections.

> The Twelfth Commandment—
> "Thou Shalt Not Harm Or Abuse Me—
> Thy Love For Me Is My Only Protector."

("Humane Societies for the prevention of cruelty to animals with all their worthwhile and commendable work are not in the least interested in what happens to fish in captivity, or any other fish for that matter. IT IS UP TO YOU.")[67]

The ambivalent bargain of captivity—paternalism and relative safety versus confinement and constant surveillance—is the subject of Raymond Z. Gallun's "Davey Jones' Ambassador," a science fiction story published in 1935.[68] This "imprisonment by sea creature" tale is remarkable for its reconfiguration of aquarium fish-human relationality, particularly around the issue of confinement. In the story, biologist Cliff Rodney escapes his damaged submersible only to awaken in an undersea "aquarium," where he must stay imprisoned by an underwater culture of marine fauna till he rots. His only companion is the Student, a fish who learned English, keeps a small museum of human detritus, and is eager to study humans—unlike others of his culture who have no desire to interact at all, as human proclivities have been deemed too dangerous. The Student helps Rodney escape, motivated not by empathy but, rather, scientific curiosity as to what he is capable of. When Rodney eventually does escape, the Student, now imperiled in his home world, which forbids human contact, bobs to the surface in a glass bubble, eagerly anticipating his future life in an aquarium as an ethnographer.

This same ambivalence characterizes aquarium hobbyist humor about captivity. One cartoon, published in the *Aquarium*, features a large and rather rough-looking fish telling his tank mates, "Pass the word. Ten o'clock, we're busting out of this crummy tank."[69] One of his potential coconspirators looks shocked; the other looks frankly worried. A snail on the bottom appears oblivious, and the tank itself, such as it is, doesn't look half bad. In another cartoon, also published in the *Aquarium*, two fish regard their owner on the other side of the glass. He wears a big, goofy smile, perhaps an indication of the very protective love noted in the "Twelfth Commandment." The fish are unimpressed. One says to the other, "Kind of depressing when you think that he's all we have to look forward to."[70] The humor and pathos here revolve around the reality that these creatures are stuck right where they are, and their "voices" sound unsettlingly familiar. They can't escape, any more than the harried worker can be free of a boss's gaze or the circle of production and consumption in which she or he is immersed. As the formulation "busting out" suggests, the tank may have been styled as a pastoral parlor pond and the home of a "happy family," but it was also, however well appointed, a prison, one that resonated uncannily with modernity's own confinements. In a reversal of what Steven M. Gelber calls "ideological spillover" from work to leisure, anthropomorphizing fish and seeing captivity and constant surveillance from "their" point of view threatened to reproduce the core conditions of modernity that the aquarium was supposed to help the hobbyist at least momentarily escape.[71]

Similarly, the harmony of the bucolic parlor pond and its happy family inside and out was to serve as an antidote to both the rigors of industrial capitalism and untamed wilderness red in tooth and claw. The "safety" of pet fish in the home tank, as opposed to "the Amazon, the Congo, or wherever," both mirrored and contributed to that of the family at home. Yet again, however, the actual mechanics of aquarium keeping raised anxieties as well as soothed them, by exposing the raw dynamics of consumption, including the fact that who eats and who gets eaten is often largely arbitrary and potentially mutable. If "the law of the sea" referred to in the "Twelve Commandments" had it that big fish ate little fish, anthropomorphism in aquarium ads and humor suggested that aquarists, like their pets, might be both. Some ads, like that for TopsAll Cannibal Mix, unabashedly assert the reality that Butler's formulation "the happy family" meant to disguise (see fig. 10).

Fish Are Cannibals

Fish is the Natural Food for Fish![72]

Underscoring the point is a large toothy predator chasing a visibly terrified tiny black fish locked in its sights. To spare the hobbyist the stark reality the copy presents, the food itself is mixed and processed, the piscine equivalent of Chaudhuri's "disappeared animal" making up hamburger.

Aquarium humor frequently raises the easy category confusion between fish as pet and fish as food, as in the *Aquarium* cartoon featuring a well-dressed woman at the store, live fish in a plastic bag, asking cluelessly, "Now, just one more thing . . . how do I prepare them?"[73] While holding the woman's ignorance up to ridicule, the cartoon points to the complete interchangeability of commodities, even (especially) those that are alive and potential companions. Anthropomorphism enables tank residents to address this directly, as in the *Tropical Fish Hobbyist* cartoon featuring a shocked and exasperated fish hanging out of his tank, yelling at a couple enjoying their fish dinner nearby: "Murderers!!"[74] If the first cartoon ridicules the nonhobbyists' inability to discern meaningful differences in a consumer economy, the second exposes a more disconcerting truth: the distinction between pet/"family" and food, like other commodity distinctions, is a movable feast. Whether you eat or get eaten is contingent on the size and type of your pond or the caprices of convenience, as in another cartoon featuring a young, shapely woman in a dress, pumps, and apron, holding a frying pan in one hand and a dip net in the other. With the net, she is reaching into a nearby aquarium, the better to move the fish inside from tank to pan. The caption reads, "I hate to do this—but I couldn't get a thing from my butcher."[75] Women are disproportionately agents of this type of category confusion in aquarium humor, a way of mocking their purported hostility to the hobby, presumed ignorance, and putatively greater immersion in consumer culture. The cartoon lays bare the fiction of love as one's only protector, exposed here by the most banal of exigencies. Another cartoon takes this formula to its extreme in reverse. A huge, serpentine, malevolent fish bursts out of its bowl, greedily eyeing a clearly terrified hobbyist, who is quickly

Fig. 10. "TopsAll Cannibal Mix," advertisement, *Aquarium Journal*, November 1956, 412.

trying to exit the frame. In the foreground sits a box of fish food: "Supra-6. High Concentrated" (see fig. 11).[76]

The representational fungibility of aquarium fish, coupled with the general slipperiness and potential reversibility of anthropomorphism, suggests that if aquarists ask, "Are fish people?" when exercising their buying power, they might also wonder uneasily if people were fish. This possibility made for entertaining cartoons like "When Things Are Reversed," published in 1916. A very well dressed fish family pauses to consider a tank of little people, some swimming, one floating on his back. A sign on the tank reads "$2.00." The young fish son begs, "Pop, Buy me one?" Father fish, who appears to be wearing top hat and tails in addition to his own tail, responds, "No. They're too much bother." Mother fish, in fur-collared coat and muff, adds, "And they're too expensive."[77] On one level, the cartoon's role reversal comments on the relative costs and labors of human relationships through conventional objections to the hobby. On a more serious note, it suggests that both captivity and cannibalism could rebound between tank mates and master, illustrating a kinship that was situational as well as evolutionary. Étienne Balibar observes that "every theoretical racism draws upon *anthropological universals*" undergirded by "the presence of the same 'question': that of the *difference between humanity and animality*," leading to the "systematic 'bestialization' of individuals and racialized human groups."[78] As chapters 5 and 6 demonstrate, there is no shortage of this bestialization in aquaria. But fishes' ambivalent animality and the fluidity of aquarists' anthropomorphism suggest another possibility. The residents of the little glass pond in the parlor might also expose their owners' predatory and/or vulnerable animality. Aquarists, too, were utterly immersed in and dependent on a highly constructed environment that promised safety through managed relations designed to obscure the realities of predation. Most hobbyists were "little fish," even if they were kings of their own domestic castles. Fishes' "thingness" made these situational similarities easy to dismiss, but aquarium humor, especially concerning captives and cannibals, suggests that these anxieties were alive and well, operating just below the surface.

"IT" FISH

Fishes' ambivalent animality and their versatility in operating as surrogates are ideologically useful, but this does not make them lovable. As Arthur Edwards's pet Minny and Paula's angelfish suggest, aquarists engaged fish—indeed, even loved them—as individuals, but some fish are more individualiz-

Fig. 11. "Supra-6. High Concentrated," cartoon, *Aquarium*, May 1969, 57.

able than others. This section explores the ways fish become individual objects of affection, fully inserted into the zooetic economy of the pet. Here again, fish are an exception to the typical processes of individualizing warm-blooded animals. As Grier notes, empathy through a sense of shared capacities was a crucial dynamic in the domestic economy of pet keeping.

> The intellectual move from recognizing the physical similarity of bodies to acknowledging alikeness in other ways was not difficult for people to make. The belief that animals were emotional and moral beings capable of inspiring the finer feelings in humans was an important justification for welcoming other creatures into the household.[79]

All aquarium fish had going for them in this regard was aquarists' insistence that they had the potential for moral uplift, though, as noted in previous chapters, this was often cast as a function of fishes' primitive differences from, rather than their physio-emotional similarities to, humans.

Toy Fish 151

Joseph Roach's discussion of "It," the indefinable allure of "abnormally interesting people," is a useful tool for examining how fish became individuals.[80] Not all fish have It, but those that do expose the characteristics that made them pets, not toys. Like their human counterparts, they were supported by publicity and promotion technologies, including photography. Techniques for successfully photographing aquarium fish were pioneered by R. W. Shufeldt at the turn of the twentieth century.[81] Photography replicated the aquarium's core function of making individual underwater residents visible and heightened it further. As with shots of Hollywood's It girls in fan magazines, photographs of It fish made them doubly visible by making them more widely consumable. Hobbyists across the country could learn about them, then demand and acquire them. Aquarium photography made fish portraiture a standard part of hobbyist discourse. Like pictures of the family dog or cat, photographs of aquarium fish at least theoretically individualized specimens. Unlike their warm-blooded counterparts, though, this could only go so far, even for It fish. In contrast to conventional pet portraiture, there could be no poses on owners' laps, no record of humorous tricks replicated for the camera, and often not even the idiosyncratic markings or collars and other accessories that designated a pet in particular.[82] If you saw one example of a species in a photograph, you had seen them all. Therefore, even the most charismatic It fish needed good press as well as good head shots. Hobbyist publications complied; they both traced and stoked fascinations with particular species and individuals.

In its human incarnations, It presents as a curious amalgam of immediacy, physical attractiveness, and what Roach calls "a kind of freakishness."[83] Above all, It is theatrical and thus relational, not entirely a property of an individual or an audience, but cocreated between them. As such, It is particularly appropriate for describing abnormally interesting tank residents because a fish's entire relational potential is created reciprocally at the intersection of how it appears and behaves and how the aquarist feels about and interprets it. Of course, fish are "its" already because of difficulties determining sex visually, their historical and technologically enhanced thingness, and their profound expressive limits. But the theatrical nature of It means that it doesn't matter whether or not the audience knows the unadorned denotative truth, the "real thing" underlying the possessor of extraordinary presence; it only matters that they feel they do. Roach cites Diderot on great actors with It; his words are especially relevant to It fish: "It's because he's everything to perfection, since his particular form never stands in the way of the alien forms he has to assume."[84] As with humans, it is easier to describe a particular example of It than to offer a comprehensive definition. Three It species demonstrate the capaciousness of the category: the Jack Dempsey, the oscar, and the puffer. Their species' distinctiveness, paradoxically, bestows individuality on them because, to reverse the cliché used earlier, once you saw them all, you saw one. All were "characters"; all had It, so, by extension, each member of the species did as well.

Boxers, Oscars, Puffers

The Jack Dempsey (*Cichlasoma biocellatum*) had It squared, its own structures of fascination amplified by association with human celebrity. Even William Innes, that normally sober paragon of the hobby, almost gushes about this "real fish personality."[85] He begins by registering this It fish's impact on a young fan. Innes himself is immersed in the task of photographing the star at a local aquarium store when he is interrupted by

> a repeated wail of a small boy, "Pop I wanna see Jack Dempsey!" . . . With open features (eyes and mouth) the youngster surveyed His Majesty. I was unable for the moment to decide whether his rapt attention was due to admiration or to an overpowering disappointment. Shortly came the explosive and eloquent decision, "Gee, ain't he a beaut!" Jack Dempsey had registered another knockout.

Named for the famous boxer, the Jack Dempsey is pugnacious and, more important, "a good showman and can be depended upon to do his act." But pugnacity in and of itself does not make It. Piranhas, for example, are sensational in a "man bites dog" type of simple reversal, but the Jack Dempsey has "personality." Mating pairs lock lips as if kissing; their spawning behaviors are complex; and they are fearless protectors of their fry, at least to a point, whereupon the aquarist must break up "a beautiful domestic scene" or risk an outburst of cannibalism. The fish is very large relative to the average tank resident and subtly but powerfully attractive: "they make the flash. They are an eyeful. They register."[86] Innes's last sentence is the key. It fish "register," as their human counterparts do, through a distinctive combination of appearance and behavior, especially the type that demonstrates engagement with fans. They are large within their respective frames. Roach quotes Elinor Glyn, author of the novella *It*, who had her own taxonomy of animals with It. Tigers and cats, "fascinating and mysterious, and quite unbiddable," were at the top.[87] Because fish always already had all three characteristics in spades, the It fish needed something more and different, a combination of "cavalier sangfroid" and affectionate availability that proved magnetic, even when it also proved troublesome.

"Never has a fish with so many disadvantages been as popular as the oscar," writes Frederick J. Kerr in an article whose title, "Personality Plus," explains why this It fish is worth the trouble.[88] Kerr goes on to enumerate those "disadvantages," which, given the often-touted limited affective capacities of fish, seem to constitute a kind of charm.

> A full grown pair requires a 50-gallon aquarium, will eat anything smaller than a medium-sized tuna, uproot any [aquarium] plant smaller than a tree, push rocks around the aquarium, move gravel from one side of the tank to the other, splash water on the carpet and bite the hand that feeds them. How does such a bundle of obnoxiousness become so popular?[89]

Like the Jack Dempsey, the oscar (*Astronotus ocellatus*) is large, both physically and affectively. They clearly recognize individuals and have "taste" of a kind. Babies will wag their tails and roll their eyes; adults will splash when they see their owners, and funny hats or accoutrements cause them to hide. They like to be stroked but, like touchy divas, also bite. And they are excessive in other ways, including gluttony and periods of panicky neurosis. They are visually striking fish that go through color changes as they age, but, as with It girls, their attractiveness is more than physical: "how many aquarists would be willing to cater to a fish like this when with much less work he could maintain fishes which are more colorful?" The answer, of course, is that many do because the oscar offers the prospect of a special relationship in return for being indulged. Indeed, as Kerr suggests, it could potentially rewrite the possibilities for meaningful fish-aquarist exchanges. Aquarists get "attached" to them because they offer responses beyond others' mute and simple longevity. They are curious, can be trained to do tricks, and exercise discretion in response to changes in their homes, whether by following their owners across a room to the extent that the tank allows or by rearranging tank plants and gravel to their liking regardless of the aquarist's efforts. Their It factor consists of being fish and not fish at the same time: "They almost reach the status of a pet cat or dog."[90] This It factor does not necessarily save the oscar from the aforementioned uglier aspects of dog-eat-dog consumption always already hovering at the edges of the hobby. Kerr notes that the oscar is reported to be tasty, "[s]o, if your oscar finally tries your patience and your pocketbook to the limit, take one cup of flour and add a pinch of salt."[91] Even It fish never seem to fully escape the contradictory responses of emotional investment and easy disposability that characterize tank residents as pets.

Roach notes that "[e]xemplary embodiment activates the 'It effect.'"[92] For the Jack Dempsey and the oscar, this is size. For the puffers (here *Tetraodon fluviatilis*), it is both their appearance and their physical potential. Diane Schofield, one of the few and most active female writers in hobbyist publications through the 1960s, describes the puffer as having "the constant appearance of a confused little fat man." Further, it is acrobatic, capable of the "carnival act of blowing himself up" when sensing a threat. It could also vomit explosively when agitated soon after mealtime. Schofield uses the same terminology employed by other hobbyists to describe It fish. Puffers have "personality plus"; they are the "baggy pants comedians of the aquatic set."[93] Like the Jack Dempsey and the oscar, they, too, are pugnacious divas, finicky eaters, aggressive to tank mates, and demanding on issues of water quality. Contrary to Mellen's assertion that aquarium fish do not merit mourning, Schofield asserts, "There is nothing much sadder than a dead puffer." Like the late lamented comedians he resembles, pathos comes from the dissonance between the flash, aura, and wit of It and the banality of mortality; the deceased fish's expression "seems to say that life wasn't really as jolly as he thought it might be." Though "hardened" to the task of dead fish disposal, Schofield sheds a tear for her puffer and buries him in the yard alongside his partners in It, her two oscars. There, in the "'family' burial plot," he merits a memorial that reflects both his extraordinary charisma as a fish and the relative expendability that characterizes even those with It. Although she is not sure the church would approve, the dearly departed "even rate[s] a small cross—for a while at least."[94]

Snoz and Blanche

Occasionally, an exceptional individual fish, endowed with sufficient affective capital, could escape the centripetal pull of genericism and claim It for itself. Like It species, these fish offer a remarkable, if not always conventionally attractive, appearance and the often-mentioned "personality plus." As opaque as It, "personality plus" is usually code for diva behavior that is pugnacious, demanding, and destructive but also ripe with the possibility of special contact between owner and pet. As if determined to flout every early aquarium book touting the putative ease of the hobby, these specimens demand special treatment. Easy keepers were generally not It fish. They seemed to insist on being noticed and, in return, assert a vigorous animality (as opposed to placid thingness) and a wide range of behaviors that can be viewed as expressive. Two celebrities from the pages of the *Aquarium Journal* exemplify It individuals. Their idiosyncrasies and adventures, detailed in multiple articles written over months and even years, illuminate cross-species bonds that continue to sustain the hobby and hobbyists like Paula quoted at the opening of this chapter. They remind us of one promise of aquariums: tanks offer not just brute mastery of a personal water world but also the chance for meaningful exchange with truly alien beings.

Snoz, or Snozolla (*Gnathonemus petersi*), a public celebrity housed in the Steinhart Aquarium in San Francisco, was the subject of multiple articles by hobbyist turned professional Donald Simpson. Simpson had an eye for It fish and was especially attuned to the ways star quality frequently marked a kind of performative "nonfishness."

> It seems whenever I write about a fish it turns out to be some weird character whose only piscine characteristic would seem to be that it lives in water ... Snoz is no exception. Snoz *does* live in the water, though there are times when he acts as if he didn't care much for it.[95]

Snoz is named for a protruding lower lip that looks like an elephant's trunk, one, Simpson notes, "that probably has Jimmy Durante hiding in a dark closet."[96] His fins "look as if they were stuck on from a do-it-yourself kit by someone who had a hard time following directions."[97] His brain is, proportionate to his weight, comparable to that of humans. Snoz is "really a weirdie" for reasons other than his appearance. He seems nervous, an observation borne out by his rapid respiration. Apparently placid at first, he proceeds to brutally dispatch two catfish who clean his tank, then turns his fury to his plants, which he methodically shreds. So begins a battle of wills with Simpson, who finally replaces the live plants with a plastic one, which Snoz then also destroys. The aquarist's exasperation is tinged with a bit of respect, albeit only partly serious. Snoz is eventually left alone with only a ceramic hippo, "and so far he hasn't been able to dream up any devilment to do to it, but he's thinking man, he's thinking, and with that brain he may beat me yet."[98] Snoz has It by virtue of his capacity to surprise. Like the oscar, his destructiveness is an asset, not a liability, because it challenges the mute thingness of his more sedate relatives. Coupled with his extraordinary physique, Snoz's seemingly adversarial relationship to the aquarist makes him all the more interesting. To paraphrase a comment originally made about It girl Clara Bow, Snoz had a way of wreaking havoc that showed and told pretty well.[99]

It fish both relied on conventional narratives designed to help audiences make sense of aquariums and exceeded them. They might conjure exotic locales, and their spawning habits might recall domestic melodramas, but their peculiarities drew focus from the plots. This is one reason individual It fish make poor rhetorical surrogates. They are too much themselves. Not all were notable for their bellicosity. Some, like Blanche the lionfish (*Pterosis volitans*), combined a truly spectacular appearance with the tenacity of life that, one hundred years earlier, was a clue to early aquarists that pet fish might offer more than a flash of color in the parlor. Blanche's owner, marine collector Robert P. L. Straughan, wastes no time in getting to the heart of Blanche's It factor. She "is a deadly creature, yet she is awesome and beautiful."[100] Lionfish are covered by feathery, striped fins and spines. They are also venomous and insatiable predators. Straughan's articles about her over four years recount a rather remarkable amount of little fish devoured by his pet. Yet it is not her voraciousness that is notable but her unique combination of vulnerability and resilience. She survives several close calls. Because "[s]he was such a show specimen," Straughan left the aquarium light of her tank on for much of the day to better accommodate Blanche's many admirers. This, he suspects, caused her to go blind. Risking stabbing by her poisonous spines, he hand-fed her, training her to accept minnows impaled on toothpicks. Later, toxins from the fumigation of a nearby store bleached Blanche white, almost killing her a second time. After being nursed back to health again, she was rewarded with her own beautifully landscaped fifty-gallon tank, fitted up like her personal reef—deluxe accommodations befitting her status as "almost a legend."[101] Ida Mellen believed it was possible to refrain from mourning fish when they died. Blanche's owner did not agree. He raised her from a juvenile and kept her for almost six years, nursing her back to health as Paula did her angelfish. On her death, presumably of old age, he wrote, in her two-page obituary,

> Blanche was a real fish friend. She never bothered anyone. Never made any noise. Always seemed glad to see me and when she felt bad, she never made herself burdensome. Instead, she quietly rested in a corner of her tank until I corrected conditions to make her happy again.[102]

Blanche was a curious combination of docility and danger, and her death was much like her life as an It fish. It registered.

It fish both embody and exceed fishness. They are the exceptions that prove the rule of fishes' relational porousness, waiting to be filled by their owners' responses to them even as they function as surrogates, filling other vacancies in the larger culture. Yet they also reveal what Donna Haraway calls "some of the knots of ordinary multispecies living," the ways people and pets form sustained and rewarding relationships through shared banalities and idiosyncrasies.[103] Aquarists read relationality into fish, whether through anthropomorphism or heightened attention to their remarkable and seemingly extraordinary presence. Fish respond by embodying some of the capricious consequences of modern capitalism, including surveillance, captivity, and unceasing circuits of consumption, so aquarists could see them and be soothed in the process.

CHAPTER 5

THE DOMESTIC AQUARIUM

> Lives there a wife with flaxen head,
> Who never to herself hath said,
> "Oh, how I wish those fish were dead!"
>
> —"A WORD FOR WIVES," *Aquariana*,
> September 1993

    The aquarium's effectiveness as a surrogate for managing modern dilemmas comes not only from its multiple visual affinities, the expansive rhetoric of early practitioners, and the representational fungibility of toy fish but also from its function as a home and the ways "home," in this context, operates as a set of nested, mutually reinforcing locations. Nowhere is this clearer than in the period covered by this chapter, 1910–70. During these sixty years, as the very idea of the typical American home was in flux, the aquarium hobby morphed from a novelty to a mainstay of middle-class leisure. Along the way, the tank had a lot of cultural work to do.

    Between 1910 and 1930 alone, an increasingly heterogeneous middle class expanded by almost 135 percent.[1] The tank grew along with it, spawning new and increasingly vocal commercial interests as well as consumer enthusiasts. The United States was now a majority urban nation, and during the 1920s, suburbanization began to intensify, increasing demand for a portable and manageable "nature" to compensate for the increasing absence of "the country" from "the city."[2] Electrification, which changed the aquarium hobby by enabling relatively efficient and consistent heating and aeration, became the norm; 85 percent of households used electricity by 1930.[3] The wages of middle-class expansion fueled a recognizable modern consumer culture by the 1920s.[4] Greater spending power was purchased through labor in increasingly automated and routinized workplaces—offices as well as factory floors—rapidly solidifying organizational hierarchies and widening experiential gulfs between an "ideology of promotion" and the challenges of increasing competition and specialization.[5] Women joined the office workforce; by 1930, over 40 percent of working women were employed in clerical/professional capacities.[6] All of these factors led middle-class and upper-middle-class men to aquarium keeping in search of respite through vicarious world-making mastery, fantasies of unalienated labor as fish breeders/artisans, and the possibility of like-minded fraternity. The tank was so effective in its ministrations to these cultural shocks, so potent a container for the shifting tides of industrial modernity, that it weathered the seismic upheavals of the Great Depression arguably better than most other domestic leisure amusements, apart from movies and radio.[7]

The quickening pace of modern consumer capitalism, the anomie of the routinized professional workplace, and, later, the rise of the cult of the nuclear family in the 1950s reinforced a vision of the home as a little private world, a refuge from the rigors of the public sphere. But these same forces also encouraged consumers, including aquarists, to recognize the mutual interpenetration of "home" and the larger "world" through, American imperial adventures at the macro level and what Kristin L. Hoganson calls the "consumers' imperium" at the micro level: collapsing "the distinction between 'abroad' and 'at home' by showing how they come together in the domestic realm."[8] The aquarium easily accommodates both. The tank in the living room was itself a living room for new generations of "happy families" and, with the advent of air travel and the rise of so-called tropical fish, a small world after all. Even conventional how-to books captured this potent interpenetration of the local and the global.

> Some species which find their way to the tropical fish market are imported, some are native, others of domestic cultivation. Swamps, ditches, rain pools, rice fields, mountain brooks, lakes, and rivers in Egypt, Australia, Asia, India, China, Siam, the United States from the Carolinas south through Florida, Panama, and South America to the Argentine have all been searched and seined by professional collectors to put into the home aquarium . . . [The aquarium] is a little world of its own—a microcosm where all sorts of events take place under Nature's guiding hand . . . Births, deaths, courtings, marriages, murders, brawls, and picnics—all the events depicted in a tabloid newspaper—take place within four glass walls.

Aquaria promised the allure of vicarious travel to exotic locales plus the juicy details of family and neighborhood gossip for "so little effort that the realization will come as a surprise."[9] Mediating between home and world was yet another domestic realm: the nation. Here, the tank proved a useful reinforcement of both imperialist and nativist ideologies simultaneously. It accommodated an imperial cosmopolitan logic by domesticating the logic of keeping exotic others at home, as well as domestic boosterism through aggressive advocacy for "real" Americans, human and piscine. This boosterism was more than rhetorical. It reflected an emerging structural-economic realignment in the hobby from loose networks of independent, relatively moneyed amateurs to more formal, market-driven relationships between producers and consumers, even if these roles were sometimes interchangeable.

The aquarium was a container of a national imagined community; this emerges with special clarity when imperial might "over here" (in the United States) was constructed using imagery, landscapes, and tank specimens from exotic foreign locales "over there" as discussed in chapter 6. The present chapter discusses the domestic aquarium more narrowly. It begins by examining the native tank in the period 1910–40. During this time, the very idea of the "native tank" was constructed reciprocally by the increasing availability of nonindigenous stock. Local specimens were now options, not necessary preconditions, for a home aquarium, and they quickly became objects of advocacy for key figures in the hobby. But native fish were not the only domestics to benefit from such patriotic appeals. During this period, leaders in the emerging aquarium industry also came to see themselves and their contributions to the marketplace as disconcertingly dispensable. Consistent with earlier metonymic slides between the tank and the sea, the idea of the native aquarium stretched to include larger-scale American breeders and retailers as well as local specimens. The very global flows that injected color and/as imperial adventure into the parlor pond threatened aquarium businesses, which responded in the pages of hobbyist journals using a variant of the xenophobic nativism that lead Calvin Coolidge to proclaim, "America must be kept American."[10] From here, this chapter turns to one of the most important and enduring components of the aquarium's cultural work: managing anxieties about sex and gender. Its status as a literal and rhetorical container, one both housing and constructing happy families inside and out, made it an ideal technology for containing gender trouble at home between 1930 and 1970.

THE NATIVE (AND NATIVIST) AQUARIUM

As indicated in chapter 3, all early American home aquariums, like their British counterparts, contained only local species. (For examples of common native aquarium fish, see fig. 12.) This practice was, of necessity, unexamined until the introduction of imported specimens in the 1910s.[11] The imports were exotic by virtue of their provenance and their appearance; they were usually more colorful than native species. They served as displays of the cosmopolitanism and aesthetic, intellectual, and financial capital of their owners. These early exotics included species that, in short order, became tank mainstays and remain so today: barbs, bettas, gouramis, guppies, rasporas, and swordtails. Relatively expensive and fragile, they were very popular, so much so that shortly after their introduction, aquarists needed to be reminded that "[t]he land of Agassiz, Audubon, Evermann, Jordan, and many other famous naturalists, ichthyologists and aquarists" was also blessed with its own attractive aquarium fish.[12] The reminder didn't take. Over the next six decades and continuing to the present, hobbyist journals repeatedly asserted the tankworthiness of native species. The rhetorical tactic most often used was a demonstration that preference for so-called exotics was based on simple ignorance, as in William Innes's account of the "rainbow minnow" (*Notropis lutrensis*).

> [T]he writer [Innes], who is fond of many of our native fishes, and who is not adverse to an occasional practical joke, sent pairs of this beautiful species to two of his aquarist friends, with the statement that they were a new species of the genus so-and-so, just imported from Africa! They were amazed by the beauty of the fishes and begged to know the source from which more could be had. On being told "Texas" they were dumbfounded, but were sports enough to stick to their statements that they had never seen a more beautiful fish.[13]

Over time, aquarists also used another variant on the cliché that an aquarium fish, like an artist, is never fully appreciated in its own country: reverse cosmopolitanism wherein the European regard for American species enhanced their cachet and countered irrational prejudices at home. Such is the case in the profile of hobbyist Frank Pierce, Jr., who, thirty years after Innes's stunt and at the dawn of the civil rights movement, "is getting set to launch a one-man attack on indigenous fish discrimination": "'It seems strange to me that we Americans almost completely ignore the beautiful native fish that surround us,' he [Pierce] said as we peered at a four-inch sunfish, who thought he was about to be fed. 'But abroad—Germany in particular—American fresh-water fish are in great demand.'"[14]

On one level, expanding networks of local tropical fish breeders often rendered "exotic" versus "indigenous" a distinction without a difference. More fundamentally though, as the market for aquarium fish grew increas-

Fig. 12. Representative American native aquarium fish. (From Chester A. Reed, *Goldfish—Aquaria—Fermeries* [New York: Doubleday, Page, 1908], 36.)

ingly profitable, ideas of which "natives" merited greater appreciation expanded beyond the specimens themselves to the breeders who supplied them and the retailers who sold them. By the early 1930s, "domestic" came to refer to the aquarium industry, not to the fish themselves. These commercial concerns became the new unjustly underregarded indigenous species. Nowhere is this clearer than in a remarkable article by Frank S. Locke that deployed another indigenous resident, the "vanishing Indian," to rail against the dumping of European-bred fish in the American pet market, undercutting prices.

> No use going into the distasteful subject of what happened to the Indian in this country, as everyone knows what befell him when he didn't have sense enough to organize himself and cash in on that which was originally his. In his place was gradually built [*sic*] a different civilization, calling themselves Americans, of which I am a part, having been born in this country. They became smug in their ideas and ideals to the extent that they have gradually lost sight of the fact that although they may not be entirely displaced as an identity, they will, if present mental and financial situations continue to an ignoble end.[15]

Published in 1933, at the height of the Great Depression, this article is notable for many reasons: casual racism couched as self-evident fact, coupled with risible blame-the-victim pieties; resonance with rhetorics of racial degeneration brought about by immigrants and other "undesirables," which fed the eugenic discourses of the period; and rage against an emerging global economic order mercilessly undermining local producers. It also focuses attention on the increasing complexities and instabilities of "aquarinomics": a curious amalgam of antimarket, artisanal rhetoric; the interlocking sets of economic relationships, real and imagined, between aquarists and dealers; and an increasingly global traffic in aquariums.

Aquarinomics offered the possibility of blending fun and profit, tempting some hobbyists to spawn cottage breeding operations in the hopes of escaping the office rat race and spurring some aquarium publications to consider the implications of these attractive agrarian-artisanal fantasies for businesses as well as individuals. It is an early precursor to "blue-green capitalism" and its own giddy promise of turning marine bioproductivity into profit through small, agile, entrepreneurial start-ups.[16] During the period under consideration here, aquarinomics marks a transitional stage in the aquarium's passage from small, unruly niche markets run by intertwined networks of amateurs to one component of large conglomerates in the pet industry: a stage that has yet to completely disappear. Aquarinomics shares with its contemporary cousin "biotech" a utopian cast and a productive ambiguity that accommodates competing, even contradictory rhetorics. For the aquarium hobby and its self-styled commercial partners during the formative period of the 1920s and 1930s, aquarinomics attempted to reconcile the profit-driven industry with explicitly antimarket appeals to exempt it from a profit motive: calls for free exchange of ideas and specimens, proposals to ban intrahobbyist commerce altogether, and attempts to construct aquaria as the pure preserve of knowledge and beauty, as in William Innes's stark admonition that "[o]ne should go in [to aquariums] for the love of it or not at all."[17]

Aquarinomics describes the tank's immersion in representational and financial flows, as well as the ways these flows converge in hobbyist discourse. Consistent with the romantic writings of nineteenth-century English aquarists, a seeming aversion to and amnesia about the commodity situation of the hobby was a crucial part of the tank's social work. Its putative status as a site apart from the rigors of industrial capitalism (as deep water and/or time, leisure, nature, and home/private sphere) disguised the fact that it was inextricably linked to and reinforced the logics it seemed to resist or remediate, particularly the transformation of both wilderness and the home into resource and market, respectively. Hobbyist publications affirm this vision as much through a disavowal of the market as through an enthusiastic embrace. In these outlets, aquarinomics was cast as an iteration of a domestic economy, with first home and then nation as the primary points of production and consumption. This enabled breeders and retailers to successfully position themselves as both fellow hobbyists sharing a parlor passion and an endangered native species in need of patriotic protection.

As noted in chapter 3, Henry Butler's *The Family Aquarium* and his partnership with P. T. Barnum demonstrate that, from its earliest incarnations, the American hobby was seen as a viable business opportunity. American readers were enthralled by the coupling of piety and pedagogy in English aquarium books, but they were also alert to the commercial potential of their pets and ready to exploit it. Forty years after the publication of Butler's book, a reader of *Harper's Bazaar* recounted her success in transitioning from simple pet owner to backyard breeder supplying a New York aquarium retailer; she reports her 1898 income as "almost $1500" and asserts that her fish "are almost no trouble, and very little expense."[18] As the hobby and its commercial potential developed, aquarinomic tensions appeared to test the tank's extraordinary rhetorical capaciousness. Specifically, the values touted as intrinsic to the hobby in both British and American contexts—construction of a space apart from the public sphere, leisurely contemplation, free exchanges of ideas between hobbyists, camaraderie, contributions to pure science, and spiritual uplift—were increasingly antithetical to a profit-driven industry. Hobbyist publications, dependent on industry revenue for advertising, deftly juggled both interests.

To be sure, relationships between hobbyists and the larger forces of aquarinomics were always more complex than most aquarium texts acknowledged. This was especially true in the positioning of the tank as antidote to the world of commerce: "The high-strung nervous business man can get what he needs as a 'let-down' or relaxation from the business tension when he gets home in the evening and can spend an hour or so, preferably before dinner, with his pets." The tank offered respite because it both drew on some core managerial skills ("close observation") and resisted others (delegating authority), while reconceiving their object. The goal was not financial profit: "Very few, indeed, are the fanciers who have made any money out of this hobby." Instead, the rewards were twofold, including both production and consumption: the artisanal self-satisfaction that theoretically came from unalienated labor, both intellectual and "mechanical," and the permission to consume, which could be satisfied by "modest sums" or vast ones with "scarcely any limit."[19] Yet even the most restorative close observations could also reveal that the rigors of predatory industrial capitalism, like those of the water world, were always hovering nearby. In rare cases, hobbyist publications made this connection explicitly, as with a 1913 ode to the muskallunge, a large pike native to the upper Midwest.

> Whence and what are you, monster grim and great?
> Sometimes we think you are a "Syndicate,"
> For if our quaint cartoonist be but just
> You have some features of a modern "Trust."
> A wide, voracious and rapacious jaw,
> A vast, insensate and expansive craw;
> And, like the "Trust," your chiefest aim and wish
> Was to combine in one all smaller fish,
> And all the lesser fry succumb to fate,
> Whom you determine to consolidate.[20]

Once again, as noted in chapter 4, the hobbyist was reminded that he could be both a big fish and a little fish, depending on the size of the tank.

Relationships between hobbyists and aquarinomics emerge with special clarity between 1932 and 1934, the period in which Frank S. Locke published his article comparing American breeders to vanishing Indians. Some accounts tout individual success despite the economic chaos of the Great Depression. Lilian A. Cotter's "How I Got My Start" eagerly advocates a career in breeding and retail. Her essay mirrors the progress from pet owner to commercial vendor offered by the anonymous *Harper's Bazaar* case over thirty years earlier.[21] But this is the exception that proves the rule. Difficult economic circumstances pitted American producers against Europeans, hobbyists against professionals, and the romantic values associated with aquaria against commercial ones, all set within larger calls for government relief.

William Innes summarizes the problem of the increasing globalization of aquarinomics: European dumping depresses prices imperiling American producers, but tariffs may raise prices for consumers, limiting the reach of the hobby into new domestic markets. His exploration of the issue reveals a rhetoric straining to accommodate aquariums as commodity: "With most of those interested in the aquarium and its problems the commercial aspect is not the first consideration," yet "[m]any have gone into the hobby past the beginner's stage with the hope of extra income from sales."[22] The tank is not primarily commercial, yet it is always imbued with a potential to generate profit, which in and of itself must be protected. To suture both together, Innes turns to a classic trope used to advance the hobby: its priceless and intrinsic dignity, which functions as the secular version of Gosse's piety, and fraternity. Neither one would benefit from a price war that, whatever its pragmatic consequences, would shift the tank from a tool of respite to an artifact of the very market logic necessitating respite in the first place—from manageable nature/home back to an unfettered economic wilderness red in tooth and claw.

Locke, as noted earlier, is much more direct and sets the commodity situation of the home aquarium into an explicitly nationalist context. The aquarinomics of the home tank paralleled that of the nation as home; what was good for the former was good for the latter. He writes, "There is no doubt but that every last one of us will be taxed for all the turmoil and strife of several European countries." Therefore, the logical conclusion for redressing geopolitical imposition is renewed domestic commitment: "Buy American" to restore order, quality, and integrity to aquariums and aquarinomics, which are one and the same in Locke's essay.[23] Just as Gosse's romantic rambles position the tank as outside the modernity on which it depended, Locke uses European imports to argue that were it not for such an obvious economic injustice, the market situation for aquariums was both rational and just.

Yet Europeans weren't the only foxes in the American aquarinomic henhouse; fellow hobbyists were perceived as such, too. In another editorial from the same period, the American retailer was imperiled not by cheap and shoddy global stock but by enterprising domestic amateurs who also undercut prices: the very aquarists Innes described as "past the beginner's stage with hopes of extra income." Against this turn on the retailer as an unjustly neglected native species, hobbyists are asked to redefine their communities to include businesses supplying stock, so as to protect those businesses' profits, while exempting themselves from the community of commerce to which many aspired. This was cast as both godly ("Love Thy Neighbor as Thyself") and "sporting." Commercial aquarinomics was reshaped as a set of premodern artisanal arrangements to remediate very modern economic dilemmas by encouraging customers to forget exchange of funds in favor of collegial "thoughtfulness," while excluding actual artisanal backyard breeders.[24] In yet another attempt to redefine the tank as outside of market forces while preserving profits for retailers, aquarinomics between hobbyists was recast as a free flow of information born of "enthusiasm," not buying and selling of specimens: "No real fancier prizes his collection for its representative money value, but, rather, for its tangible recognition of his enthusiasm and patience. Pass your enthusiasm along to others; your ideas, your observations; share them, don't hoard them."[25] Yet sharing had its limits; it didn't pay the bills. Locke reminds readers that "the individual fancier will terrorize the American breeder to desperation, with questions and hours of consumed time and will straightway patronize the impersonal importer who merely brings them in and slaps them down as it were, at a price which betokens no 'back talk' at the hands of the fancier purchaser."[26] Enthusiastic questioning, coupled with savvy shopping, was a form of predation; the individual hobbyist's demands were another muskallunge, and the American breeder/retailer was the vulnerable little fish needing protection.

These articles, written at a time of extraordinary economic upheaval, nevertheless expose the uneasy and contradictory ways nature and leisure were set into market logics.[27] Nationalist protectionism, values of kindness and sportsmanship, and apocalyptic tales of vanishing natives required hobbyists to remember the rigors of an increasingly interdependent global market and to forget them at the same time. Innes subsumed the entire aquarinomic situation under the rubric of patriotism, once again linking private consumption and national interest, which he then reframed as "enlightened self-interest." Locals who undercut prices were simply ignorant; they "lacked business training."[28] Government intervention in the form of price supports was the solution, and Innes urged vigorous backing of Franklin Roosevelt's National Recovery Act. The fish, whether real or allegorical, appeared to have the last laugh. In a cartoon initially published in the *New York Herald Tribune* and reprinted in the *Aquarium*, Uncle Sam is shown surrounded by fish in an endless array of tanks, globes, flasks, and cups stacked on chairs, books, and each other, all labeled "NRA offspring," "AAA addition," and "RFC increase." Uncle Sam, holding a dip net and clearly overwhelmed, pleads "Help!" The caption reads "Someone Gave Him a Few Tropical Fish."[29] While ridiculing the proliferation of "alphabet soup" agencies during the Roosevelt administration, the cartoon offers another discomfiting truth, one that returns to Herman Melville's characterization of fast fish claimed as property and loose fish up for grabs. When it came to stability and fixity—both of aquariums by the market and of aquarium rhetoric around market imperatives—fast fish were often much looser than they appeared.

Later hobbyist publications reflect a schizophrenic relationship to the imperatives of industrial modernity through the 1960s and to market logics in particular. On one hand, aquarists increasingly embraced bureaucratic organizational structures and even iconography of the public sphere the tank purportedly repaired. The International Federation of Aquarium Societies, for example, adopted an insignia that recalls the Pinkerton Detective Agency logo: an oval enclosing the closeup of a fish head in profile, captioned "Seeing-Eye of the Aquaria World."[30] The water world as antibureaucracy to soothe the nervous businessman was increasingly organizing itself through a rhetoric of discipline and surveillance. Aquarinomic relations between hobbyists and state and federal governments became considerably less friendly than they were in the days of the NRA, as import restrictions and laws barring release of potentially invasive species limited both the production and consumption of specimens, with particularly significant implications for breeders and retailers.[31]

Many more pages were devoted to asserting two seemingly indisputable aquarinomic facts: the hobby was expensive, and it was tough for amateurs to make any money on it. Like the consumer economy that spawned it, the hobby demanded extensive outflow with only hypothetical potential for personal profits. This vexing fusion of expense and futility was often a point of humor, as in two examples that encompass the consumption and production ends of the aquarinomic spectrum. The first is outlined in "Klee's Lemma of Maximum Perversity," a variant on Murphy's Law coined by Albert J. Klee, which highlights the fundamental points where the amateur aquarium confounds the logic of the market: inefficiency, unpredictability, and absence of any, even tenuous correlation between market value and longevity. If fish (and bureaucratic) fecundity flummoxed Uncle Sam, fishes' intractable animality was equally disruptive to hobbyists' investments: "The propensity of a fish towards the acquisition of a disease or a refusal to eat or breed, is an increasing function of its cost and/or the difficulty experienced in replacing it."[32] Even fast fish, bought and paid for, could be loose fish, regardless of the aquarist's skill, expense, or commitment. The same theme appears in a cartoon featuring two men headed to their local fish store. One is proudly holding a plastic bag and grinning broadly: "Seven years to spawn them, Harry, but now it's all gonna be worth it to see the expression on this guy's face when I offer to sell him my first batch of rare toluse tetras." Visible to the reader but unseen by our self-satisfied and profit-minded breeder is the front window of the store, featuring a tank labeled "Toluse Tetras Now 10¢."[33] The message is clear: for the home hobbyist, aquarinomics was a site of diminishing returns.

Editorials strike a similar note but go even further to argue that amateurs shouldn't even try to profit from their tanks. William Vorderwinkler reminisces about "the old days" in Germany: "We had real hobbyists then, not a lot of businessmen!" To bring back these glory days, the solution is to "go back to being hobbyists [consumers] once more. Let's enjoy our own fish, and be interested in the fish themselves."[34] The editorial's sentiments are lofty, but market pragmatics carried the day: hobbyist breeding generates gluts that depress prices. Neal Pronek is more direct, capturing the rhetorical split between aquarinomics and Gossean aquarium "purity."

> Come on now, admit it. Once in a while you let sneak into your head the idea that maybe it would be nice to make a few drachmas out of tropical fish . . . [Y]ou confess to yourself that you're more interested in selling a spawn of kribensis than you are in sitting back and ruminating on the wonders of nature as represented by the procreative activities of cichlids. So you feel dirty and degraded because you know that your unbounded venality has prevented you from grasping the TRUE MEANING, the REAL SIGNIFICANCE, the BASIC RELEVANCE of the aquarium hobby, right?[35]

Pronek's larger point is a more prosaic corollary of Klee's lemma: the free-floating nature of value in aquarinomics makes the home tank a poor business proposition. Enterprising aquarists did not need to despair, however. If the tank resisted management as a business, it could be managed as a home. In both arenas, the key to success was the happy family's ability to reproduce itself.

CONTAINING HOME

In *Homeward Bound,* Elaine Tyler May examines the intersection of American cold war politics and the domestic ideology of the period; both operated on the imperative of containment.[36] On the home front, containment had the potential to organize and regulate potentially disruptive social forces and set them firmly within the sturdy framework of the docile, patriarchal family—the "natural" bedrock of the nation. By the dawn of the actual cold war, however, the home aquarium had been managing domestic anxieties for almost a century, including women's increasing participation in the workforce and growing visibility and assertiveness in the public sphere. Its advocates celebrated its ability to construct family and community inside the tank and out. It offered opportunities for both world-making agency and private management of sex, and between 1930 and 1970, such opportunities were especially welcome. Consider, as one example from the middle of this period, Alfred Kinsey's revelation that nice middle-class women were, in fact, desiring, sexual beings, even outside the confines of marriage and procreative duty.[37] Visual and rhetorical reminders that such potentially unruly sexual potential could be easily and even attractively contained were not just pleasing diversions. For many middle-class men, they were necessary.

The tank's visual promiscuity and rhetorical capaciousness, plus its resident population of fish surrogates, were keys to its containment of domestic dilemmas, but three additional factors were also crucial. First was the nature of the literal container involved. The tank was not just situated in the home; it was itself a home, readily intelligible in domestic terms thanks to characterizations like Butler's "happy family" and the long list of the tank's household virtues, from its hygiene to its ability to serve as babysitter and tutor, extolled by enthusiasts. The tank as a whole could and did operate as a surrogate for the family independently of the spawning behaviors of individual residents. These, in turn, only enhanced its potential as container of domestic problems and potential. An aquarium had the added bonuses of captivity and perpetual visibility, ensuring that nothing, not even the most intimate acts, escaped the vigilant aquarist. An untitled 1954 cartoon captures the tank's ability to serve as a surrogate for the home by making the relationship literal. In the first frame, a male enthusiast is shown bent over, head in the tank, trying to observe the goings-on. The second frame shows a smiling viewer gazing appreciatively at an aquarium identical to a family ranch home; fish are clearly visible in the windows.[38] In this new turn on the relationship between the tank, the sea, and the home, it was no longer sufficient for the aquarium to be just an iteration of the sea; fully immersive voyeurism was as inconvenient in the former as in the latter. As a home, however, it offered the equivalent of spying on one's neighbors or even managing a model home, with no closed doors and no complex negotiations with the residents.

On one level, the tank as surrogate home reinforced the naturalness of the family as a social unit, one so organizationally potent that it could even be imposed unproblematically on fish of different species. At the same time, the tank also exposed the constructedness of the category, the maintenance required to make it function, and the sometimes brutal consequences of shortfalls from the ideal. Such is the representational fungibility of the aquarium-home that it could construct disparate residents as a family of fish and serve as a conceptual container for the improvised human family as well.

Perhaps the most notable early example outside of Butler's aquarial "happy families" is Mark Twain's Aquarium Club, his "collection" of "pets," surrogate granddaughters. According to John Cooley, editor of Samuel Clemens's "angelfish correspondence," Clemens admired a large aquarium while on a trip to Bermuda, the angelfish in particular, and

> quickly made the connection between these colorful, angelic fish and the bright young ladies who were beginning to swim around him. They were to be his angelfish, and he would need an aquarium . . . By the time Clemens returned home in April he could count ten angelfish in his aquarium. He quickly had little enameled angelfish pins made up by Tiffany's and sent one to each of his fish, inviting her to become a member of his Aquarium Club.[39]

Cooley leaves unanswered the crucial question, why was Clemens drawn to the image of an aquarium and angelfish rather than to a myriad of other possibilities, like a cage of canaries or a corral of little ponies? Part of the answer may be biographical. Clemens was certainly familiar with P. T. Barnum and his various constructions of "happy families," even referring to this explicitly in a mock "Barnum's First Speech in Congress."[40] The self-evident artifice of the formulation and its easy applicability to both the aquarium and his relationships to his "pets" may have appealed to him. The aquarium, rather than the menagerie, might have seemed like the ideal happy family, given the circumstances. Clemens had lost two daughters to disease and was estranged from another. Recalling Mellen's formulation that fish might show affection but spare the owner from mourning their deaths, Clemens might have found the equivocal animality of fish a relief from the messy animality that enabled mammals to both leave and inspire grief in those left behind. Aquarium dynamics and the easy surrogacy of fish could also contribute a rationale. Certainly, his cheery young angelfish were multiply other to Clemens, as well as soothing and pleasing—everything tank promoters assured consumers aquarium residents would be. Fish had no obvious sexuality if not caught in the act of spawning, and they had no visible markers of sexual difference or age. They offered a kind of respite from more blatant animal sex; they were "innocent." They might be able to recognize their caregivers, but they couldn't talk back or bite. Above all, fish's obvious dependence, along with the aquarium's self-evident function as a container and a home, gave rhetorical coherence to this peculiar "hobby," a "family" that was highly circumscribed, populated by beings who could not exist outside its strict confines. When a girl turned sixteen, she could no longer be a member of the club. The tank was a world-making endeavor, a personal realm both immersed in and apart from everyday life, administered by a steward whose pleasures came from observing and maintaining it.

As suggested by both the cartoon of the aquarium as home and Mark Twain's club, these pleasures were highly gendered. Despite the important contributions of prominent and pioneering women, the hobby was, from its inception, overwhelmingly male. Like other hobbies, the aquarium offered men respite from both the rigors of the public sphere and the interpersonal demands of the private one. It also offered opportunities for self-expression and self-assertion, both hinging on the conceptual mutability of the aquarium. As Arthur Edwards noted in 1858, the tank was "a world in miniature" as well as a home, and both required solid patriarchal stewardship.[41] Herbert Axelrod, writing almost a century after Edwards, reminded readers, "The owner of a home aquarium takes on his responsibility with the pride and passion one would have toward a family of children."[42] But these children couldn't talk back or leave. As aquarists, men could enjoy the privileges of world making and reinscribe and control housekeeping as forms of power in/as leisure. While some of the pleasures of the activity were variants on fantasies of unalienated labor (i.e., the world made with one's own hands), world domination was certainly part of the mix. The aquarist made it and owned it, with a power to re-create and eliminate limited only by his income. In this respect, aquariums were markedly different from other mid-twentieth-century male cultures of tinkering. Ham radio operators, for example, could construct systems to access the world, but the aquarium actually *was* a world, complete with its own distinct population to be managed, added to, and disposed of at will. Sometimes, though, aquarium housekeeping ran up against the more complex dynamics of the actual family home. When this happened, hobbyist magazines identified a clear source for the friction: the spouse, almost always "the wife." Gosse tried to exempt the aquarium from modernity, but later American hobbyists attempted to exempt it from the feminine sphere of influence, using commiseration and humor to shape what Steven M. Gelber calls "domestic masculinity."[43]

Mark Twain's "aquarium" was, by all accounts, chaste. Real ones were not. Water worlds were full of sex, and breeding was the sine qua non of the successful aquarist. Jane Desmond argues, "Our stake in scrutinizing animal reproduction, called sex, is not so much to find out how they do it, but why we do it."[44] As aquarium publications amply demonstrate, hobbyists were also asking, instead, "How do we manage it?" Here, domestic masculinity, combined with the complex surrogacy of toy fish, enabled hobbyists to man-

The Domestic Aquarium   173

age gender trouble inside and outside of the tank. Taken together, the tank's ability to function as a surrogate for home and family, its construction of a domain for domestic masculinity, and its ability to contain sex offered an ideal vehicle for asserting masculine competence in the private sphere while repairing any damages inflicted by routinized, hierarchical, anomic work in the public one.

The WAF: Gender Politics and the Home Aquarium

Speaker after speaker at the 2006 International Marine Aquarium Conference mentioned an apparently vital element of an aquarist's success: the WAF. I assumed this was a measure of water quality. It was not. The acronym stood for "wife acceptance factor," a loose way of calculating how much a husband's investment in aquariums could consume before meeting resistance. Even if such resistance materialized, there were work-arounds, including trade-offs (new fish or a protein skimmer for him, new shoes for her), promises of eventual profitability, and outright lying. The tongue-in-cheek tone with which much of this was delivered seemed to underscore, not diminish, its seriousness and relevance for the overwhelmingly male attendees. I hadn't heard so many references to "the wife" (almost always generic, like "the old ball and chain"; rarely "my wife") since my childhood viewing of *The Flintstones*.

To be sure, over the history of aquaria, there were couples who enjoyed their hobby together. "Fish guy" Donald Simpson and his wife, Helen, were partners in endless aquarium collecting, breeding, and maintenance adventures. Though before she met him she "had never come closer to a fish than a tuna sandwich," she was "a natural"; an indication of how intimately the hobby figured into their marriage is the discussion of the pet octopus they kept in a tank in their bedroom.[45] Helen does not passively "accept" aquariums; Simpson indicates she is an enthusiastic and equal partner in everything—from driving to exotic locales; to identifying specimens; to sharing his deep fondness for "Louie," the aforementioned octopus. Yet in hobbyist publications, such matches made in aquarium heaven seemed to be very few indeed.

Understanding "the wife" as the serpent in the aquarial garden requires recognition of the time, money, space, and potential mess involved in aquariums, all of which can tax domestic resources and a partner's patience. Further, "the wife" also functions as a handy rhetorical brake on the hobby's potentially addictive excesses. But more than this, the WAF exposes precisely how profoundly the tank functions as respite for male enthusiasts, one that merited "protection," even from one's spouse. An especially illustrative example is a 1935 article, "Fish Pulled Me Out," remarkable for its intricate connections between homosociality, aquarinomics, and the classic values of aquaria, going back as far as Gosse. The author, Don Norman, begins by describing the exigency from which his fish benevolently extracted him: the debilitating effects of modern business.

> On the golf field, at lunch—everywhere—the villain of business conditions, the depression, and kindred subjects pursued me. Obviously, the result was that I was rapidly developing into a nervous pain-in-the-neck, uninteresting to talk with, a caged lion in the home that shouted, crabbed and yelled at the stomp of a cat's paw on the carpet.[46]

He is saved by the artistry of constructing the tank, the opportunity to exercise his individual taste, and the pleasures of viewing and maintaining the results. Fish become a kind of living drug that treats depression (with both lowercase and uppercase *d*), and as they heal Norman, they heal the home made tense by his escalating anxiety. The friendly confines of the tank release the lion within the man. In another reminder of the persistence of its visual affinities, the key to the tank's restorative power is the seeming replacement of accounting and its discontents by the peaceful panorama and the theater.

> [F]ish do not argue, bark, chirp, purr, give static trouble, consume oil or gasoline, nor argue labor costs . . . There is beauty and rhythm in constantly changing panoramic pictures not possible to describe or picture. Monotony is out. The eye forgets the debit and credit figures of the day. There is romance, tragedy and humor constantly being unfolded, not a single act of which is without interest.

Though the tank is the result of individual effort and taste, it is not a solitary pursuit; "brotherhood" is integral to its healing effects. Further, in contrast to discussions of "labor costs" that expose unsettling truths about how dispensable some of the brethren actually are, "class distinctions" are "out."[47] Norman illustrates the "cosmopolitan" and "share-the-wealth" ethos of fish enthusiasts, alongside the fiction of the hobby's class democracy, with an anecdote detailing a janitor's generosity (with information and white worms) in providing the crucial expertise a distinguished (and presumably very wealthy) citizen needs to ensure successful breeding of an exotic specimen. He concludes, "To me, there's something stimulating and invigorating in the camaraderie of exotic fish men—possibly because values become things not always measured by dollars and cents, which is (maybe, after all) the true standard of measurement." In his respite from "labor costs," within the putative egalitarianism of aquarium fraternity, Norman seems blissfully unaware that the upward flow of value from laborers to wealthy businessmen is precisely what dollars and cents measure and precisely the ur-value of the hobby in his own testimonial: it so "cools" and revives his "business-driving apparatus" that he receives two raises.[48] Indeed, Norman's ultimate affirmation of the hobby is cast in the very "debit and credit" terms the tank purports to repair: an aquarium might be expensive to set up and maintain, but it's "'bout half the price of a respectable funeral."[49]

It is both true and too simple to dismiss testaments to the restorative and fraternal benefits of aquaria as reinscriptions of class position and the infusion of market values into leisure time. The aquarium also offered middle-class and upper-middle-class men a variety of identities—nurturer, artist, amateur scientist—without the significant demands of any of them. In particular, it provided a way to maintain intellectual and managerial authority through domestic masculinity that included housekeeping as a crucial component. Gelber, Mary Ann Clawson, Mark Carnes, and others have argued that homosocial formations like athletics, fraternal organizations, and do-it-yourself projects ease male gender anxieties in industrial modernity.[50] According to Gelber, domestic masculinity "was practiced in areas that had been the purview of professional craftsmen, and therefore retained the aura of preindustrial vocational masculinity."[51] This was always part of the aquarium's repertoire for managing modern anxieties, but two other interrelated elements were also important. First, relationships with fish and the logistical rituals of caring for them provided possibilities for affective investment that were both personally rewarding and, compared to relationships with human family, undemanding. Second, nurturing and artisanal components could be subsumed under "science," which had increasing mainstream cachet through radio and television popularizers. The opportunity to narrate his own tank—the lives of its residents and the life of the setup itself—made every enthusiast an emcee and producer of his own personal *Zoo Time* and *Wild Kingdom*.[52]

The WAF maintains aquariums as a male respite in part by failing to acknowledge that women, too, shared the aquarium's pleasures, though they were decidedly in the minority in hobbyist history and publications. One cartoon—the exception that proves the rule—even suggests that a "husband acceptance factor" might be an issue for some. On the front lawn of a typical family home, a sign reads, "SALE! DISPOSING OF TROPICAL FISH—G. J. BROWN." A smaller sign next to it reads, "IF HE SELLS EVEN **ONE** I'LL KILL HIM—MRS. BROWN."[53] Rebecca Stott and Bernd Brunner separately note that women were central to the engineering, refinement, biology, and propagation of the home aquarium in Europe, England, and the United States, including Jeanette Power de Villepreux, Anne Thynne, and Elizabeth Emerson Damon.[54] In his history, *Toy Fish*, Klee adds Ida Mellen, who, as noted in previous chapters, served as aquarist and ultimately chief at the New York Aquarium from 1916 to 1929 and authored a number of significant aquarium books that ran into multiple editions. Thynne, who raised and researched scores of madrepores (a type of coral) in glass tanks at her residence in the cloisters of Westminster Abbey, where her husband was subdean, was recognized by Gosse as a worthy interlocutor; he credits her with introducing marine "vivaria" to London.[55] She was the first urban reefer. Power de Villepreux was dismissed outright by Gosse's American contemporaries through a remarkable rhetorical sleight of hand with the very definition of the aquarium.[56] Elizabeth Emerson Damon, whom Klee credits with owning the first American freshwater tank and whose brother William was the author of an early (1879) aquarium book, receives only brief acknowledgment.[57] Without this, she would be entirely absented from the history of the hobby. Mellen fared better, gaining esteem for her position and publications. Later in life, however, she was ambivalent about her association with aquariums and did not keep a tank in her home.[58] As the hobby grew, women occasionally contributed to publications, generally detailing travels to sites of international exotic specimens or offering personal narratives of the "How I Got My Start" variety. If these women's aquarial excesses troubled relatives, it goes unremarked.

Diane Schofield, a regular contributor to the *Aquarium Journal* beginning in the late 1950s, was exceptional for her time, a women hobbyist who forthrightly announced her intoxication with the pleasures of keeping aquariums and her readiness to remake her home to accommodate them. Schofield was a married, suburban mother of two and so did not pose the challenge to the tank as a wholesome family activity that a single woman might to a fraternity of family men; in this, at least, she was typical. Those few women hobbyists represented in aquarium publications are explicitly identified as married and as entering aquariums through husbands or sons. In addition to her journal submissions, which include an almost prodigious output of humorous fish-themed doggerel, Schofield served as editor of the newsletter *Fin Fun* and wrote her own book on tropical fish. A representative example of Schofield's poetry is "Ode to a Piranha Who Was Not a Vegetarian," which includes a guide to phonetic pronunciation to enhance appreciation of the rhyme. It begins,

> Hail, oh, hail, little baleful piranha
> > (pee-ron-ya)
> Does it annoy you to have people gaze
> > Upon ya?[59]

Schofield's challenges to the gendering of leisure didn't stop with her adoption of the traditionally male pastime of the aquarium. She was also an enthusiast for aggressive and demanding, versus "decorative," fish, including piranhas. In "Biting the Hand That Feeds Them!" she describes the fish in ways that suggest empathy and the possibility that the piranha might share adaptive strategies with the suburban housewife, including herself: "All tropical fishes are not the benign, simpering, terribly grateful things that they are cracked up to be. Some of them are just biding their time, waiting their chance."[60] Her articles offer an interesting glimpse into the gender politics of the white middle-class hobby in the years immediately preceding the publication of *The Feminine Mystique* in 1963.

Fish keeping enabled Schofield to indulge one of her "first loves—writing," giving her opportunities for a voice and a platform that few female aquarists or middle-class housewives of the time enjoyed.[61] She had more formal training than many hobbyists, majoring in zoology at her local community college. She ultimately turned instead to interior decorating and was good-humored about the seeming incompatibility of this choice and her devotion to her pets; the new, more conventionally feminine pursuit "has proved of inestimable benefit in my days of aquarium keeping as I have the only tanks interiorly decorated in 18th-century Guppy and Early Mollie periods." But her insights into the gendering of the hobby go beyond recognition of the comparative frivolity of decor: "Sometimes I feel rather alone in a world of masculine fish lovers" who "seem to outnumber females by at least ten to one."[62] Yet Schofield's solution was not to forge a sorority of female keepers of fish to offer "egalitarian" companionship of the sort so sustaining to Don Norman. On the contrary, in an essay entitled "Arise Men!" she goads henpecked husbands to man up: "[A]fter all, who pays the bills around your house, fellas? Stand up for your rights."[63] On the surface, this is clearly a case of a male-identified "exceptional woman" casting her lot with those who lent her a modicum of expressive capital. A closer look, however, reveals that the essay is less a defense of male hobbyists than Schofield's own attempt to justify a nontraditional and resource-intensive diversion at the height of domestic containment. Further, that justification is rhetorically routed through Schofield's various "awfully squishy, slimy" fish.[64] Men must be mobilized to "march" not just to assert their inherent patriarchal right to all the tanks they could reasonably support; they also needed to "protect the feelings" of unjustly maligned and misunderstood fish and, by extension, the few women who cared for them.[65]

Schofield begins by expressing her surprise at the lack of women in the hobby, given its beauty and the fact that "hefting tanks . . . is a mere bagatelle compared with the lifting that must be done by anyone raising small children."[66] Men from the time of P. H. Gosse turned to the tank over seemingly more manly hunting because, as Don Norman put it, "there is a sense of repulsion in 'killing.'"[67] Schofield uses a similar rationale for favoring aquariums over "staid civilized," traditionally female crafts she describes as brutally violent, even perverse: "torturing wretched little bits of paper into artificial flowers, beating innocent little bits of glass into insensibility to make mosaics, or knitting."[68] She reasons, seemingly tongue in cheek, that other women must prefer such abominations to the more obvious rewards of aquarium keeping because they have an irrational prejudice against things that appear "slimy" and "squishy." In another example of fish surrogacy, Schofield rehabilitates her pets as a way of justifying her own nontraditional pleasures, arguing that they are "good housekeepers," television-Western-loving family members, and, to the open-minded, "big butterflies." These fish stories comprise the bulk of the essay. It is very difficult not to read them as allegories advocating the inclusion of such disdained slimy ones into the conventional family—appropriate objects of a woman's affection—and as stand-ins for the misunderstood female hobbyist herself. The essay's humor hides a deeper rage against the rigid gender proscriptions of leisure time that reassured the socially squeamish about everyone knowing their proper places. For Schofield and women hobbyists like her, the tank was not simply an Eden, a respite, a miniature version of the undersea, or even a happy family. It was a little glass box exposing and containing her own ambitions for world making, beauty, self-expression, and a turn on a larger social stage. It was a way to acknowledge what she shared with her finny friends—captivity, the aversion of the ignorant, perhaps "good housekeeping"—while being a fish out of water, as alone among male fish lovers as among female knitters.

During the late 1950s, when Diane Schofield was exhorting male aquarists to claim what was rightfully theirs, "[c]ompromise, accommodation, and lowered expectations were solutions for many disappointed people who still clung to the ideal of domestic containment."[69] Variations on the WAF during this period expose the mechanics of such negotiations and suggest ways domestic containment itself operated through the aquarium as container. Rhetorical tactics used to manage the WAF included everything from complete capitulation (almost always on the part of "the wife"), to duplicity, to all out war, each aimed at resolving competing claims to domestic space, resources, and authority. Even at their most outrageous, advice on how to work around "the wife" hints at self-consciousness on the part of the male hobbyist, a recognition that an obsession with aquariums (versus sports, woodworking, or other "manly" diversions) was still somewhat odd and that some of the desires of the zealous husband aquarist might seem a bit beyond the pale.[70]

Albert Klee frankly advises a wife's absolute acquiescence to the caprices of her "addicted" mate, as well as her collusion in the requisite dishonesty that accompanies the addiction. Representative examples from his ten-point list include implicit and explicit extortion, a new iteration of "debit/credit" aquarinomic transaction in the home. His first point reads,

> Be optimistic and believe everything your dear man tells you about the purchases of his fish, plants, aquaria and other equipment. True, that fish he told you cost only 50¢ may actually have cost $3 but remember, sooner or later he will voluntarily suggest that you buy a new hat or dress as a salve to his overburdened conscience.

His ninth point reads,

> Be deceitful and untruthful when facing aquarist visitors. When your husband blandly announces that the water in his breeding tanks is at least 6 months old when you know that they were filled only the night before, look his visitors straight in the eye and back him up. The blackmail you practice later may not be moral but it is legal between spouses and the profits are enormous.[71]

Klee ultimately advocates an "if you can't beat 'em, join 'em" solution to the purported domestic turmoil caused by "the addict," but the overall humor of this piece and others like it suggests that these conflicts, while undoubtedly real and frequent, also figure into the homosocial pleasures of the hobby.[72] In this view, complaining about or getting one past "the wife" is its own kind of fish story, replete with the same exaggerations and bravado present in traditional fish tales. These tales of domestic conflict offered occasion for self-assertion in the telling that paralleled and reinforced owners' self-expression in the design and management of their tanks. They were a narrative tool for fraternal bonding, and the worthier the foe, the greater the victory or the more understandable the defeat.

Robert J. Wyndham carries the trope of domestic combat to a new extreme in his essay from the same period entitled "On the Aquarium Front—For Men Only: Don't Be a Mouse Facing Your Spouse." As the reference to "the front" suggests, Wyndham explicitly deploys the rhetoric of statecraft, both martial and diplomatic, though the difference between the two is negligible. For example, a "master diplomat" offers one set of possibilities for extracting concessions like more tanks in the living room. For clarification, the "master diplomat" is defined as "the rare type of man who can do anything to a woman and make her like it."[73] The connection to rape is hard to miss, one of the slippages between sex in the aquatic and terrestrial family homes. The overall goal is "breaking down by hook or by crook (or both) her will to resist." Yet despite the admonition against mousiness in the title and the testosterone-infused military formulations, the actual tactics advocated are more weaselly than warriorlike. They include "perfidious subversion" (making a new tank seem like her idea), playing on guilt rooted in the conflation of the tank and the home ("it's a shame [hatchlings] can't enjoy family life in the community tank"), getting her to feed them ("women can't help developing a tender attachment to those they feed"), and easing into additional tank acquisition ("Remember the introduction of the Federal Income Tax?").[74] Winners of this "war of the sexes . . . have made Machiavelli look like a fumbling schoolboy," but to conclude the piece, the author seems to morph into that same schoolboy, caught in some untoward act: "Pardon me for ending this article rather abruptly. Suddenly I remember that the little woman is due home any moment now. I must get this piece out of the house and in the mails [sic] right now. Oh no, not that I am afraid. But . . . well . . . You know." The last paragraph completely undercuts the martial vigor of the preceding pages. It suggests a humorous way of managing another key feature of domestic containment: resignation in the face of the inevitable compromises of autonomy demanded by family life. Feigned fear of "the little woman" is one way of asserting and deferring to the limits on time, funds, and attention that circumscribed the pleasures of the male aquarist.

It offered an "opt-out" clause exempting him from any unwelcome demands of fraternity even as it reinforced homosociality through narratives emphasizing shared sufferings at the hands of "the wife."

As noted earlier, the aquarium was managing such dilemmas even before cold war domestic containment in the 1950s. The marketing of the tank as decor or pedagogical amusement for the whole family persisted throughout its history to the present, but beginning with the increasing popularity of the tank in the 1920s, such appeals took a backseat to those directed at an implied audience of male hobbyists. This shift was particularly noticeable in aquarium publications of the 1930s and 1940s. As three examples from this period demonstrate, "the wife" also enabled aquarists to manage concerns about scarcity and excess; she was another version of the spoilsport, but she was also the voice of conventional wisdom, through rarely acknowledged as such. An article in *Home Aquarium Bulletin*, "The Mrs. and the Hobby," by "Mostof Us," addresses both elements.

> It seems just bad that the Mrs. does not see the hobby in the same light as we do . . . She cannot figure out why we must purchase a male *Sclahokum* at a time when we cannot afford new shoes for the youngest heir. She doesn't realize that the youngster will need the shoes next pay day more than he does today. I can't understand how the Mrs. can be so unreasonable.
>
> Last season we raised four black swordtails and sold them for three dollars—and I gave her the three bucks, too. The black swordtail parent [sic] were a beautiful pair.—I got them cheap at eight dollars.[75]

The humor of the piece rests on two points: the often-mentioned aquarinomics of diminishing returns and the self-evident eccentricities of the hobbyist, rendered even more extreme by "the Mrs.'s" "unreasonable" insistence on human family first and fiscal good sense. "The Mrs." is once again the rhetorical brake on the hobbyist's enthusiasm, but unlike the "war of the sexes" rhetoric of the late 1950s, this article, published in 1931, presents her as less an opponent than a stand-in for the domestic reality of financial limits and household priorities at a time of economic constriction.

Excess, specifically the uncontrollable fertility of tropical fish that so vexed Uncle Sam in the previously mentioned NRA cartoon, was another source of domestic friction, as in a "Suggested Song (?)" for San Francisco–area aquarium society meetings from 1947. "Fish, Fish, and More Fish" was to be sung to the tune of "Home on the Range."

> First one pair I had. Then a dozen or
> two,
> Until now it is thousands galore;
> And where it will end,
> I can not tell to you,
> But it troubles me plenty and more.
> Fish, fish and more fish;
> I do spawn them by day and by
> night;
> From basement to roof,
> Tanks do fill up my house,
> And my wife does complain more and
> more.[76]

The wife's complaints are more than the refrain to this song and, by extension, the male aquarist's life. They function as the family reality principle, asserting itself lest the hobbyist burst the confines of domestic propriety with the fruits of his unruly aquarial desires.

Sexual Containment in the Tank

The WAF marked the limit of what "the wife" would accept, and it is unsurprising that those limits were most vigorously challenged by sex, specifically fish sex and its inevitable results. As Frank Locke observed, "Rearing a full and hardy spawning to maturity, is many times responsible for caustic remarks on the part of one's wife, (if one has one) who may not be in perfect accord with your latest breeding accomplishments."[77] Vigorous pursuit of "breeding accomplishments" was a source of small tensions mimicking the potentially seismic ones produced by generating offspring outside the nuclear family, heedless procreation unchecked by the confines of domestic containment. Spawn were themselves pregnant with the prospect of yet more tanks and even more spawn. Fish fecundity was a mark of an aquarist's success and a challenge to domestic resources, especially money, space, and attention. Further, though fishes' runaway fertility might trouble the male aquarist and "the wife" over the logistical nightmare of fish, fish, and more fish, the opposite problem could also alienate him from his family, with even more dire consequences. William Vorderwinkler captures this situation in his poem "Father's Dilemma," which begins,

> Since Father's started breeding Ramirezi,
>   Mother hardly sees him any more;
> His absent-minded eyes are getting hazy
>   When he comes home from the local dealer's store.

Mother's dilemma is that Father seems to be obsessed with fish porn. "He just sits and watches by the hour" as the family tiptoes around him.[78] Father's dilemma is aquarial impotence: the Ramirezi are stubbornly refusing to do what nature and the aquarist intended. As "Father's Dilemma" humorously suggests, aquarium fish, sex, and a male hobbyist's obsession were a potent combination, comparable to a mistress in the ability to seduce a man away from his family and disrupt his home life. The combination also did important ideological work, managing fears about sexual chaos in times of social change by using fish as surrogates for traditional gender roles and behaviors.

Writing about displays in the Monterey Bay Aquarium, Jane Desmond argues,

> The culturalization of nature proceeds here in casting biological reproduction as "sexual encounters" and in continuously reasserting the categories of male and female even when such divisions are basically meaningless. Such explanations of reproduction attempt to make bodies which are radically different from our own comprehensible by inscribing a sexual difference even when none is visible. This construction of the natural as the sexual obversely functions as evidence of what is natural in the cultural. Ideologically, such discourses of nature naturalize the attachment of sex as a gendered activity to sex as a biological category.[79]

In the home aquarium and supporting publications, the symbolic forces of nature and science could be mobilized in service of domestic sexual containment, particularly the reinforcement of traditional gender roles. The aquatic family home offered a template for intimacies in the terrestrial one. In addition, the tank, as home within the home, enabled the male aquarist to revel in the pleasures of surrogate fatherhood through his breeding successes. May notes the importance of fatherhood in postwar masculinity: "On television, upward mobility into respectable middle class life emerged in the form of fatherhood, when men ceased to be workers and became 'dads.' In fatherhood, a man could exert true authority and manliness." In that other glass box in the home, mechanics of managing breeding tanks enabled men to usurp maternal gestational privilege, too; they could be both mother and father, with none of the "undercurrents of uncertainty" that circulated around the father's proper role in child rearing.[80]

A 1955 advertisement for "Miracle Filter" (see fig. 13) captures this dynamic in graphic terms. On one side of the ad, a man reclines, eyes closed, smoking a cigarette as he relaxes in front of the tank. The copy tells us, "This chap doesn't know the difference between a Lebistes reticulatus [a guppy] and an Oranda and he doesn't care. He wants a beautiful aquarium with the least possible work." Like a disengaged father who sees home simply as a respite from the rigors of the workplace, he provides basic support, and that is sufficient. The adjoining frame features a man smiling broadly before a downward cascade of tanks. In the first, two fish kiss. The second is labeled "Maternity," with two more below that are designated "Nursery." Our happy aquarist is helping little fish jump from one to the other. This hobbyist is a provider and more: he facilitates maternity itself. He is "proud of his success in breeding and raising the real problem fish—he knows that water conditions have to be just right—and that the babies have to be literally swimming in food, without danger of fouling the water."[81] In short, he is mother and father; he is incubator, nurturer, and housekeeper as well as scientist, engineer, and naturalist. As breeding birthed more and more tanks, the hobbyist became more than a worker or even mother/father. Through his own intellectual and logistical potency, he was populating his own ecosystems, all under his complete control.

One potential danger of sexual containment through the tank is the chance that, like "Father" in Vorderwinkler's poem, the male aquarist would be so diverted by the reproductive potential of his fish that sex in his own home was contained only too well. It could drain libidinal investments from the household, not reinforce them. Of course, the home aquarium was not the only hobby with such potential. Writing during World War II and citing no clinical or empirical evidence, psychiatrist William Menninger posited that these leisure activities provided an outlet for suppressed sexual energies but, when obsessively pursued, "produce[d] feelings of guilt because the hobby is symbolic masturbation."[82] The issue here was not evidence but a scientifically endorsed suspicion of non(re)productive energies directed outside of work or the family, one that was heightened even further during cold war domestic containment. Here, the (re)productive family unit was the state's bulwark against the communist menace, a restorative partner to American enterprise. The potentially disruptive rerouting of such energies into cross-species investments was cause for nervous self-recognition in the

WHICH ONE HAS THE MIRACLE FILTER?

THIS CHAP Doesn't know the difference between a Lebistes reticulatus* and an Oranda and he doesn't care. He wants a beautiful aquarium with the least possible work.

THIS FELLOW is proud of his success in breeding and raising the real problem fish — he knows that water conditions have to be just right — and that the babies have to be literally swimming in food, without danger of fouling the water.

BOTH USE THE MIRACLE FILTER, the perfect answer to greater success and MORE PLEASURE WITH LESS WORK.

*Guppy

Injection molded plastic... Stronger... more rigid than before! No glass wool needed when No. 3 or coarser gravel is used.

Ideal for MARINE AQUARIA ... Easy to maintain ... No extra aeration needed.

NEW SIZES:

No. 2 — 2 gallon	$3.45	No. 10 — 10" x 20"	$5.95
No. 3 — 3 gallon	3.95	No. 15 — 12" x 24"	6.95
No. 5 — For all 5, 6, 7 & 8 gal.	4.95	No. 25 — 12" x 30"	9.95

Custom sizes also. Prices on request.

At better pet shops everywhere or write for free brochure

Dealers — Write for FREE DEMONSTRATOR offer.

MIRACLE FILTER COMPANY
1007 East 10th Street, Long Beach 13, California

Fig. 13. "New Miracle Filter for Aquariums," advertisement, *Tropical Fish Hobbyist*, September–October 1955, n.p.

hobby even after cultural ruptures to the cold war domestic containment of the 1960s, as in a 1970 cartoon of a bride and groom apparently headed off to their honeymoon. The groom is hugging his aquarium, which sits in his lap. His bride, her arm around him, pleads, "Well I know you'd miss them Dear, but it's only for one week."[83] In contrast, "Picture of a Happy Hobby" invited hobbyists to imagine the ideal scenario: a circuit running between love of the tank and love of family, linking one organically to the other. It featured a well-dressed couple and a child, presumably their son, all beaming at their well-stocked tank—a prosperous happy family outside birthed by one inside.[84]

Fish breeding had its own complexities, not the least of which was the difficulty in telling males and females apart. Numerous corollaries to "Klee's Lemma of Maximum Perversity" involved situations where members of expensive "breeding pairs" turned out to be the same sex or where local water quality made mating conditions impossible.[85] There were problems posed by what was seen as excessive hybridization resulting in "freaks" or diluting reliable bloodlines, though in 1941, at least one aquarist was aware that appeals to "Nature's purity of strain" might sound uncomfortably similar to those "proclaimed by certain neurotic members of our own species."[86] The mechanics of fish breeding would certainly seem to support Desmond's assertion that "[a]n enormous discursive and imaginary effort is required to translate information about species reproduction into . . . highly sexed tales of mating."[87] Fish did not have intercourse and were dimorphic, though, as William Innes observed, "[i]t is almost as difficult convincing a confirmed aquarist that a fish can change sex as it is to persuade the uninformed that some fish have their young born alive."[88] Such difficulties suggested that it was imagining fish *outside* of human gender categories that actually required the discursive and imaginative work. As hobbyist publications amply demonstrate, the utility of fish as surrogates meant that inserting them into human idioms to contain anxieties about sex and gender roles seemed to take no effort at all.

The most obvious examples of the aquarium as an institution containing both piscine and human sexual issues involve the transposition of mating into marriage. Two cartoons by Albert J. Klee illustrate that such transpositions were useful, even when they were held up to ridicule. One features a middle-aged couple with an aquarium between them; the woman is tossing something into the tank. The man, presumably her husband, observes, "I know they are thinking of spawning, Martha, but rice won't help!"[89] The second represents the opposite dilemma: having spawned, the prospective "father" needs encouragement to "do the right thing." Seated on the floor near a jug of moonshine, a bearded and barefoot aquarist, the very stereotype of the "hillbilly," points his shotgun at his tank, admonishing, "One uh you boys gotta marry her!"[90] On the surface, both cartoons reflect the seeming absurdity of subjecting "nature" in the tank to the demands of culture. However, with fish fertility under the command of the watchful aquarist and contained in the home within a home, the underlying and reassuring message is that though attempts at domestic containment may be the ultimate exercises in futility, they are also central to the well-regulated, productive household.

Even without the explicit transposition of "mating" into "marriage," breeding fish are surrogates for traditional gender roles of husband and wife, father and mother. Here, "Amazons" get their comeuppance by being killed or put in their place, and manly, responsible "family men" get their due. Coincident with the rise and consolidation of industrial modernity and the entry of women into the workforce, the aquarium itself was replete with "gender trouble," "scandal[s] with the sudden intrusion, the unanticipated agency, of a female 'object' who inexplicably returns the glance, reverses the gaze, and contests the place and authority of the masculine position."[91] The tank was one arena in which such scandals could be managed "naturally," as in the remarkable account "That Siamese Amazon," detailing the domestication of an exotic oriental temptress (a betta) that seduces the aquarist and potential piscine mates alike.

> Bored to the uttermost she looked, brooding at the bottom of a diminutive glass jar . . . She never stirred, just rolled her eyes up at me once and then lost interest. I had no use for her, had no idea of adding another fish to my lot, but "What a fish!" and I was lost. Dark red all over, finned well enough to make a male fish hang his head in shame and with a productive promise I could not resist, there was no denying her charms.

The seductive fish leads the sober aquarist astray with her beauty and "productive promise," and he quickly identifies a "worthy" mate: an equally striking "great red brute." When they were introduced, however, "it was no love light that blazed from her eyes; it was the joy of battle if I ever saw it." Sure enough, the Amazon batters her potential suitor, necessitating his retreat to another tank to "recover his dignity" and repair his shredded fins, which the aquarist dabs with "mercurochrome" like a cut-man in a boxer's corner.[92] This has all the makings of a gender scandal, except for the fact that the Amazon's biological clock is clearly ticking: she is building a bubble nest.

In a sign that even the toughest "termagant" can be won over by Mr. Right, she is introduced to another "real battler," "far from a beauty but all fish." She melts immediately, with the happy result that "a cloud of husky infants" is soon filling the tank.[93] The hobbyist's own seduction has a happy ending. Productive potential is realized as the Amazon succumbs to her biological destiny by yielding to a deceptively dull but worthy match in this aquatic variant on the plots of movies from the 1930s and 1940s in which a sexy, feisty heroine is tamed by the stolid hero and domesticity.[94]

Male aquarists seemed particularly fond of fish they could characterize as "regular guys," "all fish," and "gentlemen." These mannerly but macho tank residents prove their mettle by putting females in their place, if not through the mutual seduction of the "Siamese Amazon" and her match, then more violently. In most of these cases, domestic order is restored, ensuring that the stubborn rigidity of traditional gender norms imposed on the tank could work reciprocally to stabilize the home. Occasionally, though, the happy heteronormative narrative arc is disrupted by both gender trouble and male caprice, as in an account of the breeding habits of *Arcara curviceps* (see fig. 14), which merits quoting at length.

> Speaking of gentlemen, Arcara curviceps is entitled to all the glory that surrounds the term [. . .] Most marriages among them, to be successful, are invariably made in Heaven; and in this instance, necessitate a real prayer on the part of their owner to hope for stabilization to the point where the first honeymoon brings real results in the shape of a rousing crowd of youngsters. The subject of divorce is a matter which is usually handled in a workmanlike manner by the male fish; but on some occasions a real Amazon develops who will toe the mark with her supposed lord (but not master), battle it out on an even basis, and in the end leave him floating at the surface in such a mess that he will likely not be of further use to any other lady of his particular genus.
>
> On occasion, it is necessary to supply a particularly pugnacious male with from two to four females before one of them possesses the proverbial "it," in his estimation. This choice might not always be for the best either, as he might decide to embark on his new venture with the most unseemly appearing hussy in your possession.[95]

If this description requires "work" to insert *Arcara curviceps* into conventionally gendered behaviors, it's hard to detect it. The passage reads as an allegory for domestic romances gone both right and wrong. In the former, the happy marriage "made in Heaven" is rewarded with "a crowd of offspring," and the unhappy one is dealt with by dispatching the "wife." In the latter, pugnacity and/or the bad taste to consort with "hussies" are suboptimal, leading to male injury or inferior stock. It's hard for contemporary readers to see the gentlemanly aspects in either scenario. The stickleback (see fig. 14), in contrast, has been a model of male fish decency for over a hundred years. Henry Butler describes him as "dapper," "belligerent," "courageous," and an "affectionate and attentive mate": "His gallantry is perfectly *exemplaire*."[96] Like *Arcara curviceps*, this fish is pugnacious, but his breeding behaviors, including constructing a bubble nest and guarding the fry, make him "a great family man" and a do-it-yourselfer who is a "conscientious and reputable builder."[97]

These descriptions and others like them pull in two directions that parallel the demands on middle-class masculinity from the 1930s through the 1950s. On the one hand, an emerging culture of domesticity and the economic and social capital involved in being a "good family man" encouraged middle-class men to channel sexuality into the family. The tank was one way to experience domestic potency while alleviating human relational obligations: it offered world-making potential in the tank and the allegorical potential of gendered fish that, depending on the account, accommodated or ruptured structures of sexual containment. Male fish could have their "hussies" and their "husky infants," too, and still be "gentlemanly." On the other hand, though, the tank offered opportunities to vicariously indulge one's inner beast. As these accounts indicate, pugnacity and toughness often carry the day, ensuring domestic bliss through a "natural" exercise of force. It's important that these "gentlemanly" fish are brutes, belligerents, and battlers; they ensure that good manners are not mistaken for effeminacy inside the tank or out. Toughness counts. To take one more example, the beautiful blue gularis (*Aphyosemion coeruleum*) is "not a sissy" because he is so resilient he can survive a jump to the floor more than ten feet from his tank and an hour out of water on the floor.[98] Responsible "family men" inside the tank reassured responsible middle-class aquarists outside that they would prevail because they adhered to conventional norms of domesticity and, more important, because they were fiercer and hardier than they looked.

The aquarium was domestic in two senses of the word: an indigenous industry and a home within a home. Aquarinomics, gender politics, and sex came together around dubious promises of financial profit and (re)productive promises of spawning happy families. The tank was also a battleground. Inside, Amazons met their matches; outside, male aquarists asserted command over household space and resources, as well as their own leisure time,

Acara curviceps
(*Acara thayeri*)

A do-it-yourself fan
and great family man —

Meet Mr. Stickleback!

Fig. 14. Aquarium fish as "family men": *Acara curviceps* and "Mr. Stickleback." (*Acara curviceps* illustration from *Aquariana* [November, 1932], 107 [author: Frank S. Locke; illustrator uncredited]; "Meet Mr. Stickleback" illustration from *Aquarium Journal*, December, 1958, [author: Robert J. Wyndham; illustrator uncredited].)

through the enabling fiction of the WAF. The aquarium demonstrates domestic containment at work as early as the 1930s. As a world-making project confined to little glass boxes, it both reproduced and alleviated the strictures regulating self-expression in the modern workplace and the sex and gender proscriptions in the home.

In 1856, Shirley Hibberd asked his readers, "How will future poetry be affected by the revelations of the aquarium, and how far will the sober facts of scientific research influence the pictures and incidents of romance."[99] He could not have anticipated that almost two hundred years later, in 2002, the aquarium would instead birth "Firemouth," the monster truck (scientifically named "Chevyus Kickus Buttus") of the fish food company Tetra. Here, the aquarium as an extension of male pastoral reverie, antidote to male cruelty, or incarnation of paternal potency morphs into the aquarium as testosterone-saturated boxing ring. Gone are the adjectives aligning the "gentlemanly" *Arcara curviceps* and that "good family man" the stickleback with norms of docile domesticity. On the first page of a three-page spread, Tetra informs readers of *Aquarium Fish Magazine*,

> When your name is
> Firemouth, Convict
> or Jack Dempsey,
> you want a food
> you can sink
> your teeth into.

Characterizations of the animals themselves leave no doubt as to the new muscularity of the tank, whose residents are now characterized not as a happy family but more like members of a fight club: "These omnivores don't nibble politely—they strike ferociously at food."[100] Just in case the reader misses the point about the ferocity of these macho fish, she or he can turn the page to read equally macho quasi-scientific descriptions of the three cichlids named previously: "Smaller fish beware. Mauls plants, gravel and unsuspecting species."[101] The piscine pugnacity that served as surrogate for terrestrial family men's frustrations while affirming the manliness of the hobby is still in force, only more so, and absent any, even token connection to the domestic sphere. Here, too, aquaria reflect shifting norms in domestic containment, and in post-9/11 America, muscularity itself was the preferred strategy.

CHAPTER 6

"FOREIGN IN THE DOMESTIC SENSE": TROPICAL FISH AND THE TRANSNATIONAL AQUARIUM

With the introduction of so-called tropical fish in the 1910s, the American home aquarium gained the potential to contain the global south and a whole new set of relationships, tropes, and visual affinities. Its prior associations were not abandoned. On the contrary, the garden, the window, the stage, the home, the seeming immutability of biological difference, slippage between the tank and the sea, the restorative antimodernity of manageable nature, and the queer alterity of the fish themselves were all part of the crucial conceptual infrastructure for the new transnational tank. As increasingly global networks transformed the nineteenth-century "happy family" into a community of specimens from "Egypt, Australia, Asia, India, China, Siam, . . . and South America," aquarists drew on the full measure of their existing rhetorical repertoire.[1] But they were also innovative, further demonstrating the tank's representational capaciousness by reactivating old imperial clichés and setting these alongside new iterations of familiar genres. In their efforts to imagine the hobby within a set of expanding global networks, aquarists operated as a domestic microcosm mirroring the geopolitical movement of the United States as it asserted itself on the world stage and inserted itself into imperial logics with increasing vigor. The aquarium benefited from these imperial logics and returned the favor by domesticating and naturalizing them, rendering them part and parcel of daily routines.

The home tank was both a product of the consumers' imperium and an agent of its reproduction. It stretched the hobby's elastic, ambivalent relationship to cosmopolitan modernity—particularly its "incomprehensible size" and increasingly global interconnections—even further.[2] As indicated in chapter 5, aquarists themselves decried the perils of an increasingly global consumer capitalism as early as the 1930s. In their view, relentless pursuit of cheaper stock cast worthy native breeder/retailers as vulnerable little fish left to the tender mercies of predatory aquarinomic networks based first in Europe and later in the global south. This increasingly transnational modernity was a pernicious and deleterious force. It required a personal water world as a palliative, even as it provided the necessary preconditions for organizing and displaying "nature" as a mass-market middle-class consumable. But the idea of transnational modernity itself was also a way of celebrating racial and national superiority under the rubrics of technological and scientific prowess. The configuration of the tank as container/world and the representational fungibility of toy fish domesticated an imperial chronopolitics wherein colorful fish from the global south stood in for the hemisphere's "colorful" peoples—alien, primitive or outside of time, docile or curiously aggressive, requiring the care of benevolent and technologically superior custodians.[3] In the home and on the pages of hobbyists' magazines, the tropical tank relied on transnational networks to minister to the very dislocations those networks produced. The tropical aquarium relied on global networks to offer even more ways to revel in modernity while disavowing it at the same time. Anna Lowenhaupt Tsing proposes "friction" as a metaphor for examining "the awkward, unequal, unstable, and creative qualities of interconnection across difference" that characterize contemporary global exchange.[4] By the mid-twentieth century, tank water was a powerful lubricant for the frictions required to sustain transnational modernity. It relieved anxieties about the consequences of geopolitical expansion and adventures by substituting manageable Edenic water worlds for the messy complexities of terrestrial ones and, often, by substituting fish for the vexing alterity of native peoples.

The title of this chapter is taken from Amy Kaplan's analysis of *Downes v. Bidwell* (1901), an important element of the legal framework justifying American imperialism.[5] The case established that Puerto Rico was a possession of the United States, not part of it, and thus was not covered by the U.S. Constitution. Justice Edward Douglas White reasoned that "whilst in an international sense Porto [sic] Rico was not a foreign country since it was subject to the sovereignty of and was owned by the United States, it was foreign to the United States in a domestic sense, because the island had not been incorporated into the United States, but was merely appurtenant thereto as a possession."[6] The circumlocution "foreign in the domestic sense" is ideal for describing the ways the tank alleviates imperial anxieties while reinforcing imperial logics, through a visual and rhetorical legerdemain that exposes the leaky borders between "foreign" and "domestic" while upholding their putative distinctiveness at the same time. The equivocality of the term *domestic* conflates the nation as home, the family home, and the tank as home. But the aquarium was also another world, an insular case—ironically the opposite of an island, with water surrounded by land—and, when preceded by the adjective *tropical*, a metonym for a generic global south. The "tropics" stood in for and homogenized countries in four continents, as well as multiple elements of difference. "Tropical fish" thus came from a generically, often fictively, foreign place—somewhere else, but also nowhere in particular. The foreignness of "the tropics" parallels that of the underwater world and the queer alterity of fish, with their curious customs and manners. The tank's job was to contain the foreign in a domestic sense, to transform a potentially anarchic group of exotics into a docile community if not a "happy family," always available—because always visible—for the hobbyist's private psychospiritual succor. This chapter begins by examining the tropes of tropicality that organized the transnational tank, then turns to travel narratives that literally set aquarists into the geographic tropics.

TROPES OF TROPICALITY

The tropical fish tank both drew on and contributed to tropes of tropicality operating in Western art, science, and public discourse over centuries.[7] In so doing, they actively contributed to the growth of "the tropical" as a transnational brand in everything from a leisure destination to home decor.[8] The tropics are defined by the circles of Cancer and Capricorn, at latitudes 23 27' north and south of the equator. Many, though by no means all, tropical fish originated in this region of the globe, though their entrée into the American market was due mainly to European breeders. Most of the early tropicals actually came from Germany. As this geographic amnesia demonstrates, mentions of "the tropics" in aquarium hobbyist discourses do not always refer to a particular geographic designation. Moreover, the "tropical" in reference to "tropical fish" has remained stubbornly generic, not distinguishing between the Amazon rain forests, African lakes, or Southeast Asian rivers, much less specific countries. Such genericism is useful, not the least because it precludes aquarists' linking specific fish explicitly to specific geopolitical developments and thereby preserving the tanks' restorative potential as (because) exempt from such developments.

References to "tropical" fish required hobbyists to establish the exotic bona fides that simultaneously underlined and erased species' origins and paths to the tank. These strategies are similar to those governing the slippage of the adjective *native* from references to indigenous American species to references to American wholesalers and retailers, as discussed in chapter 5. In a complex set of partial erasures and substitutions, the designation "tropical" first functions as shorthand for fish originally found any place in the global south. Next, the decontextualized and generic designation "tropics" preserves the affective residue of these origins, particularly their exoticism, however distant from the site of fishes' actual production. The designation is neither scientifically precise nor as pragmatically informative as the admittedly equally generic "warm-water fish," but it is evocative as well as useful, drawing on preexisting images of bountiful faraway lands that are the fictive antitheses of modernity but also of that same modernity's seemingly miraculous ability to extract and transport this bounty to the American home. These tropes of tropicality constructed a fluid set of "imaginal, pictorial, and textual spaces" often interchangeable with other compelling but generic locations, especially "the jungle."[9] Such spaces worked lexical and visual magic, allowing the aquarist to conjure exotic locales and at least theoretically reproduce them in the tank.

Tropics of Color

The tropics inserted new dimensions of differences into the home aquarium through preexisting visual and rhetorical shorthand for the global south as colorful, exotic, fecund, and primitive—a veritable riot of alterity. But the overarching difference organizing all other tropes of tropicality in the tank is color. Tropical fish are more colorful than native species, and their exoticism derives directly from their pigmentation. In hobbyist publications, fishes' colors are attributes to be maximized through special diets and attention to water chemistry. Vibrant colors testify to aquarial expertise. Michael Taussig argues that "color is what sold, and continues to sell modernity."[10] He is referring to the chemical industry's production of synthetic dyes, but aquarium fish, modernity's found objects, were naturally vivid and thus authentic, like flowers or parrots. If all color was "creaturely"—tactile and sensual—tropical fish made this literal.[11] The fluidity of their movements became actual flows of color. Their small size, easy containability, and self-evident "naturalness" were inoculations against Western chromophobia and the dismissal of the colorful as garish bad taste.

The tank domesticated color as it domesticated underwater worlds. Technological and rhetorical frameworks made color consumable and intelligible. Tropical fish were one way "vivid color [passed] through the toll gates of the West," as part of a larger strategy of creating and managing differences from the global south.[12] Moreover, fish were a conduit for, as well as possessors of, color. They could stand in for "colored" peoples. And because both fish and color were representationally fungible, people of color entered the pages of aquarium publications as stand-ins for fish—equally authentic and exotic, often seemingly equally docile, and always containable. In a move enabled by both images of the anthropologist in popular culture and aquarists' own travel narratives, tropical fish became the hobbyist's own personal tribe, and native peoples could be imagined as possible pets.[13] Yet this representational fungibility was also potentially disconcerting. It raised the specter of white American aquarists being swamped by global flows from dark continents in a colorful world made smaller by technology and travel. It suggested uneasy connections between color "over here" and "over there," especially as postcolonials increasingly began to challenge imperial logics during the period covered here, 1930–70. Aquarium publications managed these anxieties using another iteration of the tank as domestic containment. Exotic and, by extension, local color was held fast within a frame, whether it was a graphic box, a set of genre conventions, a moldy imperial bromide, or the tank itself.

The cover of the November 1934 issue of the *Aquarium* seems more appropriate for *National Geographic Magazine*. Typically, the journal featured attractive but comparatively muted fish on its covers. In this issue, these have been replaced by a striking color photograph of four dark-skinned, seemingly naked men, immersed to their hips in an unidentified body of water; gentle ripples of that water are echoed graphically in the gentle undulations of the boxes that frame both the title of the magazine and the cover as a whole. The lush greenery of the impenetrable vegetation in the photograph is answered by the more muted industrial greens sparingly added to highlight the page. The men are busy deploying a yoke, seine net, and large gold-hued basket. A caption informs us of both their location and the object of their labors: "Catching Aquarium Fishes in Ceylon [Sri Lanka]" (see fig. 15). An especially eye-catching element in the photo is the vibrant pink bundle one of the men wears on his head. The accompanying article inside the magazine notes, "We are not advised as to what the gentleman has in the precious pink parcel poised on his head," but it doesn't really matter.[14] Its waves of fabric, knotted at the top, make it seem almost as large as the collecting basket and as elaborate, organic, and, above all, colorful as any fish these men might seine from the water. The fish themselves are not pictured, but the deep chocolate brown of the men's skin, the verdant green, and this shock of pink enliven the

Fig. 15. "Catching Aquarium Fishes in Ceylon," cover illustration, *Aquarium*, November 1934, 145.

restrained palette of the cover, which is mostly white, with black and light green accents. In contrast to the fluidity of the text boxes framing the magazine title and cover page, the photograph itself is surrounded by a precisely incised black rectangle. The borders, colors, and placement of the photograph on the page recall the decorative borders and variegated residents of the home tank that housed the fruits of these fishermen's' labors and, by extension, the entire scene, including themselves.

At first glance, the absence of fish images is puzzling, especially since Sri Lanka has some notably colorful specimens that would have been particularly photogenic.[15] Here, the specimens to be inspected and appreciated for their vibrant exoticism are the men themselves; their color vouches for that of their unseen quarry. As in *National Geographic*, which adopted color photography during this same period, these images highlight the tactility and availability of the scene. Color suggests that the viewer could actually possess both fish and fishermen.[16] Further, the fishermen's apparent nakedness and their partial immersion testify to their "naturalness," interchangeable with that of the tank residents they might supply. The dark-skinned natives bring authentic nature to the home aquarium in more ways than one: not just by catching the raw materials, but also by joining them. Their brilliantly tinted bodies contribute directly to the image of the aquarium as a "natural" respite from the bland rigors of industrial modernity and as a world-making exercise in "natural" mastery of exotics of all sorts. But these same bland rigors also policed the borders of color, insisting that it stay boxed in—safe, manageable, and leakproof.

The cover image of "Catching Aquarium Fishes in Ceylon" demonstrates another trope of tropicality that characterizes the hobby and another way color organizes difference: exotic, colorful sites were also primitive. Refinement meant "disinclination" toward color, which was for children, peasants, or savages.[17] This coupling of the exotic and the primitive in the tropical tank was particularly potent and persistent. Modernity generally requires "the primitive" to construct and affirm its modernness; the white hobbyist's technologically enabled leisure both depended on and bested colored natives' manual labor: brown people a world away worked for home aquarists as naturally as aquarists tended their pets. Moreover, the idea of the primitive does important ideological work.[18] As di Leonardo observes, "The one provable fact about 'primitives' across many populations is precisely the point that the assertion of their temporal distance from us disallows: that they have been, and are, entangled on the losing ends of varying institutions of international political economy."[19] The aquarium asserts this fictive temporal divide and doubles it through the surrogacy of tropical fish. Here, evolutionary distance of aquarium inhabitants from humans stands in for putative temporal and developmental distances between Western hobbyists and the populations of "exotic" locales who occupy both the geographic south and, as their lack of Western dress and preindustrial fishing methods imply, the primitive past. This shared "primitivity" of fish and non-westerners reassured white male aquarists of their comparative supremacy abroad and natural mastery at home.

As another example, the article accompanying the cover image reinforces the visual encoding of primitivism with its reassurance that though "native methods of fishing are effective, no matter how primitive they may be," "no early peoples" used the hook and line preferred by westerners; "Anglo-Saxons invented it."[20] In addition, the primitive is coded as always already available for viewing and for viewership that is not reciprocal, the audience's privilege to look versus the consumable curiosity's "to-be-looked-at-ness." The aquarium actively reinforces the fiction of geotemporal distance and differential visual privilege through a frame that appears as simultaneously innocent, pedagogical, scientific, and spiritual, like the pleasures of viewing exhibited indigenous peoples and/or a seemingly virgin landscape. Indeed, in hobbyist publications, these two pleasures often converged in surprising ways.

But the tank did not just assert seeming temporal distances. It also demonstrated industrial modernity's ability to collapse geographic ones for domestic consumption. The tropics and its colorful inhabitants were not actually remote. They were extensions of the transportation revolution and the neighborhood fish store and could be easily and completely contained in the family home. The productive liminality that positioned the tank as both not the sea and not not-the-sea also rendered it as a tropical microcosm simultaneously very nearby and very far away.

The interchangeability of exotic people and exotic fish via the generative genericism of "the tropics" brought new elements of difference to the tank while underscoring those that were there all along. In a 1959 *Tropical Fish Hobbyist* cartoon, one raspora commiserates with another, as a betta, popularly known as the "Siamese fighting fish," floats by. The raspora complains, "I couldn't understand a word he said . . . Siamese, you know."[21] The exchange illuminates two critical operations using fish surrogacy. First, geographic designations of fish stabilized associated human differences, including exoticism and unintelligibility. Second, because these differences were routed through fish bodies, they appeared biological, immutable, and insurmountable, as well as geographic. Yet that very genericism, coupled with fishes' queer potential for surrogacy, could also expose just how arbitrary these same elements of difference actually were, as in a 1969 cartoon appearing in the *Aquarium*. Standing before a packed tank, an aquarist identifies his prospective purchase to the store clerk nearby, net in hand: "I'll take that one, he seems more tropical."[22] He points to one fish, distinct from the rest. This specimen wears a pair of board shorts in floral print and a wide-brimmed straw hat. "He" is strumming a guitar and appears to be singing. Drawn in a stronger, darker line than his sketchier tank mates, he is an underwater Harry Belafonte. On one level, the cartoon mocks the confusion of tropicality as it is understood in popular culture with its biological counterpart. On another, however, it exposes both "tropicals" as mutually reinforcing enabling fictions. "Tropicality" was a set of performances and costumes that produced an exotic effect, not a literal quality of a particular place. Throughout the mid-twentieth century, the tropes of tropicality in popular culture imbued fish with exotic potential, and they, in turn, offered tropicality and aquarists' jungle visions a "natural home" in the tank.

Fictive Travels, Jungle Dreams

Tropes establishing tropicality as colorful, primitive difference combined with the obvious alterity of water worlds to establish the tropical tank as a getaway: simultaneously "at home" and very much "somewhere else," it offered a warm, uncomplicated, yet familiar natural respite from sterile, unyielding, and demanding modernity. The tropics injected new life into the long-standing affinity between aquaria and fictive travel. This affinity persisted into the mid-twentieth century, aided and refined by middlebrow media like *National Geographic Magazine* and travelogues on film and, later, television.[23] As discussed in chapters 1, 2, and 3, the aquarium as travel operated along a representational continuum from the novelty of an undersea voyage with Captain Nemo to the reassuring nostalgia of childhood rambles or pastoral scenes. The tropics were sufficiently exotic to replace the undersea, sufficiently primitive to replace rural villages, and seemingly simple enough to replace the innocent pleasures of youth. If, as Taussig suggests, color sold modernity, vicarious travel to the vibrant tropics via the tank meant that color also sold modernity's antidote. Often, though, that antidote required people of color to disappear from the scene.

The role of the tropics as a marker of difference leading to both an embrace of and respite from modernity emerges with special clarity in two examples, one from before and the other from after World War II. In 1932, at the height of the Great Depression and amid growing international instability, Wm. Tricker, Inc. demonstrated the affective accretion of fish, "natives," exotic (if undifferentiated) locales, and the American home, all harmonized in the tank, in its ad "Exotic Pigmy Fish," which ran in multiple versions as the back cover of the *Aquarium*.[24] The ad copy begins by conjuring a panoramic undersea view: "Fishes in gay patterns with pigments run riot, a waving plume of plant, a mollusk moving over the sea bottom—all before your very own eyes." Here, the aesthetics of the gaily-colored fish and leisurely waving plume of sea flora—a scene from the depths of both space and time—are coupled with an acknowledgment of modern scientific literacy in the invocation of the slow-moving "mollusk" (vs. "snail"). If the implicit prospect of actual global transit proved too disconcerting, the reader is reassured that some advances of modernity make others optional: "No glass-bottomed boat, no diving helmet, not even a short trip to the sea—for all this water lure is home."

The ad is dominated by two images, with the eye moving from the lower left to the upper right in a sweep from a premodern "past" to the well-appointed American home. In the lower left corner, a male figure looks toward the viewer, expressionless. His eyes appear closed; he looks back, but he doesn't seem to see and certainly does not return the viewer's gaze. He is brown, but his ethnicity is indeterminate. His clothes read like a composite wardrobe of the global south: brimmed straw hat, cinched-up robe, short pants, and sandals. The copy mentions an "Amazon collection of tropical fishes," but the background is filled with sails like those of Chinese junks, suggesting an "oriental" locale. The man carries a yoke over one shoulder. Two globes with fish in them are suspended from one side; a basket hangs from the other. As if to emphasize his inevitable disappearance from the modern scene, the landscape surrounding him fades underneath some copy and the framed image of two white children, proportionately larger than the "native," staring at a home aquarium. Color flows from the fish in gay patterns into the American living room via the colored body of the native, who is blanched in the process. The third paragraph of copy states, "From the far corners of the earth we have gathered these fishes with their exotic appeal, odd forms and delightfully interesting habits." Is the native part of the "we" who have "gathered" these odd and exotic creatures with a skillful toss of the net, or is he another of their kind? Under the man's feet, the copy assures the reader that the aquarium housing these exotic others and this timeless, placeless primitive pastoral is itself chromium-plated, especially designed for windows, and "strikes a modernistic tone."

If the figure in the lower left establishes the difference supporting descriptor "exotic pigmy" in this ad for "exotic pigmy fish," the image on the upper right, clearly framed and more vigorously colored, establishes the reassuring confines of home and the possibility that the man, like the fish, may be foreign but in a domestic sense. The effect is one of progressive miniaturization and domestication, with the box around the image paralleling leaf-covered drapes that frame a window revealing foliage outside, which in turn becomes an extension of the aquarium inside. We see over the heads of the two children, witnessing both the aquarium and their fascination with it. The boy and the girl are formally dressed; the boy is larger in the frame; the little girl is resting her hand on his shoulder. Two angelfish, one of five pairs of fish visible in the tank, are centered in the image between the heads of the children. They appear to meet the boy's gaze. This happy scene can be replicated within the tank as well as without as the fish "become at home, . . . breed, and rear their families," in a mirror of domestic reproductivity. Here, the pleasures and the dangers of regressive alterity, figured as both racial and biological others, are domesticated as iterations of the picture window, one making "exotics" of all sorts safely available for visual consumption. Both the modern home and foreign fauna could be peacefully and productively domesticated if the former could contain the latter.

The anxieties and promises of post–World War II globalization emerge with special clarity in 1947. This year featured the twin births of the first global passenger airline and the Truman Doctrine, pledging to aid governments resisting communism. The United States signed a military bases agreement with the Philippines in that same year. Transnational mobility was both an adventure and a defensive reflex to secure the nation/home. An editorial in the January 1947 issue of the *Aquarium Journal* anticipated and drew on these elements of possibility and anxiety to explain the virtues of the home aquarium as "a bit of the jungle."[25] The essay begins by vividly invoking a sylvan scene "at the edge of the Amazonian savannah": " . . . brilliant butterflies as large as swallows flutter drowsily in the noonday sun . . . The air is still, the rain has passed and there is the brooding peace and quiet of the midday rain forest." Remote both geographically and seemingly chronologically, the jungle is an Edenic fantasyscape wherein timeless "dainty fish tinted like the rainbow" dart about "after the way of their kind," until collected by a passing "native" for a canoe, then an intercontinental plane trip to the home of a "nerve-tired office worker" in the concrete jungle: "Outside there is the clanging noise of the great city and the nauseating odor of burnt gasoline. Inside there is quiet, and to the drab apartment . . . there has been brought a colorful bit of life." The native, having discharged his duty to provide the specimen and authorize its exoticism, disappears from the text. The jungle is a color line that only fish and the Western consumer can cross.

The enervated worker, dehumanized from his bureaucratic labors, is restored through his vicarious immersion in a primitive and pristine state, one reassuringly enabled by his own ability to access the resources of global modernity. This curious combination of mastery and respite hinges, in part, on the equivocal nature of his pets. They are animals but are more radically other in their animality ("colorful bit of life," "drop of color"), and this alterity itself reassures the viewer that he is exempt from, because higher than, their elemental daily dramas that so restore him.

> Before his eyes the elements of life are portrayed for him in jewelbox microcosm. There is the struggle for food, the antagonisms and rivalries for space and a home, the play of the sexes, birth, growth, the ripening of old age, and death. As his interest grows . . . the worries of the business day gradually fade from his mind, his nerves at long last relax and he is freed of the cares of life for a brief moment.

The editorial's appeal also depends on the "new owner's" simultaneous identification with and difference from "the native . . . in his canoe." Both are anonymous. Both deploy "a brief dip of [the] net" to access their "brilliant drops of color" beneath the surface. The aquarist performatively reproduces this same native operation as part of routine tank maintenance; each dip into the parlor pond recalls that primal collection scene. Both occupy jungles: one concrete and cacophonous, the other serenely quiet and pristinely beautiful. The native brings healing peace, quiet, and color to the drab and fetid urban jungle, with tropical fish as the conduit, giving new meaning and directionality to the emerging field of "tropical medicine."

In his discussion of tropicality and late nineteenth-century European public health scares, "Returning Fears: Tropical Disease and the Metropolis," Rod Edmond observes, "Global imperialism had opened up a new kind of material space within the metropolis, and metropolitan constructions of the tropics were strongly influenced by fears for the health of the national body."[26] This was one example of the tropics as imagined site of degeneracy, a motif that also emerged in American texts. Yet the aquarium, which was itself a tropical space within the metropolis, was remarkably immune to this rhetoric, at least until the late 1950s and travel accounts that operate according to a familiar imperial dualism: the richness of nature versus the degeneracy and corruption of the indigenous population.[27] Still, both before and after these narratives, the imagined tropics persist as an aquarist's utopia, complete with obliging natives. In "The Aquarist's Dream,"[28] for example, the helpful others are the tropical fish themselves. The poem begins by describing the diligent hobbyist's efforts to construct a tank

> For fish of every kind and creed
> That in my life would fill the need
> For beauty and for jungle streams
> That I explored in all my dreams[.]

His efforts are rewarded with a fantastic nocturnal voyage to the very source of his imagined "Promised Land."

> As I on moonlit seas set sail
> I drifted through a jungle land
> And dropped my anchor in the sand[.]

This dream jungle is his home aquarium, now life-size and no longer a facsimile; it is as expansive as the generic tropics and accommodates fish from danios and gouramis to scalares. Moreover, in a testament to the jungle's potential for healing revelation, magic, and mystery and for nature in all its wild and glorious excesses, these fish can communicate. The aquarist can learn more about his pets, be chided by them (the catfish doesn't like feeding only on "seconds"), and receive their thanks.

> . . . old Scalare [angelfish] he had no gripe
> Just mentioned that his wife was ripe
> That both of them were satisfied
> They realized that I had tried
> To make their home a pleasant place . . .

Ultimately, our voyager wakes to find that his dream "was partly true." It reinforced the slippage between the tank and the tropics and repaired biosocial estrangement from his pets. It confirmed his sound aquarium practices, not because his aquarium literally replicated streams from the Amazon basin to Southeast Asia, but because the fictive jungle authorized his good work as if it came straight from the gourami's mouth.

TANK TRAVELS

Michel de Certeau posits that every story is a travel story.[29] Fish stories are no exception. Fish themselves were travelers, living representatives that were both natives in situ and souvenirs, despite the fact that they were often local products. Contrary to Susan Stewart's contention that the "souvenir is by definition always incomplete," fish immersed in their water worlds seemed fully at home.[30] Unlike human natives, they did not talk back. Fish travels were the mirror opposite of aquarists'. Where the latter drew on narrative conventions of dark continents, tropical trials, and feckless natives to frame journeys as radical departures back in time to the heart of darkness, fish always moved forward from that same primitive past into a future actualized in the home tank. Their very presence in the local pet store thus established the triumph of modern consumer culture over the source of the materials on which it depended. Accounts of fish as natural resource reinforced aquarists' connections to public paragons of importation, from Teddy Roosevelt and his trophies of animal heads to Henry Ford and rubber.[31] Aquarists were at the top of the global pyramid: agents of civility and commanders of dark-skinned laborers, they were largely removed from the day-to-day unruliness of foreignness.

Fishes' tropical provenances were important to hobbyists. They demonstrated access to aesthetic, financial, and intellectual capital, as well as the worthiness of the specimens themselves. Recall William Innes's practical joke (detailed in chapter 5) centering on the false claim that a colorful Texas native was really from "Africa." The reported colorful beauty of the fish made its exotic origins seem logical. Yet beyond often generic identifications, details of fishes' actual native habitats are presented sparingly in hobbyist publications before the 1970s, which is surprising given recurring appeals to scientific rigor in the construction and observation of home tanks. Thus, the Jack Dempsey's "original home is in Guatemala, where it lives in slow-moving streams where the water is none too clear."[32] The *Trichopsis pumilis* (sparkling/pygmy gourami) "is said to occur in Siam, Cambodia, and throughout the Malay Peninsula in swamps, rice fields, ditches, and the lowlands of the mouths of rivers."[33] Aquarist Fritz Mayer observed, "According to scientific studies, *Micropoecilia parae* [Two-spot

Livebearers] are found in near-coastal regions of Northeast South America, ranging from the mouth of the Amazon River as far as British Guiana."[34] The qualifications in these descriptions ("original home," "is said to occur," "according to scientific studies") are both typical of the first decades of tropical tanks and illustrative. As noted earlier, many of these species were actually introduced to American hobbyists by German aquarists. By the 1930s, when these accounts were published, they were being produced by American breeders. The ecological awareness of the 1970s had not yet affected the average hobbyist; these descriptions were neither calls to replicate actual "slow-moving streams" in the tank nor testaments to firsthand knowledge or research in the field. Rather, they were totemic, ways of asserting a connection to the tropics both textually and through the living bodies of fish themselves. The designation "tropical" organized specimens from a range of places into a tribe, a transnational version of the "happy family" aquarium that substituted elasticity for specificity. The tank didn't just contain a finny collage of individuals from "Siam," "Guatemala," or "Africa." Under the homogenizing rubric of the tropical, it contained them all. The designation "tropical" established one difference—the modern aquarist, stand-in for the industrialized West—while subsuming others: warm-water fish as surrogates for "the rest."

The management of the tropics and/as difference through literal travel was not limited to reinforcing the exotic origins of particular species. It included accounts of the contact zones where the "primitive" tropics met the "modern" aquarium industry. Such accounts stabilized the "imaginative geography" of the tropics and the logistical superiority of the west for the home aquarist.[35] In these narratives, tropical people, again usually generic, were sites of both identification and estrangement, but modernity itself was the hero.

Innes offers a representative "brief outline" of collecting and transportation techniques, which, he assures the reader, will be more informative than what "can be told by the use of maps."[36] The site of the collecting operation is not given; the absence of maps reinforces that it is once again an unspecified foreign place. This lack of specificity was crucial to the experience of the tank as a site of reverie, a primal landscape dependent on modern technology to relieve owners of modern stresses. The "use of maps" had the potential to remind aquarists of potentially unsettling geopolitical particulars and entanglements in actual places. A fictive geography of the tropics was far more soothing because it contained no such perils. Aquarists could construct their own tropics from this cartographic blank slate as they designed and managed their own underwater worlds and those worlds' complex interconnections. The only two specific locations mentioned are New York and Hamburg, suggesting that tropical fish enter specific geographies as they are routed through the West.

The bulk of Innes's essay concerns shipping logistics. The fish travel to American aquariums on ocean liners, whose efficiency is in stark contrast to the premodern transportation required to get them to port from their homes in unspecified slow-moving streams: "it is often necessary to place the carrying cans on pack animals, for many of the roads are mere crude paths, impossible to automobiles."[37] Innes describes the regular stock checks and import-export mechanics needed to ensure a safe and profitable arrival, but the briefer discussion of native collecting is especially interesting. "Enterprising men of foreign lands" collect the fish "according to conditions and custom," using, among other methods, a large cast net "so successful . . . that in most parts of our own country its use is forbidden."[38] The reader, presumably an enterprising hobbyist who collects from local retailers, is both aligned with the foreign collector as an exotic counterpart and reassured that "custom" and the gross efficiency of a technology banned in the United States, not the agency of personal decision making, accounts for the latter's success. Aquarists, in comparison, did not need custom to design homes for their tropical "raw materials." Their humane mastery of strategy, science, and innovation, as well as exercises of personal capital and taste, enabled them to insert fish into modernity for personal pleasure, just as the importer inserted them into the ocean liner for personal profit.

Two images frame the essay. They are in the reverse order of the collecting and transport processes and work as a temporal move from the present back to the past, a way for hobbyists to look through their tanks to the geographically and temporally distant living raw materials comprising them. In the first image, a close-up inside the cargo hold of a transatlantic liner, metal cans containing fish are nestled in baskets of varying sizes, shapes, and colors. Hoses connect these composite containers to air pumps; the caption reassures the reader that an "abundance of electric current" also enables lights and heaters for the fishes' protection. The layering of these vessels, one inside the other, is visually analogous to relationships between modernity and tropicality that circulate in hobbyist discourse. The streamlined metal cans, air pumps, and electricity, as well as the liner itself, testify to modernity's mastery of the water world and its inhabitants, one shared on a small scale by aquarists. The baskets, comparatively idiosyncratic and seemingly primitive and artisanal, function as a veneer that continually reminds hobbyists of distant slow-moving steams and rice fields, the antitheses of and thus antidote to the corporate concrete jungle.

The second image, at the conclusion of the article, is captioned "Skilful [sic] Throw of a Cast Net."[39] It features a dark-skinned, bare-chested native in a loincloth and head wrap, hurling a large weighted net into the water in which he stands, immersed to the knee. His facial features are barely discernible; the location is unidentified, the body of water (river? lagoon?) unnamed. The man stands on one leg, the other bent and crossed over the standing leg at the knee—almost balletic, like a move through *passé* frozen in time. The unfurling net expands away from him; the weight in the center gives it the appearance of a large, translucent flower in bloom. It is a startlingly aestheticized image. Set into a graphic box at the very conclusion of the essay, it is itself aquariumlike in its promise of an exotic other safely domesticated for comfortable viewing. The native fisherman is the representational equivalent of the baskets in the first image, a residue of the actual and fictive tropics that adheres to tropical fish. He reshapes the tank as a vessel for vicarious voyages to timeless, elemental Edens in the opposite direction from the liners steaming toward New York or Hamburg, as well as a version of that same liner.

Without the presence of the native, tropical fish are simply one more banal commodity, a trickle in the global flow of commerce rendering aquarists small fish. Tank residents could as easily come from New Jersey as Brazil, but that would make them nothing more than fellow commuters, a net loss of fantasy and healing potential. The anonymous "skilful throw of a cast net" makes the difference that, in turn, makes the "tropical" meaningful. It was not just a shorthand for colorful warm-water fish. It was a reassuring template for a global order that cinched the aquarists' transnational supremacy: dark-skinned people and the full force of modern infrastructure both worked for them, just as their fish did.

Later, in the mid-1950s, as tropicals became the norm in home aquariums, natives disappeared from accounts of industry logistics altogether, to reemerge in hobbyist travel narratives, as discussed shortly. They were no longer needed as authenticators of fish provenance and also carried the risk of reminding aquarists of actual postcolonials who, unlike their surrogates in the tank, were making actual demands. For example, in "Flying Fish" (1954), detailing the airfreight logistics of British Overseas Airways Corporation (BOAC), no natives appear. The article is an unqualified celebration of the humane efficiency of modern shipping. Presumably, in hobbyist circles, the fish themselves were sufficiently familiar as exotics by this point to serve as synecdochal stand-ins for "India, Ceylon, the West Indies, [and] Malaya," without the visual or textual support of human counterparts.[40] But nonwestern peoples did not disappear from aquarium narratives altogether. As in wildlife documentaries of this same period, they were reclassified. They had been so synonymous with nature that they were interchangeable with tank residents; now they were serpents in the aquarial garden, whose hostility, indifference, irrelevance, or ineptitude threatened the enlightened aquarist's ability to consume nature's wonders.[41]

Tank Travels on Dark Continents

The increasing affordability and availability of intercontinental travel meant that aquarists did not need to settle for the fictive tropics. They could visit the real thing, where they could confront actual messy materiality, including actual difference. Fish offered opportunities for jungle adventure as well as jungle dreams, a way for hobbyists to reproduce or vicariously participate in expeditions like those of earlier elite American big game hunters, collectors, and anthropologists. Aquarists' voyages to dark continents were more banal iterations of "Teddy Bear Patriarchy," early twentieth-century journeys to Africa to shore up the American Museum of Natural History's collections along with white Anglo-American male supremacy.[42] These were not Gossean romantic rambles through a timeless rural landscape; they were manly exercises that relied on timeworn tropes of tropical adventure. To ensure that these were sufficiently manly, images of the healing tropics were replaced by those of jungles red in tooth and claw, where aquatic abundance sometimes contrasted sharply with terrestrial decay.

Accounts of actual travels to exotic destinations begin to appear regularly in general interest aquarium books and hobbyist publications in the 1930s, offering readers the combined pleasures of vicarious adventure and information about foreign fish and peoples. Authors of these accounts were not typical middle-class or even upper-middle-class hobbyists, particularly in the period before 1960. Their very ability to marshal the capital and logistics for relatively exotic travel—even, in some cases, at the height of the Great Depression—suggests that most were both moneyed and leisured, the aquatic equivalent of the country clubber on safari or the elite gentleman adventurer. In rare cases, a scientist or pet industry executive would contribute an account, but generally amateurs offered travel writing as an extension of their hobby, a pleasant diversion involving an alien world. Their accounts held the same appeal for middle-class and upper-middle-class male readers that fashion magazines featuring couture creations held for their female counterparts. Aquarium travel accounts were prototypes for aspirational consumption, vehicles for vicarious journeys to actual wilds conjured by domestic(ated) tropicals, and extensions of revivifying but wholly fictive jungle dreams.

The narratives themselves share common features. First, movements are chronological as well as geographic: the destination is outside modernity as well as outside the United States. Here, the evolutionary distance of fish from the Western aquarist finds its analogue in that between the wealthy American aquarist and foreign interlocutors: both fish and foreigners remedy his ennui. Thus, "four pals" visit Egypt to collect tropicals for their tanks and satisfy their longings for "the silent lure of far-away places" imagined in the "small confines of office—engulfed by the whirlpool of industrial activity in the metropolis."[43] Their Charon on this adventure is "a boatman, who is so evidently an ancient Egyptian that we find ourselves wondering how he escaped being mummified four or five thousand years ago." The boatman is not an idiosyncratic character: "The life and physique of the modern Egyptian is little changed from what it was centuries and centuries ago."[44] The serene waters of the Nile dissolve the whirlpool of industrial activity, and broad expanses of timeless Egypt free the travelers from their office confines. There are also more literal rewards from their travels along the Nile: "What a nice school of *African cichilids* [sic] (*Hemichronis bimorculatis*) are captives in the bucket. When success crowns our efforts, as it does with a pail peopled with a mass of this gorgeously-colored fish I contend that the game is worth the candle." The brilliantly colored "peopled pail" parallels the streets of Cairo, where "every store front, every street corner, every turbaned group of people is a ready-made picture."[45] A successful aquarist-traveler can extract local color from both terrestrial and aquatic realms. Further, in one more illustration that the game is worth the candle, the rewards will multiply. Cichlid courtship and mating back home is an important component of this travel narrative, demonstrating the intimate connections between reproducing the foreign and/as the domestic in the tank through literal reproduction.

This journey along the Nile is a relative idyll compared to other accounts of collecting trips. Another common feature of aquarium travel narratives is a list of bracing rigors that must be endured in order to wrest rewards from the tropics. These trials cast the global south as a place of perils as well as pleasures and portray the intrepid aquarist as a great explorer-anthropologist. To exorcise any lingering characterizations of the tank as a toy, writers drew on conventional tropes of jungle adventures to ensure that this alternative to hunting was still sufficiently manly, particularly in general interest books geared toward expanding the hobby. As the previous example suggests, collecting adventures were affairs between men, even in the very rare cases when they were accompanied by their wives. Whatever the perils, the collector hero of these adventure tales was always handsomely compensated, even if not monetarily.

> Every trip is a new adventure and the collector becomes a true explorer... The beauty of a calm sea, a spectacular undersea garden, sunken Spanish Galleons, and the myriad of exotic tropical fish are commonplace to the collector, but never cease to amaze. Life under the sea, however, is not always serene: man-eating sharks, giant green moray eels, vicious barracuda, and other predators of the sea are ever present and may suddenly make an appearance when least expected... Fierce tropical storms, poisonous jellyfish, stinging coral, and long spined sea urchins add still another touch of danger to the life of the collector, but in our hectic world with its traffic jams and smoky cities, and crowded beaches, these dangers seem but a small price to the skin diving collector when he heads out to sea in his boat on a quiet tropical night, under a star studded sky.[46]

The collector-explorer in a boat reproduces and bests the glories of empire, here recalled in the sunken galleon. Sharks and storms add a revivifying "touch of danger," which is less than that of the deadening urban traffic jam. And the rewards are intellectually and aesthetically superior to mere imperial booty: personal agency, solitude, the production of new knowledge through the rigors of exploration.

This same trope of travel trials also appears in Christopher Coates's book *Tropical Fish as Pets*. The adventures he recounts are certainly more harrowing than trips to the local pet store and add to the tank's exotic pleasures the possibility of dangerous natives easily vanquished by white collectors' mere appearance.

> In the new territory, the collector frequently arouses the militant suspicion of the natives since they are often the first white men to visit obscure villages and backwaters. The appearance they present, with their knee boots for wading and their assortment of cans and nets jangling about, must be terrifying indeed.[47]

Here, modernity is not a cramped, noisy prison to be escaped but a visual marker of white supremacy, one that causes the "natives" to shrink back from the aquarist in awe and terror. There is a vague nostalgia about this description: it seems more of a piece with far earlier accounts of imperial discoveries, an effect reinforced by its anonymous, generic quality. That does not diminish its insistence on perils as the price of progress, however, nor the manly stoicism with which these are to be regarded: "Another collector, up the Amazon, was almost eaten alive by piranhas, the famous man-eaters, but three or four inches long. Such are the vicissitudes of collecting that his brother, with him on the occasion, did not think it worth mentioning."[48] Finally, like accounts of fish traveling humanely and comfortably by sea and air, tank travel narratives are replete with modern triumphalism, presented here as the inevitable yielding up of dark continents' riches to the disciplined scientific gaze: "The waters of the tropical world are rapidly revealing their finny secrets. If the present rate of exploration continues, there will not remain a stream or pool unvisited or a species of suitable size untried."[49] Carefully observing the tropicals in their own tanks, hobbyists were a vital link in a global chain joining exploration, science, commerce, "the unmapped jungles of the Amazon or Congo," and the suburban living room.[50]

The trope of tropical trials does more than inject a frisson of danger into the parlor pond. It also establishes value in multiple ways. First, the novelty of specimens could be assessed as a function of the risks undertaken in order to procure them. This was particularly important as the giddy potential of yesterday's global exotica threatened to become today's commonplace. The transnational small world was becoming a banal one; as one aquarist noted in 1959, "It is an ancient and out of date cliché to refer to the Congo chief who gets 'The New Yorker' by airmail."[51] Novelty, one of the hobby's core values, was now a function of white discomfort, not the representation of native labors. If cosmopolitan Congo chiefs no longer sufficed to establish exotic provenance, "a broken leg, snake bite, pneumonia, and flies by the thousands in one's tea (just after the filthy things have just swarmed off a half buried corpse)" would have to do. Second, as noted in chapter 5, assessing fishes' commercial worth was a notoriously opaque proposition. The aquarist's personal "dog-hard work" finding untapped pools by bumping along paved roads "about as good as those in Aroostook County, Maine, 35 years ago" and unpaved ones that were "murder," while braving crocodiles and warm beer, helped rationalize retail prices.[52] The natives are still a hazard, not because they are necessarily hostile, but because, with the possible exception of the *New Yorker* reader, they stubbornly refused to recognize that fish and water are not hobbies.

> In unfamiliar territory you may stop 25 feet from the fish-mine of the century to ask a native if he knows of any good fishing spots thereabouts. He will laugh and say "No, Bwana—you waste time round here. Nearest good fish three day's walk back way you come." The native's idea of fishes and yours almost never coincide. He thinks of his stomach, you of your aquarium.
>
> The time when short lived pools contain the best fishes is, of course, the time when they are least accessible and hardest to push or swing a net through—if the natives have not already fouled it up by washing themselves and their cattle in it.[53]

There is useful capital to be mined from these divergent views of fish and water. The ventriloquated natives' use of *bwana* (master/sir) and the "fouling" done by washing self and cattle in the same pool suggest that collecting in the global south reaps dividends in white supremacy. In the late 1950s, with the increasing visibility of the civil rights movement at home and anticolonial independence movements abroad, accounts like the preceding one reassured readers that reproducing imperial voyages of discovery, with all their rigors, would reproduce imperial privilege as well. Their pets, jungle jewels extracted from the bush and saved from the fouling of primitive cattle grazers, were living proof.

Travel narratives in aquarium publications secured color outside the tank as well as inside it by linking the traveler to the hunter/explorer and, increasingly through the 1960s, to the intrinsically noble but beleaguered colonial administrator. Fish surrogacy was crucial here, as was the hobby's well-established rhetoric of stewardship for so-called lower beings. No text is more remarkable in this regard than Herbert Axelrod's "Africa in Color," published in 1970.[54] The color here does not actually come from the fish: " when you've fished Brazil as much as I have, going to Africa is like going to the desert."[55] Instead, as if to illustrate Taussig's argument that color is a colonial subject, it comes from some black Africans in tribal garb who are represented alongside the wildlife in a series of photos making them interchangeable spectacles or, more typically, happy primitives who know their places as distinct from others, set in vivid descriptions of postcolonial decay and mendacity of which they are, by implication or direct attribution, the agents.[56] Thus, a "matron of the Zulu tribe" in traditional ceremonial dress calls forth admiring comments about a "disciplined," "proud, well-organized people"; fixed by vibrant costumes that in turn fix their absolute difference, these natives know their place as embodiments of "tradition" and acceptably framed local color.[57] Encountered outside of that frame, however, they are corrupt extortionists, if they are encountered at all. Their petty treachery is set against honesty and/as international white solidarity, a stand-in for civility and the rule of law: "the only person I didn't have to bribe was the white manager of the hotel."[58] The essay is replete with unabashed colonial nostalgia, a way of warning readers of the consequences if color refuses to stay fixed within the frame. In stark contrast to his admiring visit to colonial Leopoldville ("a paradise") preindependence, in 1957, the renamed Kinshasa is reduced to "a humid stench." It is, simply, "horrible."[59]

Apartheid South Africa, though, is another matter entirely. Axelrod, who confesses "mixed emotions" about visiting the country, writes, "What a surprise I had in store for me!"[60]

> Having traveled in almost every black country in Africa and being fairly well informed on the condition of black minorities in such places as Haiti, Brazil, Atlanta, and London . . . I can safely say that the black people in Jo'burg are the best-dressed, best-looking, and most satisfied I have ever seen.

Axelrod concludes that the system is just great for everybody; his rhetorical fusion of black minorities in and outside the United States leaves the reader to conclude that such a fine arrangement might solve color problems over here as well as over there. Though it is "difficult to administer"[61] and thus more a problem for white leaders than black subjects, he is an unabashed fan, using a logic that parallels the argument for captivity made by Vorderwinkler against charges that aquariums are cruel: tank residents live "the life of Riley, and . . . are pampered plutocrats" compared to the "poor relations" left to their own devices.[62] This paternalistic logic of captivity, combined with the putative primitivity of fishes/natives, reminds readers that aquariums might model ways to keep color out as much as hold it in.

> Apartheid . . . allows the black man to live under his own rules and laws. It allows the native in the bush to practice his own way of life, provided it doesn't include cannibalism, murder, robbery, or crimes of violence against his neighbors . . . [H]ere the black MAJORITY groups can practice their own ways of life without interference from whites . . .and it is here that the whites can practice their own austere ways without being embarrassed by the tribal habits of native South Africans.

Like tropical fish, "the black man" is always already amodern; he can be "allowed" to live according to his nature, but he occupies an alien realm: "the bush." And he can provide manageable local color for chromophobic whites who might be "embarrassed" by his excesses. Like careful aquarists who manage and segregate incompatible species, transforming them into happy families, apartheid administrators guard against cannibalism by proving good stewards of their charges who live alongside them but irreducibly and insurmountably differently. Axelrod, an authority on the community tank, concludes that "the world should pay attention to what is happening in South Africa."[63] Of course, some were paying attention; the International Olympic Committee, to take only one example, had banned South Africa from the Olympics in 1964. But Axelrod suggests that apartheid operated as the tank did, as a microcosm of the possible, a way to tame and manage an alien world through the atavistic rhetoric of good stewardship of putative "inferiors" and recognition of differential "natural" potentials.

This odious passage is remarkable for the baldness of its racism, which, while not typical for aquarium publications of the time, was also not unknown in tank travel narratives. Most publications made race conspicuous by its absence, a tacit acknowledgment of the real and assumed whiteness of the hobby. But there were other accounts of aquarist visits to the global south featuring white collectors seeking racial solidarity with colonials against uppity or hostile natives.[64] Axelrod's Africa also reveals the extent to which tropes and rhetorics of tropicality aligned middle-class aquarists so completely with the interests of white global elites that aquarial logics of containment could be unproblematically applied to people of color in a hobbyist journal at the height of the American civil rights movement. Joseph Roach notes that "imagined communities perpetuate themselves through transmission of their prohibitions and entitlements."[65] "Africa in Color" demonstrates that the entitlement to tropicality inside the tank found a natural analogue in an ideology of color containment outside. The aquarium in South Africa of 1970, as in the United States even to the present, "is a white man's hobby."[66] Colorful fish did more than vivify the American home. Surrogation (where fish were interchangeable with nonwesterners), coupled with fictions of benevolent stewardship, made a white hobby ideologically even whiter, a seemingly international solidarity of whiteness mediated and enabled by water, like an imperial alliance and all the more potent because it was so everyday and so wholly unexamined.

The peripatetic Axelrod had his own reckoning with captivity twenty-five years after he saw Bantustans as models of self-governance. He served sixteen months in the Monmouth County Jail in New Jersey for tax evasion, after initially fleeing the charges and sailing to Cuba. Though he enthusiastically proclaimed in 1970, "If I couldn't live in America, I'd want to live in South Africa!" it was reported that, after his release in 2005, he was moving to Switzerland.[67]

Of course, not all natives represented in hobbyist publications were awed by collectors' clanking cans or shaking down a few pounds from aquarist wannabe colonials. A 1960 *Aquarium Journal* cartoon features two white male collectors wearing pith helmets, the classic headgear of great white hunter/explorers. Each is up to his shoulders in a black pot on the boil; flames leap from the fires beneath. They are surrounded and held at spear point by heavily colored black "natives" whose savagery and primitiveness are signaled by their dress (lack of tops or bottoms), complete absence of facial features, and bodies that are basically stick figures, in addition to their apparent cannibalism. One aquarist says to the other, "Don't blame me! You're the one who wanted to collect his own Discus."[68] The cartoon explicitly links aquariums with discourses of tropicality and native savagery going back to the earliest voyages of imperial discovery, still present ten years later in Axelrod's implication that the rationality of apartheid staves off cannibalism. Like "Africa in Color," the cartoon's potency resides in its ability to insert fantasies of dark continents and dark people into the hobby and, as a result, into the everyday intersections of work and play suffused with world-making energies, personal aesthetics, and appeals to scientific rigor. Operating alongside other long-standing popular representations of journeys to the heart of darkness, aquaria contributed to an overarching American imperial logic: the global south and its people, like its colorful fish, were resources to be exploited, blank slates for self-fashioning, and potential dangers to be carefully managed.

But the market, not the cooking pot, was both the collector's ultimate terror and the native's best revenge. In "The Tragic Tale of Professor Lee," William Vorderwinkler, second only to Diane Schofield in the ability to produce rhymes using fishes' species names, describes a hapless enthusiast's journey to "a dismal African bog" in search of the rare and elusive "Whistling Goby."

> He struggled through jungles, and marshes, and mire,
>   He was bitten by tsetse flies, bugs and ticks too.
> His feverish brow felt as though 'twas on fire
>   And cannibals almost caught him for stew.[69]

None of these rigors deter him; he finds his quarry and transports it home, only to be completely undone by a villain more threatening than a dusky nonwesterner with a spear and an empty kettle on the boil: that inevitable aquarium law of diminishing returns. The professor's local fish store has a sign offering "Whistling Gobies: 79 Cents a Pair!" Over a decade later, the natives themselves are in on the act. One white aquarist, knee-deep in the by-now-familiar anonymous lagoon, warns another, who is wielding a dip net and a pail: "Oh, oh, Professor, I'm afraid the natives may have beaten us to the new species."[70] Behind them is the evidence: not a dark, seminaked primitive skillfully tossing a net, but a tastefully appointed hut with a long line out the door. It sports a large sign that reads, "Jungle Joe's Tropical Fish." Here, the fluidity and vicissitudes of the global marketplace are the real savages.

The tropical aquarium illustrates the domestication of imperial presumptions through the intimacy of a hobby: both were pleasurable modern routines at the intersections of work and play. Kaplan writes of the anarchy of empire in the making of U.S. culture, but the aquarium offers a very different promise: the ability to contain global flows between northern centers and southern peripheries like it contains domestic plays of gender and (re)productivity. This is not just a matter of housing pets in glass boxes. It also involves mastering an entire repertoire of genres and tools: the color palette of the racialized tropics, the mechanics of travel and ethnographic narratives, rhetorics from aesthetics and science, the savoir faire of the seasoned traveler, and the bonhomie of a buddies' adventure. The tank, of course, could never fully deliver on its promise to contain the global south once and for all, but that very failure was part of its rhetorical utility: it reminded aquarists that managing foreign investments was an ongoing operation that required diligent management, even as it upheld and stabilized the position of the managers.

CONCLUSION: REEFER MADNESS

> Our bodies are coral reefs teeming with polyps, sponges, gorgonans, and free-swimming macrophages continually stirred by monsoon climates of moist air, blood, and biles.
>
> —ALPHONSO LINGIS, "Animal Body, Inhuman Face," in *Zoontologies: The Question of the Animal*, ed. Cary Wolfe

> Keeping fluids in shape requires a lot of attention, constant vigilance and perpetual effort—and even then the success of the effort is anything but a foregone conclusion.
>
> —ZYGMUNT BAUMAN, *Liquid Modernity*

The faithful assembled at the halfway point of the 2006 International Marine Aquarium Conference (IMAC) to hear featured speaker Mike Paletta describe "setting up a LARGE aquarium."[1] How large? So large he could actually submerge in it; so large that it required consultation with a structural engineer and the sides had to be individually fabricated. It took up his garage—now a fish room. It was so large that husbands were told to cover their wives' eyes—the "wife acceptance factor" (WAF) was going to be stretched to the breaking point. A slide flashed, giving the setup cost as thirty thousand dollars, not including fish and other stock. It took four months to complete ("You have to tell your wife it will only be a mess for two weeks," Paletta explained).

This was a reef tank; the complex lighting required to ensure the viability and vivid coloration of the coral was so august that it cast a blue glow onto the snow-covered hill outside his Pennsylvania home. This, in turn, attracted the attention of the local police, who assumed Paletta was growing something other than coral, and he didn't help himself later when an officer came to his door to ask about the light. "Oh," he said. "That's just my reef tank." The officer, it seems, was not a fellow hobbyist. "Reefer" meant a different kind of intoxicant to him, and he jumped to the wrong conclusion. Then, Paletta said, the real nuisance commenced: "I had to show him the tank and he stayed for two hours." But, Paletta concluded, it was worth it all: the lying to the "Mrs.," the huge diversion of funds, the inconvenient brushes with the law. Judging by the enthusiasm of the packed, overwhelmingly white, overwhelmingly male audience, none would disagree. After all, Paletta noted, he was a "coral addict." This way, he reasoned, "I could get every single coral I wanted."

Three years later, at the 2009 IMAC, "Joan," one of relatively few women reefers in attendance, told me how her tanks have taken over the family home, and she doesn't plan to stop. She now has ten; they occupy every room, including the bathroom. In a formulation I've heard applied to everything from designer purses to classic muscle cars to greyhounds, she described the hobby's "potato chip factor": you can't be satisfied with just one tank.[2]

Abstemiousness is not a notable trait of dedicated aquarists. Even Philip Henry Gosse, who has been depicted as practically a Puritan zealot, stuffed a truly prodigious number of creatures into his tank while counseling restraint on this very issue.[3] From its earliest inception, it seems as if the home aquarium opened the floodgates of a unique and curious desire; the results threatened to swamp its glass walls and even the family home. Paletta joked (again deploying the WAF) that spouses feared aquarists "would seal up the house and fill it with water—which," he added after a pause, "we would do." Paletta's insatiable longing to have every coral he wanted was a logical answer to Henry Butler's rhetorical question, posed almost 150 years before, "With the bountiful contents of the wide ocean and the flowing river made so accessible, where is the taste, however *bizarre* or capricious, that must perforce go ungratified?"[4] The move from simple gratification to full-on addiction is not merely a function of the ubiquity of addictologia in contemporary popular discourse. In 1956, the American Medical Association declared that alcoholism was an illness. The tank was described in similar terms well before, as in the opening paragraphs of S. S. Van Dine's remarkable foreword to Alfred Morgan's *Tropical Fishes and Home Aquaria* (1935).

> The breeding and raising of tropical fish is both a scientific pastime and a virulent disease. It is as fascinating as it is malignant. It is uplifting and edifying—and also bothersome and heart breaking. But whatever the disadvantages may be, they are more than compensated for by the zealous ecstasy which simultaneously invades the aquarist's bloodstream and inflames his hormones.
>
> The disease of aquaritis is practically incurable, although there are

records of occasional recovery where the disease was mild. In its usual malign form there is no hope for the patient. No antidote has yet been found. No cure has yet been discovered. And the curious and illuminating thing about this piscatorial malaise is that the victim does not desire surcease.[5]

The fact that women were often impediments to free indulgence in aquariums did not mean that they were immune to such intoxications. Consider "Alice," "a lovely woman who was recovering from an accident. A friend (?) gave her a couple of guppies in a brandy snifter. Two years later she had 71 tanks."[6] Morgan, somewhat more sober, describes the hobby as "therapeutic."[7] Diane Schofield agrees, though not without adding her customary idiosyncratic spin.

> The use of tropical fish tanks seems to be gaining a wide foothold as a therapeutic device in mental hospitals. Many hospitals for those who are not physically ill, have tanks sitting around in the wards—but maybe they are not really for therapeutic treatment, maybe the people who were brought in for odd and irrational behavior, insisted on taking their tanks with them.[8]

Home aquariums were both an enslaving disease and the cure.

Why? The tank has offered a reassuringly containable version of the nation and/as home. It stabilized gender, racial, and national privilege, offering reassurance to its primary American constituency: white, middle-class men buffeted by the shifting currents of social change. It provided opportunities for collegiality and creativity outside the demands of the workplace. Home aquariums were vessels for fictive travels to exotic locales and windows through which to spy on domestic melodramas. The remarkable equivocality of toy fish—both full of relational potential and undemanding of specific emotional investment—made them useful surrogates for filling a wide range of psychic and social vacancies. Their representational fungibility meant that they could be easily inserted into any number of plots, as gentlemen, aliens, mute testaments to owners' intellectual and financial capital, inveterate brawlers, distant relatives, or baggy pants comedians.

The aquarium's uncanny ability to contain modern anxieties through its impressive visual and rhetorical capaciousness, as well as the uncanny animality of its residents, explains its ideological utility and perhaps its longevity, but surely one per home could do the job. What accounts for this pervasive discourse of all-consuming excess, sometimes even in rhyme?

> My boat no longer lifts its sails,
> For now I'm raising Ramshorn Snails.
> Let Rudy Vallee play and croon,
> I'd rather breed a fine Blue Moon.[9]

Aquarists themselves offered theories. Another speaker at the 2006 IMAC, Bob Fenner, divided hobbyists into three types, each based on the specific personal need satisfied by the tank.[10] The "adventurer/wanderer" continues the tank's historic relationship to real and fictive travels. "Tinkerers" revel in solving the endless technical challenges posed by complex setups. Those with a "deity complex" ("I brought you into this world and I'll take you out!") seek power and control through their little or not-so-little water worlds. All three positions both depend on and remedy modernity's putative isolation and emasculation, but the aquarium's addictive potential was more than a function of individuals' unfulfilled psychic needs. What of the intoxicants themselves: the configuration of the tank, with its multiple visual affinities; the water; the liquid flows of the inhabitants?

Even from the earliest accounts, it is clear that the tank is not just a passive vessel for adventurer/tinkerer fantasies or opportunities for exercising personal grandiosity. It seems to reach out to ensnare hobbyists whatever their proclivities. Indeed, as in an account from nineteenth-century hobbyist William Damon, grandiosity, ingenuity, and adventure do not lead enthusiasts to aquariums; it is the other way around. The tank produces these qualities and fantasies. Damon's commitment to the hobby led him to publish *Ocean Wonders* in 1879. He caught aquarium fever after a visit to Barnum's museum, writing,

> From fish to fish I traveled, and from those fishes I never stirred for the whole day; and when finally dragged away from the place by my companion, my first thought was, "*I must have an aquarium!*" At first I wanted one as big as the Central Park, where could be kept every kind of fish I had ever heard of; then, successively, I felt obliged to reduce the size to that of Union Square and of the Everett House; and thought I was very moderate when I had compressed my imagination to the limits of two city lots, and mentally flooded them for the purpose of fish culture! But, finally, on reflection, it became apparent to my sobered thought that in so large an aquarium as I had been imaging, I should not be able to *see* my fish, any more than if I should drop them into the ocean. So away went my dreams and, sad sobriety, I at last concluded to content myself with a tank of *the largest possible size!*[11]

Sad sobriety compresses the aquarist's imagination, but the result is still the same: the biggest tank possible is the best. Resonance with Paletta's "LARGE aquarium" is hard to miss; the fish, like the corals, are the catalyst. Damon wants to see his fish. He wants to observe fish culture in a vessel both like the ocean, holding the same mysteries, and unlike it, offering greater intimacy.

Tank residents in their "natural" environment are crucial to understanding the aquarium's rich roster of enticing promises. First, the aquarium promises to make underwater worlds visible and thereby intelligible. These worlds are familiar in their literal surface contours but also profoundly mysterious, replete with even more promises: of dazzling beauty, utopian models of community, new knowledge, sensational violence, even profitable biocapital. Second, the aquarium promises relationality enabled by this intelligibility; it is a place where species meet, inside the tank and out. Third is the promise of possession, which is not the same as a "deity complex." An owner is not necessarily a god. As aquarists will tell you, the promise of possession generates actual day-to-day obligations—feeding, cleaning, and routine maintenance of all sorts. These are the pleasures, not just the chores, of tank keeping. These rituals of possession are among the reasons that mere owners who keep tanks for display but outsource the maintenance to others are largely disdained, except as sources of livelihood for far worthier, genuine fish people.

The aquarium is addictive because it almost, but not quite, delivers on these promises. The gaps between what is promised and what is delivered and between what *can* be delivered and what *might* be entice the aquarist to push for bigger, better, more. To finally fulfill the promise is to close the gap and really, actually *have* a perfectly accessible parlor pond or mimic sea big enough, yet intimate enough, to effectively house every sea creature an aquarist ever wanted. The aquarium is addictive because it is asymptotic. It approaches the limit of what modern consumer culture can do to reproduce nature in the home (and, aquarists would say, vice versa) but never reaches it, even as it beckons the hobbyist to continually try to get closer and closer to the limit—to the real thing.

This is, of course, the classic promise of mimesis: that well-known intoxicant decried by Plato. Michael Taussig writes that mimesis is "the nature that culture uses to create second nature, the faculty to copy, imitate, make models, explore difference, yield into and become Other. The wonder of mimesis lies in the copy drawing on the character and power of the original."[12] Taussig might be defining the aquarium here. He might also be talking about the theater, which bequeathed to the tank more than a perceptual logic and time-tested plotlines. The aquarium shares the theater's foundational condition, as not the "original" but not not-it either.[13] And it shares theater's promise of the possible: by engaging the copy and surrendering to it, the original can be fully seen, understood, perhaps changed. Further, the potential to create a second nature as good as the original, maybe even better, is also the siren song of modernity itself and particularly of modern consumer capitalism. Here, unceasing exploration, better and better technology, more money, and scientific rationality will result in tangible progress—in this case, back to a copy of our evolutionary home, where, as in T. S. Eliot's "Little Gidding," we will come to know it for the first time. The aquarium opens a mimetic gap between the parlor pond and the sea, between the rural countryside, the tropics, and the home. It beckons the aquarist to close it—to actually possess all of these locales and their inhabitants once and for all—if only she or he has enough money, space, and time and a sufficiently indulgent spouse. No wonder aquarists are an obsessed and intoxicated lot.

Reefers try to close this mimetic gap between copy and original with realism. No melodramatic crabs, gentlemanly sticklebacks, or plastic hippo aerators for them. Lighting that is timed to mirror the phases of the moon and manage color, devices to ensure appropriate water flow, and other attempts to wholly reproduce this complex ecosystem offer the same tantalizing prospects as realist theater—the generative interchangeability of the representation and/as "reality," which, in turn, becomes all the more real by being represented. As nineteenth-century theater critic George Henry Lewes put it, "[I]ncidents, however wonderful, adventures however perilous are almost naught when compared with the deep and lasting interest excited by any thing like a correct representation of life."[14]

Unfortunately, this reefer realism may prove to be as much an exercise in nostalgia as Gosse's rural idylls. Reefs are disappearing. Rising ocean temperatures, pollutants, and their destructive spawn, including more severe hurricanes and coral bleaching events, have decimated them. Alarms sounded at the 2006 IMAC were even more frantic in 2009, but these concerns were not new. Hobbyists were raising environmental issues in their own publications decades before, as in a 1970 cartoon in which a pied piper leads a numberless horde of rats to the water's edge. Meanwhile, two unsuspecting fish are commiserating beneath the surface. One says to his grimacing interlocutor, "Oil—chemicals—detergents . . . what else could they possibly dump in here?"[15] Sobriety now means compressing one's imagination to accommodate a new sobering reality: Henry Butler's "bountiful ocean" is not so bountiful anymore. Both IMAC meetings were interventions of sorts, as speaker after speaker delivered bad news.[16] In the Caribbean, an estimated 50 percent of the coral population is gone. What remains is declining rapidly. Wild *Acropora palmata* coral populations are down 90 to 95 percent. Fish don't fare better. The overwhelming majority of marine tank species are wild caught, and they are in trouble. Clown fish, of *Finding Nemo* fame, have been overharvested; cardinal fish are imperiled for the same reason. Fellow aquarists gave a long and sorry litany of losses.

Critical theory reminds us that there are no purely innocent pleasures, and the metaphor of addiction reminds us that malignant intoxication ultimately goes badly, first very slowly, then very quickly. Aquarists have something to answer for in this. The desire to close the gap between nature and the home has opened other gaps, this time in entire ecosystems, that will surely be very difficult to close, if they can indeed be closed at all. Some aquarists meet these realities defensively, asserting, not entirely without merit, that the hobby has a minor impact at best but becomes an "easy scapegoat" because it is a "luxury."[17] Many more are actively working to advance captive breeding, fashion guidelines for sustainable fish and invertebrate management, and advocate for increasing collaboration between hobbyists, the domestic aquarium industry, international suppliers, and environmentalists. It is too soon to gauge how successful these efforts will be, but the hobby is certainly opening up to the realization that the tank, so accommodating of the day-to-day dilemmas of modernity, might ultimately be one of its time capsules and not just home to some of its found objects. In this new and unfortunate capacity, the tank is still a vessel for fictive travel, but now sadder, gesturing back to a vanished abundance.

One hundred fifty years ago, Shirley Hibberd wondered about the ways the aquarium might shape future romantic poetry. Bernd Brunner ends his recent illustrated history of the tank in a similar utopian key.

> Maybe in the not too distant future humans will decide to move into the ocean. Often enough they have spun dreams about it and even created architectural plans for submarine palaces. If this were to happen, the last phase of the aquarium's design history would bring about a complete reversal of the relationship between humans and the ocean: no longer would the swimming pool be the only aquarium for humans, but the ocean itself would perform this role.[18]

Aquariums seem to inspire such musings, whether as jungle dreams of fish-human communication, rustic rambles back in time, or happy families of all kinds. Brunner's fantasy is the ultimate suture closing the mimetic gap, but if ontogeny recapitulates phylogeny, this ocean-aquarium, too, will no doubt spawn its own addictive excesses, its own peculiar productions of difference, and its own unique ideologies of containment. Hopefully, it will also include the same beauties and colorful characters—piscine and otherwise—collected together by terrestrial tanks. Hopefully, too, the full spectrum of relations it enables will be better—more humane, egalitarian, and environmentally sound—than what we aquarists have so far managed to produce.

NOTES

Introduction

1. "Aquaria" is not a plural of "aquarium" but is more inclusive. Admittedly a bit arcane, it is used by enthusiasts to indicate discourses, accoutrements, and other supporting structures for the hobby. Throughout the book, "aquaria" is used to describe this broader set of structures; "aquariums" is used as the plural of "aquarium."

2. *Rustic Adornments for Homes of Taste* is the title of one of the most influential British aquarium books, discussed in detail in chapter 2.

3. David Allen, "Tastes and Crazes," in *Cultures of Natural History*, ed. N. Jardine, J. A. Secord, and E. C. Spary (Cambridge: Cambridge University Press, 1996), 405.

4. Ibid., 406.

5. The formulation "cultural work" was used by Jane Tompkins to discuss noncanonical works of American literature as they impacted the public sphere. See Jane Tompkins, *Sensational Designs: The Cultural Work of American Fiction, 1790–1860* (New York: Oxford University Press, 1985).

6. Walter Lippmann, *Drift and Mastery: An Attempt to Diagnose the Current Unrest* (1914; New York: Henry Holt, 1917), 211. See also Michael Clarke, *These Days of Large Things: The Culture of Size in America, 1865–1930* (Ann Arbor: University of Michigan Press, 2007); Tom Lutz, *American Nervousness, 1903: An Anecdotal History* (Ithaca: Cornell University Press, 1991).

7. Marshall Berman, *All That Is Solid Melts into Air: The Experience of Modernity* (New York: Simon and Schuster, 1982), 345.

8. Zygmunt Bauman, *Liquid Modernity* (Cambridge: Polity, 2000), 119–20.

9. Zygmunt Bauman, *Liquid Life* (Cambridge: Polity, 2005), 9.

10. For a history of the aquarium, including its antecedent the Ward Case, see Albert J. Klee, *The Toy Fish: A History of the Aquarium Hobby in America; The First One-Hundred Years*, rev. ed. (Pascoag, RI: Finley Aquatic Books, 2003).

11. For an extensive survey of aquarium types with particular attention to variations patented in the United States, see Albert J. Klee, *A History of Aquarium Inventions: The First Hundred Years* (Pascoag, RI: Finley Aquatic Books, 2007).

12. Arthur M. Edwards, *Life Beneath the Waters; or, The Aquarium in America* (New York: H. Balliere, 1858), 22.

13. Ibid., 111. Edwards was specifically challenging the anemone-centered tank so enthusiastically advanced by H. Noel Humphreys in his book *Ocean and River Gardens*, discussed in detail in chapter 2.

14. Klee indicates that the first American patent for a mechanical aerator went to James Ambrose Cutting, Henry Butler's partner in the Boston Aquarial Gardens, in 1861 (*Aquarium Inventions*, 5).

15. H. Noel Humphreys, *River Gardens* (London: Sampson Low, 1857), 17.

16. Nina Quart, "Keeping Your Aquarium Alive," *Tropical Fish Hobbyist*, June 1959, 39.

17. Ibid. See also J. M. Bellanca, "Designs for Aquarium Décor," *Tropical Fish Hobbyist*, October 1968, 93–94; M. D. Bellamy, "Dyeing Your Anemones," *Aquarium Journal*, December 1960, 592.

18. James A. Secord, *Victorian Sensation: The Extraordinary Publication, Reception, and Secret Authorship of "Vestiges of the Natural History of Creation"* (Chicago: University of Chicago Press, 2000), 439.

19. For two especially noteworthy critical studies of public aquariums, see Susan G. Davis, *Spectacular Nature: Corporate Culture and the Sea World Experience* (Berkeley: University of California Press, 1997); Jane C. Desmond, *Staging Tourism: Bodies on Display from Waikiki to Sea World* (Chicago: University of Chicago Press, 1999), 144–250.

20. Paul Krugman uses the distinction between freshwater and saltwater aquariums to answer the question "How did economists get it so wrong?" (*New York Times Magazine*, September 6, 2009, 40). The "it" here is the great recession of 2008. In Krugman's article, two stacked cartoons illustrated by Jason Lutes feature, first, a "freshwater" economist in a white suit writing on a blackboard and, below, a "saltwater" economist in a black suit writing on a white board; the latter seems unaware of a nearby shark fin. Both economists draw curves that, in their optimistic upward trajectories, are essentially the same. The terms *freshwater* and *saltwater* here stand in for a distinction without a difference, something with which many dedicated aquarists might disagree.

21. Erma Bombeck was an American humorist whose work centered on the absurdities of suburban family life and, particularly, the irritants, absurdities, and triumphs confronting the modern housewife.

22. Hayden White, "Bodies and Their Plots," in *Choreographing Histories*, ed. Susan Leigh Foster (Bloomington: Indiana University Press, 1995), 234; emphasis in original.

23. It is not clear if goldfish are included in the category "freshwater fish." See http://www.americanpetproductions.org/press_industrytrends.asp.

24. http://www.census.gov/econ/census02/data/industry/E45391.HTM.

Chapter 1

1. H. Noel Humphreys, *Ocean Gardens: The History of the Marine Aquarium and the Best Methods Now Adopted for Its Establishment and Preservation* (London: Sampson Low, 1857), 9; emphasis in original.

2. William Innes, editorial, *Aquarium*, November 1932, 191. See also Todd Newberry, "A Visit to the Aquarium," in *Aquarium*, by Diane Cook, Len Jenshel, Todd Newberry, and Lawrence Weschler (New York: Aperture Foundation, 2003), 11.

3. Jonathan Crary, *Suspensions of Perception: Attention, Spectacle, and Modern Culture* (Cambridge, MA: MIT Press, 1998), 33. Crary examines processes of con-

structing attention cognitively and sensorially in alignment with the imperatives of modern rationalism. The aquarium is certainly one element of consumer culture that contributes to the management of modern attention, particularly because it extends practices and norms of institutional observation into the domestic sphere as it reframes them as leisure. A full discussion of the aquarium's contribution to the construction of attention exceeds the scope of this work.

4. J. E. Taylor, *The Aquarium: Its Inhabitants, Structure, and Management* (London: Hardwicke and Bogue, 1876), 24. For Crary, distraction and attention are intimately linked as a function of modernity. The aquarium deploys this link to both reassure viewers of the medium's modernity and soothe them as an antidote to this same modernity.

5. Crary, *Suspensions*, 77; Michel Foucault, *Discipline and Punish: The Birth of the Prison*, trans. Alan Sheridan (New York: Vintage, 1995), 295.

6. W. J. T. Mitchell, *Iconology: Image, Text, Ideology* (Chicago: University of Chicago Press, 1986), 3.

7. W. J. T. Mitchell, "Imperial Landscape," in *Landscape and Power*, ed. W. J. T. Mitchell, 2nd ed. (Chicago: University of Chicago Press, 2002), 5. Most of Mitchell's nine "theses on landscape" support the present book's overall argument about the aquarium's cultural work. For example, his assertion that "landscape is a particular historical formation associated with European imperialism" resonates with the power of the aquarium to manage American imperial anxieties (see chapter 6 in the present book). On one point, though, aquarists would take Mitchell to task, vigorously disagreeing with his statement that aquariums, to the extent that they are landscapes, are "boring."

8. Angela Miller, *The Empire of the Eye: Landscape Representation and American Cultural Politics, 1825–1875* (Ithaca: Cornell University Press, 1993), 13.

9. David C. Miller reads the prevalence of this imagery as a register of anxieties about the ship of state, cast in elemental terms. See his "The Iconology of Wrecked or Stranded Boats in Mid to Late Nineteenth-Century American Culture," in *American Iconology*, ed. David C. Miller (New Haven: Yale University Press, 1993), 186–208. Whaling and shipwrecks converge in the paradigm case of the water world as a place of peril: the wreck of the *Essex*. See Nathaniel Philbrick, *In the Heart of the Sea: The Tragedy of the Whaleship Essex* (New York: Penguin, 2001). As the nineteenth century unfolded, whaling and aquarium keeping followed opposite trajectories, with the former in steep decline after the 1870s and the latter increasing in popularity. The aquarium is in visual or rhetorical dialogue not with whaling or shipwrecks per se but with representations and fictions of underwater realms that highlight their alienness. For more on whaling, see Eric J. Dolan, *Leviathan: The History of Whaling in America* (New York: Norton, 2007).

10. Herman Melville, *Moby Dick*, ed. Harrison Hayford and Hershel Parker (New York: Norton, 1967), 331.

11. Albert J. Klee, *A History of Aquarium Inventions: The First Hundred Years* (Pascoag, RI: Finley Aquatic Books, 2007), 5, 19.

12. Henry D. Butler, *The Family Aquarium; or, Aqua Vivarium: A "New Pleasure" for the Domestic Circle* (New York: Dick and Fitzgerald, 1858), 18.

13. Ann Bermingham argues that the mastery/independence dynamic that characterized English domestic economy also underlies its landscape tradition. See her *Landscape and Ideology: The English Rustic Tradition, 1740–1860* (Berkeley: University of California Press, 1986).

14. For recent critical studies of gardening and/as the domestication of landscape, see Christopher Grampp, *From Yard to Garden: The Domestication of America's Home Grounds* (Chicago: University of Chicago Press, 2008); Robert Pogue Harrison, *Gardens: An Essay on the Human Condition* (Chicago: University of Chicago Press, 2009); Stephanie Ross, *What Gardens Mean* (Chicago: University of Chicago Press, 1998).

15. Amy M. King, *Bloom: The Botanical Vernacular in the English Novel* (Oxford: Oxford University Press, 2003), 48

16. Daniel T. Rodgers, *The Work Ethic in Industrial America, 1850–1920* (Chicago: University of Chicago Press, 1979), 28.

17. Ross, 6.

18. Newberry, 7. For discussion of the perceptual dynamics underlying zoo viewership, see Elizabeth Hanson, *Animal Attractions: Nature on Display in American Zoos* (Princeton: Princeton University Press, 2002); Randy Malamud, *Reading Zoos: Representations of Animals and Captivity* (New York: New York University Press, 1998); S. L. Montgomery, "The Zoo: Theatre of the Animals," *Science as Culture* 21 (1995): 565–602; Nigel Rothfels, *Savages and Beasts: The Birth of the Modern Zoo* (Baltimore: Johns Hopkins University Press, 2002). Though they do not discuss the specific visual affinities that shaped aquarium viewing in its formative stages, two excellent books discuss the visual dynamics of contemporary public aquariums: see Susan G. Davis, *Spectacular Nature: Corporate Culture and the Sea World Experience* (Berkeley: University of California Press, 1997); Jane C. Desmond, *Staging Tourism: Bodies on Display from Waikiki to Sea World* (Chicago: University of Chicago Press, 1999).

19. Shirley Hibberd is one early aquarist who specifically links the aquarium and the "menagerie," albeit with some qualifications, perhaps because zoos were well established in England at the time of his writing (1856). Yet even here he alludes to the alterity of the occupants. He characterizes the home tank as

> a water garden in which we cultivate choice plants, and it is also in some sort a menagerie, in which we see living creatures of kinds hitherto the least studied by naturalists, displaying to our close gaze their natural forms, and colours, and instincts, and economy, as freely and as happily as if they were still hidden in their native depths.

See *The Book of the Freshwater Aquarium; or, Practical Instructions on the Formation, Stocking, and Management, in All Seasons, of Collection of River Animals and Plants* (London: Groombridge and Sons, 1856), 2–3. Admittedly, Hibberd is fairly indiscriminate in his use of metaphors; as indicated later in this chapter, he also sees the tank as a panorama and a museum.

20. Krzystof Pomian in Shirley Teresa Wajda, "'And a Little Child Shall Lead

Them'": American Children's Cabinets of Curiosities," in *Acts of Possession: Collecting in America*, ed. Leah Dilworth (New Brunswick, NJ: Rutgers University Press, 2003), 45.

21. Susan Stewart, *On Longing: Narratives of the Miniature, the Gigantic, the Souvenir, the Collection* (Durham, NC: Duke University Press, 1993), 151.

22. Shirley Hibberd's popular *Rustic Adornments for Homes of Taste* is discussed in chapter 2.

23. As the hobby developed, the idea of the collection increased in importance and became even more relevant, as conservation was added to the aquarium's potential virtues. In the late twentieth and twenty-first centuries, reef tanks in particular came to function as "Noah's arks," both because they erased and recontextualized their original contexts in their own displays and because those original contexts were being erased on a global scale.

24. Arthur M. Edwards, *Life Beneath the Waters; or, The Aquarium in America* (New York: H. Balliere, 1858), 21. Edwards's book was one of the first two published on aquariums in America and is discussed in chapter 3.

25. Dennis Doordan, "Simulated Seas: Exhibition Design in Contemporary Aquariums," *Design Issues* 11, no. 2 (1995): 8.

26. Jonathan Crary, "Géricault, the Panorama, and Sites of Reality in the Early Nineteenth Century," *Grey Room* 9 (Autumn 2002): 7.

27. Humphreys, 9.

28. This argument appears across multiple aesthetic, critical, and theoretical approaches to modernity. For two representative examples, see Martin Jay, "Scopic Regimes of Modernity," in *Vision and Visuality*, ed. Hall Foster (Seattle: Bay Press, 1988), 3–23; Anthony Vilder, *The Architectural Uncanny* (Cambridge, MA: MIT Press, 1992), 219–25.

29. Two examples from the opposite chronological poles of the hobby are illustrative: Arthur Edwards's formative 1858 book and a column from a popular contemporary hobbyist magazine. See Edwards, 16; Lovel and Joy Tippit, "Bowled Over: Get Inside the History of the Goldfish Bowl," *Freshwater and Marine Aquarium* 30, no. 3 (March 2007): 136–39.

30. Klee, *History of Aquarium Inventions*, 3–5.

31. Anne Friedberg, *The Virtual Window: From Alberti to Microsoft* (Cambridge, MA: MIT Press, 2006), 38, 103.

32. Ibid., 111.

33. Isobel Armstrong, *Victorian Glassworlds: Glass Culture and the Imagination, 1830–1880* (Oxford: Oxford University Press, 2008), 11; see also Friedberg, 113.

34. Armstrong, 361.

35. Newberry, 8.

36. In Bernd Brunner, *The Ocean at Home: An Illustrated History of the Aquarium* (New York: Princeton Architectural Press, 2003), 8. Jäger built his aquarium in 1860.

37. Newberry, 8.

38. *Aquarium*, January 1914, 82.

39. William Innes, *Goldfish Varieties and Tropical Aquarium Fishes* (Philadelphia: Innes, 1917), n.p.

40. Klee, *History of Aquarium Inventions*, 11, 99.

41. Friedberg, 113–14.

42. Armstrong, 139.

43. Ibid., 27; Elaine S. Abelson, *When Ladies Go A-Thieving: Middle-Class Shoplifters in the Victorian Department Store* (Oxford: Oxford University Press, 1992), 27.

44. Abelson, 90.

45. Ann Blair, *The Theater of Nature: Jean Bodin and Renaissance Science* (Princeton: Princeton University Press, 1997), 155, 54.

46. For discussion of performance and nineteenth-century British science, see Aileen Fyfe and Bernard Lightman, eds., *Science in the Marketplace: Nineteenth-Century Sites and Experiences* (Chicago: University of Chicago Press, 2007); Bernard Lightman, *Victorian Popularizers of Science: Designing Nature for New Audiences* (Chicago: University of Chicago Press, 2007); Ralph O'Connor, *The Earth on Show: Fossils and the Poetics of Popular Science, 1802–1856* (Chicago: University of Chicago Press, 2007). For discussions of performance, theater, and the construction of science in the United States in the twentieth and twenty-first century, see Sue-Ellen Case, *Performing Science and the Virtual* (New York: Routledge, 2007).

47. "Gosse's Aquarium," *Littell's Living Age*, July 29, 1854, 229, American Periodicals Series Online.

48. Neil Harris, *Humbug: The Art of P. T. Barnum* (Chicago: University of Chicago Press, 1973), 36–37. For more on Barnum and his spectacular entertainments, including animal acts, see Bluford Adams, *E. Pluribus Barnum: The Great Showman and the Making of U.S. Popular Culture* (Minneapolis: University of Minnesota Press, 1997).

49. Harris, 167.

50. J. E. Taylor, *The Aquarium: Its Inhabitants, Structure, and Management* (London: Hardwicke and Bogue, 1876), 162, note.

51. Edwin G. Burrows and Mike Wallace, *Gotham: A History of New York City to 1898* (New York: Oxford University Press, 1999), 943. British aquarists might have been dismissive of Barnum, but their public aquariums functioned much like those in the American Museum—as entertainment venues featuring a wide range of performances and performers. The Westminster Aquarium, opened in 1876, is an especially interesting case. When the residents themselves proved insufficiently enticing to London audiences, the directors hired the Great Farini as entertainment manager. Lewis Carroll attended a children's dance recital there in 1877, noting that the "rather pretty morris-dance by a dozen children" was "a marvel of grace and dexterity"; see Morton N. Cohen, "Alice and the Reverend Dodgson," Ballet Reference Production Notes, 1995, http://www.ballet.org.uk/reference/notes/alice/dance.html. Accessed July 5, 2005. Another such "marvel" was the gymnast/acrobat Zaeo, whose performances generated a scandal in the venue.

52. This brief program announcement invites further critique. It mentions both "Kaffir" and "Hottentot" songs, the latter dismissed as "merely a chorus of sounds without any intelligible words." No ethnic attribution is given for the "wedding," "war," "hunting," or "battle" songs, which are transcribed phonetically and trans-

lated. These translations include "We will kill our enemies" and "They come! they come! take care! oh, we will kill them all." Perhaps the putative absence of intelligibility was, among other things, a reassuring palliative accompanying these translations.

53. Butler, 19.

54. Ibid., 19–30. "Jeremy Diddler" is a stock figure, a swindler. He appears in James Kenney's farce *Raising the Wind* (1803) and Melville's *The Confidence Man: His Masquerade* (1857).

55. "My Aquarium," *Atlantic Monthly* 1, no. 4 (1858): 429. See also Butler, 19–20.

56. Taylor, 288.

57. "My Aquarium," 431.

58. Butler, 21.

59. Hibberd contrasts the freshwater tank/panorama with the marine aquarium, which he characterizes as a "museum" warranting study and providing instruction; see *Rustic Adornments for Homes of Taste*, rev. ed. (London: W. H. and L. Collingridge, 1895), 255.

60. For histories of the panorama, see Ralph Hyde, *Panoramania! The Art and Entertainment of the "All-Embracing View"* (London: Trefoil, 1988); Stephan Oettermann, *The Panorama: History of a Mass Medium*, trans. Deborah Lucas Schneider (New York: Zone, 1997); Gillen D'Arcy Wood, *The Shock of the Real: Romanticism and Visual Culture, 1760–1860* (London: Palgrave Macmillan, 2001). For a discussion of the panorama as immersive experience, see Oliver Grau, *Virtual Art: From Illusion to Immersion*, trans. Gloria Custance (Cambridge, MA: MIT Press, 2003).

61. For discussion of the ideology of the panorama in American painting, see Leo G. Mazow, "Panoramic Sensibilities in Nineteenth- and Twentieth-Century American Painting." http://tfaoi.com/aa3aa502.htm; for the panoramic sensibility in American literature, including Emerson, see William W. Stowe, "'Property in the Horizon': Landscape and American Travel Writing," in *The Cambridge Companion to American Travel Writing*, ed. Alfred Bendixen and Judith Hamera (Cambridge: Cambridge University Press, 2009), 26–45.

62. Grau, 57.

63. Crary, "Géricault," 21; see also Grau, 57.

64. Stewart, 75.

65. In "Main-street," Hawthorne's showman is, in one sense, an abject failure in this regard, taunted mercilessly by a nameless "critic" who decries the panorama's many mimetic shortfalls. Yet it is precisely this discrepancy between celebratory self-presentation of the civilizing path of progress and the unrelentingly bleak, even perverse "nature" of New England cultural and spiritual life that advances Hawthorne's larger critique of Puritan mores. See Nathaniel Hawthorne, *Tales and Sketches*, 4th ed. (New York: Library of America, 1982), 1023–50.

66. Grau, 59.

67. Crary, "Gericault," 21.

68. See Lightman in Fyfe and Lightman, 117–21; O'Connor, 265–72.

69. Butler, 11; emphasis in original.

70. Grau argues that theaters and dioramas—and presumably, by extension, aquariums—are not truly immersive because "[t]hey leave the observer outside and are thus unsuitable for communicating virtual realities in a way that overwhelms the senses" (14). This view neglects the liminal aspect of immersive experience common to all virtual realities—the subjunctive mood denoting not the scene but not not-the-scene, central to the play of the vicarious in the production and reception of reality effects. In this view, articulated most forcefully by Richard Schechner, there is no simple "outside" for these spectators. See Richard Schechner, *Between Theater and Anthropology* (Philadelphia: University of Pennsylvania Press, 1985), 109–12. For a discussion of the vicarious, see Judith Hamera, *Dancing Communities: Performance, Difference, and Connection in the Global City* (Basingstoke: Palgrave Macmillan, 2007), 35–44.

71. O'Connor, 273. See also Sally Metzler and John McCarter, *Theatres of Nature: Dioramas at the Field Museum* (Chicago: Field Museum of Natural History, 2008); Stephen Christopher Quinn, "The Worlds Behind the Glass," *Natural History* 115, no. 3 (2006): 48–53, WilsonWeb: http://vnweb.hwwilsonweb.com.lib-ezproxy.tamu.edu:2048/hww/results/results_single_ftPES.jhtml.

72. For connections between taxidermy, dioramas, and the construction of modern nature viewership, see Carla Yanni, *Nature's Museums: Victorian Science and the Architecture of Display* (New York: Princeton Architectural Press, 2005).

73. Donna Haraway offers a bracing critique of the class dynamics that sustained the diorama and particularly the adventures of big game hunting that fed them. See her "Teddy Bear Patriarchy: Taxidermy in the Garden of Eden, New York City, 1908–1936," in *Cultures of United States Imperialism,* ed. Amy Kaplan and Donald Pease (Durham, NC: Duke University Press, 1993), 237–91. See also Stephen Christopher Quinn, *Windows on Nature: The Great Habitat Dioramas of the American Museum of Natural History* (New York: Abrams, 2006), 144–45, for an example of one research narrative: the tedium and danger of the dives to produce the Andros coral reef diorama, first completed in 1935. The narrative exemplifies key themes in home aquarium literature, including the difficulties of actual underwater journeys and the diligence of dedicated collectors.

74. Quinn, 14–16.

75. Stephen T. Asma, *Stuffed Animals and Pickled Heads: The Culture and Evolution of Natural History Museums* (Oxford: Oxford University Press, 2001), 240.

76. The most recent iteration of the conversion of the television set to the aquarium involves the increasingly obsolete "box" set. See "How to Convert an Old TV Into a Fish Tank," http://www.wikihow.com/Convert-an-Old-TV-Into-a-Fish-Tank.

77. O'Connor, 199; see also Grau.

78. Kristin L. Hoganson, *Consumers' Imperium: The Global Production of American Domesticity, 1865–1920* (Chapel Hill: University of North Carolina Press, 2007), 11.

79. Ibid., 165–66.

80. "Aquariums—No. 1," *Godey's Lady's Book* 54 (June 1857): 525, American Periodicals Series Online.

81. Ibid.

82. Jules Verne, *Twenty Thousand Leagues Under the Sea*, Everyman's Library, no. 319 (London: J. M. Dent and Sons, 1908), 287.

83. Ibid., 79.

84. E. G. Boulanger, *The Aquarium Book* (London: Duckworth, 1925), 9. In an indication of how thoroughly the emerging aquarium industry drew on the novel, the frontispiece features a Verne-esque battle captioned "Octopus vs. Lobster."

85. Simon Lake, "Voyaging under the Sea," *McClure's Magazine* 12, no. 3 (January 1899): n.p., American Periodicals Series Online.

86. Eugene Smith, *The Home Aquarium and How to Care for It* (New York: Dutton, 1902), 184.

87. "The Aquarium," *North American Review*, July 1858, 156.

88. "Some Sea-Side Pets," *Harper's Bazaar*, July 30, 1881, 491, American Periodicals Series Online.

89. "Our Babies among the Butter-Cups and on the Sea-Shore," *Harper's Bazaar*, July 27, 1878, 483, American Periodicals Series Online.

90. Alfred Morgan, *Tropical Fishes and Home Aquaria* (New York: Scribner's, 1935), 121.

91. Ibid., 100.

92. In Philip J. Pauly, *Biologists and the Promise of American Life* (Princeton: Princeton University Press, 2000), 44.

93. "Customs and Manners under the Water," *Littell's Living Age*, August 26, 1854, 414, American Periodicals Series Online. This piece is a review essay devoted to Philip Henry Gosse's *The Aquarium: An Unveiling of the Wonders of the Deep Sea*. The sheer number of similar articles in U.S. publications of this period devoted to Gosse's aquarium writings attests to his popularity and importance to the hobby on both sides of the Atlantic.

94. Ibid.

95. Mary Louise Pratt, *Imperial Eye: Travel Writing and Transculturation*, 2nd ed. (New York: Routledge, 2008), 15–52.

96. "Customs and Manners," 414.

97. Ibid.; emphasis in original.

98. Hoganson, 153–208.

99. The term *deep time* was coined by John McPhee to describe the remote recesses of geologic time. See his *Annals of the Former World* (New York: Farrar, Strauss and Giroux, 1998), 90.

100. Butler, 10.

101. Ibid., 11.

102. In Thomas M. Allen, *A Republic in Time: Temporality and Social Imagination in Nineteenth-Century America* (Chapel Hill: University of North Carolina Press, 2008), 10.

103. Ibid., 154.

104. See W. J. T. Mitchell, *The Last Dinosaur Book* (Chicago: University of Chicago Press, 1998), 134–35; O'Connor, 426; Steven Conn, *Museums and American Intellectual Life, 1876–1926* (Chicago: University of Chicago Press, 1998), 45–53.

105. Mitchell, *Last Dinosaur Book*, 67.

106. Washington Irving in Alfred Bendixen, "American Travel Books about Europe before the Civil War," in Bendixen and Hamera, 108.

107. Dana Seitler, *Atavistic Tendencies: The Culture of Science in American Modernity* (Minneapolis: University of Minnesota Press, 2008), 2.

108. W. P. Pycraft, *The Story of Fish Life* (London: George Newnes, 1901), 15.

109. Ida M. Mellen, *The Young Folks Book of Fishes* (New York: Dodd, Mead, 1946), 2–4.

110. "Surrogacy" is Joseph Roach's term for operations of cultural reproduction, where stand-ins for vacancies in webs of relations never quite fill the gap. I discuss aquarium residents as surrogates more fully in chapter 4.

111. Mellen avers on natural selection, "Whether Nature, throughout the struggling ages, had a definite scheme of producing Man at the top of the scale, or whether Man arose as an accidental growth, is a question that we must leave for future generations to answer. We have not gathered enough evidence yet to make any intelligent guess" (3). She does deploy evolution as a trope frequently, including descriptions of typical progressions in hobbyists' tastes in stock.

112. Millicent Washburn Shinn, "The Biography of a Baby," *Puritan* 6, no. 3 (1898): 398; Neil Shubin, *Your Inner Fish: A Journey into the 3.5-Billion-Year History of the Human Body* (New York: Pantheon, 2008), 41.

113. Hawthorne, 1024.

114. Humphreys, 4.

Chapter 2

1. Sarah Ahmed, *The Cultural Politics of Emotion* (New York: Routledge, 2004), 44.

2. Susan Scott Parrish, *American Curiosity: Cultures of Natural History in the Colonial British Atlantic World* (Chapel Hill: University of North Carolina Press, 2006), 7; Mary Louise Pratt, *Imperial Eyes: Travel Writing and Transculturation*, 2nd ed. (New York: Routledge, 2008), 15–36. See also Michel Foucault, *Discipline and Punish: The Birth of the Prison*, trans. Alan Sheridan (New York: Vintage, 1995).

3. For overviews and critical studies of British natural history, see David Elliston Allen, *The Naturalist in Britain: A Social History* (Princeton: Princeton University Press, 1976); Lynn Barber, *The Heyday of Natural History, 1820–1870* (London: Jonathan Cape, 1980); P. M. Harman, *The Culture of Nature in Britain, 1680–1860* (New Haven: Yale University Press, 2009); N. Jardine, J. A. Secord, and E. C. Spary, eds., *Cultures of Natural History* (Cambridge: Cambridge University Press, 1996); Lynn L. Merrill, *The Romance of Victorian Natural History* (New York: Oxford University Press, 1989).

4. Thad Logan, *The Victorian Parlor* (Cambridge: Cambridge University Press, 2001), 105.

5. For a fuller discussion of the politics of the enclosure acts and the increasing spread of industrial disciplinary imperatives across both work and leisure activities

during this period, see E. P. Thompson, *The Making of the English Working Class* (New York: Vintage, 1963).

6. Gregg Mitman makes a similar argument about nature films. See his *Reel Nature: America's Romance with Wildlife on Film* (Cambridge, MA: Harvard University Press, 1999), 1–4.

7. In one respect, Swainson was most emphatically not representative. His favored system of species classification was highly idiosyncratic. See D. E. Allen, 90.

8. William Swainson, *A Preliminary Discourse on the Study of Natural History* (London: Longman, 1834), 100; emphasis in original.

9. Ibid., 101.

10. See also ibid., 98–99.

11. Ibid., 103.

12. M. R. Goodrum, "The British Sea-Side Studies, 1820–1860: Marine Invertebrates, the Practice of Natural History, and the Depiction of Life in the Sea" (PhD diss., Indiana University, 1997), 7.

13. Adrian Desmond in Merrill, ix. Swainson was not isolated from these institutions by choice; his attempts to secure institutional position were unsuccessful, possibly due to his advocacy of his highly idiosyncratic classification scheme.

14. Amy M. King, "Reorienting the Scientific Frontier: Victorian Tide Pools and Literary Realism," *Victorian Studies* 47, no. 2 (2005): 153–63. See also Merrill, 51–74; Ralph O'Connor, *The Earth on Show: Fossils and the Poetics of Popular Science, 1802–1856* (Chicago: University of Chicago Press, 2007), 106–7.

15. D. E. Allen, 65–66.

16. Ibid., 65.

17. The reference to him as "indefatigable" is from H. Noel Humphreys, *Ocean Gardens: The History of the Marine Aquarium and the Best Methods Now Adopted for Its Establishment and Preservation* (London: Sampson Low, 1857), 7.

18. Philip Henry Gosse, *The Romance of Natural History* (New York: New Amsterdam, 1902), iii. The book was initially published in England in two series in 1860 and 1861.

19. The allusion is to Thomas Gradgrind in Charles Dickens's *Hard Times*, who famously begins the novel, "Now, what I want is, Facts. Teach these boys and girls nothing but Facts. Facts alone are wanted in life. Plant nothing else, and root out everything else. You can only form the minds of reasoning animals upon Facts; nothing else will ever be of any service to them" (ed. George Ford and Sylvère Monod, 2nd ed., Norton Critical Editions [New York: Norton, 1990], 7).

20. Ann Thwaite, *Glimpses of the Wonderful: The Life of Philip Henry Gosse* (London: Faber and Faber, 2002), 171.

21. Ibid., 181–82. There are an extraordinary number of American reviews. In fact, the aquarium is introduced largely as the object of Gosse's book. For only a small sample, see "The Aquarium," *North American Review*, July 1858, 143; "Customs and Manners under the Water," *The Friend: A Religious and Literary Journal*, September 23, 1854, 14 American Periodicals Series online; "Gosse's Aquarium," *Littell's Living Age*, July 29, 1854, 229, American Periodicals Series Online; "Liter-

ary Notices: *The Aquarium* by P. H. Gosse and *The Common Objects of the Seashore* by the Rev. J. G. Wood," *Atlantic Monthly* 2, no. 9 (1858): 253.

22. W. J. T. Mitchell, ed., *Landscape and Power*, 2nd ed. (Chicago: University of Chicago Press, 2002), 2.

23. Philip Henry Gosse, *The Aquarium: An Unveiling of the Wonders of the Deep Sea*, 2nd ed. (London: Van Voorst, 1856), vi. The first edition of the book was published by the same company in 1854.

24. Ultimately, a deeply chastened Thomas Gradgrind, the "Dr. Dryasdust" equivalent in Dickens's *Hard Times*, makes his "facts and figures subservient to Faith, Hope, and charity" (Dickens, 218).

25. Susan Stewart, *On Longing: Narratives of the Miniature, the Gigantic, the Souvenir, the Collection* (Durham, NC: Duke University Press, 1993), 75.

26. Gosse, *Aquarium*, 249.

27. Ibid., 72.

28. King, 156.

29. According to his son Edmund, "The Mimic Sea" was the original title Gosse chose for the book that became *The Aquarium*. See Edmund Gosse, *The Naturalist of the Seashore: The Life of Philip Henry Gosse* (Charleston, SC: Bibliolife, 2009), 251.

30. Pierre Bourdieu defines the habitus as "principles which generate and organize practices and representations that can be objectively adapted to their outcomes." They are "transposable dispositions." Gosse's construction of the habitus for the home aquarium persists to the present, particularly by positioning it as antithetical to the structures of urban modernity on which it depends. See Pierre Bourdieu, *The Logic of Practice*, trans. Richard Nice (Stanford, CA: Stanford University Press, 1980), 53.

31. As already cited, Gosse uses the genre designation "personal narrative" explicitly (*Aquarium*, iv).

32. On evolution, Gosse was, in fact, unconventional, not in his refusal to accept it but in his attempts to explain the fossil evidence as planted by God to give the appearance of an old earth. See Philip Henry Gosse, *Omphalos/Creation* (London: Van Voorst, 1857).

33. Gosse, *Aquarium*, 117.

34. Ibid., 119.

35. Ibid., 117.

36. See also Gosse's description of his precautions when exposing his tank to the London soot (*Aquarium*, 11), a "machine in the garden" moment, as indicated in note 40.

37. Charles Dickens, *Bleak House*, ed. Stephen Gill, Oxford World's Classics (New York: Oxford University Press, 2008), 1.

38. William Wordsworth, "The Prelude," 7.592–97, in *William Wordsworth: The Major Works, Including "The Prelude,"* ed. Stephen Gill, Oxford World's Classics (New York: Oxford University Press, 2000), 483.

39. Raymond Williams, *The Country and the City* (New York: Oxford University Press, 1973), 150.

40. "Machine in the garden" moments are intrusions of urban infrastructure into otherwise pastoral, preindustrial scenes, as described by Leo Marx. See *The Machine in the Garden: Technology and the Pastoral Ideal in America* (New York: Oxford University Press, 2000), 1.

41. Gosse's descriptions can be set in a larger context of the celebration of the rustic and picturesque in visual art. That tradition is discussed in detail in Anne Bermingham's *Landscape and Ideology: The English Rustic Tradition, 1740–1860* (Berkeley: University of California Press, 1986).

42. Gosse, *Aquarium*, 22, 52, 120.

43. Ibid., 23.

44. Ibid., 76–77.

45. Contrast Gosse's descriptions with Herbert Axelrod's dismissal of the natives in his travels, as discussed in chapter 6.

46. Thwaite notes that Gosse's staunch antievolutionism is sometimes undermined by his prose (214–15).

47. Logan, 157.

48. Thomas Hardy, *The Return of the Native* (Hertfordshire: Wordsworth Classics, 2000), 7. Hardy is speaking of the heath specifically, but his imagery is strikingly similar to Gosse's in descriptions of fierce and timeless rustic scenes.

49. Anthony Low, *The Georgic Revolution* (Princeton: Princeton University Press, 1985), 12.

50. D. E. Allen, 66.

51. O'Connor, 346–47.

52. Della Pollock, "Performing Writing," in *The Ends of Performance*, ed. Peggy Phelan and Jill Lane (New York: New York University Press, 1998), 94. Interestingly, though O'Connor does not use the term *performative writing* to describe the specific works he analyzes, he does identify them with performances.

53. O'Connor, 347.

54. Gosse, *Aquarium*, 14.

55. Elaine Scarry, *On Beauty and Being Just* (Princeton: Princeton University Press, 1999), 9.

56. For more on citational solidarity as relational infrastructure, see Judith Hamera, "Regions of Likeness: The Poetry of Jorie Graham, Dance, and Citational Solidarity," *Text and Performance Quarterly* 25, no. 1 (January 2005): 19.

57. Gosse, *Aquarium*, 210; ellipses in original.

58. Ibid., 177.

59. Ibid., 63, 179, 50.

60. Ibid., vi.

61. Ibid., 16, 91.

62. Chapter XI of *The Aquarium*, the how-to section adapted for the *Handbook*, actually does begin with a poetic epigraph (249), not reproduced in the later work. It is six stanzas and unattributed, though the final stanza's celebration of the glories of God, coupled with the scientific names for specimens, argues strongly for Gosse himself as the author. The first stanza beckons readers to enter the aquarium as a

way of visiting the sea itself, yet another example of the slippage between the two. It also entices the reader with vivid descriptions of the aquarium's (and/as the sea's) underwater beauties.

> Let's visit the caves of a miniature ocean,
> The gorgeous sea-flowers and worms to behold:—
> Actinae, rose-finger'd, ever in motion;
> Phyllodoce, liveried in emerald and gold.

63. Gosse, *Aquarium*, vi.
64. Ibid., iii.
65. Ibid., v.
66. Ibid., 44, 40.
67. Keith Thomas offers three definitive characteristics of the English pet between 1400 and 1800: the animal was allowed into the house, individually named, and not eaten. Katherine Grier adds a fourth, more subtle characteristic: status as a companion or comforting presence. Gosse's tank residents met only one of these criteria. See Grier, *Pets in America: A History* (Chapel Hill: University of North Carolina Press, 2006), 7
68. Logan, 157.
69. Gosse is somewhat more restrained than many of his contemporaries in recounting these bloody tales of the tank. Both what Logan calls "the erotics of the aquarium" (157) and the complexities of using tank residents as rhetorical surrogates are central to the tank's ideological work, as discussed in the remaining chapters.
70. Thwaite, 297–300.
71. Gosse, *Aquarium*, 131.
72. Ibid., 64–65.
73. Ibid., 190.
74. Ibid., 127.
75. Ibid., 155.
76. Salter in Gosse, *Aquarium*, 163–64.
77. Merrill, 211.
78. Gosse, *Aquarium*, 154.
79. Gosse, *Aquarium*, 251; *A Handbook to the Marine Aquarium* (London: Van Voorst, 1856), 4.
80. Gosse, *Aquarium*, 21–22.
81. Gosse, *Aquarium*, 261; *Handbook*, 13.This description makes it much easier to understand pragmatics that, in addition to sexism, account for the relative dearth of women in the hobby. Class and gender pressures meant that those with the requisite leisure and disposable income were not likely to be negotiating with ship's stewards. Anna Thynne was the exception that proves the rule, but she relied frequently on her servants for aquarium logistics. For a discussion of Anna Thynne's aquariums, see Rebecca Stott, *Theatres of Glass: The Woman Who Brought the Sea to the City* (London: Short Books, 2003).
82. Gosse, *Aquarium*, 276; *Handbook*, 24. Despite the cautions, Gosse admits to

being highly immoderate himself, stocking his own tank with about one hundred residents (*Aquarium*, 97–98). This early example of the intoxicating excess that characterizes the hobby to the present exemplifies how the technomanagerial counsel to be prudent succumbs to desire.

83. Gosse, *Aquarium*, 281; *Handbook*, 27; emphasis in originals.

84. The popularity of the aquarium led some authors to release works in different forms. Hibberd is the classic example. In addition to his *Rustic Adornments for Homes of Taste*, which went through multiple editions, he published *The Book of the Aquarium*, which contained two separate sections, one on freshwater and one on marine tanks. Versions of these sections were also published separately as paper volumes. In addition, Hibberd complains of plagiarism, charging that writers were not only copying him in part but also reproducing entire chapters and representing them as their own. See *The Book of the Aquarium; or, Practical Instructions on the Formation, Stocking, and Management, in All Seasons, of Collections of Marine and River Animals and Plants*, rev. ed. (London: Groombridge and Sons, 1860), v–vi. Humphreys also published *Ocean Gardens* and *River Gardens* as separate volumes and, with some alterations, in one volume.

85. Gosse, *Aquarium*, 4–5.

86. Shirley Hibberd, *The Book of the Freshwater Aquarium; or Practical Instructions in the Formation, Stocking, and Management, in All Seasons, of Collections of River Animals and Plants* (London: Groombridge and Sons, 1856), n.p.

87. J. E. Taylor, *The Aquarium: Its Inhabitants, Structure, and Management* (London: Hardwicke and Bogue, 1876), 27.

88. This was acknowledged explicitly by Taylor (11).

89. The titles of H. Noel Humphreys's books *Ocean Gardens* and *River Gardens* underscore the point.

90. Shirley Hibberd, *Rustic Adornments for Homes of Taste*, rev. ed. (London: W. H. and L. Collingridge, 1895), 1

91. Ibid., 247.

92. H. Noel Humphreys, *River Gardens* (London: Sampson Low, 1857), 27; Humphreys, *Ocean and River Gardens* (London: Sampson Low, 1857), 112.

93. Hibberd, *Book of the Freshwater Aquarium*, n.p.

94. Shirley Hibberd, *The Book of the Marine Aquarium; or, Practical Instructions on the Formation, Stocking, and Management, in All Seasons, of Collections of Marine Animals and Plants* (London: Groombridge and Sons, 1856), n.p.

95. Humphreys, *Ocean Gardens*, 11.

96. Humphreys, *Ocean and River Gardens*, 108–9.

97. The "black hole of Calcutta" refers to a tiny cell with one small window that purportedly held the failed European defenders of the British East India Company's Fort William. The Nawab of Bengal attacked the fort on June 19, 1756, imprisoning, by one account, 146 men in a room of eighteen by fourteen feet; 123 of them reportedly died of suffocation. That the "black hole" may have been fictive rather than actual did not diminish its potency as an explicit imperial rallying point and an indicator of imperial anxiety. For "black hole" references in English aquariums, see Gosse, *Aquarium*, 276; Taylor, 27. For use of the image in American publications,

see Arthur M. Edwards, *Life Beneath the Waters; or, The Aquarium in America* (New York: H. Balliere, 1858), 17; D. C. Beard, *What to Do and How to Do It: The American Boys Handy Book*, new ed. (New York: Scribner's, 1893), 63. For a discussion of the circulation of the image through imperial discourse, see Jan Dalley, *The Black Hole: Money, Myth, and Empire* (Brighton: Fig Tree, 2006).

98. Humphreys, *Ocean Gardens*, 11–12.
99. Ibid., 17; emphasis in original.
100. Hibberd, *Book of the Marine Aquarium*, n.p.
101. Taylor, 2.
102. D. E. Allen, 159–60.
103. Taylor, 24.
104. Hibberd, *Rustic Adornments*, 256.
105. Humphreys, *Ocean Gardens*, 4.
106. Taylor, 25.
107. Ibid., 255.
108. Hibberd, *Rustic Adornments*, 256.
109. Taylor, 26.
110. Hibberd, *Rustic Adornments*, 236.
111. D. E. Allen, 124.
112. In ibid.

Chapter 3

1. "Customs and Manners under the Water," *The Friend: A Religious and Literary Journal*, September 30, 1854, 18, American Periodicals Series Online.
2. "The Wonders of the Shore," *Eclectic Magazine of Foreign Literature*, February 1855, 205.
3. Ibid., 206.
4. This argument is indebted to Kristin L. Hoganson, *Consumer's Imperium: The Global Production of American Domesticity, 1865–1920* (Chapel Hill: University of North Carolina Press, 2007).
5. "Aquariums—No. 1," *Godey's Lady's Book*, June 1857, 525, American Periodicals Series Online.
6. "Editors' Book Table: Sea-Side At Home," *Independent*, September 24, 1857, 8, American Periodicals Series Online.
7. Chas. E. Hammett, Jr., "The Aquarium or Aqua-Vivarium," *Scientific American*, September 26, 1857, 19.
8. "Interesting to Ladies," *Home Journal*, October 6, 1855, 4, American Periodicals Series Online.
9. There are rare exceptions to the avoidance of natural history in early aquarium articles by Americans. For example, the tank's utility for both botanists and zoologists is noted in "Parlor Aquarium," *Friends Weekly Intelligencer*, September 18, 1852, 204.
10. Editor's note to Hammett's "The Aquarium."
11. "Editors' Book Table."

12. "Parlor Aquarium," 203.

13. "Interesting to Ladies"; "A New Pleasure," *New York Observer and Chronicle*, September 24, 1857, 1; "Aquaria," *Ballou's Pictorial Drawing-Room Companion*, September 26, 1857, 197, American Periodicals Series Online.

14. "Interesting to Ladies."

15. P. Barry, "The Aquarium," *Horticulturalist and Journal of Rural Art and Rural Taste*, July 1, 1855, 304.

16. William C. Cutter, "Uncle Hiram's Pilgrimage," *Merry's Museum and Parley's Magazine*, July 1, 1857, 137, American Periodicals Series Online.

17. "Aquariums—No. 1."

18. "A New Pleasure."

19. Barry, 304.

20. "Customs and Manners under the Water," *The Friend: A Religious and Literary Journal*, September 30, 1845, 18. American Periodicals Series Online.

21. Hammett, 19.

22. Cutter, 139.

23. "Customs and Manners under the Water," *The Friend: A Religious and Literary Journal*, September 23, 1854, 14, American Periodicals Series Online.

24. Hammett; Cutter, 137–38.

25. "Wonders of the Shore."

26. "Gosse's Aquarium," *Littell's Living Age*, July 29, 1854, 229, American Periodicals Series Online.

27. Ibid., 230.

28. Hammett.

29. "Aquariums—No. 1," 527.

30. Arthur M. Edwards, *Life Beneath the Waters; or, The Aquarium in America* (New York: H. Balliere, 1858), 21, 40.

31. Henry D. Butler, *The Family Aquarium; or, Aqua Vivarium: A "New Pleasure" for the Domestic Circle* (New York: Dick and Fitzgerald, 1858), v.

32. Ibid., 15.

33. Ibid., 16. Though Butler did not see it as a worthy competitor, England lends its Old World aura to the American aquarium and to Barnum's in particular. Butler is careful to mention that the tanks in the American Museum "are the handiwork of artificers originally taught and employed at the Royal Zoological Society of London" (v).

34. Ibid., 17.

35. For an intertwined history of Barnum, Butler, and Cutting and the institutions they owned or managed, see Jerry Ryan, *The Forgotten Aquariums of Boston*, 2nd ed. (Pascoag, RI: Finley Aquatic Books, 2002).

36. Stanley Buder, *Capitalizing on Change: A Social History of American Business* (Chapel Hill: University of North Carolina Press, 2009), 84.

37. Ibid., 94.

38. For a discussion of the emerging middle class during this period, see Stuart M. Blumin, *The Emergence of the Middle Class: Social Experience in the American City, 1760–1900* (Cambridge: Cambridge University Press, 1989), 139–57.

39. Edwards, 153.

40. Steven Conn, *Museums and American Intellectual Life, 1876–1926* (Chicago: University of Chicago Press, 1998), 423.

41. As Buell, Parrish, Pratt, and Pauly indicate, there was no dearth of early American natural history writing. Buell in particular gives a useful account of the "mythical reduction" of "literary naturism" to Thoreau. See Lawrence Buell, *The Environmental Imagination: Thoreau, Nature Writing, and the Formation of American Culture* (Cambridge: Harvard University Press, 1995), 397–423, especially 398–99; Susan Scott Parrish, *American Curiosity: Cultures of Natural History in the Colonial British Atlantic World* (Chapel Hill: University of North Carolina Press, 2006); Philip J. Pauly, *Biologists and the Promise of American Life: From Meriwether Lewis to Alfred Kinsey* (Princeton: Princeton University Press, 2002), 15–43; Mary Louise Pratt, *Imperial Eyes: Travel Writing and Transculturation*, 2nd ed. (New York: Routledge, 2008), 15–36; Robert E. Kohler, *All Creatures: Naturalists, Collectors, and Biodiversity, 1850–1959* (Princeton: Princeton University Press, 2006).

42. James Fenimore Cooper, *The Prairie*, ed. Donald Ringe, Oxford World's Classics (Oxford: Oxford University Press, 1992), 70–71.

43. Ralph Waldo Emerson, "Blight," in *The Norton Anthology of Poetry*, 3rd ed., ed. Alexander W. Allison et al. (New York: Norton, 1983), 672.

44. Butler, v.

45. Edwards, 14.

46. Butler, 29.

47. Edwards, 46.

48. Philip F. Gura, *American Transcendentalism: A History* (New York: Hill and Wang, 2007), 4.

49. Angela Miller, *The Empire of the Eye: Landscape Representation and American Cultural Politics, 1825–1875* (Ithaca: Cornell University Press, 1993), 10; Barbara Novak, *Nature and Culture: American Landscape and Painting, 1825–1875* (Oxford: Oxford University Press, 1980), 3–33; William W. Stowe, "'Property in the Horizon': Landscape and American Travel Writing," in *The Cambridge Companion to American Travel Writing*, ed. Alfred Bendixen and Judith Hamera (Cambridge: Cambridge University Press, 2009), 29–35.

50. Butler, 18; Edwards, 111.

51. Henry David Thoreau, *Walden; or, Life in the Woods, and On the Duty of Civil Disobedience*, Harper Classics (New York: Harper and Row, 1965), 132.

52. Oliver Wendell Holmes, "Brother Jonathan's Lament for Sister Caroline" (1861), in Miller, 10.

53. Butler, 119–20.

54. In a move typical of the often-contradictory rhetoric establishing the aquarium's virtues, Butler does not hesitate to refer to books to authorize the tank when it suits him. See, for example, his reference to "erudite books" in his preface (v).

55. Emerson, "Each and All," American Transcendentalism Web, http://www.vcu.edu/engweb/transcendentalism/authors/emerson/poems/each.html.

56. Edwards, 16.

57. Miller, 18.

58. Miller calls this strategy in mid-nineteenth-century American landscape painting "synecdochic nationalism" (17).
59. Butler, vi.
60. Pauly, 32. The South was not an afterthought in Butler's career as a public aquarist in Boston. The Boston Aquarial and Zoological Gardens included specimens from the South, as discussed later in the present chapter.
61. Butler, 44, 83, 85.
62. Ibid., 83.
63. Ibid., 85.
64. Buder notes the increasing use of the phrases *I reckon* and *I calculate* for *I believe/think* during the antebellum period from 1840 to 1860, one indicator of the increasing importance of both precision and time in the emerging urban industrial consciousness. See Buder, 85.
65. Buell sees this same positive relationship between modernity and nature as underlying nature writing generally (411).
66. Edwards, 154.
67. Ibid., 117.
68. Ibid., 45.
69. Recall here Butler's lengthy discussion of the tank as a theater (19).
70. Ibid., 21, v, vi.
71. Ibid., 121, 98.
72. Ibid., 98.
73. Ibid., 21.
74. Ibid., 24.
75. Hicks was inspired by Isaiah 11:6 (King James Version), which begins, "The wolf also shall dwell with the lamb, and the leopard shall be down with the kid, and the calf and the young lion and fatling together . . ." For a reproduction of Hicks's 1829–30 *Peaceable Kingdom*, see N. F. Karlins, "Peaceable Kingdom," http://www.artnet.com/magazine_pre2000/features/karlins/karlins11-2-99.asp. For the 1846–48 *Peaceable Kingdom*, see Carol Vogel, "Inside Art: A 'Peaceable Kingdom' Comes to Auction," *New York Times*, April 18, 2008, B28.
76. Barnum included a color illustration of a peaceable kingdom in his children's book *Barnum's Menagerie* (New York: White and Allen, 1888). After the Civil War, the peaceable kingdom was, perhaps, imaginable once again as it was not thirty years before.
77. Neil Harris, *Humbug: The Art of P. T. Barnum* (Chicago: University of Chicago Press, 1973), 166, 191, 227.
78. Boston Aquarial and Zoological Gardens programs, 1859[?], February 3, 1861, Special Collections, Mayr Library, Harvard University. Unlike bird families, which were also of interest to amateur naturalist collectors during this period, the aquarium (and/as the peaceable kingdom) is rhetorically potent precisely because it is *not* a biologically reproductive unit.
79. The 1859[?] "Catalogue of Animals" is especially indicative. Here, as if to underline the geographic exoticism of certain residents, local species are unmarked. In a move reinforcing Angela Miller's synecdochic nationalism (17), those outside ei-

ther the northeast or the nation seemingly required geographic identification, as in the (presumably) ubiquitous lobster versus the "Loggerhead Turtle from Florida" or the "European Carp" from Sicily. The only local species so geographically designated are "undescribed . . . from Boston Harbor," with the location standing in for a specific name. Names are important on this program; it included common and scientific names, as well as "the abbreviated name[s] of the author from whom it is taken." These names were august, including Cuvier, Agassiz, and Audubon, among others. In this sense, the venue offered a veritable happy family of naturalists contributing to a global ark to complement the happy families of specimens.

80. Butler, 12.
81. Ibid., 25.
82. Ibid., 68.
83. Ibid., 66, 63.
84. Ibid., 65, 64.
85. Edwards, 24, 72.
86. Ibid., 21.
87. Ibid., 15, 75.
88. Ibid., 112.
89. Thomas J. Schlereth, *Victorian America: Transformations in Everyday Life* (New York: Harper Perennial, 1991), 119; Katherine C. Grier, *Culture and Comfort: Parlor Making and Middle-Class Identity, 1850–1930.* (Washington, DC: Smithsonian Institution Press, 1988), 64.
90. Butler, 30–31.
91. Edwards, 16.
92. "The Diary of Horatio Nelson Taft, 1861–65," http://lcweb2.loc.gov/ammem/tafthtml/tafthome.html.
93. Later aquarium books in this period tend to ignore Edwards altogether and to present Butler as dealing solely with marine tanks, which was not the case. One exception was Osburn, who presents Butler accurately. See Raymond C. Osburn, *The Care of Small Aquaria* (New York: New York Zoological Society, 1914), 11. As early as 1858, some were reframing the history of the hobby in American terms, as in the *North American Review* essay crediting William Stimson of the Smithsonian as the true founder of the practice. That essay argues that because Stimson's work preceded Robert Warrington's by a year (1849 versus 1850), "[t]o him may safely be assigned the credit of having made the first attempt at constructing an aquavivarium," despite the fact that "[h]e made no account of his success" ("The Aquarium," *North American Review,* July 1858, 146, 145).
94. J. H. Collier and J. Hoop, *The American Parlor Aquarium; or, Fluvial Aqua Vivarium* (New York: John H. Collier, 1866), v.
95. Pauly, 56–60.
96. Collier and Hoop, vi.
97. Clifton L. Hodge, *Nature Study and Life* (Boston: Atheneum Press, 1903), vii; 393.
98. Hall, in particular, was an ardent opponent of coeducation and the concomitant "educational 'sissification' of American boys." See Gail Bederman, *Manliness*

and Civilization: A Cultural History of Gender and Race in the United States, 1880–1917 (Chicago: University of Chicago Press, 1995), 111.

99. G. Stanley Hall, introduction to Hodge, xiii–xv.

100. Bederman, 87.

101. Bederman argues convincingly that neurasthenia, "frequently associated with superior intellect," struck both men and women, though in different ways. Women were done in because the mental demands of modernity undermined their reproductivity. Men were "drained" of their "nervous force until they were as weak and useless as worn-out batteries." See Bederman, 85–90.

102. Hodge, viii.

103. Ibid., 12.

104. While tank residents are characterized favorably as "guests" and "lodgers," the tenement also remains a cautionary space. Smith issues the recurring caution against overstocking by arguing that "[f]ishes, like human beings, refuse to thrive in an overcrowded tenement." At least in this one case, the tenement replaces the aquarists' earlier fetish, the "black hole of Calcutta." See Eugene Smith, *The Home Aquarium and How to Care for It* (New York: Dutton, 1902), 74.

105. Herbert Croly, *The Promise of American Life* (New York: Macmillan, 1909), 400.

106. Ibid., 434.

107. Smith, 1–2.

108. Gregory C. Bateman and Reginald A. R. Bennett, *The Book of Aquaria* (New York: Scribner's, 1902), 1.

109. Osburn, 13.

110. Margaret Hamilton Welch, "Domestic Topics," *Harper's Bazaar*, June 1902, 555, American Periodicals Series Online.

111. Smith, 184.

112. Louisa May Alcott, *Little Men* (New York: Grosset and Dunlap, 1977), 165; Arthur Henry, "For the Children of the Streets," *Puritan* 9, no. 1, 1900, 145–49.

113. Shannon Jackson, *Lines of Activity: Performance, Historiography, Hull-House Domesticity* (Ann Arbor: University of Michigan Press, 2000), 87.

114. W. A. Poyser, *Aquarium,* April 1913, 6.

115. J. H. Wagner, *The Home Aquarium or "House Pond,"* Hobby Series, no. 20 (Baltimore: August M. Roth, 1915), 1–2.

116. Ibid., 25.

117. Butler, 11. Ready-made aquarium decorations were both commercially available and featured in general interest aquarium books. See, for example, Chester A. Reed, *Goldfish—Aquaria—Fermeries* (New York: Doubleday, Page, 1908), 36.

118. In a compelling illustration of the hobby's ability to consume personal time and space to one's detriment as well as create it for one's pleasure, Smith, who was also a founder of the New York Aquarium Society, died suddenly and unexpectedly not even a full year after assuming editorship of the *Aquarium.* William Innes, the acting editor who replaced him, noted that he had "through overwork . . . impaired his health" ("Important," *Aquarium,* December 1912, 60). Smith must have died as this issue went to press ("Eugene Smith," *Aquarium,* December 1912, 61). In a com-

pelling illustration of the small world of American aquaria, Smith mentions in one of the lead articles in that same issue that his formative encounter with the practice had come as a small boy when he was taken to Barnum's museum (Eugene Smith, "Public Aquaria in America," *Aquarium*, December 1912, 55). This journal is not to be confused with a later *Aquarium*, first published in May 1932 and running until 1971.

119. This list is by no means intended to be exhaustive.

120. The societies were the Brooklyn Aquarium Society, the Chicago Fish Fanciers' Club, the New York Aquarium Society, the Philadelphia Aquarium Society, and the Milwaukee Aquarium Society. All posted their officers and advertised their meetings in the pages of aquarium journals, including, in this case, the *Aquarium*.

121. See Osburn, 61; [Eugene Smith?], "From the Fatherland," *Aquarium*, September 1912, 71.

122. ["The balanced aquarium . . ."], *Aquatic Life*, August 1916, 163.

123. Poyser, *Aquarium*, April 1913, 6.

124. Ibid.

125. W. L. Brind, "Aquarium Fishes from Our Own Country?" *Aquatic Life*, September 1915, 19.

126. Ibid.

127. Hugo Mulertt, "The New York Aquarium," *Aquarium*, July 1895, 184.

128. For more on Mulertt's career in the hobby, see Albert J. Klee, *The Toy Fish: A History of the Aquarium Hobby in America; The First One-Hundred Years*, rev. ed. (Pascoag, RI: Finley Aquatic Books, 2003).

129. D. L. Semann, "How I Became a Fish Fan," *Aquatic Life*, December 1915, 49–50.

130. G. S. Myers, "Foreward to First Issue," *Ichthyologica*, January 1966, 3.

131. Donald A. Simpson, "How Do They Get That Way?" *Aquarium Journal*, June 1956, 209.

Chapter 4

1. For the evolution of American pet keeping, see Katherine Grier, *Pets in America: A History* (Chapel Hill: University of North Carolina Press, 2006); for a discussion of the notion of "companion species," see Donna J. Haraway, *When Species Meet* (Minneapolis: University of Minnesota Press, 2008), 15–19.

2. The major works of the animal studies literature focus on mammals. See Virginia DeJohn Anderson, *Creatures of Empire: How Domestic Animals Transformed Early America* (Oxford: Oxford University Press, 2006); Arnold Arluke and Clinton R. Sanders, *Regarding Animals* (Philadelphia: Temple University Press, 1996); Lorraine Daston and Gregg Mitman, eds., *Thinking with Animals: New Perspectives on Anthropomorphism* (New York: Columbia University Press, 2005); Jennifer Ham and Matthew Senior, eds., *Animal Acts: Configuring the Human in Western History* (New York: Routledge, 1997); Elizabeth Hanson, *Animal Attractions: Nature on Display in American Zoos* (Princeton: Princeton University Press, 2002); Harriet Ritvo, *The Animal Estate: The English and Other Creatures in the Victorian Age* (Cambridge: Harvard University Press, 1987); Nigel Rothfels, *Representing Animals*

(Bloomington: Indiana University Press, 2002); Cary Wolfe, ed., *Zoontologies: The Question of the Animal* (Minneapolis: University of Minnesota Press, 2003). Jane C. Desmond notes the mammal bias in animal studies in *Staging Tourism: Bodies on Display from Waikiki to Sea World* (Chicago: University of Chicago Press, 1999), 149. Erica Fudge notes the peculiar status of fish as nonmammalian and as food in *Animal* (London: Reaktion, 2002), 51. One exception to this pervasive mammal bias is performance studies scholar Alan Read's brief discussion of Bob Carroll's "Salmon Show" in "Editorial: On Animals," *Performance Research* 5.2 (2000): 111.

3. Irene Pepperberg, interview by Terry Gross, *Fresh Air*, NPR, November 12, 2008, http://www.npr.org/templates/story/story.php?storyId=98659373&ft=1&f=13.

4. Una Chaudhuri, "Animal Geographies: Zooesis and the Space of Modern Drama," *Modern Drama*, Winter 2003, 646; Steve Baker, *Picturing the Beast: Animals, Identity, and Representation* (Champaign: University of Illinois Press, 2001), 77.

5. Chaudhuri, "Animal Geographies," 646.

6. Akira Mizuta Lippit, *Electric Animal: Toward a Rhetoric of Wildlife* (Minneapolis: University of Minnesota Press, 2000), 1; emphasis in original.

7. Una Chaudhuri, "(De)Facing the Animals: Zooesis and Performance," *TDR: The Drama Review*, Spring 2007, 13.

8. Gosse himself credited Joseph Priestley's discovery of oxygen with beginning the hobby. See Philip Henry Gosse, *The Aquarium: An Unveiling of the Wonders of the Deep Sea*, 2nd ed. (London: Van Voorst, 1856), 5. For a discussion of Priestley, his discovery, and modernity, see Steven Johnson, *The Invention of Air: A Story of Science, Faith, Revolution, and the Birth of America* (New York: Riverhead / Penguin), 2008.

9. Lippit, 184, 185.

10. Baker, 77.

11. This is even truer of invertebrates, particularly those lacking faces of any kind. See Desmond's discussion of the thingness of jellyfish in the Monterrey Bay Aquarium (167).

12. Jacques Derrida, "The Animal That Therefore I Am (More to Follow)," trans. David Wills, *Critical Inquiry*, Winter 2002, 380.

13. Ida M. Mellen and Robert J. Lanier, *1001 Questions Answered about Your Aquarium* (New York: Dodd, Mead, 1935), 7.

14. Blennies are an exception that proves the rule. They have eyes closer together on the head and so have a curious, quizzical, human appearance that most fish do not.

15. Alphonso Lingus, "Animal Body, Inhuman Face," in Wolfe, 17.

16. Desmond, 167; emphasis in original.

17. This is one underlying problem in Randy Malamud's assertion that Julio Cortázar's "Axolotl" illuminates dynamics of aquarium spectatorship. The axolotl is a salamander, an air-breathing amphibian, with feet and eyes at the front of its head, closer in physiognomy to Derrida's cat than to Paula's yellow angelfish. I do not argue that people cannot narcissistically identify with fish, but such identifications are more complex perceptually than Malamud suggests, and zoo spectatorship and

aquarium spectatorship are not simply interchangeable. See Randy Malamud, *Reading Zoos: Representations of Animals and Captivity* (New York: New York University Press, 1998), 245–53.

18. See "How Old Are Your Fishes?" in *Aquarium Highlights,* ed. William T. Innes (Philadelphia: Innes, 1951), 83; Albert J. Klee, "Beginner's Corner: Longevity of Fishes." *Aquarium Journal,* March 1960, 162–63.

19. John Berger, *About Looking* (New York: Pantheon, 1980), 14; emphasis added.

20. Donald A. Simpson, "Something Fishy" (unpublished manuscript, California Academy of Sciences, 1961[?]), 4.

21. Fishes' supposed primitiveness hinged on confusion about evolution and the "great chain of being," wherein evolutionary processes were seen as teleological, leading inexorably from "lower" to "higher" and "more perfect" forms. A full discussion of evolution and associated confusions is found in Steven Jay Gould, *Wonderful Life: The Burgess Shale and the Nature of History* (Harmondsworth: Penguin, 1991).

22. Grier, 182–230.

23. See "Screaming Fish," *Littell's Living Age,* July 20, 1861, 186, American Periodicals Series Online; "Tenacity of Life in a Fish," *Saturday Evening Post,* February 15, 1862, 6, reprinted in *New England Farmer: A Monthly Journal,* March 1862, 141. These curiosities were not limited to the early days of the hobby. Almost one hundred years later, an "appallingly ugly" fish's tenacity for life is credited with birthing a whole family of hobbyists who were impressed by its resilience. See Ouida Verizzo, "Nine Lives of a Catfish," *Tropical Fish Hobbyist,* June 1959, 26–28.

24. "The Fish World at Home," *Eclectic Magazine of Foreign Literature,* November 1862, 387.

25. Ibid., 390.

26. Ibid., 391.

27. Hugo Mulertt, "Exhibition Aquariums," *Aquarium,* July 1895, 185.

28. Ibid., 185, 187.

29. Ibid., 187.

30. Desmond, 150; emphasis in original.

31. Two examples represent the two general categories of "fish as healer" discourse. In the first, the home aquarium and its residents serve as tonic for individual maladies, as in the case of Doris Bialk, who credited her aquarium with curing her of "problems with nerves and hyperactivity that I doctored for years." See Ed Gralewicz, "Meet the Hobbyists: Dolores and Joe Bialk," *Tropical Fish Hobbyist,* February 1970, 22–26. The second category touts the beneficial effects of aquarium fish on institutions, particularly their ability to calm and regulate behavior, as in John W. Haas, "Tropical Fish Help Cure the Mentally Ill," *Tropical Fish Hobbyist,* September 1958, 30–32.

32. A recent *New York Times* article suggests that the jury is still out, at least in the minds of one key aquarium constituency, on a fish's capacity to suffer. Brendan I. Koerner writes, "Next to bickering over whose dad is tougher, playground intellectuals may love nothing more than debating whether goldfish can feel pain" ("Chas-

ing the Joneses, in a Fish Tank," *New York Times*, July 3, 2005, section 3, p. 2).

33. Gregory C. Bateman and Reginald A. R. Bennett, *The Book of Aquaria* (New York: Scribner's, 1902), 111.

34. Grier, 153.

35. "Protection of Goldfish," *Aquatic Life*, September 1915, 6. For Lloyd's colorful career in the aquarium hobby, see Klee, *Toy Fish*, 129–30.

36. Rev. Paul Wagner Roth, "My Polyacanthus," *Aquatic Life*, August 1916, 153; W. A. Poyser, "Reason and Instinct," *Aquarium*, May 1915, 13. The question of fish intelligence continues to resonate in contemporary science. See, for example, Sean B. Carroll, "For Fish in Coral Reefs, It's Useful to be Smart," *New York Times*, October 20, 2009, D1+. Carroll begins the article by reflecting on fish behavior in a childhood aquarium as an indicator of fish intelligence.

37. Poyser, "Reason and Instinct," 13.

38. Dana Seitler is particularly clear in her argument about photography and film as visual carriers of atavist preoccupations. See her *Atavistic Tendencies: The Culture of Science in American Modernity* (Minneapolis: University of Minnesota Press, 2008), 55–57.

39. Roth, 153.

40. In a particularly potent collision of aquariums and atavistic racism, Ida Mellen was herself a rabid advocate of eugenics, arguing that "a truly civilized state" would "euthanize" "idiots, . . . then the hopelessly and criminally insane, then incurable criminals, sex perverts, and other undesirables." She stated that Hitler's willingness to execute "idiots. . . . was one gesture immensely to his credit" ("Order for Euthanasia," April 27, 1947, Box 2, "O," Ida Mellen Papers, New York Public Library).

41. Daston and Mitman, 12.

42. Joseph Roach, *Cities of the Dead: Circum-Atlantic Performance* (New York: Columbia University Press, 1996), 2.

43. Yi-Fu Tuan, *Dominance and Affection: The Making of Pets* (New Haven: Yale University Press, 1984), 163.

44. Edward C. Symmes, "The Fishy Little World of Edward C. Symmes, Jr.," *Aquarium*, July 1968, 56–57, quoted in Albert J. Klee, "A History of the Aquarium Hobby in America," part 2, *Aquarium*, October 1968, 54.

45. For a discussion of anthropomorphism and modernity, see Akira Mizuta Lippit, ". . . From Wild Technology to Electric Animal," in *Representing Animals*, ed. Nigel Rothfels (Bloomington: Indiana University Press, 2002), 124.

46. Desmond is correct in her assessment that fish are anthropomorphized in discussions of reproduction, as discussed in chapter 5 of the present book. However, this is not "against all odds," as she suggests (184).

47. "Are Fish People?" advertisement, *Tropical Fish Hobbyist*, September 1959, 30.

48. Daston and Mitman, 11.

49. "Anthropomorphism," *Sea Creatures & Me* (blog), January 4, 2008, http://nanoreef.wordpress.com/2008/01/04/anthropomorphism/.

50. Steve Baker, "Sloughing the Human," in Wolfe, 147–64.

51. Ibid., 158.

52. Simpson, "Something Fishy," front cover.

53. Levinas posited the face-to-face relation as the foundation for experiencing irreducible alterity and thus for ethical responsibility for the other's ability to respond. For a discussion of Levinasian ethics and animals, see Wolfe, xvii–iii.

54. Tuan, 7–17.

55. "Fish Are Like Humans," advertisement, *Aquarium Journal*, November 1957, 42

56. Grier, 155–56.

57. Hugo Mulertt, "Use Mulertt's Condensed Fish Food," *The Aquarium: Information for the Care of the Parlor Aquarium* (Brooklyn: Hugo Mulertt, 1909), back cover.

58. "President Roosevelt's NRA Gives Us a Square Deal ," advertisement, *Aquarium*, December 1933, xx.

59. "Boss, I *Love* That Frozen Brine Shrimp . . . ," advertisement, *Aquarium Journal*, May 1959, n.p.

60. "Please Tropi-Cure Me!" advertisement, *Tropical Fish Hobbyist*, November 1958, 59.

61. "Boy . . . Am I Hot!" advertisement, *Aquarium Journal*, June 1956, 227.

62. Joseph M. Bellanca, editorial, *Tropical Fish Hobbyist*, November 1968, 3.

63. "I Know How You Feel . . . ," *Aquarium*, March 1971, 53.

64. Rube Goldberg, "If You Haven't Got a Collection . . . ," reprinted in *Aquarium*, January 1934, 220.

65. Newberry, 8.

66. William Vorderwinkler, *Tropical Fish Hobbyist*, November 1959, 2+.

67. Juan Echevarria, "Twelve Commandments," *Tropical Fish Hobbyist*, May–June 1953, 12. The "Twelve Commandments" also belies Vorderwinkler's characterization of the aquarium as an almost intrinsically benign alternative to the wild. Reminders like "Thou Shalt Keep Me With Brothers Of My Own Stature (The law of the sea: 'Big Fishes Feed on Little Fishes')" reinforced the reality that fishes' relative safety was clearly a function of the aquarist's prudence, while further reinforcing the slippage between the tank and the sea through invocation of shared "laws."

68. Everett F. Bleiler, "Davey Jones' Ambassador," in *Science-Fiction: The Gernsback Years* (Kent, OH: Kent State University Press, 1998), 138.

69. "Pass the Word . . . ," *Aquarium*, July 1971, 55.

70. "Kind of Depressing . . .," *Aquarium*, March 1971, 69.

71. Steven M. Gelber, *Hobbies: Leisure and the Culture of Work in America* (New York: Columbia University Press, 1999), 19.

72. "TopsAll Cannibal Mix," advertisement, *Aquarium Journal*, November 1956, 412.

73. "Now, Just One More Thing . . . ," *Aquarium*, April 1971, 65.

74. "Murderers!" *Tropical Fish Hobbyist*, June 1969, 83.

75. "I Hate to Do This. . . ," in Innes, *Aquarium Highlights*, 87.

76. *Aquarium*, May 1969, 57.

77. In Klee, *Toy Fish*, 109.

78. In Wolfe, xx; emphasis in original.

79. Grier, 158.
80. Joseph Roach, *It* (Ann Arbor: University of Michigan Press, 2007), 1.
81. See Klee, "A History of the Aquarium Hobby in America," part 7, *Aquarium*, June 1968, 52–53.
82. For more on the history and conventions of pet portraiture, including photography, see Grier, 96–103.
83. Roach, *It*, 11.
84. Joseph Roach, "It," *Theatre Journal* 56, no. 4 (2004), http://muse.jhu.edu/journals/theatre_journal/v056/56.4roach.html.
85. William T. Innes, "The Jack Dempsey," *Aquarium*, May 1932, 1.
86. Ibid.
87. Roach, *It*, 4.
88. Frederick J. Kerr, "Personality Plus: The Oscar," *Tropical Fish Hobbyist*, November 1969, 5–9.
89. Ibid., 5.
90. Ibid., 6.
91. Ibid., 8.
92. Roach, *It*, 127.
93. Diane Schofield, "Comedians of the Aquarium: I'll Huff and I'll Puff," *Aquarium Journal*, January 1960, 48.
94. Ibid., 52.
95. Donald A. Simpson, "Snozolla Comes to the Steinhart," *Aquarium Journal*, July 1956, 263. See also "Some Further Notes on Snozolla at the Steinhart," *Aquarium Journal*, November 1956, 405; "You Tell Me," *Aquarium Journal*, February 1960, 64–65.
96. Simpson, "Snozolla Comes to Stienhart," 263. The results of my decidedly unscientific survey suggest that Jimmy Durante is the celebrity It fish are most often said to resemble. Diane Schofield says her puffer also resembled the late comedian, despite its lack of a proboscis ("Comedians," 48).
97. Simpson, "Snozolla Comes to Steinhart," 264.
98. Simpson, "You Tell Me," 65.
99. In Roach, *It*, 78.
100. Robert P. L. Straughan, "Blanche the Lionfish," *Aquarium Journal*, July 1958, 250. See also "Marine Collector Keeps Lionfish for Four Years," *Aquarium Journal*, November 1959, 158–59; "Blanche, Lionfish, Dies," *Aquarium Journal*, March 1961, 150–51.
101. Straughan, "Blanche, Lionfish, Dies," 150.
102. Ibid.
103. Haraway, 3.

Chapter 5

1. Hobson Dewey Anderson and Percy E. Davidson, *Occupational Trends in the United States* (Stanford, CA: Stanford University Press, 1940), 592.
2. Peter G. Rowe. *Making a Middle Landscape* (Cambridge, MA: MIT Press,

1991); see also Kenneth T. Jackson, *Crabgrass Frontier: The Suburbanization of the United States* (New York: Oxford University Press, 1985).

3. Ibid. For a discussion of heating and aeration improvements brought about by widespread electrification in the 1920s, see Albert J. Klee, *The Toy Fish: A History of the Aquarium Hobby in America; The First One-Hundred Years*, rev. ed. (Pascoag, RI: Finley Aquatic Books, 2003), 152–60.

4. Stanley Buder, *Capitalizing on Change: A Social History of American Business* (Chapel Hill: University of North Carolina Press, 2009), 234–35.

5. C. Wright Mills, *White Collar: The American Middle Class* (New York: Oxford University Press, 1951), 275; David Savran, *Highbrow/Lowdown: Theater, Jazz, and the Making of the New Middle Class* (Ann Arbor: University of Michigan Press, 2009), 138–45.

6. Alba M. Edwards, *Sixteenth Census of the United States, 1940: Population; Comparative Occupation Statistics for the United States, 1870–1940* (Washington, DC: Government Printing Office, 1943), 183.

7. Klee, *Toy Fish*, 152.

8. Kristin L. Hoganson, *Consumers' Imperium: The Global Production of American Domesticity, 1865–1920* (Chapel Hill: University of North Carolina Press, 2007), 12.

9. Alfred Morgan, *Tropical Fishes and Home Aquaria* (New York: Scribner's, 1935), 4.

10. In Dana Seitler, *Atavistic Tendencies: The Culture of Science in American Modernity* (Minneapolis: University of Minnesota Press, 2008), 134.

11. Albert Klee offers a humorous account of early travails in fish importation, including categorizing stock for purposes of assessing import duties (*Toy Fish*, 85–87).

12. W. L. Brind, "Aquarium Fishies from Our Own Country?" *Aquatic Life*, September 1915, 19.

13. William T. Innes, "*Notropis Lutrensis* (Rainbow Minnow)," *Aquarium*, May 1934, 3.

14. Robert Gannon, "Meet the Hobbyist: Frank Pierce, Jr.," *Tropical Fish Hobbyist*, February 1960, 57. The German endorsement of American species would have carried particular weight, as Germany was seen as one of the cradles of the hobby, as well as of scientific innovation in and beyond aquariums.

15. Frank S. Locke, "Speaking of Americans," *Aquariana*, February 1933, 198.

16. The formulation *aquari*-points to the relative containment of this industry, as opposed to the "sky-high promise" of biotechnology. Though the U.S. aquarium industry is highly profitable, its points of production and consumption are more institutionally circumscribed (with comparatively smaller companies, infrastructure, government and university connections, etc.) and less speculative than that of marine biotechnology. See Helmreich, *Alien Oceans: Anthropological Voyages in Microbial Seas* (Berkeley: University of California Press, 2009), 107. For an excellent history of the pet industry, including aquariums, see Katherine Grier, *Pets in America: A History* (Chapel Hill: University of North Carolina Press, 2006).

17. William Innes, "The Editor's Letter," *Aquarium*, July 1934, 67.

18. "Women's Work," *Harper's Bazaar*, November 18, 1899, 46, American Periodicals Series Online.

19. *Aquarium*, January 1914, 82.

20. [E. J.?] Wilcox, "The Muskallunge," *Aquarium*, November 1913, 58. In another testament to the muskallunge's ferocity, the U.S. Navy launched a submarine with the same name in 1942.

21. Cotter, who eventually opened her own store, clearly had far easier access to capital, even by the relative standards of the well-off aquarist. See Lilian A. Cotter, "How I Got My Start," *Aquariana*, June 1933, 279–80.

22. William T. Innes, editorial, *Aquarium*, October 1932, 161.

23. Locke, "Speaking of Americans," 201–2.

24. Herbert A. Dulfer, editorial, *Aquariana*, May 1933, 242; Innes, editorial, October 1932, 161.

25. Herbert A. Dulfer, editorial, *Aquariana*, February 1933, n.p.

26. Locke, "Speaking of Americans," 199.

27. Gelber discusses the commercialization of hobby culture, locating it in the 1950s. The aquarium puts this much earlier, a full century earlier if Butler's book is included. Further, it demonstrates that such aggressive commercialization persisted even during times that severely tax leisure-based consumption. See Steven M. Gelber, *Hobbies: Leisure and the Culture of Work in America* (New York: Columbia University Press, 1999), 23–56.

28. William T. Innes, editorial, *Aquarium*, July 1933, 75. *Aquariana* also explicitly supported Roosevelt's NRA, in the September 1933 edition (44).

29. Edward S. Brown, reprinted in *Aquarium*, June 1934, 44.

30. "T.I.F.A.S. Insignia," *Tropical Fish Hobbyist*, March–April 1957, 32.

31. An excellent summary of state legislation and the perceived stakes for the hobbyist is "Big Brother is Watching," *Aquarium*, December 1967, 30–32.

32. Albert J. Klee, "Beginner's Corner," *Aquarium Journal*, July 1961, 339.

33. *Tropical Fish Hobbyist*, April 1970, 98.

34. William Vorderwinkler, "Editorially . . . ," *Tropical Fish Hobbyist*, March 1960, 2.

35. Neal Pronek, editorial, *Tropical Fish Hobbyist*, June 1969, 2.

36. Elaine Tyler May, *Homeward Bound: American Families in the Cold War Era*, 20th ed. (New York: Basic, 2008).

37. Alfred C. Kinsey et al., *Sexual Behavior in the Human Female* (Bloomington: Indiana University Press, 1998).

38. *Tropical Fish Hobbyist*, September–October 1954, 17.

39. John Cooley, ed., *Mark Twain's Aquarium: The Samuel Clemens Angelfish Correspondence, 1905–1910* (Athens: University of Georgia Press, 1991), 94. See also Ron Powers, *Mark Twain: A Life* (New York: Free Press, 2005), 610–20; Karen Lystra, *Dangerous Intimacy: The Untold Story of Mark Twain's Final Years* (Berkeley: University of California Press, 2004). Despite the obvious potential for scandal, the Aquarium Club was not among Clemens's "dangerous intimacies." All three sources conclude that the club was born of nostalgia for his own daughters' child-

hoods and the longing for grandchildren. Klee sees it as an extension of an innately human impulse to collect (*Toy Fish*, 189–90).

40. Neil Harris, *Humbug: The Art of P. T. Barnum* (Chicago: University of Chicago Press, 1973), 190–91.

41. Edwards, 15.

42. Herbert Axelrod, *Tropical Fish as a Hobby*, rev. ed. (New York: McGraw-Hill, 1952), ix.

43. Gelber, 205–11.

44. Jane C. Desmond, *Staging Tourism: Bodies on Display from Waikiki to Sea World* (Chicago: University of Chicago Press, 1999), 192.

45. Donald A. Simpson, "Something Fishy" (unpublished manuscript, California Academy of Sciences, 1961[?]). Simpson fittingly dedicates his manuscript to "Helen, naturally."

46. Don Norman, "Fish Pulled Me Out," *Aquarium*, September 1935, 102.

47. Ibid., 103.

48. Ibid., 102.

49. Ibid., 103.

50. Gelber, 205; see also Mary Ann Clawson, *Constructing Brotherhood: Class, Gender, and Fraternalism* (Princeton: Princeton University Press, 1989); Mark C. Carnes and Clyde Griffen, eds., *Meanings for Manhood: Construction of Masculinity in Victorian America* (Chicago: University of Chicago Press, 1990). Domestic masculinity was distinct from masculine domesticity, wherein men took on jobs traditionally gendered female. The aquarium offered opportunities for both.

51. Gelber, 205.

52. *Zoo Time* and *Wild Kingdom* are only two examples of a genre of shows centering on wildlife in and outside of captivity. Often locally produced, such shows emerged on radio as early as 1925. For more on *Zoo Time* and the *Radio Nature League*, see Marcel Chatkowski LaFollete, *Science on the Air: Popularizers and Personalities on Radio and Early Television* (Chicago: University of Chicago Press, 2008), 27–44. For more on *Wild Kingdom* and its relatives, see Gregg Mitman, *Reel Nature: America's Romance with Wildlife on Film* (Cambridge, MA: Harvard University Press, 1999), 132–56.

53. *Tropical Fish Hobbyist*, August 1971, 61.

54. Rebecca Stott, *Theatres of Glass: The Woman Who Brought the Sea to the City* (London: Short Books, 2003); Bernd Brunner, *The Ocean at Home: An Illustrated History of the Aquarium* (New York: Princeton Architectural Press, 2003), 20–29, 35–37.

55. Philip Henry Gosse, *The Aquarium: An Unveiling of the Wonders of the Deep Sea*, 2nd ed. (London: Van Voorst, 1856), 7.

56. The anonymous author of the *North American Review* essay "The Aquarium" (July 1858) both establishes and dismisses Power de Villepreux's contributions thusly: "The cages made by Mrs. Power, a learned French lady residing in Messina, in 1832, although she gave to some of them the name of Aquaria, were merely receptacles suspended in the waters of the bay to enable her to watch the habits of marine animals" (145). The essay includes another interesting gender dismissal when it

critiques the anonymous author of "My Aquarium" in *Atlantic Monthly* (1, no. 4 [1858]: 426–31), assigning female gender and linking it explicitly to inadequacy and ignorance: "The pleasant writer of 'My Aquarium,' in the *Atlantic Monthly*, does not appear to know why her third attempt [at keeping aquarium residents alive] succeeded after two failures, although the fact of the presence of Infusoria is distinctly stated" (149). One dismissal, at least, did not go unchallenged: also writing in the *North American Review*, Matilda Joslyn Gage identified Power de Villepreux as the inventor of the aquarium, challenging the conventional wisdom that women "possess no inventive or mechanical genius" ("Woman as Inventor," May 1883, 478–90).

57. Klee, *Toy Fish*, 29.

58. Consider, for example, Mellen's seemingly testy response to an invitation from H. E. Dando, editor of *Pets Magazine*, by declining his offer to give her a column on tropical fish.

> Leaving the Aquarium has unfortunately not meant getting away from aquarium business. It seems as if everyone who has a sick aquatic animal or a problem in fish culture or who wants to build a public aquarium in any part of the world still thinks it necessary to correspond with me on the subject! . . . I am out of the "Aquarium game" and do not keep tropical fishes in my irregularly heated home. (January 4, 1930, Box 3, Folder: *Pets Magazine*, Ida M. Mellen Papers, New York Public Library)

Over twenty years later, Mellen, who writes almost constantly about her lack of funds, is contacting publishers to pitch a new book on aquarium fish.

59. *Aquarium Journal*, December 1957, 434.

60. Diane Schofield, "Biting the Hand That Feeds Them!" *Aquarium Journal*, October 1958, 355.

61. Diane Schofield, "This is Your Life: A Brief Autobiography," *Aquarium Journal*, January 1959, 58.

62. Diane Schofield, "Arise Men!" *Aquarium Journal*, August 1958, 299.

63. Ibid., 308–9.

64. Ibid., 306.

65. Ibid., 309.

66. Ibid., 299.

67. Norman, 103.

68. Schofield, "Arise," 306.

69. May, 175.

70. One rich area for future investigation is the resonance between the seemingly queer investments of hobbyists in aquariums, its homosocial potential, and the queer alterity of fish and reef invertebrates.

71. Albert J. Klee, "Beginners Corner," *Aquarium Journal*, March 1958, 112–13.

72. The "if you can't beat 'em, join 'em" strategy resurfaces regularly in aquarium publications. In "A Word for Wives," published in 1933, the anonymous author recommends that "Mrs. Aquariist [*sic*]" take up the tank as an adjunct to painting and "Japanese Flower Art" (*Aquariana*, September 1933, 28–30). Donald Simpson hu-

morously speculates that it was the same strategy that initially led his wife, Helen, to join him in aquarium keeping, in what emerges as one of the most remarkable partnerships in the hobbyist literature ("Something Fishy," 12).

73. Robert J. Wyndham, "On the Aquarium Front—For Men Only: Don't Be a Mouse Facing Your Spouse," *Aquarium Journal*, September 1961, 418.

74. Ibid., 423–24.

75. "The Mrs. and the Hobby," reprinted in Albert J. Klee, "A History of the Aquarium Hobby in America," part 19, *Aquarium*, June 1969, 52–53.

76. "Fish, Fish, and More Fish," *Aquarium Journal*, April 1947, 33.

77. Frank S. Locke, "Arcara Curviceps," *Aquariana*, November 1932, 106.

78. William Vorderwinkler, "Father's Dilemma," *Tropical Fish Hobbyist*, January–February 1955, 9.

79. Desmond, 186.

80. May, 139.

81. "New Miracle Filter for Aquariums," *Tropical Fish Hobbyist*, September–October 1955, n.p.

82. In Gelber, 31–32.

83. Wickman, *Aquarium*, November 1979, 61.

84. Wardley Products, "Picture of a Happy Hobby!" *Tropical Fish Hobbyist*, January 1959, 77.

85. Klee, "Beginner's Corner," July 1961, 340.

86. Henry A. Nichols, "The Penalties of Aquarium Progress," *Aquarium Journal*, March 1941, 22.

87. Desmond, 185.

88. William T. Innes, *Exotic Aquarium Fishes: A Work of General Reference* (Philadelphia: Innes, 1935), 447.

89. Albert J. Klee, *Aquarium Journal*, January 1957, 31.

90. Albert J. Klee, *Aquarium Journal*, June 1961, 272.

91. Judith Butler, *Gender Trouble: Feminism and the Subversion of Identity* (New York: Routledge, 1990), vii.

92. Thomas H. Bauchle, Jr., "That Siamese Amazon," *Aquarium*, August 1933, 98. Betta are known colloquially as the "Siamese fighting fish."

93. Ibid., 99.

94. See, for example, May's discussion of *Blonde Venus* (37–38). See also Molly Haskell, *From Reverence to Rape: The Treatment of Women in the Movies* (Chicago: University of Chicago Press, 1987); S. J. Kleinberg, *Women in the United States: 1830–1945* (New Brunswick, NJ: Routledge, 1999), 277–81.

95. Locke, "Arcara Curviceps," 106.

96. Henry D. Butler, *The Family Aquarium; or, Aqua Vivarium: A "New Pleasure" for the Domestic Circle* (New York: Dick and Fitzgerald, 1858), 63–64.

97. Robert J. Wyndham, "Meet Mr. Stickleback!" *Aquarium Journal*, December 1958, 482, 484.

98. Robert J. Wyndham, "Western Aquarist Says the Blue Gularis is Not a Sissy!" *Aquarium Journal*, September 1958, 322–23.

99. Shirley Hibberd, *The Book of the Marine Aquarium; or, Practical Instructions*

on the Formation, Stocking, and Management, in All Seasons, of Collections of Marine Animals and Plants (London: Groombridge and Sons, 1856), n.p.

100. Tetra Company, "When Your Name Is . . . ," *Aquarium Fish Magazine*, July 2002, 9.

101. Ibid., 10.

Chapter 6

1. Alfred Morgan, *Tropical Fishes and Home Aquaria* (New York: Scribner's, 1935), 4.

2. Walter Lippmann, *Drift and Mastery: An Attempt to Diagnose the Current Unrest* (1914; reprint, New York: Henry Holt, 1917), 211.

3. For a discussion of chronopolitics as part of Western strategies of colonial representation, all of which can be seen operating in the home aquarium, see Dibyesh Anand, *Geopolitical Exotica: Tibet in the Western Imagination* (Minneapolis: University of Minnesota Press, 2007), 31–32.

4. Anna Lowenhaupt Tsing, *Friction: An Ethnography of Global Connection* (Princeton: Princeton University Press, 2005), 4.

5. Amy Kaplan, *The Anarchy of Empire in the Making of U.S. Culture* (Cambridge, MA: Harvard University Press, 2002), 1–12.

6. In Kaplan, 2.

7. The following discussions of tropicality contributed to this analysis: David Arnold, "Inventing Tropicality," in *The Problem of Nature: Environment, Culture, and European Expansion* (Oxford: Blackwell, 1996), 141–68; Denis Cosgrove, "Tropic and Tropicality," in *Tropical Visions in an Age of Empire*, ed. Felix Driver and Luciana Martins (Chicago: University of Chicago Press, 2005), 197–216; Nancy Leys Stepan, *Picturing Tropical Nature* (Ithaca: Cornell University Press, 2001); Beth Fowkes Tobin, *Colonizing Nature: The Tropics in British Arts and Letters, 1760–1820* (Philadelphia: University of Pennsylvania Press, 2005).

8. For the idea of the tropical as a transnational brand, I am indebted to Melissa Blanco Borelli and her work on the figure of the mulatto in Cuban popular dance, particularly "Power and Hi(p)-stories: Dancing in Cuba's Academias de Baile (1920s–1950s)," paper presented at the joint conference of the American Society for Theatre Research and the Congress on Research in Dance, Seattle, WA, November 2010.

9. Cosgrove, 198.

10. Michael Taussig, *What Color Is the Sacred?* (Chicago: University of Chicago Press, 2009), 25.

11. Ibid., 19.

12. Ibid., 10.

13. For a discussion of the relationship between popular figurations of the anthropologist and American modernity, see Micaela di Leonardo, *The Exotic at Home: Anthropologies, Others, and American Modernity* (Chicago: University of Chicago Press, 1998).

14. Milanius De Almeida, "Catching Aquarium Fishes in Ceylon," with William Innes, *Aquarium*, November 1934, 145.

15. For comparison purposes, see Albert W. Herre, "A Fish Collector in Ceylon," *Aquarium Journal*, September 1947, 12–17. The colors of the local specimens are described in detail. Interestingly, as in the *Aquarium* article, the fish are not pictured. Seemingly premodern indigenous fishermen comprise the illustrations, excepting only a picture of the author himself. The colorful premodern scene stands in for the absent colorful fish.

16. Catherine A. Lutz and Jane L. Collins, *Reading National Geographic* (Chicago: University of Chicago Press, 1993), 31–32.

17. Taussig, 3–9.

18. Especially relevant examples for my argument include W. J. T. Mitchell's *The Last Dinosaur Book*, Dana Seitler's *Atavistic Tendencies*, and di Leonardo's *The Exotic at Home*.

19. Di Leonardo, 35.

20. De Almeida, 146.

21. *Tropical Fish Hobbyist*, May 1959, 44.

22. *Aquarium*, September 1969, 53.

23. See Lutz and Collins, 1–46; Jeffrey Rouff, ed., *Virtual Voyages* (Durham, NC: Duke University Press, 2006).

24. "Exotic Pigmy Fish," *Aquarium* 1 (April 1932): n.p.

25. W. M. Chapman, "The Editor's Page: A Bit of the Jungle," *Aquarium Journal* 1 (January 1947): 23.

26. Rod Edmond, "Returning Fears: Tropical Disease and the Metropolis," in *Tropical Visions in an Age of Empire*, ed. Felix Driver and Luciana Martins (Chicago: University of Chicago Press, 2005), 194.

27. In this, the American home aquarium lags behind representations of the same regions in American travel writing. See, for example, Terry Caesar, "South of the Border: American Travel Writing in Latin America," in *The Cambridge Companion to American Travel Writing*, ed. Alfred Bendixen and Judith Hamera (Cambridge: Cambridge University Press, 2009) 185.

28. H. Carl A. Andersen, "The Aquarist's Dream," *Aquarium Journal*, September 1947, 23.

29. Michel de Certeau, *The Practice of Everyday Life*, trans. S. Rendall (Berkeley: University of California Press, 1984), 115.

30. Susan Stewart, *On Longing: Narratives of the Miniature, the Gigantic, the Souvenir, the Collection* (Durham, NC: Duke University Press, 1993), 136.

31. For a discussion of Henry Ford's machinations around rubber importation, including his establishment of a colony in Brazil to enable circumvention of import duties, see Greg Grandin, *Fordlandia: The Rise and Fall of Henry Ford's Forgotten Jungle City* (New York: Metropolitan Books, 2009).

32. William T. Innes, "Jack Dempsey," in *Aquarium Highlights*, ed. William T. Innes (Philadelphia: Innes, 1951), 8.

33. John Arnold Paul, *"Trichapsis pumilis,"* in Innes, *Aquarium Highlights*, 45.

34. Fritz Mayer, "A Contribution to the *Micropoecilia* Problem," in Innes, *Aquarium Highlights*, 67.

35. Cosgrove, 197.

36. William T. Innes, *Exotic Aquarium Fishes: A Work of General Reference* (Philadelphia: Innes, 1935), 455.

37. Ibid., 457.

38. Ibid., 455, 456. Innes's book does include small maps showing the origins of specimens. These generally function as snapshots, showing locales in isolation, without the explicit global interconnections that were beginning to define the industry.

39. This image is actually reprinted from De Almeida's "Collecting Aquarium Fish in Ceylon." In the original, the caption reads, "Primitive cast net, requiring great skill for the throw. Will Rogers could not sling a lasso more beautifully" (146). The original caption's transformation of the native fisherman into Will Rogers underlines a highly aestheticized "frontier" skill, reinscribed for popular entertainment.

40. "Flying Fish: B.O.A.C. Has Pioneered Large Scale Carriage of Tropical Fish by Air," *Tropical Fish Hobbyist*, September–October 1954, 39.

41. For discussion of changing representations of Africans in wildlife and conservation documentaries in the mid-twentieth century, see Gregg Mitman, *Reel Nature: America's Romance with Wildlife on Film* (Cambridge, MA: Harvard University Press, 1999), 190–202. Mitman's analysis resonates powerfully with aquarists' depictions of natives in travel narratives about Africa during this same period.

42. Donna J. Haraway, "Teddy Bear Patriarchy: Taxidermy in the Garden of Eden, New York City, 1908–1936," in *Cultures of United States Imperialism*, ed. Amy Kaplan and Donald Pease (Durham, NC: Duke University Press, 1993), 280.

43. L. H. Hahn, "Four Pals Do Far-Away-Lands in Quest of Tropicals and Things Aquatic," *Aquariana*, May 1933, 243, 244.

44. Ibid., 244.

45. Ibid., 245.

46. Robert P. L. Straughan, *Adventures in Marine Collecting* (Cranbury, NJ: A. S. Barnes, 1973), 13–14.

47. Christopher Coates, *Tropical Fishes as Pets* (New York: Liveright, 1938), 7.

48. Ibid., 6.

49. Ibid., 7.

50. Ibid., 1.

51. Henry A. Nichols, "90¢ Is Way Too Much! Scouting the Fish Collecting Country of Equatorial Africa," *Aquarium Journal*, April 1959, 138.

52. Ibid., 139.

53. Ibid., 140.

54. Herbert R. Axelrod, "Africa in Color," *Tropical Fish Hobbyist*, June 1970, 5–43.

55. Ibid., 7.

56. Taussig, 159.

57. Axelrod, "Africa in Color," 19; see also 20, 38, 39.

58. Ibid., 39; see also 10.
59. Herbert Axelrod, "In Passing," *Tropical Fish Hobbyist*, September–October 1959, 11+; Axelrod, "Africa in Color," 35.
60. Axelrod, "Africa in Color," 18, 26.
61. Ibid., 27–28.
62. William Vorderwinkler, *Tropical Fish Hobbyist*, November 1959, 67.
63. Axelrod, "Africa in Color," 29.
64. Another example is Albert W. Herre's reliance on a "very pleasant Englishman" to dress down and "make short work" of a "negro soldier who delays him at the customs office in Zanzibar. See "Fishing Along the East Coast of Africa," *Aquarium Journal*, December 1947, 8, 9.
65. Joseph Roach, *Cities of the Dead: Circum-Atlantic Performance* (New York: Columbia University Press, 1996), 55.
66. Axelrod, "Africa in Color," 29.
67. Ibid.; Robert Strauss, "Briefs: Justice; Axelrod Leaves Jail," *New York Times*, October 16, 2005.
68. Albert J. Klee, *Aquarium Journal*, April 1960, 203.
69. William Vorderwinkler, "The Tragic Tale of Professor Lee," *Tropical Fish Hobbyist*, March–April 1957, 48–49.
70. *Aquarium*, July 1971, 65.

Conclusion

1. Mike Paletta, "Setting up a LARGE Aquarium," paper presented at the International Marine Aquarium Conference, Rosemont, IL, April 29, 2006.
2. The "potato chip factor" refers to an advertising slogan used by Lay's Potato Chips: "Bet you can't eat just one."
3. In *Father and Son* by Edmund Gosse, his father, Philip, is literally described as a "joyless Puritan." See Ann Thwaite, *Glimpses of the Wonderful: The Life of Philip Henry Gosse* (London: Faber and Faber, 2002), xv–xvi. Yet Philip Gosse's housing of over one hundred residents in his own tank argues against the literal accuracy of such passages, as does his own exuberant prose and use of citational solidarity. For a list of Gosse's tank residents, see Philip Henry Gosse, *The Aquarium: An Unveiling of the Wonders of the Deep Sea*, 2nd ed. (London: Van Voorst, 1856), 97–98.
4. Henry D. Butler, *The Family Aquarium; or, Aqua Vivarium: A "New Pleasure" for the Domestic Circle* (New York: Dick and Fitzgerald, 1858), 17; emphasis in original.
5. S. S. Van Dine, foreword to Alfred Morgan, *Tropical Fishes and Home Aquaria* (New York: Scribner's, 1935), v. Van Dine himself is an interesting figure in aquaria. "S. S. Van Dine" was the pseudonym of Willard Huntington Wright, editor and art critic for the literary magazine *The Smart Set*. In the 1920s, "Van Dine" turned to fiction writing, creating the immensely popular Philo Vance mysteries. Van Dine's testament to the addictive pull of the home aquarium was born of personal experience. The two-floor New York penthouse he shared with his wife contained

sixty-eight aquariums, with more than a thousand tropical fish. Aquarium fish figure prominently in his novel *The Dragon Murder Case* (1933). The book was made into a film, which, in turn, stimulated its own aquarium craze. For more on Van Dine, see John Loughery, *Alias S. S. Van Dine: The Man Who Created Philo Vance* (New York: Scribner's, 1992), especially 224–38. Thanks to Alfred Bendixen for recognizing the connection between aquariums, Van Dine, and Philo Vance.

6. Henry Kalb, "For Fish Lovers Only!" *Aquarium Journal*, March 1957, 93.

7. Morgan, 4.

8. Diane Schofield, "But I'm All Right—NOW!" *Aquarium Journal*, May 1959, 194.

9. "Another Poor Fish," *Aquarium*, October 1932, 152.

10. Bob Fenner, "Organism Selection for Saltwater Aquarists," paper presented at the International Marine Aquarium Conference, Rosemont, IL, April 28, 2006.

11. William Damon in Albert J. Klee, "A History of the Aquarium Hobby in America," part 1, "The Stirrings of the Hobby," *Aquarium*, December 1967, 55; emphasis in original.

12. Michael Taussig, *Mimesis and Alterity* (New York: Routledge, 1993), 5.

13. Richard Schechner, *Between Theater and Anthropology* (Philadelphia: University of Pennsylvania Press, 1985), 109–12.

14. In Marvin Carlson, *Theories of the Theatre: A Historical and Critical Survey from the Greeks to the Present* (Ithaca: Cornell University Press, 1984), 230.

15. *Aquarium*, June 1970, 51.

16. Examples include Anthony Calfo, "A Call to Farms," paper presented at the International Marine Aquarium Conference, Rosemont, IL, April 28, 2006; Mitch Carl, "SECORE: From Collection to Colonies," paper presented at the International Marine Aquarium Conference, Long Beach, CA, August 1, 2009; and Matt Pedersen, "Captive Bred Fish and You," paper presented at the International Marine Aquarium Conference, Long Beach, CA, August 2, 2009. This list is very partial. Particularly in 2009, virtually every speaker addressed habitat disappearance in his or her presentation.

17. Matt Pedersen repeated this argument to refute it in his presentation.

18. Bernd Brunner, *The Ocean at Home: An Illustrated History of the Aquarium* (New York: Princeton Architectural Press, 2003), 132.

INDEX

Agassiz, Louis, 43, 69, 122, 162, 246n79
Ahmed, Sarah, 50, 236n1
Alcott, Louisa May, 119, 247n112
Allen, David Elliston, 1, 56, 66, 80, 83, 227n3, 236n3, 237n7, 237n15, 239n50, 242n102, 242n111
American Museum, the, 21, 29, 30, 33, 88, 91–92, 103, 104, 109, 232n51, 243n33
American Parlor Aquarium, The (Collier and Hoop), 113, 246n94
American Society for the Prevention of Cruelty to Animals, 134
Animal studies, 126–27, 248n2
Anthropomorphism, 48, 71, 129, 137–50
Apartheid, 215–16
Aquarinomics, 164–67, 169–70, 175, 182, 190, 194
Aquarium
building, 26–27
as collection, 22–23, 34, 49, 52, 119
contemporary ownership of, 13
decorations for, 8
as diorama, 24, 28, 37–38, 45, 234n70, 234nn72–73
and evolution, 45, 47, 49
excess and, 1, 3, 11–12, 174, 182, 221, 226
as garden, 17, 19–20, 22, 23, 29, 49, 75, 87, 89–90, 120, 126, 193
as "happy family," 9, 80, 85, 103–13, 119, 124, 125, 140, 147–48, 160–61, 170–72, 179, 187, 190, 192–93, 195, 207, 216, 226
as landscape, 17–24
and modernity, 2–4, 8, 10, 12–13, 16, 24, 43, 45, 49, 50–51, 52, 55, 66, 69, 76, 79–80, 83, 84–85, 102, 114, 127–30, 135–36, 137–38, 145, 147, 160, 167–68, 173, 176, 188, 193–94, 196–99, 201, 204, 207–8, 211, 213, 222, 224–25
nativism and, 121–22, 161–70, 194
as panorama, 2, 3, 17, 24, 28, 34–38, 40, 44, 47, 102, 175, 230n19, 233nn59–61, 233n65
picture frame construction in, 19, 27
as prison, 82–83, 85, 107–9, 147, 213

as science, 2, 8, 11, 27–28, 37, 61, 80, 85, 90, 94, 111–20, 122–24, 128, 139, 145, 165, 176, 184, 195, 208, 213, 218
as the sea, 10, 17, 19, 42, 44, 51, 55, 57–63, 75, 83, 87–90, 96, 98–101, 107, 109, 111, 117, 124, 140, 161, 171, 193, 200, 224
sex in, 170, 172–74, 181, 183–90
as television, 8, 17, 38, 234n76
as theater, 8, 9–10, 11–12, 17, 21, 24, 28–34, 37, 85, 102–3, 107, 109, 118, 120, 127, 175, 224
as travel, 24, 29, 36, 39–49, 63, 75, 127, 160, 201–18, 221–22, 225
typical configurations of, 4–8
as window, 3, 17, 24–28, 36, 37, 117, 133, 193, 203, 221
as world, 2, 9–10, 12, 16, 19, 21, 23, 36, 58, 75, 80, 88–90, 101, 106, 110, 120, 141, 144, 160, 170, 173, 179, 190, 192, 194–97, 199, 201, 208, 216–17, 222
versus zoos, 20–21
Aquarium (journal), 121, 132, 146, 147, 148, 168, 197, 201, 202, 247n118
Aquarium, American
and British antecedents, 85–86, 90
during the Civil War, 109–11
Great Depression and, 11, 141, 160, 164, 166, 202, 210
progressivism and, 85, 111, 112–22
societies, 111, 120–22
transcendentalist rhetoric and, 95–96
as urban, 8, 92, 101–9
Aquarium, reef, 12, 17, 66, 108, 127, 177, 219–20, 224–25
Aquarium: An Unveiling of the Wonders of the Deep Sea, The (Gosse), 51, 57–74, 262n3
American reviews of, 235n93
citational solidarity in, 66–69
depiction of aquarium residents in, 69–72
practical advice in, 72–74
rural and urban imagery in, 59–66
Aquarium craze, British, 1, 55, 63, 76, 91, 109, 121
Aquarium hobby
demographics of, 8–9

265

Aquarium hobby (*continued*)
  ecological consequences of, 11–12, 224–25
  profitability of, 13
Aquarium Journal, 121, 123, 156, 177, 203
Aquarium journals, 10–11, 111, 117, 120–23, 130, 161–62, 248n120
Arcara Curviceps, 189–91 (fig. 14), 192
Armstrong, Isobel, 25, 27
Atavism, 47–48, 54
Audubon, John James, 43, 53, 122, 162, 246n79
Axelrod, Herbert, 173, 214–18, 239n45

Baker, Steve, 128, 139
Balibar, Étienne, 150
Barnum, Phineas Taylor, 21, 29–32, 91–93, 103–4, 111–12, 165, 172, 222, 232n48
Barnum's Aquarial Gardens (Boston), 30
Bateman, Rev. Gregory, 6 (fig. 3), 118, 134
Bauman, Zygmunt, 3, 219
Bederman, Gail, 246n98, 247n101
Berman, Marshall, 2
"Black hole of Calcutta," 78, 83, 144, 241n97
Blair, Ann, 28
Blanche (lionfish), 13, 126, 135, 155, 157
Bleak House (Dickens), 61
Book of the Aquarium, The (Hibberd), 241n84
Boston Aquarial and Zoological Gardens, 21, 30, 31 (fig. 5), 32 (fig. 6), 92, 104
Bowls, goldfish, 24–26, 88, 133
Brunner, Bernd, 24, 177, 225–26
Butler, Henry D., 19, 21, 30, 32, 33, 37, 45–47, 84, 86–88, 90–113, 120, 121, 124, 126, 128, 148, 165, 171, 190, 220, 225

Chaudhuri, Una, 127, 129, 148
Citational solidarity, 13, 58, 66–69
  in aquarium writing, 76, 78, 94, 120
  critique of, 66
  in works by P. H. Gosse, 13, 58, 66–69, 71
Civil War, U.S., 2, 84, 95, 109–11, 112
Collier, J. H., 113, 123
Cooper, James Fenimore, 93–94
Coral, 4, 12, 61–64, 68, 101, 107, 127, 177, 219–20, 223, 224–25
Cotter, Lilian A., 166
Cowper, William, 67
Crary, Jonathan, 16, 24, 35, 229n4
Cutting, James, 21, 30, 91, 227n14, 243n35

Damon, Elizabeth Emerson, 177
Damon, William, 222–23, 263n11
Daston, Lorraine, 136, 138
"Davey Jones' Ambassador" (Gallun), 146–47
Davis, Susan G., 228n19, 230n18
de Certeau, Michel, 206
Department stores, 26–28, 35, 133
Derrida, Jacques, 128–30
Desmond, Jane C., 129, 132, 138, 173, 184, 187, 228n19, 230n18
Dickens, Charles, 61–62, 237n19, 238n24
di Leonardo, Micaela, 199
Doordan, Dennis, 24
Downes v. Birdwell, 194–95

"Each and All" (Emerson), 98
Edmond, Rod, 204
Edwards, Arthur M., 4, 8, 23, 84, 87–88, 90–103, 106–11, 124, 173, 227n13, 231n24, 231n29, 241n97, 246n93
Emerson, Ralph Waldo, 35, 94, 98, 122
Essex, the, 229n9
Evolution, 45, 47–48, 54, 61, 79–80, 130, 135–36, 236n111

Family Aquarium; or, Aqua Vivarium, The (Butler), 45, 84, 90, 165
"Firemouth" (Monster Truck), 192
Fish, aquarium
  animal cruelty discourse and, 133–34, 146
  animality of, 126, 127–36
  anthropomorphizing and, 48, 129, 138–50
  as evolutionary relatives, 45, 47, 49, 51, 130
  as modernity's found objects, 127, 196
  as pet versus food, 131, 148
  representational fungibility of, 137, 150, 159, 171, 194, 197, 221
Friedberg, Anne, 25, 27

Gallun, Raymond Z., 146
Gélber, Steven M., 147, 173, 176, 255n27
Gender and aquarium hobby, 11, 75, 83, 103, 114, 174–83, 240n81
Glass, 4, 23, 24–28, 29, 36, 73, 89, 127
Grier, Katherine, 107, 131, 133–34, 141, 151, 240n67, 254n16
Goby, the, 33, 88, 120, 217
Gosse, Edmund, 238n29, 262n3
Gosse, Philip Henry, 4, 13, 25, 42, 51, 55, 56–74, 79, 81–82, 85–89, 92, 94,

101–3, 123, 167, 173, 175, 177, 179, 220, 235n93, 237n21, 238n29, 238n31, 238n32, 239n41, 239n45, 239n62, 240n69, 240n82, 262n3
Grau, Oliver, 36, 233n60, 234n70

Hall, G. Stanley, 114–16, 246n98
Handbook to the Marine Aquarium, The (Gosse), 57, 60, 63, 69, 72–73, 239n62
"Happy family," 9, 80, 85, 103–13, 119, 124, 125, 140, 147–48, 160–61, 170–72, 179, 187, 190, 192–93, 195, 207, 216, 226
as form of "peaceable kingdom," 104
Haraway, Donna, 158, 234n73
Harris, Neil, 29
Hawthorne, Nathaniel, 36, 49, 89, 233n65
Hibberd, James Shirley, 19, 25, 34, 51, 64, 65, 74–79, 81–83, 92, 94, 95, 192, 225, 230n19, 233n59, 241n84
Hicks, Edward, 104, 245n75
Hodge, Clifton, 114–17, 119, 122
Hoganson, Kristin L., 39, 242n4
Holmes, Oliver Wendell, 96, 97
Home Aquarium or "House Pond," The (Wagner), 119, 121
Humphreys, H. Noel, 15–16, 19, 24–25, 51, 74, 77 (fig. 7), 79, 83, 87, 94–95, 227n13, 241n84, 241n89

Ichthyologica, the Aquarium Journal, 123
Innes, William, 15–16, 55, 153, 162, 164, 166–68, 187, 206–8, 247n118, 261n38
International Federation of Aquarium Societies, The, 169
International Marine Aquarium Conference (IMAC), 219–20, 222, 224–25
"It," 150–53

Jack Dempsey, the, 153–55, 192, 206
Jackson, Shannon, 110

Kaplan, Amy, 194, 218
King, Amy M., 56
Klee, Albert J., 27, 169–70, 177, 180, 187, 227n10, 227n14, 254n11

Lake, Simon, 40
Levinas, Emmanuel, 140–41, 252n53
Lewes, George Henry, 224
Life Beneath the Waters; or, The Aquarium in America (Edwards), 84, 90–100, 102
Lingus, Alphonso, 129
Lippit, Akira Mizuta, 127, 251n45
Lippmann, Walter, 2

Little Men (Alcott), 119
Lloyd, S. Chichester, 134, 251n35
Locke, Frank S., 163, 166–68, 183, 191 (fig. 14)
Logan, Thad, 65, 70, 240n69

"Machine in the Garden," 63, 102, 238n36, 239n40
Malamud, Randy, 230n18, 249n17
May, Elaine Tyler, 170, 184, 258n94
Mellen, Ida M., 47–48, 125–26, 128–30, 134, 155, 157, 172, 177, 236n111, 251n40, 257n58
Melville, Herman, 18–19, 168, 233n54
Merrill, Lynn, 72, 236n3
Miller, Angela, 18, 95, 99, 245n58, 245n79
Miller, David C., 229n9
Milton, John, 68
Mimesis, 127, 223
Mitchell, W. J. T., 17, 46, 58, 260n18
Mitman, Gregg, 136, 138, 237n6, 261n41
Modernity, 2–4, 10, 12, 13, 16, 24, 43, 45, 46, 65, 69, 76, 79, 83–85, 102, 127–30, 136, 138, 145, 160, 167, 168, 193–94, 196, 199–204, 207–8, 211, 213, 222, 224–25, 229n4, 231n28, 238n30, 245n65, 247n101, 249n8, 251n45, 259n13
atavism and, 47–48, 54
masculinity and, 135, 173, 176, 188
middle class and, 8–9, 80, 114, 147
natural history and, 50–55
Morgan, Alfred, 220–21
Mulertt, Hugo, 121–22, 132–34, 141, 142 (fig. 8), 248n128
Muskallunge, the, 166, 168, 255n20

National Geographic Magazine, 197, 199, 201
National Recovery Act, 11, 141, 143 (fig. 9), 168
Natural history, 20, 23, 34, 43–44, 50–56, 58, 61, 66–69, 80–81, 85–87, 89, 93, 95, 100, 112, 236n2, 242n9, 244n41
Natural theology, 34, 53, 85, 92
Nature Study and Life (Hodge), 114
Newberry, Todd, 21, 25, 145
New York Aquarium Journal, 121
Norman, Don, 175–76, 178, 179
Novak, Barbara, 50, 78, 95

Observation, aquarium as tool for teaching, 2, 8, 15–16, 22, 27, 43, 45, 49, 54–55, 59, 74, 79, 87, 95, 97, 106, 108, 111–12, 120, 165–66, 168, 206, 229n3

Ocean Gardens: The History of the Marine Aquarium and the Best Methods Now Adopted for Its Establishment and Preservation (Humphreys), 15, 19, 54, 77 (fig. 7), 87, 241n84, 241n89
Ocean and River Gardens (Humphreys), 227n13, 241n84, 241n89
O'Connor, Ralph, 66–67, 232n46, 239n52
Oscar, the, 153, 154–55, 156

Paletta, Mike, 219–20, 223
Panorama, 2, 3, 17, 24, 28, 34–38, 40, 44, 47, 102, 175, 230n19, 233nn59–61, 233n65
Parrish, Susan Scott, 52, 244n41
Pauly, Philip J., 100, 112, 244n41
Peaceable Kingdom, The (Hicks), 104, 245n75
Percival, James Gates, 68
Performance, 9–10
    aquariums as settings for, 29–30, 232n51
    popularization of science and, 28, 232n46
Pollock, Della, 67
Power de Villepreux, Jeanne, 177, 256n56
Prairie, The: A Tale (Cooper), 93
Pratt, Mary Louise, 44, 52, 244n41
Promise of American Life, The (Croly), 117
Pronek, Neal, 170
Puffer fish, the, 153, 155, 253n96
Pycraft, W. P., 47

Quart, Nina, 8
Quinn, Stephen, 38, 234n73

Reef aquariums, 12, 17, 66, 108, 127, 177, 219–22, 224–25
Roach, Joseph, 136–37, 152–53, 155, 216, 236n110
Romance of Natural History, The (Gosse), 56, 58, 67
Roth, Rev. Paul Wagner, 135
Rustic Adornments for Homes of Taste (Hibberd), 19, 75–78, 227n2, 241n84

Scarry, Elaine, 68
Schechner, Richard, 37, 234n70
Schlereth, Thomas, 107
Schofield, Diane, 13, 155, 177–79, 180, 217, 221, 253n96
Sea anemones, 4, 8, 12, 19, 23, 41, 42, 78, 82, 86, 87, 113, 227n13
Sea Creatures and Me (blog), 138–39
Secord, James, 236n3
Seitler, Dana, 47, 251n38

Shinn, Millicent Washburn, 49, 130
Simpson, Donald A., 13, 57, 123–24, 130, 139, 156, 174, 257n72
Smith, Eugene, 117, 121, 247n104, 247n118
Snozolla ("Snoz"), 13, 126, 136, 155–57
Stephens, Carlene, 46
Stickleback, the, 4, 13, 33, 106, 131, 190, 191 (fig. 14), 192, 224
Surrogation, 136–38, 236n110
    aquarium and, 39, 70, 111, 144, 159, 240n69
    fish and, 10, 48, 81, 89, 126, 140, 143, 150, 157–58, 171–74, 179, 184, 187–88, 192, 200, 207, 209, 214, 216, 221
Swainson, William, 53–55, 237n7, 237n13
Symmes, Edward C., Jr., 137

Taft, Horatio Nelson, 109–11
Taussig, Michael, 196–97, 201, 214, 223
Taylor, John Ellor, 16, 30, 33, 51, 74, 79–83, 241n88, 241n97
Thoreau, Henry David, 96–97, 244n41
Thwaite, Anne, 57, 239n46, 262n3
Thynne, Anna, 69, 177, 240n81
Tompkins, Jane, 227n5
Transcendentalism, 95–96, 103, 112–13
Tsing, Anna Lowenhaupt, 194
Twain, Mark (Samuel Langhorne Clemens), 44
    Aquarium Club, 172–73
Twenty Thousand Leagues Under the Sea (Verne), 40

U.S. Commission of Fish and Fisheries, 112

Van Dine, S. S. (Willard Huntington Wright), 220, 262n5
Vorderwinkler, William, 146, 170, 183, 185, 215, 217, 252n67

WAF ("Wife Acceptance Factor"), 174, 176, 180, 183, 192, 219, 220
Wagner, J. H., 119, 121
Ward Case, 3–4, 69, 84, 87, 227n10
White, Hayden, 13
Williams, Raymond, 62
Wood, Rev. J. G., 55, 83
Wordsworth, William, 41, 62, 66
Wyndham, Robert J., 181, 191 (fig. 14)

Zooesis, 126–29

Made in the USA
Monee, IL
12 January 2022